/20

Spies and Other Secrets

Nicholas Bethell

VIKING

VIKING

Published by the Penguin Group
Penguin Books Ltd, 27 Wrights Lane, London w8 5tz, England
Penguin Books USA Inc., 375 Hudson Street, New York, New York 10014, USA
Penguin Books Australia Ltd, Ringwood, Victoria, Australia
Penguin Books Canada Ltd, 10 Alcorn Avenue, Toronto, Ontario, Canada m4v 3b2
Penguin Books (NZ) Ltd, 182–190 Wairau Road, Auckland 10, New Zealand

Penguin Books Ltd, Registered Offices: Harmondsworth, Middlesex, England

First published 1994
1 3 5 7 9 10 8 6 4 2
First edition

Filmset by Datix International Limited, Bungay, Suffolk
Printed in England by Clays Ltd, St Ives plc
Set in 11½/14 pt Monophoto Ehrhardt

A CIP catalogue record for this book is available from the British Library

ISBN 0–670–85161–2

Contents

List of Illustrations

Acknowledgements

I want first of all to thank my wife, Bryony. Since our marriage two years ago she has had to put up with a husband who was about to give birth to a book. A book in embryo is a spouse's burden. I also thank her for correcting the proofs.

My assistant, Harriet Sharrard, was invaluable. She guided me not only through the research, but also through the workings of the word processor, the writing machine to which I graduated in this book's early months. She made sure that conditions for writing were always as favourable as they could be, and that no line was ever 'dumped' into oblivion.

For several months James Coomarasamy, a Russian scholar of considerable achievement, spent time in various libraries and houses of documentation, preparing my raw material. I am very grateful to him and I wish him well as a leading member of the new substantial British colony in the new Russia.

Several people mentioned in the book, for instance Tatyana Yankelevich, Alexander Dolberg, Oleg Gordievsky and Marta Ličkova, have allowed me to run the book past them. They have helped me to iron out mistakes and I am grateful to them for giving me their time.

I have probably been too unkind to the Foreign Office. As these pages show, we worked along different lines. They are diplomats by profession. I am laity and I have no doubt that they dislike my use of the megaphone in making *démarches* that have little in common with the rules of diplomacy. Still, they are a Rolls Royce machine and they are excellent allies.

Our differences were over tactics. Foreign Secretary Geoffrey Howe wrote to me on 30 June 1985, 'Our experience indicates that publicity is not normally helpful in personal (Soviet) cases.' My experience was exactly the opposite.

I would lastly like to thank many friends and brothers-in-arms from the second cold war for contributing the facts on which this book is based. I look forward to seeing them all one day at some great 'old "anti-comrades" reunion'.

1. *The Window Opens*

The nastiest letter I ever received in my life was from Alexander Solzhenitsyn, the famous Russian dissident and (in 1970) winner of the Nobel Prize for Literature. Written from Zurich on 25 April 1975, it began, 'I ask you to explain to me by what right you peddled my manuscript *Cancer Ward* and sold it in my name. You never had any authority to do this from anybody and you know yourself how such an acquisition of another person's literary property would be viewed in court ... Why did you allow to appear a slovenly and inaccurate translation of the work, which has caused me irreversible harm in the eyes of the English reader? Unless I receive satisfactory explanation from you immediately, I will make this whole matter public, or else the subject of legal proceedings.'

It was nearly enough to make me give up what had become an abiding emotional involvement as well as a political crusade and professional interest, the struggle waged by a small group of Russians and others under Soviet rule to change or discard the Soviet communist system that governed their lives.

I became interested in Russia as a young man through study of its language and literature, but I soon realized that in the Soviet Union literature and politics could not easily be separated. A Soviet writer was an instrument of state policy. If he helped the system, he was richly rewarded. Royalties were generous and there was a fine writers' club in Herzen Street, Moscow, that served good food at reasonable prices. There were also writers' *dachas* to be had at low rent in Peredelkino, a pleasant Moscow suburb.

However, any writer who attacked the Soviet system in his work was seen as more dangerous than a terrorist, his typewriter as more dangerous than a machine-gun. Then, at best, his work would never be published. He would not be shot, as many were in Stalin's time, but at worst he would be arrested and sent to a labour camp or, even more frightening, to a psychiatric hospital. This was his dilemma. He could lie and live well as a trusted servant of the regime.

He could avoid controversial issues and, if he was talented, survive by merit. Or he could resist and suffer for sticking to the truth.

It was the liberal writers, not 'dissident' trade unionists or scientists or journalists, who led the opposition to Soviet practice in those first years after Stalin's death in March 1953. I thus came to sympathize especially with them, those few Soviet writers who chose the path of opposition, of a struggle for freedom, who wanted to write without censorship. And I included among those I admired also those writers who, while not opposing the system outright, were ready to criticize certain aspects of it, whose highest hope it was to reform the system, to replace the type of communism that ruled them with a communism that was more gentle. In those days, this was the height of my hopes, a more liberal communist system, not for my own country of course but for the Soviet Union and its empire. I envisaged nothing beyond it to be possible.

I absorbed much propaganda on both sides of the conflict and I knew that there was no absolute in the good or bad of it. But in the end I was forced to conclude that, whatever valid basis there may have been for the revolutions of 1917, in terms of the working people's struggle for justice, there could be no excuse for the perversions later spawned by Lenin, Stalin, Brezhnev and Andropov. The followers of Marx and Lenin, so the joke went, had ended the exploitation of man by man and created the reverse. To be more serious, they had succeeded in crushing the spirit of their nation, having previously exterminated many millions of their citizens physically.

I am sometimes asked what drew me into this strange un-English area of study. Was it religious belief, or a commitment to the political right wing, or a Russian grandmother, or a Polish girlfriend? We in Britain were famous for Byron and our philhellenes, for Kipling and our other lovers of India, for our poets who travelled to Rome. But we had no tradition of British involvement in Slav culture. It was, in fact, based on no more than chance and guesswork, arising from opportunism. I chose to study Russian at school, not as a major subject but as a sideline from Latin and Greek. We learnt the alphabet and not much more. I remember reciting Samuel Marshak's 'Leningrad Postman' on Harrow School speech day on 30 June 1956. A review in *The*

Harrovian[1] said, 'The Russian of N.W. Bethell was everything that a contemporary Russian would wish it to be, incomprehensible to westerners . . .' In fact, it was probably incomprehensible to Russians too, since it was my first semi-public use of the language and I understood little of the grammar or structure of the poem. I just learnt the sounds off by heart. I then left Harrow and three months later, a few weeks after my eighteenth birthday, I joined the army for two years of national service.

It seemed to me that Russian was an important language, the basis of one of the world's great cultures. Although the Soviet Union was a backward land, Russian literature was second to none. And now Russia was a superpower and its language was likely to grow in importance. And hardly anyone in Britain knew it. Even at that young age, I could tell that there would be opportunities for those who did. This is why, when the army offered me the chance to spend almost all my two years on a Russian interpretership course, I grabbed the chance with both hands.

The study of any language opens a window on to a previously unseen world. In the case of Russian, it was an unusually wide and colourful new world. We were being trained for the Third World War. We were to participate in Armageddon. I started the course a few weeks after the Soviet army crushed Hungary and Britain was humiliated at Suez. There was talk in the British army, even at my lowly level in Catterick Camp in Yorkshire and then at the army's language school at Crail in Scotland, of what was going to be done 'when the balloon goes up'. It was going to be our job, they kept telling us, to use our training to translate radio traffic and captured documents and to interrogate prisoners. We were made to practise drill commands on each other, so that when the time came we could march Soviet army prisoners from place to place, then (as gently as possible) extract information from them. We did as we were told, though we wondered whether in the alarming eventuality of nuclear war there would be time for us to be taken to where the enemy, the Soviet army, was to be found and captured. And, if they were to be evacuated to Britain, how much of Britain would there be left to receive them?

Happily our teachers, most of them former Soviet officers from the Second World War, were allowed to teach us not only drill commands and the parts of the Kalashnikov machine-rifle, but also the delights of Pushkin and Lermontov. Our teachers used the Russian language to teach us Russian history and we used Russian to enact plays by Chekhov and Gogol, both in the classroom and after class. We thus came to know the magnificence of Russia as well as its horrors. As for the latter, our teachers were keen enough to tell us about the tortures inflicted by Stalin on millions of his fellow countrymen. Many of them had lost relatives in his purges, or had suffered themselves, and their hatred of the regime was intense. The Russians had wounded themselves and their neighbours so cruelly, we thought from time to time, that they must be a people without heart, which made it all so surprising when some masterpiece of beauty revealed the depth of the nation's soul.

It was only when I got to know the language better, in the spring of 1958 at Crail, that I first became aware of something terrible about the part played by our own country in helping Stalin to kill so many. In the course of those long Scottish summer evenings, after the consumption of alcohol, our ex-Soviet teachers would begin to tell us of the miracle by which they had escaped the fate of most of the other Soviet soldiers who had fallen into British or American hands in 1945.

Several million Russians and Ukrainians, they told us, including many women and children, had found themselves in western Europe at the end of the war. They had been afraid to return to the Soviet Union and had asked the West for asylum, for resettlement of any sort, anywhere. We had refused to help them and had bundled almost all of them back to the Soviet 'Motherland' and to Stalin's tender mercies, which in many cases meant a slow death through cold and starvation in the labour camps, or else a bullet through the head. I was told also that British and American troops had used considerable violence to force their prisoners back into Soviet hands. There had been deaths and suicides. I was shocked to hear this, that the British were accomplices in Stalin's terror, that we had used 'German methods' to implement an inhumane policy. At the time I did not quite believe it. I certainly did not want to believe it.

In September 1958 the army gave me a certificate of competence and said goodbye. I was now one of the army's 'bank' of Russian interpreters, to be called upon when the cataclysm took place. A few weeks later, by which time I was a Cambridge student, they sent me a railway warrant and a postal order for £1, pointing out that my orders as a reservist were to use the railway warrant to get back to my old unit as soon as there was a nuclear attack on Britain or any similar emergency. The £1 was for refreshments en route.

I never had occasion to use the warrant or cash the postal order, but I was by now committed to the notion that the Soviet system was an evil force that threatened us all. The invasion of Hungary, with its 60,000 Hungarian deaths, combined with stories told by our Russian teachers, had convinced me. The Soviet system was a 'plague bacillus', as Winston Churchill had pointed out, and it was a tragedy that we had not destroyed it in its infancy, as Churchill had wanted, that our help to the White side in the Russian civil war had been too little and too late.

And now, triumphant in the Second World War, enjoying the gratitude of all Europe for having torn the guts out of Hitler's armies, the Soviet Union had been allowed by western laziness, or treachery, to become a dangerous military giant, always on the prowl and making mischief, too powerful to kill or even to tame, a deadly machine that might one day overrun and imprison us all. Its socialist ideology was meant to be its strength. It certainly helped the Soviet Union to win friends among western intellectuals, trade union movements, and in the Third World. It claimed to offer dignity to the workers, freedom to those downtrodden by imperialism. In 1956 Nikita Khrushchev announced that his country had overtaken the United States in the production of grain and milk. He also said that he would 'bury' us. Then, when we became alarmed, he reassured us that this would all be done peacefully, making use of the socialist system's economic superiority. In those heady post-Stalin days there were, amazingly, many who thought that he would succeed.

It was a lie. The Soviet system was shot through with weaknesses. The Soviet economy, controlled with massive inefficiency by a huge central bureaucracy, was never going to match the achievements of the industrialized world. Soviet science, limited by the restraints of Soviet internal policy, would never reach the highest level. The years passed and eventually I came to see that sooner or later the system, crushed by its own weight, might implode upon itself.

This was not a popular point of view among many in the West. I remember, for instance, the well-known MP Enoch Powell visiting the Soviet Union in 1977, at the height of Brezhnev's anti-dissident campaign, and returning full of admiration for the nation 'which by its past honours itself and its future'. He approached the problem of Soviet internal policy with the right-winger's belief in the pure sovereignty of the state and admiration for the government that 'ran a tight ship'. He deplored especially 'interference' by human rights bodies. The Soviet Union believed that the citizen was the property of the state, he wrote: 'To try to shame or cajole or negotiate the Russian state into abandoning these convictions is like standing by the Volga and asking it to be so obliging as to flow north instead of south.'[2]

There were similar thoughts at the other extreme of the political line. For instance in November 1977 the British trade unionist and future Chairman of the Labour Party, Alex Kitson, told his Soviet hosts in Moscow at a celebration of the 1917 Revolution's sixtieth anniversary: 'It is pleasant to be in a country where the situation differs from the position at home . . . You have achieved much that we are still far from achieving . . . ' I replied, 'Indeed they have. In their sixty years of power they have built a great empire. They have learnt how to make guns, but not how to give their people butter, and with those guns they rule a dozen unwilling foreign nations . . . This is the socialist society on which Mr Kitson has put the British Labour Party's seal of approval.'[3]

Alex Kitson was of the traditional pro-Soviet Left. His views were of course predictable. But there were many others, politically 'progressive' but far less left-wing, who simply believed that the West was going to lose the great fight. For instance, I remember being interviewed for a profile in the British parliament's journal, the *House Magazine*, about my hopes and dreams for the future. I said, 'I'd like to be able to achieve something, or help to be able to achieve something, in Eastern Europe – I think by convincing the people in Russia and her satellites that society cannot flourish and industry cannot be efficient under the system that they have now. This must be a matter for the people themselves in Eastern Europe, but they look out to the West through the little windows that exist and, since I speak Russian and Polish and have many contacts there, I do what I can to make them understand what they are missing.'[4]

I will never forget the look on the journalist's face. She thought me mad and dangerous. Every educated person knows, she seemed to be saying, that the Soviet system is impregnable. It is part of history's army on the march. The West's free enterprise will always be the system at risk and anyone who refuses to accept this simple fact is playing with matches and liable to ignite nuclear war. The West's ruling classes may perhaps be able to contain communism's advance for a number of years, but they can only postpone the inevitable. The advance will soon be resumed and there is a ratchet effect ensuring that the process can never be turned back. Communism will win in the end and Khrushchev's heirs will bury us as he promised they would, hopefully without too much bloodshed.

In retrospect, I see that my views were expressed too moderately. In 1983, when the interview happened, I hoped merely for the Soviet Union's evolution towards a more liberal socialism. I did not envisage its collapse, at least not in my lifetime. Even so, she clearly dismissed my views as the result of upper-class nostalgia, as unfit for sensible debate.

At Cambridge I became aware of the very tragic Polish dimension of this conflict. The Poles were the only people who fought against Hitler from the war's first day right to its last day. They fought to defend their own country, then in British uniform at Narvik, in the Battle of Britain and in Italy, at Monte Cassino and elsewhere, and at Arnhem. Their only reward was to be handed over to Stalin as a Soviet satellite in February 1945, through that same ignoble Yalta agreement that had allowed Britain and the United States to deliver so many Russians to imprisonment and death in Stalin's labour camps.

At the Victory Day parade in London on 8 June 1946, Poles who had fought in British army uniform were not invited to take part. The invitation went instead to the communist Polish army. Winston Churchill spoke in the House of Commons of his 'deep regret' at the decision and Harold Macmillan wrote of his 'shame'. It was only put right after Margaret Thatcher visited Poland in November 1988. It was typical of the indignities that were heaped on Poland not only by its neighbours to the East and West, but by Britain also.[5]

Decades of injustice followed. In Africa and Asia country after country was winning its freedom from imperial rule. Everybody approved. But in central and eastern Europe, it seemed, the Soviet Union was being allowed to maintain its empire, to ring itself with 'friendly' countries, all governed by communist parties that by law enjoyed a monopoly of power. It attacked and occupied its neighbours in order to defend itself, with hardly a squeak of protest from world opinion.

In 1956 the Poles had rebelled, making it clear that they would not accept a repeat of Stalin's excesses and electing a more independent communist leader, Władysław Gomułka. They remained nevertheless a Soviet colony, and a most unwilling one. Could anything be done to help them? Was Poland condemned to remain forever in this unenviable state? Again, anyone who even posed such a question was likely to be put down as a wild right-winger and destabilizing influence. Soviet control over Poland, we were assured, was inescapable, because of the communication requirements of the Soviet army. And anyone so bold as to challenge the need for such requirements was a warmonger. Still, with the same depth of feeling that inspired Lord Byron at Marathon, I profoundly hoped that Poland would one day be free.

In August 1959 I went to the Soviet Union for the first time, with a group of fellow Cambridge students. The people were friendly, in some ways friendlier than they are now. After all, the cold war was over. Stalin was dead and millions had been released from the labour camps. In spite of the Hungarian atrocities of three years earlier, East–West relations were on a far more correct basis than they had been since the Second World War.

We were an amazing sight to them, a group of foreign students, one of the first since the thaw that followed Stalin's death, and they were in awe of us. We were greeted with flowers at Moscow railway station and ushered to the front of the queue to see Lenin in the bowels of the Red Square mausoleum, with Stalin in full Marshal's uniform lying beside him. There had been no groups like ours while Stalin was alive. It was an exhilarating three weeks, but I was shocked by the shoddiness of it all and by the naïvety of the propaganda.

I had with me a copy of Boris Pasternak's famous novel *Dr Zhivago*, which had caused such a furore when the author won the Nobel Prize for Literature in 1957. Our young Soviet guide was fascinated to see it, asked if he could borrow it and devoured it in every spare moment of our tour, although on the day we were due to leave he had still not finished it. 'Sasha, don't worry, I'll mail you a copy from London,' I told him in all innocence. His reaction was one of terror. 'No, you must not', he said. I insisted and he protested, until finally the penny dropped into my brain that the arrival of such a book, mailed to him at his Moscow address from London by 'an English friend', would damage him most horribly.

In December 1960 I made my first visit to Poland, invited by another Cambridge friend, Eryk Infeld, the son of a well-known Polish professor of physics. This was a pleasant experience. I stayed in a flat, not in a student hostel, and I could meet Polish people as friends, rather than relying on state-employed guides. Still, I was shocked and disturbed by the depth of the resentment, anti-Russian as well as anti-Soviet, that every Pole in 1960 seemed to feel the need to communicate to visitors from the West such as myself, almost as a cry for help, based on the fact that we in the West were responsible for their sad state of affairs, since we had signed the Yalta agreement.

When I spoke to Poles in Russian, there being no other common language, they would pretend not to understand, although they understood quite well, or they would castigate me for speaking 'a dog's language'. It was clear to me at that early point that, if I wanted to learn about Poland, I would have to speak Polish too. Russian was not enough. If anything, it was a disadvantage, since it reminded them of what they had lost.

These beginnings of Slavic knowledge came in useful when I joined the *Times Literary Supplement* as a sub-editor in 1962. The erection of the Berlin Wall in August 1961 was fresh in our minds, as indeed was Hungary and 1956, but in many other ways it seemed then that the system might be on the road to reform. The 20th Congress of the Soviet Communist Party had revealed Stalin's crimes to an astonished Soviet people. Millions poured home from the labour camps. The new leader, Nikita Khrushchev, removed Stalinist leaders from positions of power and Stalin himself from the mausoleum. Stalin's internal affairs minister Lavrenti Beria was shot and his foreign minister Vyacheslav Molotov sent as ambassador to Outer Mongolia. The poet Yevgeni Yevtushenko was allowed to read verses attacking communist dogma to crowds of 100,000 in Moscow's Luzhniki sports stadium – poems like 'Babi Yar' about Russian anti-semitism, or 'Stalin's Heirs' and 'Dead Hand' about the horrible Stalinist past. In November 1962, most amazing of all, Khrushchev allowed publication in the Moscow monthly *Novy Mir* (New World) of Alexander Solzhenitsyn's *One Day in the Life of Ivan Denisovich*, a short novel about a day of toil and privation endured by an innocent man imprisoned in a Siberian labour camp. It was based on the author's own experience as a camp inmate between 1945 and 1953. (In 1962 Solzhenitsyn was a name from nowhere, in print for the first time.)

There were two ways of looking at this event. The first was that of Alexander Tvardovsky, the editor of *Novy Mir*. He wrote in his political introduction to the novella that Stalin's excesses were violations of socialist legality, breaches of the norm, untypical of communist practice, and that the Communist Party could only be congratulated on its courage in bringing these most unfortunate matters to light. Never before in history had a great movement made such a full and frank confession of past misdeeds. And such misdeeds would of course never recur.

The second point of view was that expressed later by the dissident Vladimir Bukovsky, then twenty years old: 'Here was a government that had killed 20 million or maybe 40 million of its own people. It was not enough for them simply to say that they were sorry and that it would not occur again. In the first place it was unconvincing. In the second place it was insulting.'[6]

In my *TLS* book reviews of Solzhenitsyn's early work, I was inclined to give 'liberal communists' like Tvardovsky the benefit of the doubt. It was superb, I wrote,[7] that a communist leader (Khrushchev) and a former camp inmate (Solzhenitsyn) were now on common ground. It must mean that the reforms were meaningful, that the neo-Stalinists were fighting a losing battle.[8] It was wishful thinking, but there seemed no other way forward. I hoped that the emergence of Soviet leaders like Khrushchev would bring an understanding of civilized values to the power that ruled the world's last great empire and now challenged our own democratic system. If it did not, what hope was there for us all?

We could not destroy their system ourselves. Our power to do that was the power of the kamikaze pilot. On the other hand, if Khrushchev was prepared to allow a novel like *Ivan Denisovich*, there must be some good in him and there must be some hope that he and the other Soviet leaders were going to soften their dictatorial behaviour. And this was all that we could reasonably expect, a 'nicer' sort of communism living side by side with our western democracies, in competition with us and no doubt subverting our allies, challenging us at every turn, making trouble for us in the Third World, but not to the point of world revolution or nuclear war.

I was attracted to the Polish example, not because I saw any merit in their socialist economic system, which was inefficient to the point of absurdity and produced very low living standards, but because their new leader, Gomułka, had lessened police terror and abolished (except rarely) imprisonment for non-violent dissent. They were still part of the empire. They were in the military pact. Officially they were still bound by Marxist dogma, but there was flexibility and one had the feeling that not even the communists really believed in communism.

Unlike Soviets, Poles were allowed to travel abroad and they were not afraid to speak their minds. I recall driving past Communist Party headquarters in Warsaw. Workmen were digging holes in the pavement beside it. 'You know why they're digging?' said the taxi driver. 'They're finding out how deep are the convictions of the people working inside.' A Moscow taxi-driver would not have made such a joke. But the Poles were happy to do so, even to foreigners, even in writing or on the stage, although each such criticism and witticism had to be squeezed past the censor's razor blade.

I visited Poland fifteen times in the 1960s. I found Polish plays that the BBC asked me to translate for radio and television, such writers as Sławomir Mrożek and the philosopher Leszek Kolakowski. Then in 1966 I was commissioned to write a biography of Władysław Gomułka, the communist leader who was expelled and arrested by the Stalinists, only to be recalled to power in the anti-Stalin surge of 1956. It was Gomułka who had made these reforms possible and I admired him for this.

The neo-Stalinists then made their comeback. Nikita Khrushchev was toppled in October 1964 and the process of liberal reform came to an end. His successors Aleksey Kosygin and Leonid Brezhnev had no time for such things, as they made clear on 14 February 1966, when Andrey Sinyavsky and Yuli Daniel, two writers little known internationally but well respected in Moscow literary circles, were sent to prison for many years for 'anti-Soviet propaganda'. This episode, one might say, marked the beginning of the second cold war. Both

Sinyavsky and Daniel had sent their work to the West for publication. A Soviet internal dissident movement had been born and the West was being drawn into it.

The movement was nevertheless meagre and disunited. A few weeks after Sinyavsky was sentenced in 1966, his wife Maya tried to enlist the support of Moscow's latest celebrity, Alexander Solzhenitsyn, then riding high in the Soviet Union of Writers on the basis of *Ivan Denisovich* and other short novels. She says, 'Timofey Resovsky, a friend of a friend of ours, took a letter of protest signed by some Soviet writers to Obninsk near Moscow, where Solzhenitsyn lived with his then wife Nataliya Reshetovskaya. He refused to sign it, on the grounds that Sinyavsky had arranged for his work to be published abroad. He said, "It is not appropriate for a Russian writer to have his work published outside Russia."'

'It was not the fact that he refused to sign that upset me. There were sixty-two who signed, but many writers refused. Some said that it would do no good. Others said that, if they signed, their families would suffer. Others simply said that they were afraid. I know many today who did not sign in 1966 and I am friends with them. It was not the refusal, it was his explanation.'

I knew nothing of this. In 1966 Solzhenitsyn was a hero to me. And the BBC still had its Third Programme and I did what I could to fill it with any survivals of good Russian literature that could be found. There was, for instance, the radio item based on the poetry of the great classical poet, the greatest of her day, Anna Akhmatova, whose husband had been killed under Lenin and son imprisoned under Stalin. I met her in June 1965 and on 15 June I was able to entice her to Broadcasting House during the one visit she ever made to London, after receiving an honorary degree at Oxford. She read a poem, 'To the People of London', written during the London blitz. It began, 'The twenty-fourth drama of William Shakespeare is now written by Fate's passionless hand . . .'

I remember how hard it was that morning to maintain an atmosphere of cool efficiency in a producer's cubicle crammed with Russian members of the BBC staff, all of them in tears as they listened to the great lady evoking tragic memories of Russia's past through recitation of her work. I planned to see her again during a forthcoming visit to Russia in June 1966, but it was not to be. She died in March of that year. The recording that she made for me ten months earlier remains in the BBC's archives.

Meanwhile I became interested in her protégé, Joseph Brodsky, a young man from Leningrad who was making a name for himself as a poet, although an unpublished one. In the early 1960s senior figures like Akhmatova and Marshak, as well as the composer Dmitri Shostakovich, came to believe that here was a great poet in embryo. He had a following among the young also. They used to meet in Leningrad flats and read his verses in typescript, circulating them from hand to hand. There was nothing anti-Soviet about them. They had no political content. But they were the work of someone on the look-out for the guiding principles of life. This disturbed the local authorities. They took the view that he ought already to have made his mind up on philosophical matters, that he ought to place any talent that he had at the service of the communist system.

In November 1963 a local newspaper[9] called Brodsky 'a semi-literary parasite' who was corrupting the youth of the city with pornographic poetry. It seemed that he was inspiring 'beatniks' to recite anti-social gibberish to one another in private apartments, meanwhile refusing to work and living off the earnings of other citizens. Brodsky was then arrested and charged with '*tuneyadstvo*' or 'parasitism'.

At his trial in February 1964 the presiding officer, Judge Savieleva, put forward the view that only a member of the Union of Writers could be a poet. 'Who gave you the right to call yourself a poet?' she kept asking him. He replied that it was a gift from God. This was not an answer that would impress a Soviet judge. Witnesses were called swearing Brodsky to be a latter-day Socrates, that he had an evil influence on their children. Finally, the judge read her decision: 'The prisoner Brodsky is not fulfilling the duties of a Soviet citizen . . . He has refused to work and has carried on writing his decadent poems and reciting them at private parties. According to the committee investigating the work of young writers, it is clear that Brodsky is not a poet . . . Brodsky is condemned to exile in a remote locality for a period of five years.'[10] He was taken far beyond the Arctic Circle and put to work shovelling manure.

I wrote a feature programme for the BBC about Brodsky and his trial, which the BBC broadcast on 12 January 1965. His treatment, as it turned out, was severe even by the Soviet standards of those days. There was widespread protest from senior figures in the cultural world and in October 1965 he was set free.

My second visit to Russia in June 1966, with my wife Cecilia, was meant to be enjoyable and uneventful. We took a cruise boat, the *Alexander Pushkin*, from Tilbury to Leningrad, where we camped in the nearby village of Repino, then drove south through Novgorod and Kalinin to Butovo, just south of Moscow, spending three weeks in tents or small huts in various approved Soviet camping sites. The mosquitoes were terrifying and the lavatories a disgrace, but the dissident movement had hardly begun and we spent most of our time seeing the sights of the two great Russian cities. My only rash act was to call at Brodsky's family apartment on Leningrad's Lityeyny Prospekt to tell him about my radio feature.

I was received, but not greeted, by his ageing father and I realized my mistake as soon as I saw the look of fear on the old man's face. He had seen too much Soviet suffering and he did not want to take further risks, for instance by welcoming foreigners into his home. It was another early experience of the guilt and fear that was such a feature of Russians under Soviet rule, as they faced the moral conflict between their natural inclination to be hospitable to guests and their duty to protect themselves and their families against KGB reaction.

I offered him some of my translations of his son's poetry. I thought that he would be pleased, but I was not asked to sit down and I left after exchanging just a few words in the hallway. I think that he informed the KGB about my visit. When we came to leave the Soviet Union at Brest-Litovsk on the River Bug, the Soviet frontier with Poland, we were refused permission to cross. We waited and eventually a van arrived with a team of ten 'customs officers' who subjected us to a five-hour search of our car, luggage and persons. Books and diaries were taken away for overnight perusal and we were accommodated in the aptly named 'Bug Hotel' for two nights until the KGB were ready to let us leave the country, having found nothing of significance.

It was a disagreeable episode, but it ended happily inasmuch as I was asked by a London publisher to translate more of Brodsky's work and in 1967 the book was published with my Introduction under the title *Elegy to John Donne and Other Poems*. It was the first publication of his work in any translation. Copies reached him, and in May 1968 he sent one copy back to me, through one of his many English girlfriends. It bore the inscription 'From Russia with Love and Gratitude . . .' It was a prized possession then and over the years its value to me has increased.

The Leningrad 'poetry committee', it seems, had poor literary judgement. Brodsky turned out to be very much a poet. He flourished after his release from Arctic exile. He attracted the attention of W.H. Auden and others, who were soon keen to promote him. Then, as Jewish emigration gathered momentum, he emigrated to a glittering academic and literary career in the United States. In October 1987 he was awarded the Nobel Prize for Literature.

I also made a BBC radio play from the short story *Graphomaniacs* by Andrey Sinyavsky, by then serving seven years in labour camps, which the BBC broadcast in September 1967, and a few weeks later, as my last BBC effort, a play out of Solzhenitsyn's *Ivan Denisovich*, which was repeated many times and sold in many countries. And so by the time I left the BBC in October 1967, these 'liberal writers', pioneers in the struggle for a free Russia, or even for a freer Soviet Union, were my life's great heroes, Solzhenitsyn foremost among them. His work had taken Russia several steps along a long road. He had made the horrors of Stalinist rule known to a wide public both at home and in the West. He had played a part in the de-Stalinization process. Post-Stalinist Soviet oppression remained, but the scale of it had greatly diminished.

Solzhenitsyn was at this stage still a loyal citizen, a respected member of the Union of Writers and of Soviet society, whereas Sinyavsky was in jail. But in those days I knew nothing of these quarrels of the liberal intelligentsia. I had no idea of the extent to which he was distrusted and disliked by the Sinyavsky family and others well known in the Russian literary world. I thought none the worse of him for his caution. He was only being realistic, I may have thought. There was no means of destroying Soviet power. He was doing the next best thing, trying to reform it from within and he had great things in store. It did not occur to me at that stage, as I was later told by Russian dissidents, that the idea of reforming communism from within was an impossibility, that it was as futile and self-defeating as an attempt to cure a woman of syphilis by making love to her.

If I had been offered one other wish in that year, 1967, after the joy of the birth of my elder son, it would have been the chance to help Solzhenitsyn in his struggle to make known the horrors of Stalinist oppression. It was a miracle that he had squeezed *Ivan Denisovich* through the bars of Soviet censorship. The bars had now sprung back together. Very little could escape, but everything that helped to spread the man's message, I thought, would make the chance of any repetition of Stalinism less likely. On the other hand, I knew that there were many in the Soviet Union who were keen to put back the clock and reimpose tough socialist discipline. I would join anyone who was brave enough to fight against them.

I little realized it, but I was soon to be given the chance of close involvement with Solzhenitsyn's best work. It would be, for any student of Russia, a most challenging opportunity, one that I was to seize most willingly, without realizing the full extent of the risks that I ran.

2. *The Translation of* Cancer Ward

In the late 1960s it began to be rumoured that Solzhenitsyn had completed two full-length novels, *Cancer Ward* and *In the First Circle*, both of them about labour-camp life. They were said to be great works, in the literary as well as the political sense. His *Ivan Denisovich* had made a massive stir both inside and outside Russia. The two new full-length novels, it was said, would be equally explosive and they were more substantial works. I had helped to promote *Ivan Denisovich* in the *TLS* and on the BBC, and I was keen to make sure that these two new works reached the widest possible readership.

Still, few westerners had ever heard of him. His name was especially difficult for foreigners to pronounce. He was living in Ryazan, 400 miles south-east of Moscow. Communication with any Soviet citizen was then a dangerous and complicated matter. In Solzhenitsyn's case it was even harder, since he had no telephone, his mail was controlled and he lived outside Moscow's fifty-kilometre ring. It was doubtful whether any westerner had ever met him and it seemed virtually impossible for anyone to contemplate doing so. Still, I sensed that he was a giant, that it was only a matter of time before he emerged from obscurity to tower over his colleagues.

In mid 1967 I was surprised to find that there was one foreigner who had visited Solzhenitsyn in Ryazan and come to know him well. This was Pavel Lička, a journalist from Bratislava in Slovakia. Lička had fought against Nazi forces during the Slovak National Uprising in 1944. After the war he worked for the Communist Party's press department, but he resigned from this post in 1951 during the Stalinist purges and joined the local magazine *Kulturny Zivot*. His wife Marta, a translator from Russian, worked for *Slovenka*, a woman's weekly magazine.

It was Marta who made the first contact. 'Towards the end of 1966 our magazine wrote to various Russian writers asking for short extracts from their work. We wanted to print an anthology. Solzhenitsyn was one of them. Rather to our surprise, he sent us an extract, a chapter from *Cancer Ward*, a novel he was just finishing. We saw at once what a remarkable piece of work it was, although hardly suitable for a women's magazine. Pavel and I discussed and decided to hand it over to the literary supplement of the Bratislava newspaper *Pravda*. It appeared there in my translation on 7 January 1967.'

Ličko had contacts with Soviet officers through the veterans' movement from the Second World War. While visiting Russia in this capacity in March 1967, he sent Solzhenitsyn a telegram, asking if he could call on him. The writer replied, 'You are welcome to call next Monday, Tuesday, Wednesday or Thursday . . .' The enthusiasm of Solzhenitsyn's reply was the result of his excitement at news that part of his book had appeared in a foreign country, albeit in the obscure Bratislava *Pravda*. Ličko therefore travelled to Ryazan, where he was warmly welcomed, on the basis of the *Pravda* extract. He quickly won Solzhenitsyn's trust and he received from him a great honour, the first substantial interview ever given by Solzhenitsyn to a foreign journalist. On 31 March it appeared in *Kulturny Zivot* under the title 'One Day in the Life of Alexander Solzhenitsyn'.

Meanwhile, according to Ličko, around 20 March the two men met to discuss an even more important matter, in Moscow at the Café Lira off Gorky Street. Ličko (according to an affidavit that he later swore in London on 1st August 1968) says, 'Solzhenitsyn personally gave me the text of Part One of *Cancer Ward* and a copy of the play *The Love Girl and the Innocent*. We discussed at this meeting the possibility of publishing Solzhenitsyn's literary works, as a whole, abroad. I asked Solzhenitsyn directly whether he had anything against this and he replied that he wanted his work to be published in the first place in England and Japan, since he believed that the English and the Japanese have the most deep-rooted culture in the world. At the conclusion of our conversation I asked Solzhenitsyn whether I was to be his western literary representative. He replied that I was and that he wanted me to arrange for publication of *Cancer Ward* and the above-mentioned play as soon as possible . . .' Ličko wore the priceless manuscripts under his shirt for the rest of his stay in Moscow and took them back to Bratislava.

Solzhenitsyn studied the *Cancer Ward* extract from the Bratislava *Pravda* that Ličko had given him in mid March 1967, and sent Ličko several friendly letters. On 1 April he wrote: 'I am very grateful to you for your precision and accuracy . . . The make-up of your *Pravda* is unusual to our eye, but very interesting, with its sketches for my chapter . . . I would just rather that you did not translate *Cancer Ward* into Slovak as "oncological department". It is too specialist and medical. There must be a Slovak work for "cancer" . . . I wish you and your wife every success in your work . . .' He went on to mention some cuts made in the chapter by the *Pravda* editors and wrote again on 21 April: 'I have received the issues of *Kulturny Zivot* that you sent me. Thank you very much . . . I am pleased that our interview appeared, although I see that a few inaccuracies crept in . . . With all my heart I wish you success in your work! I have happy memories of our meeting . . .' A third letter dated 21 May began, 'I am glad that our interview has had further success . . . However, some of the biographical details are incorrect. Nothing can be done about this now . . . But don't let this list of mistakes cloud your good mood. In all substantial points it came out very well. I wish you and Marta all success in the work you are now beginning.' By his references to Pavel's and Marta's 'work' he meant the translation of the rest of the *Cancer Ward*, which was then being prepared by Magda Takačova, Pavel's sister-in-law.

It is clear from the warmth of the language used by Solzhenitsyn in these letters, and from the fact that part of *Cancer Ward* had already been printed through the agency of Ličko's wife with the author's approval, that Ličko was trusted by Solzhenitsyn and could therefore expect to be trusted by me. There was no doubt that he had given him *Cancer Ward*, as Ličko claimed, and that it was appearing in Czechoslovakia with the author's approval.

Ličko's interview was reprinted in the Russian *émigré* journal *Grani* and drawn to my attention by Alexander Dolberg, a Russian friend and writer who had escaped from the Soviet Union in 1956 and lived in London, writing under the name David Burg. As a result I was encouraged to drive to Bratislava from Warsaw, where I was working on a biography of their then leader, Władysław Gomułka, and make myself known to him. During several meetings in October 1967 I showed him my credentials, my reviews of Solzhenitsyn's work from the *TLS*, my radio version of *Ivan Denisovich* and my translation of Brodsky's poems. He showed me the manuscripts and the letters from Ryazan, and he gave me (in Slovak) the extract from *Cancer*

Ward that had appeared in *Pravda*. In this way we established one another's bona fides. I was aware of the risks to Solzhenitsyn that might arise from any premature publication of his work. On the other hand, a boost to his reputation in the West might help him. Most importantly, I was persuaded by the evidence that Ličko enjoyed the writer's trust and had been authorized to act on his behalf, both in Czechoslovakia and elsewhere.

In December 1967, shortly after my return to London, my cousin Guy died and suddenly I had the right to sit in the British Parliament as a hereditary member of the House of Lords. In Britain under Harold Wilson this was hardly something to be advertised. A few people were impressed. More people, especially in the media and publishing world, were embarrassed by or distrustful of anyone who stood to gain through the survival of such crude unearned privilege. It made them suspicious, or even hostile. Furthermore, draft legislation to reform the House of Lords and phase out its hereditary element had already been prepared by the Wilson government. It was anyway, I recall thinking at the time, hardly something that would have any bearing on my main hope of those days, that I would one day translate *Cancer Ward.*

There was a more important political distraction. At the end of 1967 Antonin Novotny's neo-Stalinist government of Czechoslovakia had been removed and the new communist leader, Alexander Dubček, had come to power resolved to build 'socialism with a human face'. Of course I supported Dubček's aspirations. It seemed a reachable objective, whereas the idea of removing Czechoslovakia from the Warsaw Pact and the socialist camp, as the Hungarians had tried to do twelve years earlier, seemed very dangerous. Also, it became easier to communicate with Ličko. The telephone link worked better. Visas were easier to obtain. The mail was interfered with less.

I had with me in London the extract from *Cancer Ward* translated by Marta Ličkova for *Pravda* and I arranged for it to be published by my former employers, the *Times Literary Supplement*. It was a second-hand version, translated by Marta from Russian into Slovak. It was then turned from Slovak into English by Cecil Parrott, who had been British ambassador in Prague in the early 1960s, and it appeared in the *TLS* on 11 April 1968.

Although it had undergone two translations, this first Western publication of any part of the novel alerted western critics to the existence of something important. The *Pravda* publication had passed unnoticed. The journal was too obscure. But the *TLS* was read all over the world. Solzhenitsyn heard of it on 13 April on the BBC's Russian service. 'A shock! Stunning but joyful! It had started!' he writes in 1980 in his autobiographical work *The Oak and the Calf.*[1] He had not passed *Cancer Ward* to the West, he continues, 'but if it had found its own way there, then that was how it should be, God's appointed hour had come'. This was how he welcomed the fact that, as he presumably knew, Ličko had passed a chapter from his book to a British intermediary, for publication in a British weekly.

Solzhenitsyn wondered how such impudence would be viewed by the authorities so soon (two years) after the Sinyavsky and Daniel trial. He reassured himself, 'I had a presentiment that I was being carried along a path where nothing could withstand me. You'll see, nothing will happen . . . What I had to worry about was not that it was coming out, but how it would be received there [in the West]. This was my first real test as a writer . . . I wanted peace, but I must act! Not wait for them to rally for the attack, but attack them now!'[2]

Solzhenitsyn explains that in 1967–8 he still hoped that *Cancer Ward* might be published in the Soviet Union. At one stage it was even set up in type for serialization in *Novy Mir*. It was not therefore seen as anti-Soviet propaganda. It was on the borderline of what might or might not be let through by the censors. Far from being actionable, it was almost publishable. There was never any hint in the Soviet Union that he might be prosecuted on the basis of *Cancer Ward*.

The question therefore arises, why did he give Ličko the manuscript and ask him to have it published in Czechoslovakia? And why was he writing letters to him about how *Cancer Ward* should be translated into Slovak? In *The Oak and the Calf* he does not answer these questions. Indeed, neither Ličko's name nor mine is mentioned in a passage which otherwise covers the episode in some detail.

I presumed, then as well as now, that the arrangements he made with Ličko were part of his tactic, his plan to put pressure on the Soviet leaders. An edition of *Cancer Ward* appearing in a communist country, albeit in Dubček's liberal Czechoslovakia, was a less provocative action than publication in the West. On the other hand, the Slovak edition was bound to be noticed and to be followed by publication in western countries, whether authorized or not. And if the book was going to appear anyway, with or without Soviet consent, they might as well make the best of that fact and publish it themselves. This, I suppose was his plan. Also, he looked forward to his 'first real test as a writer' on the basis of *Cancer Ward*. He believed rightly that he would pass it, that the book would be acclaimed as a masterpiece, and that this would strengthen his position both in the West and in Moscow.

The London publishers Bodley Head were now ready to invite me and Dolberg to translate the novel and the play *The Love-Girl and the Innocent* into English. It was to be done, though, on a speculative basis, without a set fee and through the payment only of royalties which might or might not materialize. Max Reinhardt, of the Bodley Head, explained to us that he could not be sure that the book, in our translation, would even be published, let alone become a best-seller. We might lose the race, in which case our work would be useless and he would pay us nothing.

The Bodley Head prepared contracts which I took to Bratislava. And on 22 March 1968, in 'Zachova Chata' restaurant, twenty miles outside town, Ličko signed it in the presence of my friend the novelist Alan Williams as well as myself, asserting that he was acting with the author's consent and on his orders. Ličko later signed another paper giving the Bodley Head permission to market non-English rights in the works. I then took the *Cancer Ward* manuscript and the contract across the border and flew home from Vienna airport. This was not as hazardous as it may perhaps sound. By March 1968 the 'Prague Spring' was in full flower. A wave of freedom was sweeping across Czechoslovakia and there was little censorship or restriction on movement into or out of the country.

We believed that our contract was valid, that it was what the author had ordered, but it was based on a word-of-mouth instruction from Solzhenitsyn to Ličko, delivered in a Moscow café and we were anxious if possible to strengthen this weak link in the chain of authority. Otherwise another publisher might beat us in an unseemly race to be first into the bookshops. At the same time, we knew that Solzhenitsyn was playing a complicated tactical game with the Soviet authorities and might find it inconvenient to give such an authority openly. He might conceal his true wishes, as Boris Pasternak did when

Dr Zhivago was first published by the Italian publisher Feltrinelli in 1956. Under KGB pressure, Pasternak asked Feltrinelli not to publish *Dr Zhivago*. But Feltrinelli, following what he believed to be his writer's true wishes, went ahead and did it.

In April 1968, Ličko went to Moscow to clarify the matter and obtain the author's confirmation of the 22 March contract. They did not meet. Solzhenitsyn was in Ryazan and could not come to Moscow. But they exchanged messages through their mutual friend, the writer Boris Mozhayev, and discussed matters through an intermediary, including the publication of the *Times Literary Supplement* extract which Solzhenitsyn already knew about. Ličko wrote in a letter to me mailed in Vienna on 12 May: 'I tried to make contact with Alexander [Solzhenitsyn] . . . I informed him exactly of the position. Above all I asked him to let me have the written authority needed by Max Reinhardt of the Bodley Head . . . Alexander does not want to reveal openly his connection with me and the Bodley Head, but he *fully approves* of everything I have done. He is pleased that an edition of his book is about to appear in England . . .' On this basis Dolberg and I were encouraged to press on with our work and the Bodley Head started selling foreign rights, with some success, although in each case there was a nagging fear that other publishers might be involved. There would be few prizes for any publisher or translator who came in second in the race.

Solzhenitsyn writes[3] that in public, under pressure from the Soviet authorities and especially from his 'old friends' like Alexander Tvardovsky on *Novy Mir*, he found it convenient to denounce all publication of his work abroad. He wrote to the Italian newspaper *Unità*[4] that no foreign publisher had received any manuscript or authorization from him. This was in at least one respect untrue. He had certainly given a typescript and instructions to Marta and Pavel Ličko, at least as regards publication in Czechoslovakia.

Ličko came to London in July 1968 and under the supervision of our solicitor Peter Carter-Ruck swore the 1 August affidavit to the effect that he was acting on Solzhenitsyn's behalf. The document was then used to protect *Cancer Ward*'s copyright, to keep anti-Soviet pressure groups out of the picture, to ensure that large numbers of editions of varying quality did not appear in a confused manner, as had happened with his previous works, and to make it possible to accumulate royalties on the author's behalf. In late 1968 and again in 1969 *Cancer Ward* was duly published in Dolberg's and my translation, first Part One, then Part Two, then the combined book, as was the play *The Love Girl and the Innocent*. Other versions licensed by the Bodley Head appeared in other western countries, to the benefit of Solzhenitsyn's reputation throughout the world as well as his bank balance.

On 21 August 1968, the Soviet army invaded Czechoslovakia. For a few months, though, some of the fruits of the 'Prague Spring' remained. Dubček was allowed, theoretically, to resume his place as his country's leader. The press was still more open than in any other communist country. Westerners could enter with visas issued at border posts. Czechs and Slovaks could travel in and out on their passports, without any special difficulty. In these circumstances I kept in touch with Ličko by telephone and visited him, and he helped me to keep up a barrage of journalistic attacks on the Soviet occupation of his country. In March 1969, for instance, he took me to meet Stefan Dubček, father of the Slovak leader, in Biskupice Hospital, ten miles from Bratislava. Stefan Dubček told me in slow but clear English, a language he had not used for many decades, how he first emigrated to the United States and worked as a cabinet maker in Chicago: 'I was a good worker, you know. I make good money, forty dollars a week. But I join American communist party. And then I decide to go to Soviet Union. I wanted to go there. That was my idea.' He had taken his whole family, including young Alexander, to Kirghizia in the far east of the Soviet Union, where their work was hard and little appreciated. 'I was working without one cent.' Even after the Soviet invasion of his country the previous August he remained a true believer. 'If Lenin was alive today, he would agree with what my son did.' It was the highest accolade that he could pay. At the end of our meeting, as we were leaving, he shouted into my tape recorder in English, 'I wish all the peoples good luck!'[5]

Ličko was clearly a product of this 'liberal' communist tendency in Czechoslovakia, which Solzhenitsyn at that time appeared to support, and we had no reason at this stage to think that Solzhenitsyn was other than content with the arrangements he and I had made. *Cancer Ward* was selling steadily. *The Love Girl and the Innocent* was about to be performed in America. The Bodley Head were collecting royalties.

On 4 November 1969, he was expelled from the Union of Writers after a disagreeable argument in the Ryazan branch. It seemed clear that press attacks would continue, although he was becoming more and more defiant, and the authorities seemed confused about what to do next.

In January 1970 I visited Moscow and stayed three weeks at the Metropole Hotel. My highest hope was to meet the man whose courage and genius I so admired, whose work I had played a part in bringing before the western public. I made contact with his friends, including Boris Mozhayev. He told me of his disappointment that the 1969 Nobel Prize for Literature had gone to Samuel Beckett rather than to Solzhenitsyn. The campaign against Solzhenitsyn in Ryazan had begun, he told me, a few days after the prize was awarded in October 1969. I also met the neo-Stalinist editor of the weekly *Literaturnaya Gazeta*, Alexander Chakovsky, who told me that the Ryazan expulsion move 'merely expresses the opinion of society'.[6]

I was not able to meet the man himself. He had never been interviewed by any westerner, I was told, and he was living outside Moscow, in the annexe to a *dacha* owned by the great 'cellist Mstislav Rostropovich at Zhukovka, 100 yards from the *dacha* of Academician A.D. Sakharov. His personal politics were at a delicate stage after his expulsion from the union. For seven years he had been a Soviet liberal, a member of the writers' establishment. He was now on the way to becoming an anti-Soviet dissident. He did not want to complicate all this, Mozhayev told me, by a meeting with a foreigner. Whatever was said about him in any foreign publication, it was likely to be used against him. Mozhayev did, however, pass me Solzhenitsyn's best wishes and there was no word of reproach for anything we had done about his work.

In June 1970 Edward Heath won Britain's general election and, in spite of my limited political experience, he offered me a job as a Whip in the House of Lords, the most junior of junior ministers. It was alarming. In 1967 I had been a BBC assistant script editor. Now I was the youngest member of the government. With or without any hubris on my part, nemesis was bound to strike.

At the outset I talked to Earl Jellicoe, Leader of the House of Lords and the person who had proposed me for the modest post, about my involvement in Soviet politics and attachment to Russian literature. I wanted to know, could this be an embarrassment? Was there anything that I ought to explain before taking up a government post? No one seemed perturbed. Like all new ministers I was interviewed by a MI5 officer, who told me how important it was not to hand in Top Secret documents at cloakrooms or leave them in parked cars or in restaurants. I answered his routine questions in all frankness, but nothing was asked about my eccentric literary interests. No one apparently saw any relevance in it, or any problem in my taking up the appointment.

It was Mozhayev who had told me about Dr Fritz Heeb, a Swiss lawyer who was to represent Solzhenitsyn's interests in the West. A few weeks after my return home in early 1970 Heeb made contact with the Bodley Head and, after showing a written power of attorney, was given copies of all our contracts and accounts, together with the promise of substantial cheques. We cooperated with Heeb in every way.

In June 1970 I called on him in his Zurich office and it was there that the doubts were first cast on Ličko's good faith. Heeb showed me a handwritten letter from Solzhenitsyn suggesting that Ličko 'shamelessly abused my trust'. This was a shock. I found it hard to believe it. The idea that Ličko had deceived anyone seemed bizarre. I had letters as evidence of how deeply Solzhenitsyn had trusted him. And there was no doubt that he had given him the *Cancer Ward* extract and manuscript, with orders to have it published in Czechoslovakia, after which it was bound to have leaked out to other countries.

Our sympathies for Ličko increased when word came to me in an unsigned letter that he had been arrested on 1 September and charged with spreading anti-socialist and anti-Soviet propaganda.

None of this seemed to cloud Heeb's cooperative mood. On 9 September he wrote to me, 'I am very grateful to you for your swift and proper publication of the works. This is why I do not want to cancel the hitherto existing arrangements . . .' On 6 October we all met at the Bodley Head's offices in London to negotiate new terms. These were approved and signed by all parties some days later, at which point the Bodley Head paid Heeb accumulated royalties of about £30,000.

He was about to receive a great deal more. On 8 October, two days after our meeting with Heeb, Solzhenitsyn was awarded the Nobel Prize for Literature. Sales of *Cancer Ward* soared and even *The Love*

Girl and the Innocent, a minor play, was a smash hit at the Tyrone Guthrie theatre by the time Dolberg and I reached Minneapolis later that week. Substantial sums from a dozen countries poured into the Bodley Head's coffers and into bank accounts set aside for the author's benefit. This great success had, of course, never been foreseen when we embarked on the translation of a little-known novel by an unpronounceable Soviet writer three years earlier, risking a year's work for an uncertain reward.

If we had not tied up the copyright in 1968, there would have been a plethora of pirate editions of the two works in many languages, badly translated and producing no payment for the author, as had happened with *Ivan Denisovich*, which was in the public domain. In the event, no one paid Solzhenitsyn on anything like the scale that we did. And I believe that it was partially through our efforts, on the basis of the English version of *Cancer Ward*, now widely seen as his finest novel and, in 1994, still on sale in our translation, that he was awarded the Nobel Prize.

Then suddenly, at this moment of high unexpected achievement, I found myself faced with an accusation which, if true, made me quite unsuitable to take part in the world of Soviet study, let alone serve as a Minister of the Crown. The abrasive columnist Auberon Waugh, writing in the satirical fortnightly *Private Eye* on 24 September, claimed that by publishing *Cancer Ward* with an authorization through Pavel Ličko we had made possible Solzhenitsyn's arrest on charges of circulating anti-Soviet propaganda. The piece went on to suggest that both Ličko (who was by then in a Slovak prison charged with *anti*-Soviet activity) and Dolberg might be Soviet KGB agents. The implication was that the KGB had orchestrated the book's publication, in order to provide ground for his arrest, using Dolberg, Ličko and myself as agents or dupes in the conspiracy.

As a government minister, however junior, I was an attractive target for *Private Eye* and I was the main object of the attack. Its crux lay in Waugh's line, 'It would be an odd paradox if a Conservative minister had been unwittingly working for the KGB, would it not?'

My first instinct was to reach for my lawyer, but Edward Heath's Attorney-General, Peter Rawlinson, advised me that there was no need to sue. 'You should disdain,' he said. 'Ignore them and they will go away.' Any reply by me would stir the pot and worsen the brew.

There was also, he reminded me, a constitutional reluctance to involve ministers in any legal proceedings. Conflict between a minister and the courts was to be avoided at all costs. Ministers were therefore rarely allowed to be involved in litigation. However, *Private Eye* was busy building its reputation with fierce attacks on public figures and the prospect of linking a Conservative minister with the Soviet intelligence service was too good to miss. The revelations about Kim Philby, the KGB's most successful double agent, who had fled to Moscow in 1963, were fresh in people's minds. The *Sunday Times* had just revealed the full enormity of his betrayal. *Private Eye*'s people decided to continue the attack, some of them even having convinced themselves that they were on the track of 'the Kim Philby of the Heath government'.

'Looking back over my career to date, and at all the people I have insulted, I am mildly surprised that I am still allowed to exist,' Waugh later wrote.[7] It was a sentiment that I would fully have shared if I had heard it in September 1970. My greatest wish at that moment was to issue a writ of such magnitude as would deprive Waugh of his beautiful Wiltshire house. (It was before he moved to Somerset.) This would have been unfair. Waugh was not the main culprit. A keen observer of the British political scene, he was in this case writing of far-away matters of which he knew little. The instigators of the attack were not *Private Eye* satirists but professional rivals, 'experts' from the Sovietology world, Kremlinologists on the fringes of the CIA or MI6, other writers and journalists who specialized in Soviet issues, academics like Leonard Schapiro, rival translators like Max Hayward. They were a far weightier crew and they were gripped by the paranoia of those days, the belief in the all-conquering guile of the KGB, whose subversions of Philby and other men from the English ruling classes had rendered useless great areas of the British intelligence effort. If I sued, these were the men who would appear as witnesses for *Private Eye*'s defence.

I was up against an unholy alliance, which included dedicated men of the Left, including Paul Foot and the Irish nationalist Gerry Lawless, whose main aim was to attack the Conservative government, as well as men of the traditional Right, represented by *Eye* editor Richard Ingrams and Waugh himself. When Foot and Lawless wrote three whole pages of further attack in the 23 October *Private Eye* under the title 'Nicholas and Alexander', they were making common cause with right-wing experts in Soviet studies, jealous of our coup in having obtained and presented such an important book. Such deeds had until then been the prerogative of the CIA and the bodies of Russian émigrés in Munich and Frankfurt that they sponsored.

Also assisting *Private Eye*'s defence were Leo Labedz, editor of a CIA-funded quarterly about the Soviet bloc, *Survey*, and Peter Reddaway, a junior lecturer at the London School of Economics, a former friend of mine, a pupil of Leonard Schapiro and a young man of Christian fundamentalist conviction. These were scholars of a special kind, politically and emotionally motivated to fight the Kremlin adversary as they saw fit and ready to use tough methods against those with whom they disagreed. They were the moving force. I remember Reddaway saying, 'We are engaged in an underground war against the Soviet government. Anyone who risks damaging the underground has to be eliminated.'

It was an Old Etonian occasional book-reviewer, John Jolliffe, a man who dabbled in Soviet studies and enjoyed a ring of literary friends, who first asked Waugh to write about it in his column. He sought Waugh out and invited him, an innocent in such matters, to look into the question of how *Cancer Ward* came to be printed. I cannot say what Jolliffe's motive was, but the result was that he caused, if not a conflagration, at least enough smoke to cause confusion among people who find such things confusing. 'It was widely considered that Dolberg was a suspicious character ... It was in this general context that I suggested to Auberon Waugh that *Private Eye* might try and investigate the matter,' Jolliffe admits today.

A few weeks later Jolliffe took another strange step. He invited my colleague in the Whips' office, Lord (Charles) Mowbray, to a lunch, where he regaled the bewildered peer with stories about the suspicious circumstances of the publication of *Cancer Ward*. After the lunch, Mowbray told me everything that Jolliffe had said. He did not understand much about what he had heard, he confessed to me, but it sounded like the sort of thing in which he ought not to get involved. He had no wish to conspire against a colleague on the basis of hearsay.

Private Eye never contacted me to check any allegation. They just printed them as the Sovietologists and the literary dabblers in Russian studies gave them out, at regular intervals during the second half of 1970, inviting my friends and former friends to their famous Soho lunches in the hope that they too might be sources of damaging ammunition and, if necessary, evidence in court. The diarist Nigel Dempster was one who was invited to contribute. Another was my old friend from Harrow days, Robin Butler, then as now a high-flying civil servant, a private secretary in Heath's office. They were being lunched in the hope of acquiring more darts that could be used against the target of the moment. 'Anyone got any dirt on Bethell?' Ingrams would ask, pouring wine and turning on his tape recorder. The results were disappointing. As far as I know, none of Ingrams's chosen informants chose to cooperate. Instead they reported to me what Ingrams and the others had said at the lunch. But it was then embarrassing for all of us when I found myself compelled, since justice was the only thing that could save me from professional oblivion, to ask them to repeat in court what they had told me in confidence and friendship.

Every two or three weeks another stone was thrown. It was no longer a question of one article in a scurrilous magazine. It was a campaign. People were saying that there is no smoke without fire and Waugh described me as 'an absurd and revolting young man' who was selfishly resisting pressure to leave his government job. ('Oh dear! Did I really write that?' said Waugh in 1993.)

The fact that I was under orders as a minister not to take legal action made matters worse, until people began asking, 'Why does he not sue?' It is a question that would only be asked by someone who had never launched such a suit. I came to realize that the law of libel is an unwieldy weapon, one that can ruin the person who uses it as easily as it wounds the person being sued. I was told that I had a good case, but that there is no such thing as an open-and-shut case and that, if I was to proceed, I must be prepared to answer questions in public about every aspect of my work in the field of Soviet studies, including how I acquired *Cancer Ward* and arranged its publication. I had nothing to hide myself, but Solzhenitsyn was in the Soviet Union under siege and threat of arrest, and Ličko was in a Bratislava jail. I did not want to find myself compelled to answer questions under oath in a way that might complicate their already difficult lives.

Finally it all became too confusing and annoying for my government sponsors and superiors, especially George Jellicoe, who was becoming nervous. His protégé was in difficulty, which was a reflection on his judgement – and not for the first time. While serving as a diplomat in Washington in 1950–51, he had been friends with the notorious Philby. He had trusted him and been outraged when Philby was recalled to London for interrogation in 1951 after the defection of Guy Burgess and Donald Maclean to Moscow in May of that year. Jellicoe took the view, in all innocence, that Philby was yet another victim of Senator Joe McCarthy, whose campaign of spy-mania and paranoia in Washington was then in full flood. Though entirely without blame, Jellicoe was seen by some as guilty by association and his career had suffered.

And now, in 1970, he was again being asked awkward questions. Why did you make Lord Bethell a minister? By what strange route does a British hereditary peer, a Lord-in-Waiting to the Queen, find himself in the weird world of East–West conflict, Soviet politics and modern Russian literature? Why is *Private Eye* accusing him of links with the KGB? My enthusiasm for Kremlinological books was too unusual a hobby for some simple Conservatives to accept as credible. There must be some other motive, they felt.

By the end of 1970 Rawlinson's original advice became unsustainable. I could no longer treat these repeated allegations with contempt and inaction. It had reached the stage where, by not suing, I was giving the allegations credence and they were spreading to American journals. On 28 December an article in *Time* magazine by Patricia Blake, another devout Sovietologist, spelt the allegation out in the clearest possible terms. Although she did not mention my name, she claimed that Ličko was 'a long-time Soviet intelligence officer' and 'the key figure in this elaborate plot' to bring about Solzhenitsyn's arrest. She even quoted Solzhenitsyn as denying that he had ever given Ličko any manuscript in the first place – a claim whose absurdity emerges from the writer's own letters. She quoted Leo Labedz's prediction that the KGB might sacrifice an agent (Ličko) to obtain ammunition against Solzhenitsyn, and the writer Robert Conquest was quoted as saying that Solzhenitsyn's 'likely' arrest would mark 'a war to the death against all opposition in Russia'. By contrast, Amnesty International adopted Ličko as a prisoner of conscience, since he was in prison awaiting trial, suffering for his convictions.

I did not feel compelled to resign. My conscience was clear and more senior ministers than I were being attacked by *Private Eye* with equal ferocity, Reginald Maudling (with justification) for sharp business practice, Jellicoe (with some justification) for heavy drinking, Heath himself (without justification) for his effete manner. If every minister being attacked by *Private Eye* were to resign, it would have been impossible to form a government. However, in the Prime Minister's eyes I was a special case. 'You were being attacked on security grounds. Of course you had no alternative but to resign and sue,' was the view put forward to me by Heath in 1990.

My reply was that I did not agree, since there was no basis for the allegation of KGB involvement. I had already, at Jellicoe's request, shown all my papers on the matter to the Foreign Office's senior expert in Soviet matters, Thomas Brimelow. He had in no way queried my version of events. There was no need to take the issue to court. Indeed, it would be highly undesirable to do so, since men living under Soviet control might be put at risk.

In December 1970 Heath informed me, through Jellicoe, that the affair was now an embarrassment and that I should think of my duty towards more important colleagues, towards the government as a whole and towards my country. I remember Jellicoe's words: 'You must now defend yourself. But you cannot do that from the dispatch box.' He explained that I had no alternative but to 'do the decent thing', resign from the government, take the matter to court and clear my name.[8] I was left by Jellicoe with the clear impression that, provided that I did this and won the case, I would then be reappointed. There were precedents for such a procedure, he said. It was in my own interest as well as the government's that I should 'bite the bullet' and take this line of action. As things were, my usefulness as a minister was non-existent. As soon as I won, though, it would be different. I would be able to carry on where I had left off.

He would help to make things as easy as possible. He would explain to colleagues that my reputation was unimpaired, that I had resigned not under a cloud, but because of a legal technicality. And, as a sign of his personal confidence visible for all to see, he would soon give a small 'farewell' reception or lunch in the House of Lords. And then, when I had won my legal case, there would be a chance of my reinstatement and indeed of promotion, whereas now there was none. This was the custom, he said. I believed him and resigned from the government on 5 January 1971.

The months that followed were not easy. It would have helped if Jellicoe had done what he told me he would and given me my 'leaving party'. It would have been a sign of his support. It turned out to be inconvenient for him to do so, as a result of which the impression was given that I had resigned under a cloud, cut loose from the government without so much as a goodbye. My friend Earl (Grey) Gowrie arranged for me to meet Richard Ingrams for lunch at his flat in Covent Garden. Gowrie's excellent champagne tasted sour as Ingrams and I sat awkwardly together in Gowrie's living-room eyeing each other suspiciously while trying to find a peaceful way out of the conflict. Anyway, we failed and as a result I spent early 1971 preparing to take *Private Eye* to court. A full-blown action, I was told by my barrister, Leon Brittan, could last three years and would inevitably be a terrifying ordeal, even if I won. If I lost – and in libel actions one can never be entirely sure – it might cost every penny that I owned. There is no legal aid for libel.

I also needed to know Solzhenitsyn's views before proceeding. My Soviet visa was delayed and it was only in July 1971 that I could get to Moscow. (It was my last visit to the Soviet bloc for more than fifteen years.) I met Solzhenitsyn's sister-in-law, Veronika Turkina, and gave her some papers, which she passed to him. She came back to me with the message that I had his sympathy in the matter. Thus reassured, I returned to London ready for legal action. Writs were prepared and served on *Private Eye* as well as on Auberon Waugh personally.

I knew well that my personal difficulties were small compared to those of the man I had allegedly wronged. The campaign against Solzhenitsyn intensified and he faced it with great courage. For instance, on 12 August 1971, KGB men burgled his *dacha* outside Moscow and beat up his friend Alexander Gorlov, who happened to find them at their work. The following day he wrote an open letter to KGB Chairman Yuri Andropov: 'For many years I have borne in silence the lawlessness of your employees, the inspection of all my correspondence, the confiscation of half of it, the tracking down of my correspondents, their persecution at work and by state agencies, the spying around my house, the shadowing of visitors, the tapping of telephone conversations, the drilling of holes in ceilings, the placing of recording apparatus in my city apartment and at my cottage, and a persistent slander campaign against me from the platforms of lecture halls, when they are put at the disposal of officials from your ministry. But after the raid yesterday I will no longer be silent . . .'[9]

News of Solzhenitsyn's problems helped me to keep my own in proportion, but it was not an easy path to tread. I was being tossed about by the great interests of the super-powers. Meanwhile my former colleagues in government were bewildered and vaguely suspicious about why I had departed from the scene so suddenly, with the naïve excuse that I was 'returning to my work as a writer', in the face of strange accusations in a satirical magazine, with no excuse or explanation provided by any senior minister.

Meanwhile the Soviet side were being equally suspicious and hostile. I made plans to go to Bratislava and visit Pavel Ličko's family. Ličko was in an unenviable position. The tough Kremlinologists were accusing him of being a KGB agent, while in fact he was serving eighteen months in prison for 'anti-socialism'. But on 23 September 1971, a telegram from the Czech embassy told me that my visa was cancelled. They even returned my £1.20 fee with an apology for the inconvenience.

In January 1972 I applied again, but this time the answer came in a different form. On 7 February I returned home from dinner to find friends and journalists telephoning with the strange news that Slovak television had just shown a twenty-five minute film called 'Who is Lord Nicholas Bethell?' Using letters, papers and tapes confiscated from Ličko's apartment, the film explained that Ličko had acted as my 'henchman' in an anti-socialist and anti-Soviet campaign. The narrator quoted my letters asking for biographical information about Gustav Husak and the other anti-reformist leaders installed by the Soviet invasion. These journalistic inquiries were presented as proof of attachment to MI6. It assured the viewers of Slovakia: 'Lord Bethell is not a figure we have invented for our story. He is alive and well, and he works against us continually together with employees of the British secret service.'

It was a sad state to be in, accused by both sides in the cold war of working, albeit unwittingly, for the secret intelligence of the other. But Ličko's situation was far worse. A few days earlier he had completed his term in prison. He was back at his home on Vlčkova Street, Bratislava. The television programme now made him a pariah. He was being attacked in Slovakia for being a British agent, just as he was attacked in *Time* magazine for being a Soviet agent. At home he was publicly branded as an anti-socialist traitor and he could not be employed. Prison had worsened his chronic bronchitis. And in these strange circumstances I could not even send him a postcard, or telephone him with a word of sympathy. Any help I might offer would have made matters worse for him. In the Slovak secret police's view he had worked for the West under my 'leadership'. The slightest approach on my part would have been seen in Bratislava as an attempt to revive our 'ring of spies'. And so for years he lived a life of poverty, abandoned by many of his friends, though his wife Marta and children continued to support him.

My usefulness, whether as writer or as supporter of Heath's government, was now small. After such an outburst on an official communist television station, the likelihood was that I would never again be allowed to visit a Soviet bloc country in search of journalistic information. This was a pity, though not a tragedy, and I did not feel inclined to complain. Visa refusal was something that had to be faced by any writer about Soviet matters, unless he was willing to curb his pen in his own and the Kremlin's interest. I was not prepared to curb my pen in this way.

But my problems at home were fundamental. If I lost the case, I could be ruined financially and professionally, and in the worst instance the evidence presented in the English court could be used to embarrass Solzhenitsyn. And I would be held responsible. I was forced to bear in mind the fact that I was a mere foot-soldier caught up in what was more than a 'great game'. It was a cruel battle and I was being fired upon by very big guns on both sides.

Still, I fought my corner as best I could. The facts in *Private Eye*'s main document of defence, largely provided by Peter Reddaway, were discredited and after some negotiation in June 1972 *Private Eye* admitted in open court that their charges were 'wholly without foundation'. They also apologized to Dolberg, paying both of us damages of £1,000 each and costs in full. Peter Rawlinson wrote, 'I certainly feel that the wording [of the apology] is categorical and sufficiently purges the libel. I well appreciate what you have had to go through over this matter . . .'

Ličko, contrary to the predictions of *Private Eye* and *Time*, was never brought under KGB control. He never gave evidence or any statement against Solzhenitsyn, although (I later discovered) he was pressed to do so in prison by Soviet as well as by Czechoslovak secret policemen. Bravely, he told them nothing that they were anxious to know. At that time the authorities, it turns out, were actually thinking of printing *Cancer Ward* themselves, as a way of opening negotiations with their turbulent writer. In short, the whole conspiracy theory centred on Ličko, Dolberg and *Cancer Ward*, as suggested by the Sovietologists and passed on by John Jolliffe to Auberon Waugh and others, turned out to be a figment of their imagination.

I take comfort in the fact that the 'Bethell v. Waugh' case, which consumed large quantities of *Private Eye's* time and thousands of their pounds, is not once referred to in Patrick Marnham's history of the magazine.[10] Nor does Waugh so much as mention the matter in his memoirs, which contain a substantial section on other won and lost libel cases. I can only conclude that *Private Eye* feel shy of mentioning it. 'It was not a libel action of which we were particularly proud,' Waugh confirmed to me when we met in November 1993, after expressing regret for what he had written twenty-three years earlier.

I pocketed my damages and went home from court, waiting for the telephone call that would offer me my government job back, as I had been assured. It never came. Prime ministers, I suppose, like to avoid the shadow of bad news. They have problems of their own, too many problems, and they see no reason to add to them. Edward Heath was worried about pay policy and striking miners. He was not going to take a risk over a very junior appointment by employing someone who had recently emerged from the libel courts, whatever the rights of the matter and whatever promises might have been made.

It was nevertheless the understanding, the custom, that any minister who resigned because of a legal problem ought to be reinstated as soon as the problem was satisfactorily removed. When it became clear that I was not being reinstated, questions were asked in some government circles. Several government colleagues, for instance 'Grey' Gowrie and 'Bertie' Denham, lobbied on my behalf. And it was mainly as a result of such friendly interventions, I suppose, that towards the end of 1972, when Britain was about to join the European Economic Community, I was asked by Earl St Aldwyn, Chief Whip in the House of Lords, whether I would like to be one of Britain's first members of the European Parliament. Six Conservative peers were to be nominated, I was told, and my name would be sent forward.

Solzhenitsyn's work was still, in spite of everything, my great fascination. I obtained from the Nobel Foundation in Stockholm the text of the Nobel Prize speech that Solzhenitsyn had been due to deliver in late 1970. They gave me the right to publish it, and this I did at my own expense in Russian and English on facing pages. It was yet another indictment of Soviet practice, though it ended with the optimistic idea that violence can be overcome by truth and art: 'One word of truth is of more weight than all the world.' On 14 October 1972, my translation of the speech was printed in the *Guardian* and read by the famous actor Paul Scofield on BBC Radio 3. It was later made into a film under the title *One Word of Truth*.

I remember the telephone ringing at home just before midnight on 30 December 1972. It was St Aldwyn, friendly but embarrassed. It had not been found possible after all, he said, to include me in the EP list. This was a further disaster. The EP appointment was important to me not for its own sake, but as a sign of rehabilitation, a symbol of the government's confidence. By first offering me the job and then cancelling it, the government were showing those in the know that the murk surrounding my case had still not been dispelled.

All this time I feared the consequence of making a nuisance of myself. So I waited a year and then, on 6 February 1974, I went to St Aldwyn to seek his advice. It was at that meeting that he confirmed to me something that my friends and I had always suspected, and which had long been rumoured, that MI5 and MI6 had advised Heath against offering me even the most lowly government post. He told me how sorry he was to have raised my hopes over the Strasbourg appointment in late 1972 and he explained, 'Ted [Heath] won't have you in the team. We sent your name in for Europe, but Ted crossed it off. MI5 and MI6 have advised him against you.'

A few days later Heath was no longer Prime Minister, so I felt able to write to him on 25 April to point out that in spite of my victory in the libel action the problem still seemed to be unresolved. I asked him if he would see me. His reply was two dismissive letters, dated 10 May and 4 June, not answering my request for a meeting and suggesting that I had misinterpreted what St Aldwyn told me. His second letter ended, 'I hope we can now consider this matter closed.' He was not prepared to give his former junior employee even a minute of his time. He was busy and it was all just too embarrassing.

Of course I could not consider it closed. The libel had apparently still not been purged, at least not in the eyes of the secret services or of the leader of my party. There was at that time no means of raising a grievance against MI5 or MI6, as there is now. I had appealed to the highest political level, but the leaders of my party, Heath and Jellicoe, would do nothing to help. Their answer was to suggest that no problem existed. I could only sit tight and wait for a change. And changes had not been long in coming. In 1973 Jellicoe had to resign his Cabinet post as Lord Privy Seal because of his involvement with a call-girl called Norma. Then Heath was thrown out by the electorate as Prime Minister, and by his MPs as leader of the party, in February 1974 and February 1975 respectively. Margaret Thatcher took over from him as Conservative Party leader in March 1975. A few days later a vacancy in the European Parliament occurred. Once again my name was put forward by Peter Kirk, the leader of our MEPs, and this time the new Conservative leader did not veto it. I was allowed to take up the Strasbourg post.

From that moment on, the secret services caused me no trouble and I had no complaint against them. I lost my ambition for ministerial office, but I was happy in Strasbourg and Brussels, especially as an elected member between 1979 and 1994. Still, for many years it irritated me that such muddle and evasion had surrounded the appointment and dismissal of a British minister, and that no one was prepared to discuss it with me, even long after the event. It was indeed a murky business, of no great concern to the British people as a whole or to my day-to-day well-being, but lurking like a shadow at the back of my mind.

Twenty years passed and finally, in 1990, I wrote to Edward Heath, reminding him of what had happened in 1970, making some of the points mentioned above and asking him to see me. He agreed, even offering to go to the Cabinet Office to consult his government's papers and refresh his memory about my case. I made an appointment and arrived with my dossier at his Belgravia home on 27 September. I waited for him, but he did not keep the appointment.

A few days later (2 October) he wrote to me, 'I have nothing further to add to what I have already told you. Nor am I prepared to contribute information from confidential documents to your autobiography. And, having read your letter of 10 September, I completely repudiate your allegations of muddle, yet [sic] alone of "a murky business". Nor were any "undertakings" of "favourable consideration" for a future appointment given to you. If you wish to influence future appointments in government, you had better speak to future prime ministers.'

3. Solzhenitsyn in the West

Meanwhile Solzhenitsyn was in Moscow, under fierce attack in the press, divorcing his wife, marrying a new and much younger wife, Nataliya Svetlova, starting a new family (three sons), harassed by the KGB, but not under arrest. *Cancer Ward* had helped him to achieve the Nobel Prize and world fame. It was also collecting large sums of money in a special account that we had opened on his behalf.

In the early 1970s I heard that Solzhenitsyn had written a more explosive and politically important book even than *Cancer Ward*. It was called *The Gulag Archipelago* and it was nothing less than a history of Soviet oppression, from the 1917 October Revolution to the present day. It was not just another criticism of the Stalin period, as his previous work had been. It explained on the basis of many historical examples that Lenin had been no less of a mass murderer, that the system had been rotten from the outset, far worse than anything that the Russian people had endured before 1917.

He wrote the unwriteable: that the Soviet *system* was bad, not just the way in which it was put into practice under Stalin, and that Russia under the Tsars had been better than the Soviet Union under Lenin and his successors. This was a violation of a most sacred taboo. It went against another taboo. It defended the decision taken by those Russians who fought in German uniform against the Soviet Union and Stalin in 1941-5. In other words, his book was anti-Soviet propaganda in the clearest possible sense.

It gave the word 'gulag', an acronym for 'labour camp chief administration', to a hundred languages. The cruelty of this system of mass incarceration of tens of millions, the author explained, was inbuilt into the Marxist and Leninist ideology. It was not an aberration or distortion of socialist law. It was bound to occur, given the concentration of power in the hands of the state bodies and the helplessness of anyone who sought to challenge it, whether with the gun or with the pen.

Not all the copies of the book were in the author's hands. More than one copy had been smuggled out of Russia. Another copy was in the hands of the KGB. English translations had been done and were ready to be printed as soon as the author gave the word. By mid 1973 it was clear the Soviet leaders were in a state of panic about it – and rightly so, for it presented a great danger to them. And in December 1973 the blow fell when YMCA Press in Paris published a Russian version of the book. The writer Lydia Chukovskaya correctly predicted the effect that it would have: 'In the immeasurability of its consequences it can only be compared to an event which occurred in 1953, the death of Stalin.'[1]

The men in the Kremlin were furious. But what were they to do? They could not use traditional Soviet methods. They could not kill him as they had killed Raoul Wallenberg. Those days were past. However, if they jailed him, as they had jailed Sinyavsky and other writers, it would also make a bad impression and the matter would be a running sore in East–West relations for many years. There would be constant western demands, including from Western communists, for his release. On the other hand they knew that it was no longer possible for them to allow such a blatant 'anti-Soviet agitator' to live and work under the system that he now attacked so fiercely. He had presented them with a challenge and they would have to react.

They had solved the Sinyavsky problem in 1973. Andrey completed his seven years and shortly afterwards he and Maya were allowed to emigrate. I had just published at my own expense *A Voice from the Chorus*, Andrey's vivid labour-camp reflections. I dined with Andrey and Maya on 8 October 1973 in Paris and asked them whether Solzhenitsyn and his family would emigrate also. Choosing their words carefully, since they did not want to quarrel with him publicly while he was still in the Soviet Union, they said that they thought it unlikely. He distrusted the West, they said, and wanted as little contact with it as possible. He would never willingly leave Mother Russia. This was his principle. And it was only later that I came to know of the fundamental disagreement between Solzhenitsyn and Sinyavsky on this point, as evidenced by the former's reaction to the latter's jail sentence in 1966 (see p. 12).

The KGB acted finally on 8 February 1974. A note was delivered to the flat where Solzhenitsyn lived with Nataliya and their three young sons, Apartment 169, 12 Gorky Street, Moscow: 'Citizen

Solzhenitsyn A.I., You are requested to report to the office of the Public Prosecutor of the USSR, 15a Pushkin Street, at 1700 hrs . . .'[2] He was out of Moscow, at the Chukovsky family *dacha* in Peredelkino, and was told about it by Nataliya on the telephone. She had refused to receive it, complaining that it did not carry a proper reference number.

Nothing was done against him over the weekend of 9–10 February. 'To this day I do not understand why they did not take me at the *dacha* in Peredelkino,' he writes. But early in the morning of 11 February he travelled back to Moscow and not long afterwards an officer arrived at the flat with a fresh summons. They sat the messenger down in the hall while Solzhenitsyn typed his reply: '. . . I refuse to acknowledge the legality of your summons and shall not report for questioning to any government agency . . .'[3] It was not he who should be punished, he went on, but the NKVD and KGB people who had carried out mass killings and were guilty of 'genocide'.

He spent the next twenty-four hours waiting, expecting the KGB to come back every moment. But nothing happened. He knew from his experience in 1945 that, when waiting to be arrested, it was advisable to collect together a few simple things that would be useful in years to come. But the hours passed and they acquired a sense of false security. They listened to foreign radio stations, which were already broadcasting the statement he had just made that morning, and became almost relaxed, almost ready to believe that the authorities were confused by his demand that KGB criminals should be brought to trial for genocide, that they were ready to back off from a confrontation. They began to think that it was going to be a quiet day after all. He ate no lunch and took his youngest son, five-month-old baby Stepan, out for an 'airing'. His two other sons, Yermolay and Ignat, aged three years and eighteen months, stayed behind.

The bell rang just before 5 p.m. on 12 February. Nataliya answered it and, leaving the door on the chain, came back to tell her husband that it was the prosecutor's office again, this time two men. Solzhenitsyn went to the door and, after some discussion through the chink, they opened it. Immediately six other men appeared from nooks and crannies on the landing. A team of eight burst into the apartment, milled round him while he collected a few things, then took him down the stairs and into their car. They drove off, four men with Solzhenitsyn in the first car and four men in the car behind.

They took him to Lefortovo prison, medically examined him, searched him, took away his sheepskin jacket to be fumigated and his crucifix, since it was made of metal and could be used for self-mutilation. They then put him into a cell with two currency speculators, both of whom were puffing at cigarettes, an annoyance which inspired him to ask to be put in a single cell. He sat down, recalling the familiar details of life in a cell from his experiences more than twenty years earlier – the bright light in the ceiling in its wire cage, the black bread on the shelf, the judas window in the cell door with its cover swishing open and closed. He knew it would be cold that night and asked for his sheepskin jacket. They gave him a second blanket, a new one, which caused the speculators to be amazed at the VIP treatment being given to this weird unknown man in the long beard.

Just before nine o'clock that evening he was taken to M.P. Malyarov, the Soviet Union's Deputy Prosecutor, and told he was being charged with treason under Article 64 of the criminal code. He refused to sign the charge form. The possibility of being forced into exile did not occur to him at this stage. However, he did not know that in Bonn the Soviet ambassador had made an appointment to call at the German foreign ministry the next morning to deliver an important message. He assumed that he was to be tried and sentenced, either to death or to a long term of imprisonment. Otherwise why would Malyarov have mentioned Article 64 and treason?

Back in his cell, he instinctively picked his shoes off the floor and tucked them under his pillow, to ensure that they were not stolen, but also to lift his head into a better position. A guard spotted them through the judas window and told him to put them back on the floor. One of the speculators was unable to sleep, tormented by the thought of who might have denounced him to the police. Solzhenitsyn, with the wisdom and experience of the old prisoner, told him not to worry about such things. He must sleep, he said. Otherwise he would be in bad form for the next day's interrogation.

At the Gorky Street flat Nataliya was busy burning papers in anticipation of a search. She came upon a statement that her husband had prepared for just this eventuality: 'If such proceedings are taken against me, I will not go to the court on my own two legs. I shall have to be delivered with my hands bound and in a Black Maria. I shall not answer a single question put by such a court. If I am sentenced to imprisonment, I shall only submit to such a sentence in hand-cuffs . . .' [4] She immediately contacted the *Figaro* correspondent, who came round, collected the text and gave it out to the world's media.

The arrest was the main news item in almost every country and a brutal shock for everyone who had followed the story, like the moment in *Agamemnon* when the long-expected death-blow is struck. I was in some distress on the BBC's *Today* programme early in the morning of 13 February. It was the same sense of unreality that we had felt when the Soviet army invaded Czechoslovakia, I said. We expected it, but we were not quite ready to believe that the Kremlin leaders were capable of such brutal stupidity. Surely, I was asked, Solzhenitsyn had embarked on the course of opposition in full knowledge of what was likely to happen? I was shocked and replied angrily. Here was a man who had done nothing wrong, I told the interviewer. He had not killed anybody. He had not stolen anything. Where was his crime? He had written a book. Why should he be treated as a criminal? By what standards were we supposed to judge the Soviet government? Those of Nazi Germany? His arrest could only be seen as an act of insanity by desperate men.

In Lefortovo prison that morning it was time for reveille. Bread and tea were pushed through the cell's serving hatch, with 'some of Fidel's granulated stuff' [5] instead of the nice white lumps that he remembered from the past. He practised the long chewing routine that black prison bread requires, if indigestion is to be avoided. He asked his cellmates if they had ever heard of Ivan Denisovich. They vaguely remembered the name from the waves created by his book in 1962. 'Are you Ivan Denisovich?' they asked him. He found himself looking back at his life with detachment, not afraid, sure that he would not break under interrogation, but equally sure that he was shortly to die, either to be shot or to perish in the camps a year or two later. The thought did not alarm him, since his work was done. He had 'given them hell'. *The Gulag Archipelago* would soon be on sale all over the world. The Soviet system would never again be quite the same. He had wounded it severely.

They came for him half-way through the morning. Interrogation was about to begin, he thought. But he was taken not to the office where he had been the previous evening, but to a room where he was asked to put on a set of new clothes. Again, he asked for his sheepskin jacket. 'You are going on a journey,' they told him. He was taken briefly back to his cell, then to the office where Malyarov had seen him. He stood up in his new KGB clothes and Malyarov began reading a text: 'Decree of the Presidium of the Supreme . . .' At the mention of the word 'decree' he knew what was to happen to him. If there was a decree, it meant that there would be no trial. Therefore he was going to be sent abroad. He was right. The German government had already agreed to give him sanctuary. He was at once driven to Sheremetevo airport, where an aircraft full of passengers had been kept waiting three hours ready to fly him and his escort to Frankfurt. The aircraft took off, the KGB men goggle-eyed as he crossed himself and bowed to the receding land of Russia which he expected never to see again.

He spent the next few days at the home of his friend the German writer Heinrich Böll, with the world's press camped outside in the village streets, then moved to Zurich to be near his lawyer Fritz Heeb and to await the arrival of Nataliya and the three boys. For the next few months he was surrounded by journalists from all over the world, anxious to print anything he might care to utter. Every word he said was worth more than a piece of gold. *The Gulag Archipelago* was published. As predicted, its impact on world opinion was immense. It struck at the very root of the Marxist–Leninist thesis.

In March 1974 I wrote to him with what I thought was good news. More than 800,000 copies of *Cancer Ward* in my translation had been printed by the Bantam paperback house in New York. Of course I wanted to meet him, but I realized that there were many ahead of me in the queue. The obscure Russian writer, whose little-known work I had translated six years earlier, had become a hero, a saint and a superstar. I was happy to await his pleasure.

He and Heeb began receiving publishers, all keen to buy the rights in his books and, sometimes, but not always, to pay him for the books they had published in the past. However, the Bodley Head had already placed their accounts at his disposal and in their view had every reason to be proud of their stewardship. At last, in early November 1974, Max Reinhardt of the Bodley Head was called to Zurich to meet Heeb and his client. He set off, armed with cheques from the past and contracts for the future, fully expecting to bask in the great man's gratitude for all that we had done on his behalf.

It turned out to be one of the worst experiences of Reinhardt's life. Solzhenitsyn turned on him the full force of his matchless invective, which appears to have lost little in the interpretation from Russian into English. He told Reinhardt that all his agreements were worthless, not only the one signed by Ličko, but the one signed by Heeb also, even though it had been done by Heeb willingly and on the basis of a clear power of attorney that Solzhenitsyn had himself signed.

Reinhardt's distress emerges from the letter he wrote me on his return:[6] 'I found him [Solzhenitsyn] very upset and it will take a lot of patience and the paying of compensation to soothe him. Otherwise he threatens to make a public disclosure of the deal, which he considers unethical, when he goes to Sweden to receive the Nobel Prize at the beginning of December. He obviously has very firm views and knows his own mind . . .'

I now faced the alarming prospect of being denounced from the Nobel Prize rostrum by a man worshipped throughout the West as a saint. His name was on the world's lips. Amazed by the events of February 1974, the press were reacting to his every word immediately and without criticism. And the 'Sovietologists' of course adored him, as I did, for the grief that he had caused the Soviet government. But he was less than discriminating in his use of the great power that he possessed. With one word he was able to wound anyone who crossed his path and he was ready to use this power as he thought fit. Everyone who resisted his requests was liable to be attacked with the same vigour and in the same spirit with which he attacked the KGB.

We were not the first to feel the lash of his tongue or the sharpness of his pen. His book *The Oak and the Calf* contains many denunciations of former friends. Even his famous fellow-dissident Dr A.D. Sakharov was not spared, being accused[7] of being 'too pure' and 'pedantic', of looking 'hopelessly' on Russia's future and of placing too much emphasis on the problems of Jews who wished to emigrate. I had seen the effect of his words on those less well known, such as the biologist Zhores Medvedev and the writer Olga Carlisle, who had helped him at various times only to be rewarded with a few sentences which could do great damage to a personal reputation or to a career in the tight Sovietological world.

I had little stomach for a re-run of the legal battles of 1970–72, but there was no alternative but to prepare for them. It would have been madness, with the writer in such an ebullient mood, to give in to his threat that he would make our arrangements public, in Stockholm or elsewhere. Our whole case rested on the idea that we had nothing to hide, especially now that Solzhenitsyn was in the West and out of the KGB's clutches. Any hesitation on our part would invite further attacks and demands, perhaps even a revival of the *Private Eye* allegations. In fact, these were already beginning.[8] I had to make it clear that I too was ready to invoke the law and, if necessary, match the great man.

I knew too that I could expect little help from Reinhardt and the Bodley Head. They had their own interests in the matter. Their priority was to keep on good terms with their best-selling author. They had already in 1972 published *August 1914*, the first volume of his epic work on the First World War and the Russian Revolution, known as 'The Red Wheel'. They wanted to publish his future books.

I recalled that Solzhenitsyn had, rather surprisingly, allowed the Bodley Head to publish *August 1914* after and in spite of Pavel Ličko's 'shameless abuse' of the author's trust in facilitating the Bodley Head's edition of *Cancer Ward*. Their main concern now was to keep him as their author and, if necessary, to 'disrobe themselves' of those who had brought him to them seven years earlier. After all, Ličko was living in Bratislava, ill, unemployed and under secret police supervision. He was in no position to argue about what had been said in the Café Lira in Moscow in March 1967 (see p. 18).

I therefore sent Solzhenitsyn a long letter in Russian explaining the entire episode. His reply was the threatening letter with which this book begins.[9] I now, for the first time, wrote back angrily, pointing out that it was Solzhenitsyn who had first brought Ličko into the picture, by giving him his manuscripts as well as the first substantial interview that he ever gave to a foreign journalist, that it was on the basis of Solzhenitsyn's signature that I had trusted Ličko, and enumerating the benefits that the Ličko contract for *Cancer Ward* had brought the author, not only the money, but also the fame that had helped to win him the Nobel Prize and protect him from the KGB.

I challenged him to show that our 'slovenly and inaccurate' translation had caused him 'irreversible harm in the eyes of the English reader'. The truth was the contrary. The style of our version, I said, would have to remain a matter of taste. But it had now sold massively in Britain and other English-speaking countries over a period of seven years. It could not be that bad. In the United States more than a million copies of our Bantam edition were by now in print. Reviews had also been largely favourable and there had been no great attack on our translation, which continued to be on sale.

On the question of accuracy, I reminded him that he knew little English and that he must be relying on the advice of 'friends', whose motives in the matter I gravely suspected. There were plenty of people anxious to acquire the honour of translating the future work of such a writer. I invited him, if he really believed that the translation was slovenly and inaccurate, to prove it with facts.

A deafening silence ensued. Solzhenitsyn did not reply to my challenge and in September 1975 Max Reinhardt advised me that a 'stand-off' settlement appeared to have been reached that would allow our translation to survive. Solzhenitsyn carried out none of his fearful threats and I never wrote to him again, nor did I hear from him, but our version of *Cancer Ward* remained in print. It is still today the only one to be found on general sale in English-speaking countries, more than twenty-seven years after it was first printed, and I still receive a few pounds in royalties from it twice a year from the Bodley Head's successors, with a smaller amount from library loans.

The Bodley Head paid Solzhenitsyn part of the money he wanted and in return were allowed to publish three more of his books: *Lenin in Zurich* in 1976, *Mortal Danger* in 1981 and *Prisoners* in 1983. Sadly, though, his epic series of 'faction' designed to cover Russian history from 1914 to the death of Lenin in 1922 never achieved success. They were hardly noticed anywhere in the West and eventually he was forced to abandon the 'Red Wheel' enterprise entirely. His masterpieces *Ivan Denisovich*, *Cancer Ward*, *First Circle* and *The Gulag Archipelago*, written in the Soviet Union, remain to his eternal credit, as does his bravery in the face of the KGB's onslaughts. But his books written in the West disappeared, almost unread.

The whole seven-year episode leaves me with feelings of joy mixed with sadness. On the one hand, I am proud to have played a part in bringing to the English reader one of the great works of modern fiction. I am thrilled that our translation has stood the test of time, that copies by the million have been sold all over the English-speaking world. I also feel, even though Solzhenitsyn does not share my view, that I helped him to build up the reputation that he used in order to fight against KGB oppression and establish himself as a great writer. On the other hand, I am angry at having allowed myself to be caught up in a complicated aspect of the East–West conflict, the details of which I did not fully understand. The whole imbroglio cost me many sleepless nights as well as a question mark against my judgement and integrity.

It was not the idea of never again being able to serve as a minister in a Conservative government that disturbed me. A political career based only on membership of the House of Lords seldom makes sense. The elected House is the only serious fountain of power. I soon accepted that any politics of mine would best be done from the back benches, which meant that Edward Heath and George Jellicoe may well have done me a favour by talking me into resigning so timidly and without protest, in the expectation of reappointment after my case was won. I was able to move into other areas, writing books and articles about the Soviet bloc and helping the cause of Britain in Europe.

It taught me, though, that I would have to act with greater caution if I was to continue my involvement in the struggle to free eastern Europe from Soviet oppression. Neither the CIA/MI6 nor the KGB liked freelances. It was their private fight and they did not like outsiders joining in. They saw themselves as the professionals in the cruel game, the rest as the amateurs. Loose cannons, controlled neither by Langley nor by the Lubyanka, can damage the equilibrium of the intelligence world. Both sides are therefore keen to tip them into the sea.

David Astor, then editor of the *Observer*, told me, 'You rushed in where angels fear to tread.' I should have been more wary, he suggested. It was, after all, not only a literary matter. It was also politics at the highest international level, part of the great conflict of our age, and people's liberty and safety were at risk, not to mention the stability of both the Western and the Soviet systems. He was keen to convince me that young men, acting on their own, should think twice before venturing into such dangerous waters, where there are sharks on both sides ready to cause injury – as indeed both sides did to Ličko. Perhaps I underestimated how ruthless they can be, although I can be sure in my own mind that my motives in the matter were legitimate and that the result of my involvement was of benefit to Solzhenitsyn.

I learnt valuable lessons too about the ruthless single-mindedness of Soviet dissidents as well as about the duplicity of our own secret services and the bestiality of the KGB. And from then I worked on the Sam Goldwyn basis that verbal assurances are not worth the paper on which they are written.

As for Solzhenitsyn, I remain in two minds. There is so much about him that is admirable, his courage and the light of the genius that appears in his early novels. His achievement, literary and political, is undeniable and I would rather be thanked than insulted by such a man. I console myself with the thought that, after all he endured, he could never have been a man of reasonable and moderate views, a person who would negotiate a problem. 'East is East and West is West,' his friend Lev Kopyliev once said to me. 'You will not find Solzhenitsyn behaving with the fairmindedness of the educated westerner.' He stands on what he believes to be principle and the idea of sensible compromise is anathema to him. If he had been different, the KGB would probably many years earlier have crushed him, or deceived him into loyalty as they did so many million others, the brave as well as the craven. And so he turned on us all the anger that he had directed against them, but only briefly. He stopped, leaving us with our translation and our royalties for twenty more years. I suppose that we were one of the less important of his many conflicts and that he had other things to do. It may also be that he, in the end, understood the weakness of his case against us.

Alexander Dolberg is more of a victim of this part of the story. Only an idiot would now suggest that he was ever a KGB agent, or in any way beholden to the KGB. Yet *Private Eye*'s attacks on him caused him many years of professional grief, from which he never wholly recovered. Their libel of him was quashed by the court, but never truly reversed. Pavel Ličko was another long-term victim. His wife Marta says, 'Pavel refused to tell the KGB anything that they wanted to know. He admired Solzhenitsyn and we were both deeply wounded by suggestions that he might have wanted to cause him harm. It will always be a mystery who concocted this terrible accusation, or what their motives may have been.'

Solzhenitsyn, the man whom Ličko had supposedly damaged, lived well in the West after 1974, a multimillionaire revered by millions as a hero and a prophet. Ličko, on the other hand, paid a terrible price for his brief involvement in literary politics. It was not so much the eighteen months in prison. It was more the years of sad decline after his release in 1972. In the West he was being called a KGB agent. In his own country he was still being punished for being an agent of western intelligence. He was the nut in the cold-war nutcracker. He was never offered another job in Slovakia. The scandal slowly died away, but not enough to allow him any place amid the neo-Stalinism that followed the 1968 Soviet invasion. He and his wife never contacted me in the eighteen years between his arrest and his death in 1988. And I knew that it would be dangerous for me to take the initiative myself. Any approach by me to him, even so much as a postcard, would have been seen by the Slovak police as the first step in an attempt to re-establish some network of spies.

Ličko longed for political circumstances to change, not least so that he could sue *Time* magazine for calling him a Soviet agent in December 1970, but he became sadder and iller and died exactly one year before the November 1989 'velvet revolution' that would have freed him. In August 1990 the charge of anti-state activity against him was quashed by the Bratislava high court. In February 1991 I was invited to Bratislava, where the new democratic director of Slovak television, Roman Kalisky, apologized for the fact that his people had called me a British spy and an 'enemy' in 1972. In March 1991 they broadcast a television programme to set the record straight about my role in the matter, thus cancelling the programme 'Who is Lord Nicholas Bethell?' that their secret police had made for them to show on 7 February 1972.

In the light of what happened to Ličko between his arrest in September 1970 and his death in poverty in November 1988, it is therefore equally absurd to suggest that he ever acted on the KGB's behalf. He could have damaged Solzhenitsyn if he had wished to and benefited from denouncing him, but he did not. On the contrary, he was loyal to the man who insulted him. And communist Slovakia made him suffer for his loyalty, whereas the Western Sovietologists gave him no credit for it.

Solzhenitsyn had long-term objectives in mind and individuals who got in the way of these objectives sometines had to pay the price. He admits this in all frankness in *The Oak and the Calf* where he writes of the year 1971: 'I felt myself passing through a twilight zone in which resolution and the will to act were dimmed . . . I had not stood up for Bukovsky when he was arrested that spring. I had not stood up for [General Pyotr] Grigorenko. Nor for anyone else. I was busy planning and timing actions far ahead.'[10]

Even the columnist Auberon Waugh, whose revelations of 'KGB plots' in September 1970 had caused the whole affair to erupt, was in the end disillusioned with the man he had gone to such effort to defend. 'For a time he [Solzhenitsyn] was my hero . . .' he wrote in his diary in May 1983.[11] But the scales had now fallen from his eyes, he went on, and he now detected in his former hero a religious and national intolerance which drew him to attack the lack of spirituality of foreigners in the West almost as harshly as he attacked the Soviet communist system of his native land.

4. *After the Last Secret*

I had had enough of Solzhenitsyn and more than enough of the Heath government. Between 1972 and 1974 I gave my time to a project that I hoped would put both of them behind me. It was a book about the forcible repatriation of several million Russians and other Soviets to Stalin's tender mercies in 1945, under the terms of the Yalta agreement of February 1945. This was a little-known subject, a matter first whispered to me by my ex-Soviet Russian teachers in Crail in 1958. I could see from the outset that it was controversial, although I had no idea how controversial it was going to turn out to be, or how long the argument would last. My selection of this topic for a book had nothing to do with my involvement in Solzhenitsyn's work. On the contrary, I hoped that it would take me far away from the great writer's all-embracing influence.

It was too early, it seems, for me to escape from the man's looming presence. Unknown to me, Solzhenitsyn had also been studying the matter. And, whereas I knew about it from documents, he knew about it from personal experience. Opening the first Russian edition of *The Gulag Archipelago* shortly after it appeared in Paris in December 1973, I saw to my surprise that the author had also been studying the little-known historical events on which I had been writing for some years. He called it 'the last secret of the Second World War, or one of the last'. It was a good phrase, so good that I decided to use it as the title of my book.

Solzhenitsyn wrote that he had himself met many of these unhappy men, while himself a prisoner in the labour camps after 1945, and that they had been 'handed over in a perfidious way, typical of traditional English diplomacy'. In the eyes of the Soviet Union, they were the worst possible traitors. But Solzhenitsyn felt pity for them, and those Soviet men who had fought with General Andrey Vlasov and other Russian officers in Nazi German uniform: 'They would never had joined the Vlasovite ranks of the Wehrmacht if they had not been driven to the final extreme, beyond the bounds of despair, and if they had not nursed an unquenchable hatred towards the Soviet regime.'[1]

The Last Secret helped me to recover from the débâcle of a very short ministerial career, followed by the pyrrhic victory of the libel action. Published in 1974, soon after Edward Heath's fall from office, it provided a welcome diversion at the time from my battles against the malice of *Private Eye*, the paranoia of the secret services and the unreliability of political life.

The story began in July 1944, when London discovered that Russian men and women were being taken prisoner in large numbers on the Atlantic coast of France after the D-Day landings. Some were fighting, others working at forced labour, almost all of them in a German uniform of some sort. What was to be done with them? Were they enemies or allies? They surrendered quickly enough and they were very obviously a sad bunch of people. It was not hard to imagine what horrors they had seen, after being deported from the East by the Nazi German authorities. Still, it was undeniable that they were citizens of the Soviet Union, an allied country, captured working for the enemy.

Patrick Dean, then legal adviser to the Foreign Office, had no doubts. He explained their position in stark terms: 'This is purely a question for the Soviet authorities and does not concern His Majesty's Government. In due course all those with whom the Soviet authorities desire to deal must be handed over to them, and we are not concerned with the fact that they may be shot or otherwise more harshly dealt with than they might be under English law.' The decision was taken partly because of the burden that these large numbers of Russians were placing on scanty British resources, but also because of the overriding need to preserve the Western allies' alliance with Stalin. The whole world's future, it was believed, hinged on this alliance, which was to continue in peace as it had in war. We hoped too that our decision in Dean's sense would encourage Stalin to return Western prisoners of war liberated in the East by the Red Army. If we did the opposite, holding back Soviet citizens who wanted to stay in the West, for whatever reason, Stalin would not understand our humanitarian motives and his worst suspicions would be aroused.

It soon emerged, as the war drew to its close, that this would be a massive problem. The number of Soviets in Nazi-occupied western Europe numbered between 3 and 5 million. And many of them were very reluctant to return home to the tender mercies of Stalin's dictatorship. Even if they had not collaborated with the enemy, the mere fact that they had been in the West and seen it would be seen by Stalin as a sign of likely disloyalty in the future.

Lord Selborne, head of the subversive warfare organization known as 'Special Operations Executive', wrote to Winston Churchill, 'I greatly regret the Cabinet's decision to send these people back to Russia. It will mean certain death for them ... My officers have interviewed forty-five of these prisoners and in each case their story is substantially the same. After weeks of appalling treatment and such starvation that cannibalism was not unknown in their camps, their morale was pretty well broken. They were paraded and addressed by a German officer, who asked them to join a German labour unit. They were then asked individually whether they accepted the invitation. The first man replied no and was immediately shot. The others consequently said yes in order to save their lives . . .'[2]

The feelings of the prisoners were summed up in another report to Lord Selborne: 'We were told in Russia that the lot of the workers was better than in any country in the world. Since we have been taken prisoner we know that there is a better standard of life in France, in Belgium, in Norway for the worker than in Russia ... Stalin would never be able to have us back ... Our lives might be spared but the stigma of traitor attached to us would never be removed.'

On 22 July Anthony Eden, then Foreign Secretary, scribbled on Selborne's letter, 'What do you say to all this? It does not deal with the point, if these men do not go back to Russia, where are they to go? We don't want them here.'

Churchill was initially sympathetic to these Russians in Western hands, but in the atmosphere of the time Britain and the United States found it unthinkable to take the side of anyone who might criticize Stalin, the West's great ally, the leader of the army that had done so much to destroy Nazi Germany. The policy of forcible repatriation therefore went ahead and was confirmed by representatives of the three allies at Yalta in February 1945.

The West underestimated the desperation of those who were to become the policy's victims. On 28 March, for instance, it was reported that one Russian had hanged himself in a Yorkshire prisoner-of-war camp, while preparing to be moved to Liverpool where a ship awaited to take him to Odessa. Another Russian cut his throat on the quayside with the jagged edge of his china mug. The reaction of Foreign Office officials was confined to speculation over how such incidents could best be kept out of the press.

Ship transports of prisoners from Britain back to Russia that spring were marked by even more horrible incidents. Men who had attempted suicide were carried on to ships on stretchers. Others jumped overboard while their ships passed through the Straits of Gibraltar or the Dardanelles. Soviet liaison officers were constantly on the look-out for 'traitors' and, according to British escorts, many prisoners were being shot in quayside sheds immediately on their arrival at Soviet ports.

Violence reached its peak in the days following the German surrender in May 1945, when Western soldiers often had to use bayonets and rifle-butts, even flame-throwers, to pack reluctant Russians on to eastward-moving trains. The worst incidents took place in the Drau Valley in Austria. Just outside the town of Lienz 22,009 Cossacks – 15,380 men, 4,193 women and 2,436 children – were herded into a massive encampment. On 28 May their 1,500 officers were tricked into giving up their arms and boarding trucks for a 'conference' with British senior officers which would 'decide their future'. In fact the conference did not exist. The men were driven instead into a wire enclosure and from there, a few hours and a few more suicides later, across the bridge at Judenburg on the River Mur to Soviet-occupied territory.

The extraction of the officers, it was thought, would make the rest less reluctant to climb into the open railway cars that were sent on 1 June to collect the Cossack masses and deliver them to the Soviet zone. In fact, a battle ensued. The frenzied but unarmed crowd, led in prayer by Russian priests, resisted a battalion of Argyll and Sutherland Highlanders for many hours before being forced into the trucks which took them away to eastern Austria, then to Russia and then on to the 'gulag archipelago' in the east. Women ran to a foot-bridge and threw their small children into the River Drau. One man shot his wife, three children and himself, rather than let them fall into Soviet hands. Many other Russians died that day, either crushed and suffocated to death in the mêlée or by their own hands, so deep was their religious zeal and their resolve never to return to Stalin's evil and godless empire. Tough Scottish soldiers, hardened by years of war, were seen to be weeping openly as they carried out this most disturbing duty. A few days later almost all the 22,000, including the women and children, had been delivered to the Red Army.

Yet nothing was written about it in the British press. Nearly thirty years were to pass before the British people were made aware in 1974, through my book *The Last Secret*³ of what was done in their name at Lienz in May/June 1945.

Solzhenitsyn was serving eight years in the labour camps himself in the summer of 1945 as these men and women poured into the Siberian camps from western Europe, many hundreds of thousands of them, like shoals of herring. He shared with them the deadly privations of camp life, in particular the cold and the hunger that killed prisoners by the million, as he was to describe in *Ivan Denisovich* in 1962. He knew who these people were, why they were there and who had handed them over to the Soviet police. And he remembered it for the books that he was later to write. Meanwhile, the West knew nothing. And the British and Americans who had ordered or taken part in the operations were so worried by it all that they said nothing.

The Soviet émigrés who taught me Russian in 1957–8 were among those few who escaped forcible repatriation. They had been able to claim Polish or Baltic nationality, or they had found someone in Britain to vouch for them, or they had found their way to Britain and lain low until the policy was no longer applied. They were kind and intelligent men, but still in the shade of Soviet terror and they did not like to talk about the decision of an earlier British government that could so easily have killed them. We came to know them well, sometimes to drink with them, in which case the inhibitions would fall and they would reveal to us, very young men as we were and very innocent, how infected they were by the terror of Stalin's power to destroy. They wanted to know, for how long would they be safe in Britain? Might Britain even now, twelve years after the war's end, as part of some deal or some favour, hand them over to the Soviet rulers, who would undoubtedly kill them? Every small Soviet diplomatic gain was a matter of life or death. Every tiny improvement in Britain's relations with the Soviet Union was, to them, a hint that forcible repatriation might begin again.

Then suddenly in December 1973 the Russian version of *The Gulag Archipelago* appeared in Paris and the press published short extracts referring to this strange event. Solzhenitsyn wrote, 'It is surprising that in the West, where political secrets cannot be kept long, since they inevitably come out in print or are disclosed, the secret of this particular act of betrayal has been very well and carefully kept by the British and American governments. This is truly the last secret of the Second World War, or one of the last. Having often encountered these people in camps, I was unable to believe for a whole quarter century that the public in the West knew *nothing* of this action of the Western governments, this massive handing over of ordinary Russian people to retribution and death.'

He was not entirely right. There were a few in the West who knew at least part of the story. I had not met the victims in the camps, but for several years I had been researching the events in the newly released archives of the Foreign Office and War Office, among British soldiers who took part in the operations and Russian émigrés throughout the western world. It was indeed bizarre. There must have been several thousand British soldiers and officials who had seen the policy's results at close range. They must have known for thirty years what terrible things had happened. And yet virtually nothing had ever been written about it.

But it was all there in the war diaries of British regiments drafted in the field in Austria, the worried reports of men like Major Thomas Goode, who was escorting truckloads of Cossacks to Judenburg when 'one officer cut his throat with a razor blade and slumped dying across my feet'.[4] He told me in 1973, 'With hindsight one should probably have turned the other way and let them escape. But at the time it didn't occur to us to do that. Our orders were so clear.' I met similar reactions from Major W.R. (Rusty) Davies, whose job it had been to lull the Cossack officers into a sense of false security, to deceive them into going meekly to the 'conference that never was', and from there back to the Soviet Union. 'It truly was a fiendish bloody scheme,' he told me.

I was therefore spurred on to finish the book quickly and in October 1974 it appeared, its title suggested by Solzhenitsyn's words. It was serialized in the *Sunday Express* and in the German magazine *Stern*. The BBC made it into a radio feature and a seventy-five-minute film, which was first shown on 22 November 1975. It appeared in many languages, even in Russian (at my own expense in London in 1977), and the émigré quarterly *Kontinent* printed several chapters.

My publisher, André Deutsch, gave me back the Russian-language rights for no fee on the ground that they were worthless.

By the mid 1970s a vague feeling of British guilt was beginning to appear. We the British, it seemed, were also liable to do awful things and to justify what they did on the basis that 'orders are orders'. In his Introduction to *The Last Secret* Hugh Trevor-Roper (later Lord Dacre) wrote, 'We have heard all these arguments from German soldiers. Perhaps it is salutary also to hear them from our own countrymen. It brings the dilemma nearer home.'[5]

It emerged that we had deceived these sad people because we were ourselves deceived. Not only the Left had supported the Soviet experiment. During and after the Second World War we had almost all consoled ourselves with the myth that Stalin's Russia, for all its faults, was a lesser evil than Hitler's Germany, our enemy. And now, it seemed, the whole moral basis of our recent crusade was being called into question by Solzhenitsyn's claim that 'these prisoners were handed over in a perfidious manner, typical of traditional English diplomacy'. It was embarrassing. Our hero Solzhenitsyn was calling our other hero Winston Churchill a war criminal.

As usual, he was over-simplifying. He asks his readers 'what political or military reason could there have been' for the hand-over of so many innocent people. There were of course many political reasons, though not necessarily valid ones. Trevor-Roper writes, 'He [Solzhenitsyn] saw Churchill and Roosevelt as criminals who sent millions of Russian political refugees back to Russia to be persecuted and killed. But this is to ignore the political context and the intellectual climate of the time. It is to regret the reality of the war, the pressure of emotion and propaganda.'[6]

In February 1974 Solzhenitsyn came to the West and joined in the debate. He and I did not communicate. We were still angry with one another about *Cancer Ward* and he was to write me an insulting letter. But I shared his view about the repatriation of Soviets in 1945. We both believed that things could not be left as they were. He came to London on an 'official visit' in February 1976 and, in the tradition of Russian Slavophiles, launched a series of attacks on the West for its weakness and lack of principle in the face of the Soviet threat. 'We used to worship the West,' he said in a BBC *Panorama* interview on 1 March. But by now, he said, the West had by its cowardice forfeited all right to respect and the Soviet Union was dominant. The West had given up not just five or six European countries, but all its world positions. It was absurd for the West to argue that they were making concessions so as to avoid nuclear war. The Soviet Union was winning anyway, without nuclear war. 'They can take you with their bare hands,' he cried out to us on television. And Britain, once the kernel of the Western world, was now less significant than Romania, or even Uganda. He told us, with great emphasis, that our Western society carried within it the seeds of its own destruction, that we were doomed to be overrun by the Soviet system.

In other interviews he recalled the shameful behaviour of the famous British leftists, for instance Bernard Shaw or Sidney and Beatrice Webb, who came to the Soviet Union and praised Stalin during his reign of terror and his artificial famine. For decades, he said, British MPs and writers had contrived not even to notice the 15-million strong gulag archipelago, let alone do anything to ease the torment of its victims.

He was shown my BBC film based on *The Last Secret*, which had been shown on television four months earlier. It made an impression on him and he said on BBC Radio,[7] 'Our freedom-loving Western allies – and not least among them you British – treacherously disarmed them, bound them and handed them over to the communists to be killed. They were sent to the labour camps in the Urals, where they mined uranium to be used against you yourselves.' However, his most poignant comment was on the BBC Russian Service, where he suggested that, as a result of what the British government did in 1945, 'the whole British nation has committed a sin, since they have neither admitted it, nor apologized for it, nor asked for absolution from it'.

It so happened that during Solzhenitsyn's visit a debate was initiated (on 17 March) in the House of Lords by several former Foreign Office men who felt injured by my book and its subsequent publicity. I took part in the debate and soon found myself under attack from a galaxy of former ambassadors. Lord Hankey pointed out that 'we had our hands absolutely full' in May 1945 and that his former colleagues were 'most humane men in no way lacking in human sympathy'. Lord Coleraine, who as Richard Law had served as a junior Foreign Office minister under Anthony Eden in 1945, waylaid me in the corridor to tell me that my book was 'unworthy of a historian'. Then, in his speech, he suggested that Eden's decision had been 'agonizing but courageous'. Without it, we might not have won the war and our own prisoners in Soviet hands would have perished. Why, he asked, should ex-ministers and officials today be expected to discuss on television the decisions they had taken thirty years earlier amid the rigours of war? We should be more understanding of their dilemma.

I decided that my best argument in reply would be to read out the letter written to the BBC by Solzhenitsyn a few days earlier, after he saw the film based on my book. He praised it for 'recreating in some degree the sharp pain of our Russian suffering'. 'Some of these people perished before my eyes,' he said. 'Those who took such decisions bear the responsibility for them for the rest of their lives and before posterity. Those who carried them out, when faced by film cameras, have no other justification to offer than "I acted on orders". Let us remember that this was the argument used by the Nazi war criminals and that it was never accepted as a mitigating circumstance.' I sensed an unusual hush among the noble ex-ambassadors as I came to the end of these few words in my speech.

I felt that we had won the argument, but that the business was not yet done. True, circumstances had changed. Our Soviet allies were now our adversaries. It *was* unfair to judge the events of 1944–5 in the changed political context of 1976. But there was no denying that we had done a terrible thing, sending to death in the Siberian wastes not only those Russians who had fought in German uniform, but also many who were totally innocent of any hostile act against us, not to mention large numbers of women and children. What could one say to Solzhenitsyn, who had watched these people slowly dying? Were we indeed, as a nation, in a 'state of sin'? If so we should seek forgiveness by admitting it and apologizing.

This was what Konrad Adenauer and Willi Brandt had done. They admitted Nazi Germany's crimes fully and frankly. In December 1970 Brandt went down on his knees by the memorial to victims of the Warsaw ghetto and the photograph was printed all over the world as a sign of German repentance. The German people could therefore, in time, be forgiven for what Hitler's people had done.

By the same token the Russian people could not yet be forgiven (for instance) for their massacres of Poles at Katyń and elsewhere in April 1940. The Soviets, far from apologizing, still blamed others for a crime they had themselves committed.

British unease increased with the publication in February 1978 of another book on the same subject, Nikolay Tolstoy's *Victims of Yalta*. It covered much the same ground as mine had four years earlier and it was to some extent based on it, but it was longer and more detailed. Coming as it did at a time of heightened Western perception of Moscow's ill-treatment of dissidents, especially the Helsinki Group, most of whose members were by now under arrest, it struck an immediate chord with public opinion. The whole issue was revived and the result was far more than the sum of two moderately successful books. The effect was multiplicatory. *The Last Secret* was reprinted. The BBC film based on it was shown again. The radio programme was repeated. Each book boosted the other. And out of the furore there was emerging a widespread feeling among politicians as well as among book-readers that something must be done.

The British offences were on a lower numerical scale of mass murder than those of Hitler or Stalin, but they evoked the same principle, the idea that we had a duty to apologize as a nation for what our leaders had done. I talked to sympathizers about how this expiation of our national 'sin' could best be achieved and various ideas emerged. Britain could, for instance, pay compensation to those few dozen surviving Russians who had been sent by Britain to the Soviet camps and then, years later, released to the West. Or we could contribute to the memorial chapel that would be built at Lienz in Austria, where the most brutal acts took place. There were practical objections to every plan and its difficulty increased as the public controversy grew ever more intense, both in Britain and abroad.

Articles in the 'heavy' press and discussions in the House of Commons about the terrible things done by British soldiers in 1945 dovetailed with regular reports, every few days, of yet another non-violent dissident being arrested or harassed in the Soviet Union. Our historical view of 1945 was now beginning to fall into line with public policy in 1978, if not with that of the Labour government, at least with that of the less pro-Soviet Conservative opposition. The British people were at last beginning to understand, thanks to Solzhenitsyn's books and Brezhnev's behaviour, how deeply cruel a society the Soviet Union was. Also, the idea that we, the traditional defenders of democratic principle, had so recently been Stalin's friends, acting as accessories to his mass murders, was a terrifyingly unpleasant discovery to British people who were hearing the story for the first time.

I reminded readers of *The Times* of the harsh attitudes taken in 1944 by Anthony Eden, Patrick Dean and other Foreign Office men. I mentioned some of those who had helped to administer the policy and had refused to talk about it during our researches – Thomas Brimelow, who had risen from the post of British vice-consul in Danzig in 1938 to that of head of the entire diplomatic service in 1973–5; Henry Phillimore, a member of our Yalta delegation in 1945, who had invoked the Official Secrets Act to explain his silence; Toby Lowe (Lord Aldington), who had taken part in negotiations about senior Cossacks in Austria, but who now wrote to me that he had no memory of it. Statements from these and others personally involved, I suggested, might 'quieten a growing sense of collective guilt'.

The Times's famous leading article that same day, 20 February 1978, headed 'On Britain's Conscience', was worded even more toughly, referring to the 'cold blindness' of British officials and inviting a parliamentary committee to check whether the House of Commons had been misinformed on the issue. On 25 February I first mentioned in the *Spectator* the proposal that I thought would suit the problem best: 'A memorial can be erected to commemorate those Russians . . . who perished in the Soviet Union.'

It was the start of an enterprise that was to consume many years of work and involve many angry disputes. My first inquiries showed that Labour's Foreign Office junior minister Goronwy Roberts did not share our views. He wrote to me on 14 March, 'The government of the day cannot and should not be held responsible for the action of previous governments at a considerable distance in time.' A few days later he told Conservative foreign affairs spokesman John Davies that it was impossible, at this distance, to form a clear judgement of the real balance of the problem.[8]

Therefore, he went on, since the question of guilt was not proven to the Foreign Office's satisfaction against either government, that of 1945 or that of 1978, it would be wrong for the government of 1978 to involve itself in the sort of symbolic gesture that we had in mind, since this would be 'tantamount to acknowledging guilt'. 'These grim events at the tail end of the world's biggest war call for calm and sober analysis,' wrote Foreign Secretary David Owen to Edward du Cann on 23 March.

On 8 April the BBC film based on *The Last Secret* was shown again on television. Among those watching it at my home were the 'cellist Mstislav Rostropovich, Solzhenitsyn's protector near Moscow in the early 1970s, and his wife Galina Vishnyevskaya, the famous singer. Her English was hardly good enough for her to understand the commentary, but I recall how she wept throughout the entire seventy-five minutes of the screening. A number of others, including Winston Churchill, the wartime prime minister's grandson, also confessed to having shed many tears as they watched the tragedy unfold. And so our emotions deepened and support for our enterprise gathered momentum.

An especially strong impression in the film was made by Zoe Polanska, who as a lonely fifteen-year-old Russian refugee had been put on one of the eastward-bound trucks and only taken off by a British officer at the last moment. She had then married a Scotsman and lived near Dundee, her sufferings of 1945 forced to the back of her mind before she contacted me through an advertisement in the *Daily Telegraph* nearly thirty years later.

However, the Labour government remained unimpressed, determined not to question the Foreign Office's role. 'It would be absolutely unfair to judge people who reacted to circumstances in a critical situation and I resent it,' said the House of Lords's leader, Fred Peart, on 20 April. It was the sort of protest that any Hitlerite or Stalinist could have made. Then, when asked about the possibility of a second debate on the matter, he said, 'I do not think so. We are too busy with Scottish devolution and other matters.'

Around this time I was told by Richard Ryder, an adviser in the private office of Margaret Thatcher, then Leader of the Opposition, that she, while unwilling to go against the official line by speaking out publicly at this stage, was privately sympathetic to the idea of a 'British gesture' of some sort and ready to help when the time was ripe. She spoke to John Davies in this sense.[9]

We were sufficiently encouraged to call a meeting in the House of Commons on 7 June 1978 to discuss, under the chairmanship of Sir

Bernard Braine, MP, the proposal that 'a simple stone memorial should be put up' to commemorate the innocent victims. Our plan was not to continue the pursuit of those who had initiated or carried out the policy, but to tell a cautionary tale, to show by what means a fundamentally decent government, such as the British government in 1945, could have been misled or bullied by foreign tyrants into taking such an indecent decision.

Davies was meanwhile going through the mysterious process known as 'taking soundings' among Conservative leaders, as a result of which he wrote[10] to me that reaction was 'far from encouraging'. Any Parliamentary initiative, he was told, 'would inevitably run into major difficulties with certain eminent members of the Party'. He had in mind, of course, those 'eminent members' who had been involved in the policy of forcible repatriation.

Our little *ad hoc* committee, known as the Yalta Victims Memorial Appeal, was nevertheless resolved to proceed and on 24 July *The Times* published our letter calling for funds for the memorial. There was no trace in it of the equivocation that the Foreign Office and ministers were urging on us. The memorial, we wrote, would be 'an act of remembrance and expiation' for 'a crime without precedent in our history'.

We had an impressive list of signatories: representatives of the two major parties, leaders of three minor parties, the Liberal leader Jo Grimond, the well-known lawyer John Foster and the historians Rebecca West and Hugh Trevor-Roper. The money began to come in, mostly in small amounts, and we were soon able to commission a sculptor. Ironically, our secretary was John Jolliffe, the same man who had invited Auberon Waugh and Charles Mowbray to attack me in 1970. At the time I was not aware of the part that he had played in that conspiracy.

On 29 January 1979, Margaret Thatcher intervened for the first time. She wrote to me asking me to keep her informed about the memorial's progress. 'I admire the robust and diplomatic way in which you are pursuing your aims,' she wrote, adding in her own hand, 'I enclose an *anonymous* contribution of £10.' Inside the letter were two £5 notes.

Our sculptor, Angela Conner, continued to design her work throughout that year. It was a fountain, a water-activated tilting dish designed to symbolize the lot of the political refugee, cast hither and thither by the waves of ill-fortune. A site was made available by the Borough of Kensington and Chelsea in London, the same authority that had obstructed the Katyń memorial in the early 1970s, on a triangular piece of grass opposite the Victoria and Albert Museum, next to the Ismailia Mosque. Outline planning permission was approved by the Borough of Kensington and forwarded to Michael Heseltine at the Department of the Environment. (Margaret Thatcher had won the general election for the Conservatives on 10 May 1979.) The Department felt obliged, having considered the nature of the project and its possible effect on Britain's relations with the Soviet Union, also to seek the approval of the Foreign and Commonwealth Office. The enterprise's whole viability was now thrown into question.

By the end of January 1980 we discovered that the FCO had advised Heseltine to cancel Kensington's approval of the V and A triangle site. They argued that the triangle was Crown land and that (as Goronwy Roberts had said in 1978) any symbolic gesture such as we proposed would be tantamount to an admission by the Crown of guilt over the issue. It would violate the principle that the Crown can do no wrong. They had no objection to a memorial being built, they said, but not on Crown land.

We suggested that a site on Crown land was all the more appropriate, since the monument would commemorate what was done by agents of the Crown without the British parliament's or people's consent. We knew, though, that the FCO would not accept this argument, since Goronwy Roberts had said in 1978 that it was impossible to apportion blame or indeed to form a clear judgement on the issue at a distance of thirty-three years, and Fred Peart had said that he resented our attitude.

Mrs Thatcher was now our only hope. Would she follow the FCO's advice that 'the Crown cannot be allowed to criticize itself' and that the memorial would do little but worsen already bad British – Soviet relations? Or would she be governed by her instinctive feeling that present Soviet oppression should be challenged and resisted, and past Soviet crimes made known to the world? On 28 January 1980, I appealed to her not to allow FCO objections to kill our project, pointing out that a government veto 'in this week of all weeks' – I had in mind Dr Sakharov's arrest six days earlier – would greatly dismay our many supporters 'who feel that a terrible decision was taken in 1944 and much injustice done in Britain's name'.

On 21 February the Prime Minister came back to me with a most encouraging reply. It was a typical example of her independent approach to foreign policy and it was, one must remember, two months after the Soviet invasion of Afghanistan. After much thought, she wrote, she had concluded that our memorial on Crown land could proceed, provided that its inscription was uncontroversial, imputing no guilt to previous British governments. This verdict reversed Goronwy Roberts's earlier conviction that any symbolic gesture involving the Crown would be, in itself, an admission of guilt.

We were nevertheless thrilled to have won this bureaucratic victory against assembled ranks of FCO and other British officials, to whom the project was anathema, since it revealed their predecessors' cold-heartedness in the face of Stalin's cruelty. We were grateful to Margaret Thatcher who, as usual, seemed to us to have taken a decision based on principle rather than political expediency.

We now had to negotiate the inscription with Michael Heseltine and the Department of the Environment. We wanted the memorial's text to commemorate the thousands of innocent people who 'were delivered against their will by Britain and her allies to imprisonment and death'. But this statement, although factually correct, was ruled out by the minister as 'controversial' and therefore not in accord with the Prime Minister's order. His alternative suggestion was that we commemorate those 'who were persecuted after their return' to the Soviet Union. This was unacceptable to us. We saw it as implying that the victims were merely 'persecuted', as opposed to tortured to death, and that they had merely 'returned' to Russia, perhaps of their own free will, as opposed to being beaten back by brute force. So the weeks passed as we negotiated with senior ministers about our little stone legacy. It was obvious that any proposed text was going to be controversial from one or another point of view.

Once again it needed Margaret Thatcher to break the deadlock. She wrote to me on 3 April, 'I do not think that in a brief inscription we can hope to embrace everything. The government has already come a long way towards your position and I personally have tried to be helpful . . .' She asked us to accept a compromise wording. And this, after some discussion, we did.

And so the memorial was built. It was a great day for us on 6 March 1982, when it was dedicated in a short open-air ceremony at the V and A triangle. We stood there together amid the traffic and in the shadow of Harrods store and the Mosque, several hundred of us, British 'perpetrators' mixed with East European victims – Croatians, Serbians and Ukrainians as well as Russians. The Bishop of London led our prayers. Zoe Polanska, tearful and dressed entirely in black, turned the tap to start the fountain, Bernard Braine made a speech and we all sang the hymns, ending with the National Anthem.

It is not an official 'British government' monument. No minister was present at the ceremony and it was paid for not out of public funds, but entirely by private individuals, MPs and others. But, as the stone inscription makes clear, those individuals were 'members of all parties in both Houses of Parliament and many other sympathizers', several thousand people in all, most of them contributing small sums. And, thanks to Margaret Thatcher, it stands on Crown land. As such, it amounts to a national apology as convincing as the one made by Willi Brandt by the memorial to the Warsaw ghetto.

I hope that Solzhenitsyn and other victims of Stalin's bestiality will accept it in this spirit, as a national expression of regret and as an expiation of the sin that Britain committed as an accessory in Stalin's mass murders in 1945.

5. Early Contact with the Sakharovs

Andrey Sakharov belonged to the other Russian intellectual tradition. Whereas Solzhenitsyn is known as a devout Orthodox Christian, a Russian nationalist and a 'Slavophile', suspicious of the West, a believer in Russia's special role in world history, Sakharov was a secular 'Westernizer' of the liberal centre-left tradition, a fighter for religious freedom, although he was not himself religious, a man keen to defend the rights even of those who strongly disagreed with him.

He was the leading figure in the Soviet dissident movement after Solzhenitsyn was expelled in 1974. He then stayed in the firing line from the mid 1970s, through the dangerous days of the early 1980s, attacking his task so effectively that when he died in December 1989 the Soviet system itself was already at the point of its collapse. I think that he and his wife, Elena, did more than any two other individuals to rescue Russia from the Soviet system and give it the chance to set off along a democratic path. It is a joy in my life to have known Andrey and Elena, and to have been able to help them at times of particular difficulty.

I first met Elena Sakharov when Solzhenitsyn was already in the West, fighting not against the KGB but against publishers and other westerners who, he believed, had exploited or misused his work. I came to see her on 24 October 1975, in Florence at the home of her friend, Maria Olsufieva, who was from a leading Russian émigré family. Elena – her friends called her 'Lyusya' – was a frail woman of fifty-two, her hair already silvering, but I was immediately struck by her powerfully deep voice. I remember her glasses, as thick as pebbles, worn because of a serious eye defect caused by a wartime bomb.

She would not normally have been allowed to visit Italy. She had paid the Soviet state no compliment and so could hardly expect the 'favour' of a foreign passport. But her health problem made it difficult for them to refuse her without seeming callous and attracting criticism from abroad. She was able to establish that the eye treatment she needed could only be performed in the West and she had spent that summer persuading the Soviet government to allow her to leave the country for the specific purpose of an operation by Italian specialists.

I knew her background. Her culture was Russian, though her origins were half Jewish and half Armenian. Her mother, Ruth Bonner, was a devout communist, as was her stepfather, Gevork Alikhanov, who had brought her up. He was a senior official in the Komintern and the family lived in as much luxury as the pre-war Soviet state could muster. They had an apartment in a fine Moscow building set aside for respected foreign comrades, who included Josif Tito and the Spanish Civil War 'star' La Pasionaria, and a dacha for weekends. She and her brother Yegorka, like the children of so many political parents, were brought up mainly by housekeepers and nannies.

She was the wife of Andrey Dmitrievich Sakharov, one of his country's brilliant nuclear physicists. In 1950, with his collaborator Igor Tamm, he worked out a method of electrical discharge in a plasma located within a magnetic field, so enabling the Soviet Union to produce its first hydrogen bomb and become a leading nation in the production of nuclear energy. He thus became known as 'the father of the Russian H-bomb', a title he hated. He spent these years in the secret city of 'Arzamas 16', the Soviet equivalent of Los Alamos, where American nuclear weapons were first developed. Arzamas 16, known in Tsarist times as Savora Pustin, was a town not far from the city of Gorky (Nizhni-Novgorod) populated almost entirely by scientists, all hard at work on military projects and sworn by every possible oath never to reveal the town's whereabouts or even existence, let alone what they were doing there.

After his achievement over the H-bomb, Sakharov was awarded the Stalin Prize and made a Hero of Socialist Labour. Many other honours were heaped on him, as was every available material comfort, including a dacha, a chauffeur-driven car and a personal bodyguard. The only privilege that he lacked was the ability to travel abroad. The state feared that he might divulge the precious secrets that he possessed. Otherwise, he was one of the system's most favoured sons.

Then in 1958 he began to take an interest in what he called 'social issues', or what the West would know as 'politics'. He fought the 'Lysenko Doctrine', the rejection of the influence of heredity, an ideological absurdity that had caused great damage to the development of Soviet biology as well as to the personal lives of many scientists. He also called for a ban on nuclear testing. In 1966 he wrote a letter to the 23rd Party Congress, arguing against the rehabilitation of Stalin.

He became a fighter, especially for the rights of minorities, for the right of free movement across frontiers and of self-determination for the smallest political unit. This would mean giving independence not only to the republics of the Soviet Union, but also to less numerous peoples, for instance to such 'nations' in the Caucasus as Abkhazia and Ossetia and – of special interest to Elena, who is half Armenian – the enclave of Nagorno-Karabakh. He writes, 'The republic of Nagorno-Karabakh will not belong either to Armenia or to Azerbaijan. It will be a separate unit and will possess the right to enter into economic and other relations with any other country it chooses'[1] (see p. 348).

A sharp conflict of view emerges from the writings of the two great dissidents. In *The Oak and the Calf* Solzhenitsyn damns Sakharov with faint praise. It was a 'miracle', he writes, with that touch of sarcasm that marks every reference to Sakharov and many other well-known figures, that Sakharov emerged from out of 'the swarms of unprincipled, corrupt, venal scientists' to defend victims of Soviet oppression. He speaks of Sakharov's 'serene trustfulness that comes from his own purity'.[2] The two men had met in the autumn of 1968, shortly after the invasion of Czechoslovakia and the publication of Sakharov's short book *Progress, Coexistence and Intellectual Freedom*. It was a memorandum which, while it confirmed his belief in 'the socialist course', attacked the system for its police methods and limitations on freedom of speech.

Sakharov, then, had access to top secret material. This gave him many privileges, although it also imposed restrictions. For instance, Solzhenitsyn claims Sakharov was not allowed to use a public telephone. All his conversations had to be from telephones that the KGB monitored. And he could only visit friends in apartments or houses that were on a list that the KGB had previously approved, again where they had facilities for listening to what was said. According to Solzhenitsyn, though, in the autumn of 1968 Sakharov and he were able to find such a place and they talked for several hours about how best to promote their dissident ideas. They discussed, for instance, how to combine in a protest against the Czechoslovak invasion, but dismissed the idea as unrealistic. There was no leading Soviet figure, they agreed, who would have joined them in such a 'disloyal' act. And the seven dissidents who actually demonstrated outside the Kremlin had been quickly arrested and imprisoned.

Sakharov's book marked the end of his association with the Soviet system. As soon as it appeared, he was at once deprived of access to secret material. His privileges were curtailed and he became more and more integrated into the dissident movement.

The following year his wife died of cancer, leaving him with a son and two daughters, and two years later he married Elena Georgievna Bonner. She at once encouraged him to pursue his social work, as a result of which she was soon being portrayed in the Soviet media as an evil, manipulating woman who was leading the great academician astray from the Soviet way. This was an exaggeration. Sakharov was well embarked on the dissident path before Elena came into his life, although she certainly helped him along it, sustaining his courage at every turn, whereas his son and daughters disapproved of his political activity and remained loyal to the Soviet system.

Elena and Andrey were often in disagreement with Solzhenitsyn, although Andrey goes out of his way to express his 'profound respect for him, for his gifts as a writer, for his historic achievement in uncovering the crimes of the Soviet state'. On 13 February 1974, the day after Solzhenitsyn's arrest, a group of friends gathered in the Sakharovs' flat on Chkalov Street to draft an appeal for the writer's release. A few weeks later they were both at a farewell party for Nataliya, the writer's wife, who was about to leave to join her husband in the West.

Their relationship was soured, however, when *The Oak and the Calf* was published later that year. Sakharov soon obtained a copy and studied it. He writes in his memoirs, 'Solzhenitsyn's mistrust of the West, of progress in general, of science and democracy, inclines him to romanticize a patriarchal way of life and handicrafts, to expect too much of the Russian Orthodox Church . . .' But their differences were not only political. They were personal too: 'Solzhenitsyn's sharpest, if covert, thrusts are aimed at my wife . . . [He] claims my wife pushed me to go abroad and abandon my public responsibilities, and got me to stress emigration at the expense of more important issues . . .

Solzhenitsyn gives a thoroughly inaccurate picture of Lyusya as some sort of hysteric suffering from "nerves". I am portrayed as an utter fool and completely under her heel . . ."[3]

At the end of 1974 a German correspondent brought Sakharov a copy of *The Oak and the Calf*, newly published, with a warm inscription from the author. Sakharov took the present and remarked to the journalist, 'Solzhenitsyn really offended me with this book.' The journalist replied, 'And he just does not care.'

By 1975 Andrey and Elena, with her daughter Tatiana and son-in-law Yefrem Yankelevich, were running a one-family 'law centre' or 'citizens' advice bureau' for those with some complaint against authority or some aspect of the system. About twenty people a day were coming to their flat to seek their help. Elena's and my common interest, when we met in Italy in 1975, was our connection with the Paris-based quarterly journal *Kontinent*. It had been set up in 1974 by Vladimir Maximov and we were both on the editorial board. She told me, 'We receive visitors, people we know and people we don't know, all in need of help or advice. Sometimes it is no more than a word of friendship or sympathy. Among them are those who are called dissidents, also believers in God and people persecuted for wanting to emigrate or for struggling for their rights as members of our smaller nations.' The visitors to her flat in Moscow knew where to come after reading about them in foreign journals or hearing them mentioned on foreign radio stations. Audrey and Elena also ran a fund to help the families of political prisoners, 'adopting' certain individuals such as Edward Kuznetsov, condemned for trying to escape abroad by hijacking an aircraft, and Victor Khaustov, jailed for sending Kuznetsov's diary out of the country.

The Sakharovs were not likely to be arrested. His fame as a world figure, who had helped to develop the Soviet Union's military strength, put him in the 'non-torturable class' and protected him from the KGB's worst excesses. The President of the Soviet Academy of Sciences assured his American opposite number that 'not one hair of Dr Sakharov's head' would be touched. Elena pointed out to us, though, in 1975 that, since her husband's head was almost bald, it was not much of a promise.

They would not arrest him, for reasons of state, but even in 1975 they were doing their best to isolate the family from society. Son-in-law Yefrem, a qualified engineer, was forced to take a job as a laboratory assistant at a place ninety minutes' travel from Moscow. He was also beaten up in the street and, when he reported the incident, he was told by local police chief Major Levchenko, 'It happens because you associate with criminals, all these people who visit your flat every day. So long as it goes on, we cannot guarantee your safety.'

A KGB interrogator, Syshchikov, warned her in the same vein, 'You keep bad company. Always remember that you have children, and that you have a grandchild.' Their telephone link with abroad was cut and foreign mail stopped arriving. 'At the end of 1973 we got 500 New Year cards from abroad, but at the end of 1974 we got none.' Moreover, their limited immunity did not extend to their close friends, two of whom, Sergei Kovalyov and Andrey Tverdokhlebov, had been arrested in the past year.

There was no way of treating her eye condition in Russia, Elena said: 'One doctor told me that, if he operated on me, his academic thesis would not be accepted. Another asked me straight out to discharge myself from the hospital. She was afraid for her husband and son. These are not terrible people, not bad people at all. But the fear in our country is such that almost everyone will think seriously about how any association with us might affect him or her personally.'

Sometimes an envelope did arrive with a foreign stamp, in which case it had usually been tampered with – the letter removed and something inserted in its place, a picture of a naked woman or a photograph of Dr Sakharov with the eyes pushed out. Such petty means were devised to harass them and waste their time. For instance, sometimes they were invited to collect a registered letter from the local post office, only to find that it contained a catalogue or advertisement.

I flew home from Florence and on 8th October described the bizarre life of the Sakharov family in *The Times*. The next day, by very happy coincidence, he was awarded the Nobel Peace Prize. The KGB, I later learned, deduced from this that I was the one who, for mischievous reasons, had arranged for the award to be made to yet another 'anti-Soviet' figure. It reminded me of a similar accusation in February 1972, on Slovak television, where I was accused of arranging for the Nobel Prize for Literature to be awarded to Solzhenitsyn (see p. 34). Sadly, in neither case was the accusation true.

The award helped Sakharov and his work in the short term. His telephone link with abroad was restored and a few weeks later letters started arriving too. However, when he asked for permission to travel to Oslo and receive the prize, the authorities refused, forcing him to dictate his speech to Elena in Italy over the telephone.

After the award a BBC *Panorama* camera team filmed him secretly with a tourist's cine-camera at his Moscow flat. He told them, 'There are definitely more than 2,000 [political] prisoners here. Maybe their number is 10,000. It is probably within these limits, but may be larger.' However, the number of people persecuted in other ways was huge, he went on. He mentioned, for instance, the scientist Yuri Orlov, dismissed from his job eighteen months earlier for defending him.

The BBC showed their interview on 8 December and the Soviet authorities were furious, cancelling other agreements that the BBC had carefully negotiated and setting other BBC departments at *Panorama*'s throat. That same evening I met Elena in Rome. She was preparing to fly to Oslo, with the Nobel speech in her handbag, the following day. She talked of her joy at the prospect of seeing her family again in Moscow a few days later, combined with the dread of having to return to a life of constant pressure and discomfort.

They were a family of seven. Elena's mother, Ruth Bonner, and her son by her previous marriage Aleksey Semyonov slept in the bedroom. Her daughter Tatyana with her husband Yefrem Yankelevich and their baby son Matvey (Motynka) slept in the living-room, while Elena herself slept with Andrey in the kitchen. And so they ran their various activities out of two rooms. They had access to a larger flat, but Mayor of Moscow Vladimir Promyslov would not let them move into it. And Promyslov was a man, she complained, who travelled as an honoured guest to the great cities of the Western world, receiving hospitality and honours everywhere he went. She could not understand why the West showed high respect to a man of such low principle, a man prepared to persecute the Sakharov family merely to please the KGB (see p. 204).

This was how life was always going to be, she said, very difficult and tense. 'I would not say that I was the most unloving mother in the world, but if I heard now that my children had got permission to leave Russia, which meant that I would never see them in my life again, my first reaction would be of relief.'[4]

The next day she left for Oslo, where she delivered her husband's speech on 10 December. We said goodbye in Rome with the assumption that it would be some time before we had the chance to meet again. I was by now on the Soviet Union's black list, unable to obtain a visa. 'The answer to your application for a visa is that there is no reply,' an official of the Soviet Embassy in London told me. 'And you must understand that no reply is also a reply.'

Sakharov was not allowed to travel abroad because of the military secrets that he possessed. And Elena, I had to assume, would be accused of exploiting her 'medical' passport for political purposes. It would be a long time before she was allowed abroad again. It remained nevertheless my intention to stay in touch with her and her family, to help her in every possible way and one day, if I was lucky, to meet her remarkable husband.

6. *Vladimir Bukovsky*

I first met Bukovsky when he walked through my front door in London on 5 January 1977. He was the next thing to a ghost, his cheeks concave, as if squashed in by two tennis balls, his hair a quarter-inch of bristle, his colour the shiny grey of someone who is or has recently been very close to death. His story was one of the most amazing of the Soviet Union's last years.

As a teenage schoolboy in the 1950s, he took the extraordinary decision to 'go into politics', by which he meant to devote his life to a campaign of non-violent opposition to the Soviet government and system. Quite deliberately he embarked on a way of life that was calculated to end his education, destroy any prospect of a career and deprive him certainly of freedom, possibly of his life. He made up his mind at this young age to submit himself to the KGB's full range of brutalities. And it was, one must presume, a matter of principle. For what other motive could there have been? An opportunistic search for fame or political influence could hardly have been the reason. It would have been a very rash prophecy indeed, almost a defiance of logic, for him to think that the contest was likely to end in his favour, or even that he had much chance of surviving it.

At that time not even the keenest gambler or the most imaginatively far-sighted careerist could have foreseen a chance of escape from the personal disaster that must inevitably result from Vladimir Bukovsky's decision to embark on a direct conflict between himself and the KGB on Soviet territory.

At the age of seventeen, in his last year at school in 1959, he started a satirical magazine. It was not political. It contained nothing more dangerous than irony and literary parody – schoolchildren poking fun at their teachers. It was done on a typewriter, in only one copy and the children used to read it together and laugh. It produced an amazing reaction from the Soviet authorities. Officials from the Ministry of Education and the Communist Party descended on the school. They set up a committee of investigation. They did not see it as a joke, but as subversion. The result of it all was that the headmaster of the school was dismissed, Bukovsky was expelled and his father, a loyal Party member, was given an official reprimand. He said, 'It was one more illustration of the view I had formed several years earlier – that there could be no freedom or true happiness in a society run along the lines of the Soviet Union.'

It was a line that he pursued for the rest of his adult life in the Soviet Union. He decided to fight the system and to do so without one single compromise. This was most unusual, even for dissidents. Almost all of them compromised at some point. Sakharov, after all, was until 1968 a loyal Soviet scientist. And for several years after 1962 Solzhenitsyn supported the Soviet magazine *Novy Mir* and the Soviet 'Union of Writers' in Moscow. But Bukovsky never took a single step to meet the system's demands. 'I was the aggressor, if you like to put it that way,' he says.

He was told that he would never be allowed to go to university, that he must be 're-educated' in a workers' collective. He explains, 'Being Marxists, they professed to believe in the healing power of the proletarian collective. The meaning of their verdict was that I would have no chance of higher education and, therefore, would have to do manual work all my life.' But he said to himself at the time, 'Why should I be a toy, a thing, in other people's hands?' He found a way of beating the order and getting into Moscow University, where he studied biology for a year and organized unofficial poetry readings in the open air, as a result of which he was expelled and told for good measure that he should not have been at Moscow University in the first place.

In June 1963, as the Western world was idolizing Nikita Khrushchev for the publication of Solzhenitsyn's *Ivan Denisovich* seven months earlier, Bukovsky was caught with 'anti-Soviet material', Milovan Djilas's book *The New Class*. It was such a precious item in Moscow that he was lent it for just one night and photographed it, so as to have more time with it, and made two prints. He showed the photographed book to some of his friends, one of whom presumably denounced him. The KGB told him that, since he had made two copies, he must have been planning to read one copy and give the other to someone else. This was an aggravating circumstance. He had been 'disseminating' anti-Soviet material as opposed to merely possessing it for his own use.

He was committed to the infamous Serbsky Institute, where he was diagnosed as insane, and sent to the Leningrad 'special hospital' which treated political dissidents. Khrushchev had said, 'There is no one here who disagrees with the government. There are just a few madmen.' The police and courts took this as a signal of what they were supposed to do. It was a way of silencing the opposition without the trials in court that were reported in the Western press and caused the Soviet leadership such embarrassment.

This system was the blackest chapter in post-Stalin KGB oppression. Unlike the prisons and camps, the '*psykhushka*' was the scene of regular physical torture of the crudest type. Pain-inducing drugs were used to punish. Contraptions made of canvas were used to restrain and torment. Although he was never himself physically tortured in this way, Bukovsky says that of all his long years of incarceration his fourteen months in the special hospital were the worst of all.

His two cellmates were truly insane. One was a Ukrainian nationalist, who had gone crazy after seventeen years in solitary confinement. He spent his time shouting nationalist slogans and carving an intricate Ukrainian heraldic crest on the cell stonework. The other was a homicidal maniac who had killed his children, cut off his own ears and eaten them.

These horrors did not deter Bukovsky. Released from the 'hospital' after a few months, he returned to the bizarre form of politics to which he had chosen to devote his life. The KGB, realizing that they had a serious enemy on their hands, tried every way they knew to neutralize him through persuasion, including promises of a superb career, threats of death or mutilation and the offer of a passport to a new life in the West.

None of these interested him. He carried on his dissident activity to the ultimate conclusion. Each time he was released, he simply went back to opposing the system. It meant that he was never free for long. He was arrested in December 1965, served eight months, then was arrested again in January 1967 and served three years. He was free for just over a year before his final arrest in March 1971. In January 1972 he was sentenced to a total of twelve years, seven in labour camps and five in exile, on charges of anti-Soviet agitation.

In August 1975 his mother wrote to Amnesty International that he was facing 'a tortuous death through starvation' in Vladimir prison. He had been sentenced to six months on 'minimum' rations. The diet was worked out on a two-day basis. On the first day he would get sour bread, a little pickled cabbage, 70 grammes of salted sprats and 3 grammes of fat each day, most of which was of a type that he could not eat because of his duodenal ulcer. On the second day he had only 400 grammes of bread and some hot water. In 1976 he was reported[1] to be 'near death', with breathing problems and a liver complaint.

And all this time he knew that, if he only said the word, as soon as he agreed to cooperate with the KGB, his conditions would improve. He would then be pronounced 'cured'. His 're-education' would be deemed a success and he could be set free in a few months, since the KGB would have achieved a 'positive result'. He would not give the KGB the satisfaction, though. 'You have a greater interest in freeing me than I have in being freed,' he told the men who came to interview him.

My first involvement with his case was on 9 July 1976, when I introduced a resolution in the European Parliament asking the Soviet government to release Bukovsky, or at least to make sure that he did not die. I pointed out that less than a year earlier they had signed a document in Helsinki guaranteeing freedom of thought, conscience, religious belief, respect for human rights and fundamental freedoms, and that Leonid Brezhnev's signature on this paper would appear of little value if Bukovsky were allowed to die in prison. The EP accepted this Resolution unanimously, although no communist was at the vote.

I will never forget being telephoned by Amnesty International on 16 December 1976 with the joyful news that Bukovsky was free. He had, without warning, been taken from his cell and, in handcuffs, put on an aircraft with a substantial KGB guard. As they crossed the Soviet border, the handcuffs were removed. An hour later they landed at Zurich airport and within a few moments Bukovsky was free, exchanged for Luis Corvalan, a Chilean communist being held in a Chilean jail, a man in whom the Soviet government had an interest.

A few days after that, on 5 January 1977, I met him. He had spent eleven and a half of his previous fourteen years in various mental hospitals, labour camps and prisons. He had been released three times, but on each occasion he had at once resumed his dissident activity, in the sure knowledge that re-arrest must soon follow. He would have been forty-one when due to be freed from exile, if he had survived that long, although the release would almost certainly have been delayed, so defiant was his behaviour in prison.

He spoke reasonable English. Political prisoners had used English between themselves, when they did not want the guards to understand them. But in his weakened state it made him tired to express himself in a foreign language and so we spoke in Russian for several hours, listening to his bizarre story, which I had been asked to summarize for a British newspaper.[2]

A few days later Margaret Thatcher, then Leader of the Opposition, asked me to bring him to tea with her at the House of Commons. I remember that she was at her kindest and most solicitous. 'What can he eat?' she asked me. She had read that ill-treatment in prison had forced him on to a strict diet. She fussed over him in her most maternal fashion and he told her, much to her delight, that detente was a dangerous myth and that 'democratic socialism' was as much a contradiction in terms as boiling ice.

He despised westerners, he said, who believed in 'accepting reality', by which they meant reaching the best possible compromise with the Soviet Union. 'If I were to accept this, it would mean joining the Communist Party and the KGB.' He did not want Western leaders to sit down with Brezhnev and his men. He saw this as giving respectability to murderers.

These were not popular opinions. Acceptance of the need for detente still dominated Western thinking. The idea of 'winning' a conflict with world communism seemed wild and dangerous, evoking the nightmare of *Dr Strangelove* and world annihilation. Therefore, whereas admiration for the freed hero's courage was universal, there were not so many who agreed with his political views. On 13 January Prime Minister James Callaghan was asked in the House of Commons whether he too planned to meet Bukovsky. He replied, 'No', adding that he did not need Bukovsky's help in getting his views across and that approaches to the Soviet government were better done privately than through propaganda. Margaret Thatcher leapt at the clumsy comment: 'That is one of the most disgraceful and undignified replies ever given by a Prime Minister in this House.'

It was the beginning of my long friendship with Bukovsky, who turned out to be a clever political activist as well as a brave dissident. We cooperated on several schemes, as future pages will show, all designed to embarrass the Soviet system and accelerate its downfall. He also stayed on good terms with the future British Prime Minister, becoming one of her advisers on the Soviet Union, a spur to her resolve to challenge communism at every turn.

7. Sakharov and the Helsinki Group

It should have been an easier time for the Sakharovs after 1975. The Nobel Prize awarded to Andrey that year was a great honour. Even the Soviet government had to take account of it. And on 1 August 1975, the NATO and Warsaw Pact countries had joined with the rest of Europe and North America in signing the Helsinki Agreement, which had important human rights provisions. Then, in May 1976, some of these dissenters set up a 'Helsinki Group' to monitor the promises on human rights that Brezhnev had signed. The West had every right to expect a gentler Soviet policy towards non-violent dissenters, but the formation of the Helsinki Group was soon to lead to an even sharper degree of conflict.

I remember one happy moment in early 1976. Because of the Helsinki Agreement there was now for the first time, in theory, an automatic dialling facility between London and Moscow. Of course, it hardly ever worked. Usually the skill of the KGB combined with the incompetence of all Soviet industry unrelated to the military to make conversation impossible. One evening in early 1976, on an impulse, I picked up my telephone and dialled the Sakharovs' apartment - the number then was 010-7095-277-2720 - and a few seconds later I was speaking to Elena. Today there would be nothing strange about it. Telephones between Russia and England work well. But in 1976 it was astonishing. I talked to her and then to her husband for a full three minutes before the line went dead. It was a piece of luck, an achievement that I was not able to match for more than ten years.

The dissidents were working out ways of making use of the Helsinki Agreement and the Sakharovs were of course involved. In May 1976 I heard that a 'Helsinki Group' had been set up in Moscow. It was a few daring people who had taken it upon themselves to monitor the Soviet government's adherence to the human rights side of the agreement. Elena was a founder member. So was Alexander Ginsburg, Sakharov's good friend and helper.

The KGB's reaction was slow, but once they got moving Ginsburg was their first target. Sakharov reported, 'On 7 June 1976 police burst into my *dacha* by force, without showing any documents and preventing my family from moving from room to room. They telephoned me [in Moscow] and I spoke to the police, asking them to leave Ginsburg in peace and to leave my house. But they took him away by force to the police station . . . I demand an end to this illegal behaviour.'

Ginsburg was soon released from his 7 June arrest, but he was being harassed by police for spending too much time in Moscow with his family, instead of in Kaluga where he was registered. During the second half of 1976 the KGB began to find the group's activity intolerable.

A few days later a bomb exploded in the Moscow metro, killing four people and leaving others terribly injured. On 10 January 1977, the KGB journalist Victor Louis reported, 'Official sources hinted that the bomb may have been planted by a Soviet dissident group . . .' The aim was clear. Soviet dissidents were to be tarred with the same brush as terrorists from the Middle East or the IRA. If this plan succeeded, they would lose support both at home and in the West.

Sakharov at once rose to their defence, pointing out that Soviet dissidents rejected the use of force as a matter of principle: 'Our only weapon is publicity. It is this consistent and principled stand that has given dissidents their success and moral authority. . .'[1] He then, perhaps rashly, since it was an accusation that he could not prove, hinted that the bomb in the metro might be a KGB provocation, designed to discredit the dissident movement. The Soviet press at once counter-attacked, accusing him of 'slandering' the KGB, an accusation that they kept up for many years. Most importantly, though, no more bombs exploded in Moscow.

He came to the fore again in that same January 1977, when the new US President, Jimmy Carter, took office. Carter had taken a stand on human rights before the November 1976 election. He spoke about them in his interview for *Playboy* magazine that autumn and he showed every sign of wanting to continue this high-profile attitude. The dissidents were filled with hope and Sakharov took the unusual step of sending him a letter from Moscow: 'I welcome your election. Your decisive and unequivocal statements on human rights throughout the world give us new hope . . .' Carter even mentioned the sensitive issue of human rights in his January 1977 Inauguration Day address: 'Because we are free, we can never be indifferent to the fate of freedom elsewhere.'

'The utterances of the Carter administration already have a Wilsonian or missionary theme,' wrote the American journalist James Reston.[2] The question that emerged was whether the West might now be ready to exert economic pressure on the Soviet Union because of their oppressive behaviour towards the Sakharovs and others in the Helsinki Group, to deny them what the United States had hitherto seemed all too willing to sell them – scientific know-how, high technology and surplus grain. The Soviet government sensed this danger and decided to defend themselves against it by attacking the dissidents even more severely than before.

To the outrage of diplomatic purists, Carter sent Sakharov a reply to his letter. America would, he said, 'continue our firm commitment to promote respect for human rights, not only in our country, but also abroad'. The Soviet Union was nowhere in the letter mentioned by name, but Anatoli Dobrynin, Soviet ambassador in Washington, at once let it be known that such words, addressed in a private letter to one of Russia's great outcasts, constituted an impermissible interference in his country's internal affairs, in violation of Principle Six of the Helsinki Agreement.

The Kremlin, it soon emerged, was intent on heightening the confrontation. On 3 February, in what seemed like a direct snub to the United States and its president, the KGB launched an attack on Sakharov by arresting his close friend Alexander Ginsburg. Sakharov at once protested, 'For five years he [Ginsburg] was subjected to continual persecution. He was not allowed to live with his family. He was searched and picked upon by the police many times. The Soviet press poured streams of disgusting slander upon him. Now once again he is in prison. It is his third arrest.'

The Soviets were behaving badly and the US President was the one being blamed for his lack of caution and for provoking the Kremlin through his reply to Sakharov's letter, for (as it were) giving encouragement to the Soviet Union's enemies. What was Carter's letter, many asked, if not an act of gratuitous provocation against the Soviet Union? It would hardly help the Soviet dissidents. It was backed by no promise or undertaking. Indeed, it had probably egged the KGB on to even greater harshness.

Zbigniew Brzeziński, the new National Security Adviser, explained Carter's decision almost apologetically: 'After due reflection, the President wrote him [Sakharov] back a private letter, very general, restating in very general terms his concern for human rights, not pointed at any particular nation . . . a private communication not to be released by us . . .'[3] Its tone was that of regret. President Carter apparently felt the need to apologize for having sent Sakharov a note of encouragement.

Sakharov, although virtually alone and defenceless, living in Moscow and at the KGB's mercy, was less timid. Asked whether Carter's intervention had done more harm than good, he replied, 'Certainly not! Repression is part of our daily lives. It was under Nixon and Ford, before Helsinki, and it is so after Helsinki.' He went on to invite the United States to take limited sanctions against the Kremlin: 'To use food aid for political purposes I consider improper for moral reasons. And it would be completely wrong to make disarmament conditional, even on something so important as human rights . . . However I consider proper, for instance, a partial boycott of scientific and cultural contacts . . .'

On 5 September 1976, Elena, Tatyana and Yefrem, their daughter Anya and their son Matvey were allowed to leave for Italy. They organized 'Sakharov Hearings' in Rome. From there the young family flew to Boston, where they made their home and built new lives. It was a fulfilment of what Elena had told me in Rome in December 1975. She wanted to see her daughter safe in the West, even if it meant that she might never see her again. I was now able to communicate with the Sakharovs and write about them, not directly but by passing messages to Moscow through Tatyana and Yefrem in Boston.

Elena went through another eye operation, unable to speak to her husband by telephone or to receive his letters, and it was only on her return home to Moscow on 23 November that she learnt that her twenty-one-year-old son Aleksey was expelled from university for being her son. The Chkalov Street flat was now less crowded, but more lonely, and she had no idea how she would maintain contact with her daughter or grandson.

Sakharov carried on giving the West his advice. The mere mention of a political prisoner's name on the BBC or other Russian-language radio, he said, could sometimes lead to that person's release, or at least to an improvement in conditions of detention. The Soviet side needed trade more than the Americans did. The latter could do without vodka and other goods.

He suggested that Western policy be based on one essential maxim, that 'every instance of a violation of human rights should be made a political problem for the leaders of the violating country'.[4] I took this advice very much to heart, as an axiom of the human rights movement, and made up my mind to cause as many problems as possible for the Soviet government, until they improved their human rights record. And Brezhnev was on the offensive. He seemed to be saying that his government would continue to crush threats to Soviet internal security – for such was his view of the Helsinki Group and the 'documents' they circulated – without regard to Western criticism. He would show the United States and others who dared to attack him that he was boss in his own country in such matters. And, at the same time, he would show people at home what would happen to any of them who stepped out of line. This was Brezhnev's point of view. I saw no reason why the West should accept it.

In those difficult months, when communism was on the attack and liberty seemed an unattainable goal for the Russian people, with a weak President in the White House and Britain's governing Labour Party weak and split in its attitude to the Soviet system, some as opposed to it as we were, but others anxious to compromise with it and a few dedicated to its support, keen to import it into Britain in place of our own style of parliamentary democracy, there were those of us who seized every available opportunity of adding to President Brezhnev's problems, as Sakharov had asked us to, of chastising him for the misery that he and his men had imposed on Russian reformers and for the threat that they represented to our own democratic values.

8. The Helsinki Agreement

Détente, epitomized by the Helsinki Agreement (CSCE), may have been a pillar of government under Harold Wilson and Willi Brandt, with its main achievement, easier access to Berlin, much appreciated by Germany. But many Western experts saw it as a failure. 'It was not only a betrayal of the victims of oppression. It was a self-betrayal too,' wrote Soviet expert Edward Crankshaw.[1] President Ford's popularity declined by 7 per cent as soon as he returned from signing the agreement in August 1975. Ronald Reagan, who was thinking of running for President in November 1976, expressed his doubts about Helsinki in very simple language: 'I think it's time for us to straighten up and eyeball them [the Russians] and say, "Hey, fellas, let's go back to the track where it's something for something and not all one way." '

Many were by now sceptical of the Soviet Union's oft-repeated commitment to 'peaceful coexistence', realizing that this fine phrase meant different things to different men. Leonid Brezhnev, for one, did not interpret it as a promise to live and let live with the Western world. He meant that, although a *military* conquest of capitalism was no longer envisaged, the *ideological* struggle ought to continue unabated until victory was won according to Marx's and Lenin's teachings. The West would be 'buried' in peace but buried nevertheless. Helsinki was only the continuance of revolution and cold war by different means. It was designed to enable the Soviet Union to win the second cold war without firing a shot.

Russian dissidents and nationalists from the non-Russian republics were disgusted by it. Vladimir Bukovsky, then suffering ill-treatment in Vladimir prison, makes the most damning comment. The conditions of political prisoners' detention became worse as soon as the agreement was signed, he said. The signatures were on the paper and the KGB no longer felt the need to be gentle.

The terms of the agreement were mainly to the Soviet Union's advantage. For instance, Principle III proclaimed that 'the participating states regard as inviolable all one another's frontiers'. This was a recognition of the Soviet Union's wartime conquests. How was it meant to appear to the people of the Baltic states and the Ukraine, countries that saw themselves as occupied colonies, oppressed outposts of the Soviet empire? Most people in these countries wanted to change the Soviet Union's frontiers. They were now told by the governments in Helsinki that they could not do so.

Principle VI ordered all states 'to refrain from any intervention, direct or indirect, individual or collective, in the internal or external affairs' of another state. These words would be used again and again by the Soviet government in answer to all Western complaints about their oppressive policies. It made mockery of any attempt to enforce the UN Declaration of Human Rights. It was an assertion of total sovereignty, of complete control of the state over the citizen. It was the language of Enoch Powell (see p. 6).

Principle VII noted that states would 'respect human rights and fundamental freedoms, including the freedom of thought, conscience, religion or belief, for all without distinction as to race, sex, language or religion'. Soviet people were simply amazed by the cynicism that allowed Brezhnev to sign such a pledge, which he had no intention of putting into practice.

The Helsinki Group, a dozen or so Moscow-based dissidents, were the first to challenge this point of view. Their chairman was the well-known physicist Yuri Orlov. They included Elena Sakharov and the dissident ex-general Piotr Grigorenko. Their secretary was Ludmilla Alekseyeva. They took it upon themselves to test the Kremlin's good faith in having signed the Helsinki Agreement of 31 July 1975, and even if possible to enforce its terms. Other groups in the same vein appeared in Kiev and Leningrad, and in Georgia. I was one of those who, through my contacts with Ludmilla Alekseyeva, who emigrated to the West in March 1977, first reported in detail the significance of this group's pioneering activities.

When Alekseyeva first spoke to me after her release to the West, she confirmed what had been Bukovsky's initial view: 'I have to say that when Helsinki was first signed our first reaction was one of despair. It seemed to us a total surrender by the West to the Kremlin's demands for western technology and for the recognition of the Soviet empire.'[2]

But then, she says, the attitude changed. The agreement's text was

printed in full in *Pravda* and *Izvestiya* the day after its signature, 1
August 1975. Millions of Soviet citizens read it and they noticed that
it appeared to promise them certain human rights. 'It occurred to
them that it might mean something.' The West too had high hopes.
'There is no reason why, in 1975, Europeans should not be allowed to
marry whom they want, hear and read what they want, travel abroad
when and where they want, meet whom they want,' wrote the *New
York Times* the day after the agreement was signed. But the Soviet
Union saw it differently. Brezhnev, in Helsinki for the signing
ceremony, said, 'No one should try to dictate to other peoples, on the
basis of foreign policy considerations of one kind or another, the
manner in which they ought to manage their internal affairs.'

Soviet Georgians, Lithuanians and Jews were among those
interested in Principle VIII, which guaranteed 'equal rights and self-
determination of peoples'. It must mean, if it meant anything, that
these nationalities were entitled to greater independence from Moscow.
It seemed to be guaranteeing a range of new freedoms for the Soviet
people: 'The signatories intend to facilitate wider travel by their
citizens for personal or professional reasons ... to facilitate the
improvement of the dissemination on their territory of newspapers
and printed publications ... to contribute to the development of
contacts in the various fields of culture ... '

The Helsinki Group also included the Jewish activist and famous
'refusenik' Anatoli Shcharansky. The words obliging the Soviet Union
to 'deal in a positive and humanitarian spirit with the applications of
those who wish to be reunited with members of their families' were of
obvious interest to him. They would be used as a basis for requests by
Soviet citizens of Jewish origin to be allowed to join their families in
Israel or the United States. Among the other members were
Sakharov's friend Alexander Ginsburg, who ran Solzhenitsyn's fund
for political prisoners, and Anatoli Marchenko, author of *My
Testimony* and other important works.

The day after their inaugural press conference on 12 May 1976,
Orlov was called into the KGB, told that he was running an illegal
organization and ordered to desist. He replied that the organization
was quite legal and respectable, since its aim was to monitor an
international agreement signed by President Brezhnev himself.
Alekseyeva says, 'Of course we knew that our work would not please

the KGB, but we did not know what form this displeasure would take.'

The KGB's first attack was against Ginsburg, during the search at Sakharov's *dacha* on 7 June 1976 (see p. 84). But nothing much else happened. The authorities seemed baffled. The group were being openly defiant, but they had an obvious defence in international law and any move against them was bound to arouse the West's hostility. They started issuing their 'documents', each one a study of a particular human rights problem. The use of photocopying machines was illegal, so each document had to be laboriously typed out by volunteer helpers, using flimsy paper, so that as many carbon copies as possible, sometimes five or six, could be made each time. These copies, some scarcely readable, were then distributed to embassies and journalists.

The first, drafted by Mustafa Dzhemilyov, was about the Crimean Tartars, a community deported *en masse* by Stalin for alleged collaboration with Germany during the war. Although rehabilitated, not one of them was allowed to return to the Crimea. 'It is pure racial discrimination, which is forbidden by the Soviet constitution as well as by the Helsinki Agreement,' said Alekseyeva. 'The Crimean authorities just will not register a Tartar in an apartment. Even when one buys a house, they send in bulldozers to knock the house down. We listed several cases in the document, with pictures of their ruined houses and the family standing out in the open.'

Another document was about Soviet children being taken away from their parents. The law said that parents were obliged to bring their children up in a spirit of 'communist morality'. And the children of parents who refused to do this could be taken away into the State's care. The Helsinki Group listed six cases of parents, mainly Baptists, whose children had been taken away because they refused to obey it and brought their children up on religious rather than communist principles. 'We did not say that what was being done was against the law, only that the law was barbaric,' said Alekseyeva. Others highlighted by the group were the Pentecostals, several small communities of them, mostly craftsmen who were valuable to society. 'They believe it to be a sin to do their work badly.' Like the Soviet Jews, many of them wanted to emigrate.

The documents found their way to the West, where the press reprinted them or published summaries of them. These articles were broadcast back into the Soviet Union by Western Russian-language radio stations – the American-financed Radio Liberty, the BBC and Deutsche Welle. In spite of the jamming, large numbers of Soviet citizens thereby came to hear about them.

The Helsinki Group had discovered a way, albeit a very long and roundabout way, of communicating with the Soviet public. People started coming to see them and asking for their help from other parts of the country, often from thousands of miles away in the Far East. The American journalist Bud Korengold, then Moscow correspondent for *Newsweek*, says, 'Soviet citizens would come to my door and bring me these documents or proclamations. They would then go home and turn on their radios. Then, if they did not hear what they had given me on the radio within a day or two, I was some kind of idiot, or even a traitor.' It made the KGB even more irritated. And it was not long before they began to take action. Ginsburg was now being harassed by police for spending too much time with his family in Moscow. The family of Malva Landa, another group member, was threatened with dire retribution unless she stopped her work.

They waited till 25 December 1976, before making their move. 'They often do unpleasant things at Christmas,' said Alekseyeva. 'They know that many Western correspondents are out of Moscow, that your newspapers do not appear and that you have other things to think about than the Soviet Union.' The victims were members of the Ukrainian branch of the group in Kiev. KGB men spent all Christmas night searching their flats. They 'found' various forbidden items – 42 US dollars in Mikhol Rudenko's flat, pictures of naked women in Oles Berdnik's flat and a rifle buried in Oleksa Tikhy's garden. 'It was a bad development,' Alekseyeva told me. 'It showed that the KGB were now prepared to manufacture evidence as well as making full use of the already existing unfair Soviet laws against those expressing dissident opinions. Rudenko said that he had never even seen an American dollar before the KGB men showed him the money they had "found" in his bathroom. It was the same with the pictures of the naked women. It might be something not very important in the West, but in our country the possession of "pornography" is something that can totally ruin a person's reputation. And, as for the rifle, that was ridiculous.'

Then on 4 January 1977 the KGB searched the flats of three of the Moscow members: Orlov, Ginsburg and Alekseyeva. They took away trunkloads of papers and newspapers as well as a radio, a tape recorder and other valuable things. They also pretended to find dollars and several thousand roubles in Ginsburg's lavatory cistern.

It seemed that arrests of the group's leading members were now imminent. The first development, though, was an invitation from the Soviet visa office to Alekseyeva and her family to apply to emigrate, since her husband had family abroad. It was an agonizing decision. She and her husband were reluctant to leave for the comfort of the West while her friends were in such danger.

Then days passed, nothing happened and they thought that maybe the Soviet government might be ready to back off from further action. Orlov was a well-known physicist with friends in the influential scientific community. In mid 1977 the agreement would come up for review in Belgrade. The Kremlin, it was thought, might hesitate before making its negotiating position worse. And in the first days of Jimmy Carter's presidency Brezhnev would not lightly, it was thought, take action calculated to ruin relations with the leader of the other superpower.

The group decided that Alekseyeva and her husband could best help by leaving Russia and working for human rights abroad. Passports were issued on 1 February and they left the country, assuming that it would be for ever. I met them in Vienna a few days later, brought them to London for a meeting in the House of Commons and spent the next few weeks noting down her story, as summarized here, trying to make sure that the West knew as much as possible about the Helsinki monitors and their brave attempt to curb the KGB.[3]

The Arrests of Ginsburg, Shcharansky and Orlov

Jimmy Carter's first instinct, after a few days in office, was to defend the beleaguered group, but it soon emerged that the Kremlin was intent on confrontation. It was as if they wanted to make clear to the new President at the outset the position that they proposed to take on internal dissent in their country, to warn him that he would gain nothing if he tried to protect them.

On 3 February 1977, the KGB arrested Alexander Ginsburg. They had intended to arrest Orlov the same day, but he took a train to a village outside Moscow. 'He needed time to think and prepare himself,' said Alekseyeva. On 9 February he returned, not to his own flat, which was heavily staked out by police, but to Alekseyeva's flat, which was unguarded since she was about to emigrate. She was, as it were, crossed off the KGB's books.

He knocked at her door that afternoon. The door was opened and there was Orlov, his finger placed against his lips. The police might have gone, they supposed, but the microphones would still be there, so for several bizarre hours they communicated by pencil and paper. She even wrote down, 'Do you want tea?' Someone went out to a pay phone to summon friends and western journalists.

It would be undignified, they decided, to conduct the press conference with questions and answers in writing. Westerners in Russia did not like taking part in acts of petty deception, especially with the KGB nearby. Orlov therefore spoke to them openly for about twenty minutes. He planned to leave with them, calculating that they would not arrest him in their presence and that he would somehow manage to slip away.

The press conference was over and they opened the door. KGB men were standing in the hall. They looked out of the window. There were KGB cars in the yard. She picked up her telephone. It was dead. She was later told that it was cut off because she had used it 'for anti-state purposes'. Clearly the police alarm bells had rung as soon as Orlov started to speak. They had cut off her telephone and made their way to her flat at high speed. Orlov could not now leave without being caught.

They stayed in the flat, under siege, while the KGB waited for their orders. The next morning they rang the doorbell. Ten men entered the flat, found Orlov sitting in a chair and arrested him. 'They huddled round him while he put his coat on,' Alekseyeva told me. 'Guarding him as if he was a dangerous terrorist, rather than a fifty-three-year-old professor of physics who had written documents about human rights. A few moments later I looked out of the window and saw them drive him away – ten men and Orlov in four KGB cars.'

The KGB's fire now turned on the luckless Anatoli Shcharansky.

In his case the charge was treason. According to the Soviet press, although President Carter personally denied the allegation, he had been in contact with CIA agents and given them information about Soviet industry. In Georgia two other well-known dissidents, Merab Kostava and Zviad Gamsakhurdia (the future President of Georgia), were also arrested. Others were taken in the Ukraine. The Helsinki group could hardly continue its work in the face of such losses. Of the original members only Alekseyeva was free and in the West. Carter's initiative seemed to have failed. If anything, it had strengthened the KGB's ruthlessness and resolve.

Carter thus found himself in a most awkward position. His famous policy to protect the oppressed seemed to be doing more harm than good. He pointed out on 8 February that he had not the power to raise every individual human rights case, but he would do so when he could. 'I can't go in with armed forces and try to change the internal mechanism of the Soviet government,' he said.[4] Again, it sounded as if he were apologizing. The best he could do was to explain that he would continue to back Soviet dissidents, just as the Kremlin would doubtless carry on its support for communist parties and other pro-Soviet bodies throughout the Western world, and for leftist 'national liberation movements' such as the African National Congress and the Palestine Liberation Organization.

'Our commitment to the concept of human rights is permanent,' the President told the newly released Vladimir Bukovsky in the White House on 1 March 1977. But it was hard to see what precise commitment Carter had in mind, now that the election was safely won. An article appeared in the *New York Times*[5] with the heading: 'Human Rights: Talking is About All that Mr Carter Can Do'.

Many in the West were critical of a US President who had rushed boldly into the human rights arena, unarmed and unprepared, only to be blocked by a tougher and more skilful adversary. Talks on arms reduction vital to the entire world were put in jeopardy, it was being said, as a result of the President's inexperience and misplaced idealism. Brezhnev seemed to have outmanoeuvred the American leader at every turn. In a two-hour speech in the Kremlin on 21 March he referred to the arrested Helsinki Group members as 'persons who act against their own Motherland as accomplices and sometimes agents of imperialism'. These were people, he said, thumping the lectern repeatedly with his fist, who had broken away from Soviet society and, since they had no support inside the country, had turned to the West for help. 'Quite naturally we have taken and will take measures against them as envisaged by the law.'

With such bold statements the Soviet authorities blurred the moral issue of their cruelty towards political dissidents and confused the West into doubting the wisdom of lending support to communism's non-violent opponents.

It was, however, not entirely a defeat. Orlov and his team had achieved something unique. They had issued, between May 1976 and February 1977, nineteen public documents and seventy-seven press communiqués. They set up an organization openly critical of Soviet policy inside the country and kept it going over a period of several months, in constant contact with the Western press and radio, and through them with public opinion at home. They had, if only for a short period, been able to confuse their opponents, the KGB, into inactivity and carry on their work in peaceful opposition to Soviet policy. The attempt had, it is true, ended badly, but they had at least shown that opposition was possible, that there were ways by which a non-state group could communicate with the people and exert pressure on the Soviet government.

The Helsinki monitors played a big part in bringing Russia to democracy. Russia owes them much. At the time, though, I recall, it did not seem that they had accomplished anything. Their organization was smashed. The West had tried to help, but half-heartedly, dubious as to whether the movement was strong enough to be worth supporting. True, a very small group of brave people, ready to challenge the KGB openly, had emerged, but few Western leaders were ready to proclaim their activity as anything of political importance.

Was this the beginning of some great change, or merely a one-off dash for freedom that the KGB had successfully nipped in the bud, by arresting a few dozen people? Were the dissidents the beginnings of a popular movement or, as the KGB maintained, just a few freaks and criminals who deserved to be removed from a society that they in no way represented? I was one of those keen to support them, but even I underestimated their achievement. It seemed incredible that these few people could have launched a movement that would, within a mere fifteen years, see the Soviet Union's disappearance.

Imprisonment

Alexander Ginsburg was held awaiting his trial in Kaluga jail with twenty other men in his group of cells, twelve of them charged with murder. The KGB 'rented' a suite of rooms specially for his investigation and recruited extra guards who watched him day and night. They tried to break him with threats, telling him that, unless he cooperated, he would be charged with treason and shot and that his friends and fellow-dissidents would be arrested. These tactics did not work. He explains, 'I was an actor as a young man. When the interrogator told me that I had no hope of avoiding the death penalty, I replied that as a Christian it would be the greatest possible joy for me to die for my beliefs.'

His skill could not diminish his suffering, though. The threat of death brought on hypertension and a duodenal ulcer. He was in constant pain and the KGB used this fact to increase their pressure on him. It was the interrogators, never a doctor, who decided when or whether he received medication, using as their yardstick not his medical condition, but a judgement on how they might best persuade him to cooperate.

He had six interrogators of his own – three Lieutenant-Colonels, a Captain and two Lieutenants. He knew their ranks because, under KGB rules, one day in every week each officer was obliged to wear uniform. Officers assigned to the Orlov and Shcharansky cases also visited him from time to time. He calculated that the entire KGB team on the project must number several hundred. Under Soviet law he could have no contact with the outside world, no visits from his wife and family, no letters, not even access to a lawyer. He was thus entirely dependent on his own inner resources during the seventeen-month investigation in his battle against the KGB team. His only advantages were his friendship with Sakharov and Solzhenitsyn, who both did their best to defend him publicly. He was too well known and well supported to be tortured physically, killed without trial or allowed to die through neglect.

It upset him to know that the West, which sympathized with him, was all this time allowing its technology to be used against him. A strong directional microphone, made in the United States, had been set up across the road from his apartment in Tarusa and used to record his conversations. The man whose flat the KGB had 'borrowed' for the surveillance had shown it to him, complete with the maker's name. He noticed too how the KGB made liberal use of German tape recorders and Japanese cameras.

Some men were broken during their KGB investigation. In Tbilisi on 19 May 1978 the two main Georgian dissidents, Zviad Gamsakhurdia and Merab Kostava, admitted their guilt on charges of anti-Soviet activity and were sentenced to three years in the camps and two in exile. The reason for these lenient sentences was soon clear. That evening Gamsakhurdia appeared on television to offer public repentance for his crimes. He denounced his fellow-dissidents and expressed his deep regret for having 'defamed the Soviet state and social system'. His cooperation meant that he was in fact released in June 1979, just over a year later. All the dissidents who were to face trial therefore knew that they could, if they were so minded, escape from the prisons and labour camps quite easily. They just had to cooperate with the KGB.

Orlov was resilient. The main feature of his trial, which ended on 20 May 1978, was the appearance of fifteen prosecution witnesses explaining that the Soviet Union was not at all the grim place described by the accused and his Helsinki Group in their documents. Public opinion was portrayed as expressing its outrage against the accused's disloyalty. He was shown to have tried to humiliate his socialist motherland in collusion with the ideological enemy. He was sentenced to the maximum, seven years' imprisonment to be followed by five in exile.

Three weeks later, 12 June, I attended a bizarre meeting in the House of Commons, where a group of Soviet lawyers led by Samuel Zivs, vice-president of the Soviet Bar Association, spoke in defence of the Orlov verdict, outlining Orlov's 'anti-Soviet activity', which was in violation of Article 70 of the Russian criminal code. Zivs pointed out, 'We appreciate that you in Britain would not want such a law. But we in the Soviet Union have this law and it must be enforced.' British MPs expressed their outrage. The Soviet team paid little attention.

On 11 July it was Ginsburg's and Shcharansky's turn to come before the Soviet courts. Ginsburg, known to most as a quiet and studious man, was portrayed in testimony as a drunken debaucher living a parasitic life on money sent from abroad. Much was made of his participation in the Solzhenitsyn fund and of the foreign currency 'found' by KGB agents in his lavatory cistern.

The main character witness, Arkadi Gradoboyev, had served twelve years in jail for theft and pornography. 'God will punish you,' said Ginsburg's wife, Irina, to Gradoboyev outside the court. At once he went back to complain to the judge that she was threatening him with the vengeance of God. The judge then excluded her from the courtroom for the rest of the trial.

Ginsburg said before being sentenced, 'I do not consider myself guilty and do not ask for mercy.' As a re-offender he was liable to ten years. He says, 'They played a little game with me. The prosecutor told the court that he was only asking for eight years, because I had helped the police in the Shcharansky case. It was a lie, but it was a good piece of character assassination for them to use in their propaganda and to make life hard for me in the camps.' Shcharansky, on trial for treason, was accused of passing secrets to Western journalists, in particular Robert C. Toth of the *Los Angeles Times*, who the prosecution claimed was a Western agent. Toth denied the charge. Carter also denied that Shcharansky had any connection with the CIA. More plausibly, it was suggested that he had told journalists about Jews like himself who were not allowed to emigrate, on the grounds of access to secret material, and listed the places where they worked. In his evidence he denied that he had passed any secret to anyone, but explained to the court the need for the Soviet Union to accept the fact that some Jews wanted to emigrate to Israel. About 150,000 had already left in the eight years since limited emigration had been allowed. He was a Zionist, he said, but he was proud to have known such men as Sakharov, Orlov and Ginsburg 'who were carrying on the traditions of the Russian intelligentsia'.

The court was not impressed, especially when the accused ended his final speech with the words, 'I say to my wife and to my people, the Jewish people, "Next year in Jerusalem!"' The prosecutor's only concession was not to ask for the death sentence. Shcharansky was given a total of eighteen years: three years in prison, plus ten in the labour camps, plus five in exile. His seventy-two-year-old mother, not permitted to enter the courtroom, had spent the five days of the trial standing in the street outside.

A dozen other trials of Helsinki monitors, most of them from the smaller republics, took place in 1978. All were found guilty, all received heavy sentences and once again the West's reaction was minimal. Carter's only reaction was to cancel a high-level Soviet scientific delegation to Washington. There was talk of tougher action, even of economic sanctions, such as a ban on the sale of sophisticated computers and oil-drilling equipment, but many Americans argued that this would only benefit trade rivals, such as West Germany, France and Japan, whose leaders were often prepared to put business before principle. On 10 July David Owen was asked whether Britain should not now ban sales of technology to the Soviet Union. His answer was that this might put Britain's economic recovery at risk.

Prison Conditions

Over the years various well-known dissidents described to me in detail what it was like to be a political prisoner in the Soviet Union in the post-Stalin era. Ginsburg was taken to Sosnovka No. 1 camp in Mordovia, where he was made to grind sheets of glass: 'Lovely work! The air was constantly full of glass dust. Seriously, it was disgusting, for two reasons. First, it was nineteenth-century technology. Second, we were making ugly things. It is quite possible to produce things of beauty, even with old tools or on old machines, but we were making those big horrible mirrors that they hang in Soviet offices.

'I was entitled to a special diet because of my ulcer, a glass of milk every day and a little meat. In fact, it was too much trouble for them to give the milk out every day, so they gave me seven glasses once a week. And I did not get the meat. They claimed that they were putting it in my soup.'

Orlov was put to work on a bench, weaving wire into metal grilles, eight hours a day, six days a week. Any prisoner not fulfilling his production norm was punished – by reduction in diet, withdrawal of privileges such as letters, parcels or visits, by confinement in the camp prison and as a last resort, in the 'SHIZO', the *shtrafnoy izolyator* or punishment cell.

Most prisoners were young men, but Orlov was in his mid fifties and physically unable to sustain hard labour at the pace demanded by the camp authorities. The result was a vicious circle. His diet was reduced, so he became weaker, so his output went further down. He was sent to the prison six times, for six months each, making up nearly half his seven-year term in the camp.

He was treated in this way because of the Soviet government's special attitude to political prisoners. The camps were under orders to punish ordinary criminals, perhaps even to retrain and rehabilitate them, but the politicals had to be broken. It was the duty of the camp authorities to bring about a fundamental change in every political prisoner's attitude. Prisoner as well as commandant stood to gain materially from any such change. As soon as it was evident, conditions would improve and early release would be open to discussion, since the Soviet system's 'honour' was then satisfied. It also meant that Orlov, by refusing to cooperate, was under constant threat. The guards accused him of stealing a bar of soap and of starting a fight. He did these things, they claimed, not because he wanted soap but so as to cause disruption in the camp and sabotage production. 'There had to be a political reason for all my offences,' he says. 'Each time it could have meant a new trial and several more years in the camps. They wanted to keep up the psychological pressure.'

When his scientific papers were confiscated, quite illegally, he announced that he would refuse to work. He was given five days in the SHIZO: 'It was five days of complete isolation, with no books, nothing to read and nothing to write on. They would not even give me pieces of newspaper to use as toilet paper. They said I might read the print. They take away your clothes and give you just a light shirt, a pair of socks and linen trousers. You get very cold, especially at night, with the temperature down to 10 degrees. The problem is lack of sleep. My bunk was a line of wooden planks held together with metal strips. It folded up into the cell wall. Every night at ten o'clock the guard lets it down with a key from the outside and he closes it at six in the morning. You have no bedding or blanket, just your light clothes.

'I used to rub the planks with my hands to warm them up. Then I lay down, fell asleep, woke up ten minutes later because of the cold and started rubbing the planks again - and so on, hour after hour, getting just a few minutes' sleep at a time. Our food was 450 grammes of black bread a day and hot food, if you can call it that, every other day. I did two terms of five days, four of fifteen days, one of thirty days and one of fifty-five days. All that time I was dizzy through cold and lack of sleep. The aim is to break the prisoner's spirit. And I was not even breaking the rules. Especially during the last years, when I was afraid of being charged with another offence, I was truly trying to fulfil my norm and behave well.'

Shcharansky, a younger man, was more defiant and treated for that reason even more barbarically. The camp authorities confiscated the Psalm book given him by his wife, Avital, a few days before his arrest. They told him, 'It is our duty to protect you from the harmful effects of religious propaganda.' He retaliated by stopping working, so they put him in a punishment cell for 130 days, until he lost consciousness.

His memories of the SHIZO are similar to Orlov's: 'The first day they give you a piece of black bread and a cup of hot water - three times. The hot water is good because it warms you up. The next day you get 'hot food', which is a sort of soup, sour cabbage in water. Then you go back to bread and water. And so on. The maximum by law in SHIZO is fifteen days, for medical reasons, but in my case they kept extending it. I got weaker and weaker, mentally as well as physically, because there was nothing to do. I tried to play chess against myself, then to think about all the people I knew and all the good times I'd had. There was nothing in the cell, just a little seat to sit on during the day. And at night I felt cold and could not sleep. And the fact that I was hardly eating anything made me colder still.'

In mid 1978 these facts were available to Western readers. There was no doubting the Soviet Union's brutal treatment of many of its citizens, but the West was confused over how to react. It was not even sure whether there was a trend towards greater cruelty and aggression, or whether the Soviet Union was simply reacting in semi-legitimate self-defence.

Only very occasionally, I recall, did any chink of light emerge through the gloom of those months, and even then it happened by clever calculation on Moscow's part. On 24 April 1979, Alexander Ginsburg and four other well-known dissidents were taken without warning from their labour camp in Mordovia to Moscow's Lefortovo prison. Ginsburg told me later of the crippling tension in his body the next morning as he waited outside the prison governor's office, waiting to be told the reason for the sudden move. It could have meant another trial for some other political crime and an increased jail sentence.

Eventually the five men were admitted and the governor told them, in the presence of two Supreme Soviet officials, that they were to be deprived of Soviet citizenship and deported. Their families would be allowed to join them. They were given civilian clothes, driven to the airport and put on an Aeroflot flight. Ten hours later they landed in New York.

Meanwhile, according to KGB practice, Ginsburg's wife Irina was told nothing. She heard the news, she told me,[6] in bed that night, listening to the Voice of America: 'I heard that five dissidents were being released for two Soviet agents. Then they read the names. One was my husband. A few minutes later friends and relatives started knocking on my door. Western journalists came round and we gave a press conference at 3 am. I'll never forget the excitement.'

It was only in New York that Ginsburg was told what a heavy price the United States had agreed to pay for this act of 'clemency'. Two Soviet officials serving terms in American jails for espionage were to be released in exchange. The Soviet Union would also receive a quantity of sophisticated American computer equipment.

My happiness at Ginsburg's release was tinged with anxiety at the thought that yet again President Carter had been out-manoeuvred and forced into an agreement that was damaging to Western interests. Five dissidents had been exchanged for two intelligence officers. Soviet citizens were being exchanged for other Soviet citizens. Was this politically sensible? Could the crime of a professional spy really be compared to the 'crime' of protesting non-violently or attempting to emigrate to Israel? Was it really wise, even for clear humanitarian reasons, to give the KGB such a boost, such a clear 'positive result'? It was almost like encouraging the KGB to arrest more people. The more they arrested, the more 'capital' they would have for future deals and the easier it would be for them to buy out their own spies from western jails.

On 4 January 1980, a few days after the Soviet invasion of Afghanistan, I took Ginsburg to meet Margaret Thatcher, who was now Prime Minister. She asked Ginsburg why the Soviet government made these aggressive moves. 'Communist Russia cannot remain quiet and at peace. Like the universe, it has to keep expanding,' he told her. 'It has to be aggressive, forever demonstrating its own strength, in order to retain its credibility among the Soviet people. Every Soviet child is told about the permanent state of hostility that exists between the socialist system and "the imperialists". It is not a question of the occasional crisis happening from time to time. According to Marx and the other sacred texts that guide the Soviet rulers, it is something that is always there, caused by the inbuilt conflict between the two systems. The conflict will not end until one system defeats the other.

'This is why Russia has to attack. We have to defend ourselves by attacking them before they attack us. Even if it reached the stage where Soviet forces were surrounding the White House, even then Mr Brezhnev could explain that his policy was one of peace. He will point out that we have to attack the White House in order to defend ourselves against it.'

In later meetings he echoed the warnings and criticisms of his friend Solzhenitsyn, in whose home in Vermont he was temporarily living:[7] 'You British compete to sell them computers, some of which are used to keep MiG fighter aircraft in the air over Afghanistan. Western technology was an important part of the invasion. As Lenin might have said, you seem determined to sell the Soviet Union the rope with which they propose eventually to hang you.'

He gave the West five pieces of advice. 'You should ban sales to Russia of all scientific equipment. You should make your embassies in Moscow available to Russians of every persuasion, including dissidents, not just to Kremlin bureaucrats. You should increase your radio broadcasts to the communist world. You should end "scientific exchange programmes" that give them free know-how. And you should boycott the Olympic games in Moscow.'

In spite of all the gloom, he did not believe that the battle was yet lost. The Soviet people were waking from their sleep, both politically and spiritually. And, while they were still subject to the KGB terror, they were no longer cowed by it. He recalled how thousands had contributed to his 'Solzhenitsyn Fund' for political prisoners and how 35,000 Lithuanians had signed a protest document to mark the fortieth anniversary of the Molotov–Ribbentrop Pact the previous August.

'The process of resistance to Soviet rule is there,' he said. 'Even if it is a very slow process. The trouble is that ours is a huge country and a very sick country. It suffers, for instance, from alcoholism on a massive scale and a complete lack of the will to work – a sort of totalitarian ulcer. It means that the move towards fundamental change cannot easily be speeded up.'

Such guarded optimism seemed wholly out of place in January 1980, when the Soviet Union was spreading its influence in every direction, not only in Afghanistan, but also from Cuba to Ethiopia and Nicaragua and from there into other Central American countries on the United States's doorstep. It already dominated Angola and enjoyed moral authority in most of Africa through its sponsorship of the fight against South African apartheid. It had brushed aside (it seemed) the dissident movement, in spite of the US President's strenuous efforts to support it. Outsiders could see little evidence of any Russian 'moral awakening'. Moscow's voice was one of monolithic and immoral conformity. There was no religious opposition, except from the small non-conformist sects. The Orthodox hierarchy supported the atheist government. Opposition to Soviet power, according to official propaganda, was confined to a few weird characters paid by Western intelligence, and while few Westerners accepted such a crude judgement, there were even fewer who would recognize the dissidents and their friends as a significant political force, capable of helping to bring about any serious change.

'There will be war,' *Kontinent* editor Vladimir Maximov told me that afternoon on the telephone from Paris. 'Their next step will be to close the roads and railway to Berlin. They are ready for anything.' A few days later he elaborated: 'They face an internal catastrophe. Their economy is on the verge of collapse. Their ideology is not respected by the younger generation. So they decide to save themselves by aggression, to up the stakes, to go for broke.'

Amnesty International reported that forty key figures in the democratic movement had been arrested since October 1979. Among them were the dissident priest Gleb Yakunin, arrested on 1 October, the Helsinki Group member Malva Landa, arrested on 4 January 1980, bizarrely accused of starting a fire in her own flat, and then the scientist Andrey Sakharov, exiled to Gorky on 21 January. I telephoned a Moscow friend, one of the few whose telephone still worked, and she said to me, 'Can you send us some of your Western thermal clothing? We may have to move and there are some parts of the country where the central heating does not work as well as it does here.'

The dissidents in the West were shocked, but strangely exhilarated. At last something was happening and at last the West seemed to have acquired some of their sense of urgency over the need to mobilize psychologically. 'It was bound to happen,' said Alekseyeva from New York in early 1980. 'Our Document No. 101 predicted it last August. The sources of information are being turned off before the foreigners come here for the 1980 Olympic Games.' She pointed out that the main arrests had been in the cities where Olympic events were to take place: in Moscow where they had built the central stadium, in Tallin where the yachting events were to be held, and in Kiev and Leningrad where there would be football. 'It made no sense to arrest so many and to leave the leader [Sakharov] free,' said Bukovsky. 'Hundreds of journalists will be going to Moscow in July. He would have given dozens of interviews. He had to be disposed of.' There seemed nothing weak about what the Soviet government was doing. Rather the contrary.

To the dissidents, on the other hand, Moscow's moves were an admission of the crisis, an act of desperation by a monster writhing in its death agony. And the arrest of Sakharov was the greatest absurdity of all. 'They will not destroy our movement,' said Ginsburg. 'It is like trying to cut up an iceberg by hacking away at its tip. It does not work. The underwater mass is too great. Every time someone is arrested, two take his or her place.'

On 22 January 1980, the National Broadcasting Company published the results of a public opinion survey, showing that 82 per cent of Americans thought an outbreak of war either 'very probable' or 'quite probable' and 63 per cent were for increasing the defence budget. The West was now more united than ever before in its condemnation of Soviet policy, but as divided as ever on what the Western leaders ought to do.

The wave of persecution continued. On 30 January Naum Meiman, one of the few Helsinki Group members still free, was called to the prosecutor's office and threatened with arrest. 'We've dealt with your leader. Do you think we can't cope with little fish like you?' they told him. Lev Kopylev, a friend of Solzhenitsyn and expert on German literature, was one of those under attack in the press. 'We meet to learn about one another. We huddle together. It is an old instinct at times like this.' Three KGB cars followed Irina Ginsburg wherever she walked. 'They knew that I was going to the West and I suppose they thought that I might dash down to Gorky to get a message from Sakharov to take with me.'

On 31 January 1980, Irina flew with their sons Sanya and Alyosha to meet her husband in Paris. 'I spent yesterday morning saying goodbye to friends who may be arrested at any time. Some I shall never see again,' she told me in their Paris flat the following day. She had hardly spoken to her husband since his release the previous April. Not only her telephone, but her friends' telephones too had been disconnected, to prevent his calling her from New York. She was finally allowed to take his calls at a telephone in the American embassy. Then on 3 February, after three days together, they were separated again for some weeks as he left to carry out a long-term commitment to ferry food and medicines to the Cambodian border areas.

Ginsburg and his family were now reunited, but only through a 'spy swap' that the KGB had found advantageous. Sakharov was in exile, while Orlov and Shcharansky and many thousands of others convicted of political or religious crimes were still left with years to endure in the labour camps. It was only the very optimistic among us who would suggest, in the face of all these disasters, that we were going to win the second cold war.

9. Human Rights and Political Problems

An even more terrifying aspect of Soviet policy in the early 1980s was their belief that the United States and Britain were actively preparing for nuclear war against them. The KGB defector Oleg Gordievsky writes that KGB chief Yuri Andropov launched an intelligence operation, codenamed 'RYAN', designed to find out when the expected pre-emptive strike would take place. If he had become convinced that the strike was imminent, which he was apparently close to doing, we may assume that the Soviets would have 'got their retaliation in first' by attacking Western targets. Nuclear war was that close.

The result of Andropov's paranoia was a sudden increase in KGB activity during 1982, activity which gathered momentum when Andropov took over the Soviet leadership on Brezhnev's death in November of that year. The KGB in London were required by Andropov to send alarmist reports to Moscow in support of this theory, even though they were themselves sceptical about its existence. They encouraged the 'peace movement', with its demonstrations against the deployment of Cruise and Pershing missiles in Britain and, with little justification, claimed the credit for these 'manifestations of progressive opinion' whenever they occurred.

KGB agents were ordered to monitor lights in the windows of Whitehall buildings, as an indication as to which ministries were working late into the night. They noted the dates and frequency of Margaret Thatcher's visits to the Queen and were asked to report any increase in the price of blood for transfusions. They did not know, apparently, that in Britain donors provide their blood free of charge.

This dangerous error was increased by the US President's rhetoric. For instance, he asked Americans to say prayers for all those who lived in the Soviet Union's 'totalitarian darkness' and he called the Soviet leaders 'the focus of evil in the modern world'. In March 1983 he announced the launch of his famous Strategic Defence Initiative (SDI) known as 'Star Wars', a plan to build an electronic shield that would defend North America from Soviet missile attack.

The increase in KGB activity abroad was, as usual, accompanied by worse oppression at home. On 3 March 1983, they arrested the poet Irina Ratushinskaya and sentenced her in Kiev to seven years' imprisonment for writing bad verses and 'distorting Soviet history'. Then Valeri Senderov was jailed for trying to form a trade union. This was the moment when I was, most surprisingly, given a Soviet visa for the first time since mid 1971. However, on 18 April the visa was cancelled. It had been issued by mistake.

There was now only one point of contact between East and West on human rights issues. This was CSCE, the Helsinki agreement. Its unofficial Soviet monitors were now in jail, but the process still tried to stay alive and in early 1983 it was being reviewed at a conference in Madrid. On 10 March I was sent there with two EP colleagues to join in the debate that nurtured the forlorn hope of improving Eastern Europe's human rights record through diplomatic negotiation.

CSCE covered a wide range of issues, from army manoeuvres to exchanges of students, but its beauty lay in the fact that it contained specific promises on human rights signed by Brezhnev himself. The man was now dead, but his successor Andropov was now lumbered with them and, ironically, he was personally represented at the Madrid meeting by his son Igor Andropov, known as 'Prince Igor'. The main Soviet spokesman, the man I remember best from the various encounters we had in Madrid, was Sergei Kondryashov, a KGB colonel and a specialist in human rights inasmuch as it was his function to suppress them.

We were keen to talk to Kondryashov and his friends about Orlov, Sakharov and Shcharansky. He wanted to talk to us about the oppression of North American Indians, about Northern Ireland and about the use of torture in Turkey. I recall his anger when I raised the Shcharansky case, mentioning the suffering of the famous refusenik's wife, Avital, whom I had just taken to meet Margaret Thatcher. He seized on the fact that the couple, though married religiously by a Moscow rabbi shortly before her departure for Israel, had not been allowed any Soviet marriage ceremony. He exclaimed, 'Shcharansky must learn to behave himself. He must obey prison rules and work when he is told. And he must ask for clemency. Then maybe he can be released. And as for this woman, this friend of yours – she is not his wife. She does not have the right to bear his name. He lived with her in Moscow for only a few weeks, with her and several other women. Then she deserted him and left for abroad. The whole campaign has no legal basis.'

I reminded the Soviet team that their country had not always been so legalistic in such matters and that Lenin, for instance, had never officially married his 'wife' Nadyezhda Krupskaya. It was a point that provoked my Dutch socialist colleague Ien van den Heuvel to leap to my support. 'Marriage is a bourgeois concept,' she told the surprised KGB men. 'If they love one another, that is what counts, not some official ceremony.' I was happy that this KGB oppressor had been hoisted, in the eyes of democratic socialism, by his own middle-class petard. And I was encouraged on my return to London, a month before I was due to fly to Moscow, to record in print the outpourings of this defender of the indefensible.[1]

I had now been asked by the EP to prepare a written report about human rights in Russia. The cancellation of my visa spurred me on in these efforts. It was important, I believed, to maintain the West's barrage in the war of words now being waged against the East's ideology. It was, after all, the communist side that had begun this war, in the 1920s and before, with their suggestion that Marx and Lenin had found the key to happiness on earth. It was now up to us, if we wanted to win the new cold war, to find a 'religion' that would prevail over what the Kremlin tried so strongly to thrust upon us. The basis of the West's ideology, I believed, was human rights.

Britain is a newcomer to human rights, or 'the rights of man' as they are termed in some parts of Europe. They formed part of our great seventeenth century debate, it is true. They gave birth to the Bill of Rights and *habeas corpus* around the time of the Glorious Revolution. But Britain stood aside from the great movements in Europe and America a century later. It was the French Revolution that gave world importance to the rights of man. And the American Revolution proclaimed the idea of man's 'right' to life, liberty and the pursuit of happiness.

After the Second World War, Britain joined with other United Nations and Council of Europe members in drafting conventions on human rights. Human rights, according to the United Nations, are civil, political, economic, cultural and social. Britain signed these UN agreements. So did the Soviet Union. Then came the Helsinki

Agreement of 1975 and with it the realization that human rights could be a potent weapon for the West in its conflict with Soviet oppression. The Soviet Union had won many moral victories by suggesting that theirs was the way to abolish exploitation of man by man, to release the workers and the victims of imperialism from their chains. Many people believed them at that time. And the West was slow in finding ways of hitting back.

The Soviet Union claimed to have abolished unemployment. Every man and woman had the 'right to work'. This was what *they* meant by human rights, the principle of socialism. They had however now signed the UN Convention, agreeing in Article 5 to ban torture and degrading punishment as well as arbitrary arrest (Article 9) and even (Article 12) arbitrary interference with a citizen's privacy and correspondence. They had accepted Article 13: 'Everyone has the right to leave any country, including his own, and to return to his country.'

In the 1970s it dawned on the West that the Soviet government was in flagrant violation of this UN Convention. Their behaviour towards dissidents certainly amounted to ill-treatment. Their systematic interference with mail and telephone calls was a byword. And, when it came to every citizen's 'right' to leave the country, they simply refused without any semblance of explanation, incurring thereby the wrath of the Jews of the world and of the entire West, especially the United States.

And what could one say about their defiance of Article 19, which guarantees freedom of opinion and expression, including the right to receive or impart information through any media? It was hard to imagine the motives of the illiberal Stalin regime that had signed this enlightened document. They had, however, signed it. And either they must abide by it or, if they did not, they must be held to account for their failure to fulfil an international obligation. We thus felt fully entitled to pillory the Soviet government for its violations of human rights and so win a victory in the ideological war.

There were problems about this approach. The weakness in our case was that we were inconsistent. We were keen enough to chastise the Chinese, the Russians and the Poles. But we were allied with other torturers, for instance with Turkey, and we had turned a blind eye to the Shah of Iran's ill-treatment of his people. We also maintained close trade relations with racist South Africa. Could we then attack

Russia's record and avoid the charge of hypocrisy? Why were we not up in arms against those responsible for the 10,000 disappearances in Argentina? Thugs were to be tolerated, it seemed, so long as they were friendly, or helpful to the NATO alliance.

The tortures inflicted on the people of Iran by the Shah's secret police, known as SAVAK, were more barbaric than anything done by the KGB. A colleague of mine, recently in El Salvador, told me that he had seen victims of government hit squads lying dead in the streets. We were told that the Indonesian army had massacred 200,000 people, in East Timor and elsewhere. In Russia, to be sure, the KGB had cowed the spirit of the people. They starved their political prisoners and tormented them with cold, often ruining their health, but they did not torture people to death in medieval fashion. Soviet dissidents who had suffered the worst that the KGB could devise confirmed that physical torture was very rarely used.

We were accused of 'élitism' in our emphasis on civil and political rights at the expense of economic rights. It was no good having the right to make a speech in Hyde Park or to write to a newspaper, we were told, if as a result of the resulting chaos there was no food to eat, no housing, no health service and no free education. The implication was that the strict or even repressive authority of the one-party socialist state, if it could deliver the necessities of life more effectively, was preferable to human rights or democracy in the Western sense.

In various articles[2] I tried to answer these points. Of course we were right to pay more attention to the cruelties of a superpower than to those of a small and weak country. The Soviet Union was a great imperial nation with rockets and nuclear warheads sited only 600 miles from London. Unlike Paraguay or Zaïre, say, Russia had the power to destroy us all, to 'bury us'. And all the time it offered us its political system, communism, as an alternative to our own hard-won freedoms. And it backed up this offer with frequent threats and acts of aggression. Of course we should take the Soviet Union most seriously.

There was also the morality of the issue. Soviet dissidents were an unusual opposition group. They were non-violent. Their weapons were the pen and the typewriter, whereas the opposition in Guatemala used machine-guns. The harsh methods used by the Guatemala police could perhaps be justified as essential to national security, as part of a cruel civil war. The Soviet police, on the other hand, were using brute force against nothing more lethal than the intellect. We must therefore, while highlighting the bad behaviour of all fingernail-pulling governments, inevitably turn our telescopes most carefully towards the horrors that were taking place on own doorstep, in Europe's largest and strongest country, the one that had done so much to crush non-violent dissent within a few days' march of our borders.

The report I made in Strasbourg on 17 May 1983 listed the main areas of Soviet oppression. Political dissidents were not its only victims. Religious and national minorities were also in the firing line. Soviet citizens of Jewish and German origin, for instance, were under suspicion for alleged 'double loyalty'. Members of Protestant sects, especially Baptists and Pentecostalists, were attacked for breaking the restrictive laws governing religious worship. Homosexuals and feminists were imprisoned just for being different.

I explained the difference between the two articles of the Russian criminal code that made 'anti-Soviet propaganda' an offence. Article 70 made it a crime, punishable by seven years' imprisonment in the first instance, by ten years for a second offence, to publish material 'for the purpose of subverting or weakening the Soviet regime'. Article 190 made it a crime, punishable by three years, to publish material 'known to be false' which damaged the Soviet system, whether intentionally or not.

In theory, the court had to establish the accused's '*mens rea*', or guilty intent. He or she had to be shown either as a deliberate liar or as a deliberate anti-Soviet schemer. In practice, though, people were prosecuted for publishing any material critical of Soviet life or the Soviet leaders, whether true or false, whether designed to destroy the system or to improve it. Since 1917 no Russian on a political charge had ever been found not guilty.

Continental socialists, except for the Greek PASOK members who abstained, spoke in favour of my report, so there was little dissent when it came to the vote. The EP approved it by 134 votes to eight. The only colleagues voting against were six communists and, as usual, two British Labour MEPs, Richard Balfe and Alf Lomas. It was the same Lomas who, to the disgust of the rest of our EP committee, had spoken in favour of Andrey Sakharov's arrest on 21 January 1980.

The Soviet government's behaviour had reached the point, I felt, where its representatives did not deserve the normal courtesies of civilized behaviour. Every tiny concession had some political purpose. On 14 December 1981, Lisa Alekseyeva was given permission to leave Russia and marry Elena Sakharov's son, Aleksey Semyonov, in the United States. Was this a sign of liberalization? No, it was done to avoid worsening the Academy of Sciences's already bad relations with American scientists in the conflict over the Sakharov family. Russia needed East–West scientific contact. The concession could therefore be made. On 4 July 1982, the family of the chess champion Victor Korchnoi, his wife Bella and son Igor, were allowed to join him in the West. This was unusual, since Korchnoi was a defector. Was it some new kindheartedness? No, it was a concession to FIDE and the other world chess bodies that had threatened to ban Soviet participants from future championships.

The British MP George Walden wrote,[3] 'To the chronically insecure Russians, releasing a wife to the West is like sacrificing a SS-20 for nil return.' It was hard to see the Kremlin leaders other than as old men without heart or soul. Every good deed, even an act of basic humanity, had its appropriate price in terms of the Soviet state's military power or reputation.

On 31 August 1983, the Kremlin carried out another cruel act. A Korean airliner, flight number KAL 007, went off course while flying from Anchorage in Alaska to Seoul, the South Korean capital, with 269 people on board. Half-way across the north Pacific it veered to the west from the route that should have taken it across open seas towards Tokyo. Soon it was over Soviet territory, the south tip of the Kamchatka peninsula, then on across the Sea of Okhotsk and over the heavily fortified island of Sakhalin, just north of Japan.

Soviet monitors tracked it for two hours. Their fighters then took to the air, intercepted the airliner and shot it down, insisting that it was their legal right to do so, since the aircraft was over their territory in a military area. It could, they said, have been carrying bombs or spying. (It was, indeed, never properly explained why the airliner was so far off course in one of the world's most sensitive military areas. And the presence on board of Larry Macdonald, a US Congressman and member of the ultra-right John Birch Society, was also suspicious.) The principal fact though was the severity of the Soviet reaction, which can only be explained by their belief in Operation RYAN, the likelihood of an American pre-emptive strike. According to the *Daily Telegraph*[4] it was 'mass murder', whereas *The Times*[5] wrote of 'this callous regime that shoots first and asks questions afterwards'. What was the West to do in the face of such barbarism? It was pointed out with justice that no air force in the West would ever have shot down an Aeroflot aircraft full of passengers, even if it really had been spying.

Western leaders vowed to retaliate. A few countries banned Aeroflot from their air space, but it soon appeared that the measure hurt the West as much as it hurt the Kremlin. Businessmen, on their way to Moscow to discuss contracts, found themselves obliged to pay extra so as to re-route their flights. Aeroflot was the main gainer from this confusion. And Western businessmen still found it useful to come to Moscow with goods for sale. The Aeroflot weapon proved useless and was abandoned.

Western governments then turned their minds to the transfer of technology. This was thought to be the West's most powerful weapon. So long as the Soviet Union behaved in a hostile fashion, they would deny it the fruits of the West's research, so putting the Soviet economy under strain and eventually making it impossible for the Soviet armed forces to keep pace with the Western military alliance.

This was possible in theory. All Western sales of high technology were controlled by the COCOM agreement, which published a list of strategic goods, ranging from atomic weapons to computer parts, whose sale to communist countries was prohibited. This agreement was administered from a modest building in Paris, an annexe to the United States embassy. Their job was to monitor, report and if necessary punish any firm from a COCOM country, which meant NATO plus Japan, caught selling technology to the adversary.

But COCOM did not always work as it should. Many firms, especially in Europe, disliked having their business opportunities limited under American supervision, especially since Russia had come to rely for their food on American sales of grain. Not all firms were convinced by the overriding demands of NATO solidarity and the COCOM agreement. Many of them traded with the Soviet Union in spite of the ban, using false bills of lading or a firm from a neutral country as a point of transit. Even when a firm was caught breaking the rule, it was seldom prosecuted.

In this way Soviet industry had managed to buy gas-pipe technology from Western Europe and had set up a military truck factory on the Kama River, again based on Western equipment and know-how. More ought to be done, I believed, to curb this dangerous East–West trade, which had also given the Soviet Navy dry docks for their Kiev-class ships of the Pacific and Northern fleets and roll-on, roll-off technology for the amphibious warfare ship *Ivan Rogov*.[6] But little was done to punish Moscow for its aggressions. The West was reluctantly forced to conclude that it had no means. The West's unity was just not firm enough. Whatever economic means was tried, there was always some important group, for instance the Japanese electronics firms or the French farmers, who would refuse to go along with its implementation.

A further sign of Soviet aggression could be detected in the stridency of its propaganda. The KGB was intensifying its campaign of 'active measures', designed to discredit the United States and Britain among the Left and in the Third World. During 1982 there was a spate of 'revelations', documents appearing from an unknown source, apparently showing the aggressive nature of American foreign policy. These documents, all forgeries, were sent to influential people, politicians and journalists, usually without a covering letter, always without a return address. Sometimes the sender apologized for his own anonymity, explaining that he was afraid for his life or career. They were apparently signed by well-known American politicians and often marked with a high security classification, so as to enhance the news value of the forgery and ensure prominent local exposure.

For instance, the 'Clark–Stearns letter' surfaced in Athens in January 1982. It purported to be from Under-Secretary of State William Clark to the US Ambassador in Athens, Monteagle Stearns, and it indicated that America might be willing to support a military coup in Greece so as to secure and preserve its strategic position there. Although never published, it was calculated to worsen the United States's relations with Greece's PASOK government.

The 'Haig–Luns letter', sent over the name of the then Supreme Allied Commander to the NATO Secretary-General, suggested that NATO might 'be forced to make first use of nuclear weapons', in which case American forces in Europe would go into action. It was calculated to alarm European public opinion during the debate on the deployment of Cruise and Pershing missiles. Although an obvious forgery, it appeared in two newspapers in April 1982, the Luxembourg *Zeitung* and the Belgian *De Niewe*.

That same month the Danish Minister of Justice, Ole Espersen, announced that Soviet agents had tried to use a Danish journalist, Arne Pedersen, to manipulate opinion towards the idea of a Nordic nuclear-free zone. The Soviet embassy had given him alcohol and a trip to Russia as well as money to pay for pro-Soviet political advertisements, including a pamphlet attacking Margaret Thatcher.

In 1983, with 'Operation RYAN' in full swing, the number of Soviets expelled from Western Europe for espionage increased alarmingly. There were only four expulsions from the ten European Community countries in 1981, and six in 1982, whereas in 1983 there were sixty-eight: forty-seven from France, five from Germany, five from Britain, four from Italy, three from Ireland, two from Belgium and one each from Denmark and the Netherlands. Most were diplomats, but others were journalists, Aeroflot and Morflot (merchant navy) officials, an employee of the International Wheat Council and a diplomat's wife.

The former French interior minister Michel Poniatowski said,[7] 'In France the KGB manipulates about 10,000 individuals, whether they know it or not. One-third of Soviet diplomats are KGB. The rest are from Aeroflot or Intourist. This means about 200 agents with 400 others dependent on them, each one manipulating 15 to 20 people . . .'

I wrote in a European Parliament document later that year that the Soviet Union was of course entitled to put across its point of view, either directly or through the Western media, even in a distorted way. They were entitled if they wished to claim that Cruise and Pershing were weapons for evil, whereas SS-20s were weapons for good. They could accuse Britain and the United States of imperialism and at the same time hail their army's presence in Afghanistan and Poland as acts of kindness to a friend.

They could make their publications available at cheap rates. There were twenty-two on sale in Britain alone. It was a pity that they gave the West only one side of the case, especially since in Russia itself no one, whether native or foreign, was allowed to challenge it, but it was not improper, even when the aim was to destabilize society. Under British law and practice they were entitled to the same freedom of speech and expression as anyone else. They could also make friends with Western politicians and persuade them to serve the Soviet Union's interest. This was done, often successfully, and it was not illegal, although any Soviet citizen who served foreign interests in this way would of course have been liable to immediate arrest.

The KGB were *not*, however, entitled to use deceit, to finance such Soviet-front bodies as the World Peace Council, pretending that they were independent and giving them a non-Soviet façade, or to use forgeries to obtain anti-NATO coverage in the press, or to encourage terrorism in Ireland or Israel, or to provide the Bulgarian secret service with outlandish weapons for murderous attacks in London or Paris streets.

I had particularly in mind the murder of Georgi Markov, husband of my friend Annabel Dilke, in London in 1978. Markov had been a successful writer in his native Bulgaria, well acquainted with the country's communist leader, Todor Zhivkov. He had then defected to the West and attacked the Bulgarian leadership relentlessly on Radio Free Europe and the BBC. Several times he was warned that his life was in danger. Then one evening he came home complaining that a man had apparently stabbed him in the leg on Waterloo Bridge. He soon developed a high fever and a few days later he died.

A post-mortem examination revealed under the skin of his leg a spherical piece of metal 1.52 millimetres in diameter, made of a complicated platinum/iridium alloy, as used in the aircraft industry. It was pierced through with four tiny holes that could only have been made with the aid of a high-temperature furnace and precision drilling equipment. The pellet had been used to introduce a highly concentrated poison, probably ricin, a derivative of the castor oil plant, into Markov's bloodstream.

In 1983 it had not been proved that the murder was done by the Bulgarian secret service, but this was widely assumed to be the case. The weapon used was very sophisticated. It could not have been put together by any common thug or small political group, or even by a small country. It could only have been the work of a nation with a highly developed scientific base. I wrote that the murder must have been committed by Bulgarian agents, using a weapon supplied to them by the KGB.

When it came to the vote on my report in Strasbourg, as usual the

British Labour members were the ones most reluctant to accept such ideas. Their aim, they said, was 'to defend detente', even when this meant taking the Soviet Union's point of view, and to attack the 'cold warriors' like myself who were forever 'looking for reds under the bed'. Alan Rogers, who was soon to be made a Labour defence spokesman, described the report as 'nonsensical' and 'of no value', since 'we should be getting on with our own business, discussing farm prices'. Then, moving quickly from class warfare to homophobia, Rogers blamed members of the British secret service for having gone to public schools and for being 'a little strange or perhaps a little queer'.

Another Labour MEP, Richard Balfe, reminded the House that 'all of our major traitors have come from the upper middle class'. The report had been written, he said, not by a cold warrior, but by 'a cold-war cub' who lived in a fantasy world. The Italian communist spokesman, Vera Squarcialupi, called the report 'a crude yellow novel that will never be a best-seller'.

It was nevertheless approved by 136 votes to sixty-two and seven years later, in spite of the dismissive remarks of my left-wing colleagues, my theory about Markov's murder proved to be correct. This was confirmed in an interview for Radio Liberty[8] by ex-KGB Major-General Oleg Kalugin, who explained how in 1978, in his capacity as head of the KGB's 'Directorate K', whose 'Department 5' was responsible for all action taken against Soviet émigrés and defectors, he was ordered by the KGB's then deputy chairman, Vladimir Kryuchkov, to make suitable weaponry available to Bulgarian comrades. He gave the necessary orders, he says, and the murder was carried out by Bulgarian agents, using the KGB's guns and poisons.

The Soviet Union, it seemed, had never been stronger or more determined to stamp out dissent at home or abroad. Its armies held sway in Central Europe. The electronically equipped wall between East and West Germany was there, it seemed, for many generations. Andrey Sakharov was still in exile. Orlov, Shcharansky and others were in jail, while others had been forced abroad. The Solidarity movement in Poland was still banned and persecuted. And Soviet influence in west European socialist parties was strong.

The Soviet armed forces dominated Angola and Ethiopia. They also controlled Afghanistan and, in the view of many western analysts, would soon be ready to sweep southwards towards the Persian Gulf and the Indian Ocean, so knocking the West out of the Great Game once and for all.

10. My First Try at the Pass

The Soviet invasion of Afghanistan was another part of my interest in the new cold war. It was based on a study of Persian, Afghanistan's official language, at Cambridge from 1958 to 1961. Again, I am often asked why I read such an outlandish subject at university. And again I have to answer that the reason amounts to little more than whim or caprice. I was keen to learn Arabic, the language of more than twenty nations and the basis of the great Islamic religion. It would be a useful tool in many careers. And if I read Arabic, I was told, it would be normal to read Persian too, because of its great literature and dependence on Arabic for a large part of its vocabulary. I had no knowledge then of those great Persian poets: Hafiz, Saadi and Firdowsi. I only knew Omar Khayyam, and even then only in Edward Fitzgerald's decorated version. The others were to come later. I had some dim feeling that knowledge of the Middle East's history and languages might in due course help me to find work in the oil business.

In mid-course I spent the summer months of 1960 with a rich Iranian family in Qolhak, Tehran's northern suburb, learning Persian, teaching English and drinking vodka limes at the Park Hotel with vivacious, western-educated Iranian women. My other main memory is of a one-week visit to the city of Isfahan. The great Shah Abbas hotel was not yet burnt down, or even built. Anyway, as a poor student I stayed with my Iranian host, or *mehmandar*, in a modest but cleanish guest-house on Charbagh Avenue, the supposed model for Paris's Champs-Elysées. Isfahan is little known in the West, but it is a marvel to walk in it, with its Bridge of 33 Arches, its mosque with the trembling minaret and the great Royal Square, maybe the largest in the world, where the first polo used to be played, often with the skull of an enemy used as the ball. I also remember improving my Persian at Isfahan's cinema by watching a dubbed version of the film *Trouble in Store*, starring Norman Wisdom. I had seen the film before and therefore understood several of the jokes. All in all, the visit convinced me that 'Isfahan is half of the world', or '*Isfahan – nesf-i-jahan*', as local people remark so euphoniously.

It was an exciting taste of another great culture, involving poetry, architecture and good company. And I had no idea that in less than twenty years it would end in chaos and revolution. Moving as I was in a golden ghetto of Western culture and Western-thinking people, I believed them when they told me that Islam was a minority interest, an alien religion imposed by Arab armies, that the Koran prevailed only where it had been brought by the sword. I underestimated its influence and the depth of the region's anti-Western feeling, which spurred on its revival. I did not, for instance, realize how deeply they disapproved of their women drinking vodka limes in the bars of Tehran hotels, especially with the English, a people for whom they felt a strange mixture of admiration and resentment. I saw of course the wide difference between the rich and the poor, but there was nothing new about that in the Middle East and there was no doubt that in the 1960s and 1970s the poor were becoming less poor as the price of oil rose, and the power and wealth of Iran increased.

When I visited Iran again with a parliamentary delegation in May 1971, the country's status was transformed. We the British were no longer the semi-imperial power. We were now the ones making the requests. We were in financial difficulty, they were awash with cash from oil and our firms wanted their contracts. The Prime Minister, Ali Abbas Hoveida, seemed well aware of his high position. Flanked by twin raven-haired secretaries and sporting an impressive orchid on his jacket lapel, he received the British MPs with graceful condescension, chiding us for the errors of our imperial past and barely indicating the possibility of forgiveness. The Shah received us more kindly, charming us all, even the most sceptical Labour Party republican, into believing that the Western world was right to be giving him its wholehearted support.

The West was, however, making basic mistakes. We did not know for instance that by the end of the 1970s the Shah was dying of cancer. His French doctors kept the secret from the American government. And all through that decade we turned a blind eye to the excesses of the Shah's secret police, the infamous SAVAK. It was their job to destroy all opposition to the Shah's rule and they did their job with every refinement of cruelty. Soon they were famous for their use of physical torture of the most bestial kind. The KGB was crushing the spirit of the Russian nation, but SAVAK was breaking men and women by more old-fashioned methods. And our western foreign offices did nothing about it. It was not in our interest to interfere. It was not diplomatic. Or so we thought at the time.

We knew about regimes that used torture. Or we thought we did. Hitler's people pulled out the fingernails of enemy agents to obtain military information. Stalin's police tortured imagined 'enemies of the people' to force them into signing confessions. SAVAK, on the other hand, used torture as an extra-judicial punishment, and as a deterrent to the population as a whole. A man, perhaps a journalist or a student leader, would be arrested and charged with plotting to overthrow the government. He would then be 'fried' on a wire grill, like a bed-frame, heated up so that it burnt the skin, or beaten about the feet, or mauled by a bear. He would be ducked head downwards in filthy liquid until he was half drowned. Then, a few days later, if nothing serious was found against him, he might be released. He would not complain. Neither would his family, because they would be broken by what had happened.

His experience would usually be enough to stop his opposition activity and it would have a sobering effect on his family, friends and political supporters. They would see what had become of him, a strong man turned into a shell of a man, the change in his spirit and personality, the nervous stress, the nightmares and the feelings of guilt, and they would know what lay in store for them if they were so rash as to follow his example.

These were the years, the late 1970s, when Jimmy Carter and other Western leaders were protesting loudly against the KGB's oppression of the Helsinki group and other dissidents. But they did next to nothing about Iran and SAVAK. The Shah was such an important ally against the Soviet bloc, such a valued buyer of the West's manufactured goods, such a crucial provider of oil. It made sense not to irritate him at times such as these when the world economy was in recession, when Arab oil producers were chastising the West in the wake of the 1973 Yom Kippur war and when Iran was very powerful and one of the few friendly countries in the region.

We all knew that the Shah was under attack from a fundamentalist Islamic cleric, Ayatullah Khomeini. From his base firstly in Iraq, then in Paris, Khomeini vilified the Shah for his Western manners and sympathies, calling on the faithful to destroy the 'corrupters upon the earth' who had sold Iran to the infidel. But in the West few words of criticism were thrown. Amnesty International and the World Service of the BBC sometimes spoke about Iranian repression, in which case the Shah would react with great anger. More than once an item of criticism on the BBC induced him to cancel a billion-dollar contract for a British firm. Was it worth putting British workers out of their jobs for the sake of the bleeding hearts of the British chattering classes?

It was therefore mainly the Left who carped at the Shah's doings. But then, we were assured, it was the sort of thing that the Left was bound to do. They favoured the Soviet Union and they would always be prejudiced against a pro-Western hereditary monarch.

For instance, on 27 April 1977, a group at the House of Commons heard a talk from the young Iranian ambassador, Parviz Radji, after which Labour MPs put questions about repression and arbitrary arrest, while the Conservatives spoke about oil and trade. I was the only Conservative to mention torture.[1] Then on 24 May 1978 I went with my old supervisor in Persian studies at Cambridge, Peter Avery, to lunch with Radji at his embassy. Radji listened carefully and assured us, I am sure in all honesty, that our remarks would be passed to Tehran for due consideration. It was only very rarely, though, that anyone, other than from the Left, intervened in Iran's internal affairs in this way.

On 8 November 1978, by which time the Shah's hold on events was beginning to slip, I mentioned in a House of Lords debate that we might all be soon embarrassed 'by the fact that we did not protest sufficiently strongly against the excesses of SAVAK, the security police of Iran'. Again, no Conservative supported me and I was taken to task by my own front-bench spokesman, Diana Elles, who said, using the time-honoured Foreign Office phrase, that it was 'not very helpful' to criticize a country like Iran that was going through such difficulties.

Khomeini meanwhile kept up his anti-Shah tirade from his Paris base and the Iranian mob showed its support for him in massive demonstrations. More and more details emerged of SAVAK's cruelties and of the corrupt activity of members of the Shah's family. On

16 January the Shah fled the country, leaving it in the hands of his latest liberal Prime Minister, Shahpour Bakhtiar. But it was too late for liberals. Bakhtiar no longer had the means to govern a country whipped up by religious fervour. Khomeini returned from Paris to Tehran in triumph. The Peacock Throne was gone. Bakhtiar resigned by telephone on 12 February and succeeded in escaping across the border, probably with the help of members of his nomadic Bakhtiari tribe. Khomeini at once launched a Holy War against Israel and a reign of terror against members of the Shah's regime. Ex-Prime Minister Hoveida and many other mighty men well remembered from my May 1971 visit were put on trial as 'corrupters upon the earth' or for 'making war on God' and shot to death. I soon learnt that my host from 1960, a magazine publisher, had suffered the same fate. And so, in due course, did Shahpour Bakhtiar. On 8 August 1991, Iranian agents tricked their way into his Paris apartment and cut his throat.

It was all going to be very unpleasant, I wrote the day after Kohmeini took power.[2] It might not quite be 'The Crash of '79', as predicted by the best-selling novel of those days, but it was clearly the end of an arrangement that had greatly helped the West to overcome the difficult aftermath of the 1973 Yom Kippur war. Iran had been one of the few countries in the region to take a responsible attitude to oil prices and the investment of oil revenues. Western manufactured goods would now be harder to sell to Iran. For years we had imagined that we were their partners, but it seemed now that the arrangement had not at all been to their taste. All this time they had hated us as imperialists and supporters of Israel, and, as for the future, they were going to make us pay. I wrote, 'Defence arrangements, supplies of raw materials, markets for our industries – all these are now at risk in a dozen countries where the Koran is revered.'

Khomeini's revenge was worse than anything that the Shah had ever devised. On 17 February the former head of SAVAK was spreadeagled on the roof of a Tehran school and machine-gunned to death. Even worse, the former foreign minister, Abassah Khalatbari, was convicted of not having opposed sales of oil to Israel. His executioners were ordered to aim their machine-guns from the knee upwards.[3]

Political parties were banned, and rioting in the cities added to the terror imposed by the new regime. The Ayatullah's 'committees' were no longer rounding up the Shah's former friends. They were massacring businessmen, journalists, students and academics – anyone who symbolized Iran's pro-Western links. They were by now on their way to becoming one of the cruellest regimes in the world.

The Soviet Union, with its policy based on anti-Zionism and anti-imperialism, could not fail to benefit from this turn of events. The Iranian revolution was not a communist one, but it was certainly anti-Western and it meant that Washington had lost its most valuable ally in the region. All this was to the Kremlin's benefit.

Death to America!

The whole of Islam seemed to be rising up against the United States and the West. On 27 April 1978, revolutionary officers in Afghanistan seized power, killing the previous moderate ruler, Muhammed Daoud, and replacing him with a communist, Nur Muhammed Taraki. Afghanistan had until then been friendly to the 'northern neighbour', but neutral in the cold war. Taraki was now making it clear that he saw the Soviet Union as his country's natural ally and, in May, Moscow rewarded him with a huge aid package. But the growth of Soviet influence was not to every Afghan's taste. Although there was little feeling in favour of the West, Islam was strong and the new atheist ideals were not popular with the growing Islamic movement.

Guerrilla resistance to communist domination increased during 1979, resulting in an increase in the Soviet presence. Taraki lost the Soviet Union's confidence and on 27 March 1979 he was replaced by Hafizullah Amin as Prime Minister, though retaining the title of President. He was not satisfied and complained about the '1,500 Soviet advisers' who had flooded into the country. On 16 September he resigned the presidency on ill-health grounds in Amin's favour and on 9 October he died. Amin was in fact conducting a reign of terror throughout those last weeks of the decade. There was sporadic anti-Soviet rioting, as a result of which Kabul's notorious Pul-i-Charki prison was filled to the brim and thousands were taken from their homes, never to be seen again. In spite of Amin's cruelties, the situation in Kabul carried on deteriorating and in its present mood of adventurism the Soviet Union was not going to lose this important strategic interest. On Christmas Day, the KGB's favourite day, the Soviet army mounted a two-day airlift of troops into Kabul. This was done supposedly at President Amin's request, but this may not have been the case since the first important action taken by Soviet agents on their arrival was to kill President Amin. The real motive was to place Afghanistan under the Soviet Union's direct control, in the interest of Soviet strategic and economic policy. Troops poured south across the Oxus, the 'Amu Darya' as it is called locally, the river that runs along the Afghan–Soviet border. An occupying army of 40,000 was constituted by the end of the year, rising to 80,000 soon afterwards, and then to more than 100,000.

They appointed as their puppet ruler Babrak Karmal, who had spent most of the previous year in Czechoslovakia, and as their chief of the Afghan security service, known as 'KHAD', Muhammed Najibullah, a man known for his cruelty. Karmal at once declared his support for 'the sacred religion of Islam' as well as for the ideals of the April 1978 communist revolution. 'The Afghan people will support and develop their unbreakable fraternal relations with the Soviet Union,' announced *Pravda* on 31 December. In case there were any doubt about this, Karmal announced that it would be the duty of KHAD under Najibullah 'to neutralize under communist leadership the plots hatched by our external enemies'.[4]

So what was Carter supposed to do now? Again he seemed distressed and confused. And it sounded sad when he announced that he had 'completely changed his opinion' of the Soviet government, and that their invasion was 'the biggest threat to peace since the Second World War'. He needed now to re-establish American prestige and dispel the thought that his foreign policy was aimless, little more than a response to events initiated by the Soviet adversary.

He tried to punish Moscow with a grain embargo and an Olympic Games boycott and by widening the 'COCOM list'. None of this made any great impact on Soviet policy. He failed to win support even from his closest allies. British athletes took part in the Olympic Games in Moscow, although not under the British flag and without the national anthem. France backed the grain embargo only partially. They would not support Afghan peasants to the detriment of French farmers. 'Business is business' was the French attitude, the result being that Moscow had little trouble buying the grain and technology it needed.

There were those who argued that the crisis was exaggerated, that the Soviet Army had been acting defensively in December 1979, protecting legitimate national interests in a neighbouring country that had long been under their influence – until, that is, the position was threatened by the rise of Islamic extremism and anti-Soviet actions which President Amin was unable to control.

After all, it was argued, Afghanistan was important to Russia, a link in Russia's chain of defence and part of Russia's back yard, whereas to America it was a faraway country of little significance. Why then should we in the West be taken aback if Russia insisted on certain guarantees? Would not America do the same, if threatened by a hostile takeover in Mexico or El Salvador? Indeed, America apparently *was* doing the same in response to the emergence of the left-wing Sandinista government in Nicaragua. One 'Cuba' was more than enough. America would not tolerate a second. And by the same token, if the West challenged Soviet control over Afghanistan, we would throw down the gauntlet to the Russian bear, and in his own back yard, thus baiting him to acts of even more dangerous aggression.

I could not accept these arguments. The Soviet claim that they were 'invited in' by Amin was impossible to believe. It was easier to believe that they had their eyes on the oil a few hundred miles to the south-west and the warm water of the Indian Ocean in the south. I *was* impressed by the reaction of the *mujahedin* resistance. It was hopeless, in most people's view, to stand and fight against the Soviet army. The experience of the Hungarians in 1956 and of the Czechs in 1968 had shown, it seemed, that the Russians were so ruthless and well-trained as to be unbeatable, that it was a pointless sacrifice of the blood of heroes even to attempt to oppose them.

And yet this is what the Afghans proceeded to do, much as their ancestors had fought against the British Empire a century earlier. The more the communist forces poured in, the more the *mujahedin* intensified their struggle, armed with little more than old, cumbersome .303 Lee Enfield rifles and the exhortations of the Holy Koran. They were defending not only their own country, it seemed to me, but ours too, since they were the only ones on earth brave enough to be fighting

Soviet imperialism at a moment when its ambitions seemed likely to explode against us all.

The sceptics suggested that we were being hypocritical. Were the Afghan *mujahedin* morally any better, or any less anti-Western, than Ayatullah Khomeini's *mujahedin* across the western border? Our Afghan heroes were inspired by the same Islam that was punishing America so harshly, holding innocent men hostage in the Tehran embassy. The Afghan resistance's main leader, Golbuddin Hikmatyar, was an anti-Western zealot beside whom Khomeini was a liberal. Still, as the bombs rained down on Afghan villages and the people began to pour by the million into Pakistan, it was hard not to see the Afghans as victims of most blatant and cruel aggression, as people who deserved the support of the compassionate, and their *mujahedin* as fighters for our freedom as well as for their own.

They fought the invader fiercely and brutally, as they had fought all invaders throughout history. The US State Department's report on human rights for 1982 admitted[5] that, while some Soviet soldiers who fell into *mujahedin* hands were being transferred to Pakistan, 'a more common fate is summary execution, sometimes preceded by mutilations such as blinding, docking of ears, amputation of noses, castration and flaying'. One was easily reminded of the sobering advice reserved by Rudyard Kipling for any British soldier unfortunate enough to fall into Afghan captivity: 'Just roll on your rifle and blow out your brains and go to your God like a soldier.'

This was in response to the Soviet army's abominable behaviour, which was in due course described to me not only in press reports, but also by ordinary soldiers of the occupying army. For instance, I was told by Sergei Tseluyevsky, a sergeant in a tank unit, 'You know how they recruit men for the Afghan army? They send Soviet units into a village and, when they see a man of more or less military age, they take him. We used to grab them, put them in a tank and take them back to the Afghan barracks. One time we were collecting men up and an Afghan woman came and screamed at us to go away, not to take her husband or son or whoever it was. My lieutenant told me to give her a clout with the butt of my rifle to shut her up and, when I didn't do it, he yelled and swore at me. We collected every man we could find, anyone who didn't have time to run away.'

An even more terrible episode was described to me by Igor Rykov, another sergeant: 'We searched a village called Nargankhar, near Kandahar, and our Senior Lieutenant Anatoli Gevorkyan ordered members of our platoon to bring out a young Afghan boy, aged about sixteen, whom he described as "probably a *dushman*" or "enemy". He took his bayonet from his belt and handed it to Private Oleg Sotnik and said, "Now then, Sotnik, they tell me that you're afraid of blood. So here's my knife. Stick it into him." The soldier, eyes wide open and knife in hand, walked up to the young Afghan. For a few moments they looked into one another's eyes. Then, indecisively, Sotnik pushed the knife into the boy's chest. He let out a wild cry. Then Gevorkyan said, "What's the matter? Don't you know how to kill properly? I'll show you how it's done." He took the bayonet from the terrified Sotnik and stuck it through the Afghan boy's throat.

'The boy shuddered and died. Gevorkyan said, "That's how to do it." He wiped the blood from his knife. We just stood there and did nothing. Even after Gevorkyan left us, it was some time before we could utter a single word. Every one of us felt as if he had taken part in the killing of this innocent boy. And we knew that it would have done no good to complain about what this officer had done. We would only have harmed ourselves.'

The 1982 US State Department report told of 'thousands wounded and killed, mainly women and children' as a result of bombardment by Soviet aircraft and of torture in Afghan prisons in the presence of Soviet advisers. Prisoners were beaten with belts, given electric shocks, submerged in liquid and deprived of sleep. Large numbers of men from towns and villages simply disappeared, either conscripted into the army by a 'press gang' or arrested on some whim by a Soviet or Afghan government team.

Andrey Vaneyev, a sergeant in command of a Soviet tank, told of being ordered to open fire on an Afghan village: 'It was only because they saw a light burning in a house. They must have known there were no *mujahedin* in it. It was too close to our positions. They did it just to terrify the population and to show their superiors how keen they were to do something. That is why I deserted.'

I recall US Congressman Robert Dornan pointing out at a Washington meeting in February 1981, 'Every sin that the United States committed or was alleged to have committed in Vietnam, the Soviet forces have committed a hundred times over in Afghanistan. I was never a defender of Lieutenant Calley. It seemed to me right that he was court-martialled. I thought that he got off lightly. But there are Soviet officers in Afghanistan who commit a "May Lai" massacre almost every day.'

My interest in helping the *mujahedin* arose through Sayid Ahmad Gailani, leader of the National Islamic Front for Afghanistan (NIFA), one of the less extreme resistance groups. I met him several times in 1980 and he convinced me that more must be done by the West to help the men engaged in this David and Goliath struggle – a few ill-equipped tribesmen against the mighty Soviet army. Carter's diplomatic and economic moves were simply not enough. Blood would have to be shed if the Soviet Union's rampaging leaders, with their ambitious foreign policy, were to be stopped.

Gailani told me, 'They fight virtually with their bare hands. Their wives and children have crossed into Pakistan as refugees. They live in great hardship, bombed with napalm from the helicopter gunships, with no missiles to use against them, defenceless, with no aid other than the few dollars we get in charity, either from the West or from the Islamic world. God knows how they manage to carry on fighting.'

He described Soviet helicopter raids on villages, designed to make them uninhabitable, how the machines hovered overhead and the people ran in all directions, like fieldmice from a hawk. The helicopters would then rocket anything that moved or anything alive and growing, or even a building, any sign of civilization, scorching the earth and driving the people into the Soviet-controlled cities, where they could be registered and controlled, then conscripted into the army or sent across the northern border for communist re-education.

He predicted that, unless something was done, the Afghan people would accept any ideology rather than see their children killed in front of their eyes. The *mujahedin* would be forced to surrender through sheer lack of the basic means for survival, in which case stark necessity and anti-Western bitterness would drive them to help the Soviet Union in its onward march towards the oil of the Gulf and the warm water of the Indian Ocean. They would become the Kremlin's mercenaries, like the Cubans were, only more effectively, since fighting is the Afghan's traditional way.

'Afghanistan? It is a lost cause,' was the reply of a French MEP colleague when I raised the matter in Brussels in the summer of 1980.

This seemed to be the prevailing view and there was little stomach for any fight aimed at throwing the Soviets out. In *The Times*[6] Gérard Chailand described the Afghan resistance movement as 'one of the world's weakest', because of its lack of new ideas or revolutionary infra-structure. The writer did not understand, apparently, that it was a traditional movement based on an extremely firm foundation – one of the world's most important religions.

Waiting for Mr Reagan

Meanwhile the battle was on for the White House. The Presidential election was going to be held in November 1980 amid a widespread feeling that Carter was too soft on Soviet policy. Ronald Reagan had promised to handle the Russians differently and his advisers were happy to talk to me about it. For instance, security adviser Richard Allen confirmed to me that summer that (to the best of his knowledge) nothing significant was being done by Carter and his people to fight the Soviet occupation. On 26 August senior State Department official Jane Coon spoke to me willingly of the $44 million her government had donated to Afghan refugee relief, but when I asked her about aid to the *mujahedin* she replied, 'No, I would not want to comment on that.'

White House spokesman Tom Thornton told me, 'This is the position we take on all problems that could involve covert activity. If you deny one operation, you have to deny all of them. So we never confirm or deny.' The Foreign Office in London was similarly delphic: 'Aid seems to be getting through, but it is doubtful whether it would be helpful to the Afghan people to indicate the sources.'

Western governments were reluctant to support the resistance openly. I disagreed with this approach, but official representatives explained their policy to me frequently. They feared that the Kremlin would present the *mujahedin* as American puppets and their own occupation of a foreign land as a simple conflict between the super-powers, as a battle between a lawful government and 'bandits'. In that case the West might lose the diplomatic support of the Third World on the issue and the active support of Egypt and Saudi Arabia.

They were also worried about the effect of serious aid to Afghan allies on the stability of Pakistan, through which all aid to the *jihad* had to pass. And they were anxious not to make the Soviet Union angry and give it cause for further acts of aggression. Direct Pakistani involvement in armed conflict against the Soviet army might become just the pretext that the Kremlin needed for a massive drive south towards the warm water. Reagan's supporters apparently saw these fears as alarmist. 'This is one of the issues that we propose to review urgently on our assumption of power in January 1981,' Richard Allen told me on the telephone. It seemed, therefore, to those of us who wanted a more active American riposte to Soviet aggression, that it was a matter of 'waiting for Mr Reagan'.

I complained[7] that the West was being 'coy' about helping those involved in what I saw as a clear-cut war of national liberation. After all, when the Russians involved themselves in comparable anti-imperialist wars – for instance in Angola or South Africa – they trumpeted their interference and took pride in it. There was nothing coy about the Kremlin's support for the African National Congress in its fight against *apartheid*. The world did not object to what they did and the Third World loved them for it. It was time, I thought, for the West to strike a blow on the basis of principle and ideology, as the Soviets had done for so long and with such success, in spite of their manifest lack of principle and the weaknesses of their ideology in many other respects.

I wanted the West to support the moderate Gailani rather than the fundamentalist Golbuddin, whose ambition was not so much to free his country as to raise the green flag of Islam over cities of East and West. But the latter's Hizb-i-Islami party was close to the Pakistan government. Gailani dismissed Golbuddin as a man of no importance, but a Pakistani spokesman told me that he was '60 per cent of the *jihad*'. Golbuddin's line found sympathy with General Zia ul-Haq, the Pakistan leader, and it was the latter's Inter-Services Intelligence (ISI), which managed the *jihad*. ISI had close links with the American CIA and, according to Gailani, this was why Golbuddin got the lion's share of any finance and arms that might come from American sources, and good publicity from journalists guided to him by the Pakistanis in Peshawar.

These were Gailani's complaints, which I passed on. He told me that Golbuddin was a façade, that he (Gailani) had 14,000 fighters in

Jaji district just north of the border, but could only put 2,000 of them into the field, because of lack of weapons. He wanted SAM-7 ground-to-air missiles. They had proved their worth in 1973, he said, when used by unskilled Syrian infantrymen to shoot down Israeli jet fighters. The Soviets had given tens of thousands of them to Arab leaders, who had sold them throughout the world for cash, so that they were available in 'bargain basement' stores. The rocket launcher cost $7,000 and the missile $3,000. Each missile was capable of destroying $9-million worth of Soviet helicopter. But his men did not have these missiles, simply because they had not the money to buy them. Instead, he said, his most popular weapon was the AK-47 machine-rifle, captured in large numbers from the Soviet army and the puppet Afghan army. And some of his men did not even possess a machine-gun. They were reduced to spending $2 each on hand-made rounds for their .303 Lee Enfields, every round crafted individually in small workshops near Peshawar, any mistake in the handicraft likely to ruin the rifling inside the barrel, firing them in desperation at the murderous Soviet helicopters and watching them bounce like peas off their titanium-strengthened hulls.

'The stuff *is* getting through,' Foreign Office minister Douglas Hurd advised me at the Conservative Party conference on 7 October 1980. The tone of his voice, though, advised me not to press him for detail. He would not say publicly what Britain was doing or sending and, according to the unwritten rules of covert operations, he would not tell me anything that might confirm the truth of what he was saying. 'The rebels are getting arms and I think that the least said about how they are getting them the better,' said Lord Carrington, then Foreign Secretary, on television. I was not reassured. 'Maybe Gailani exaggerates,' I thought to myself. (He did sometimes exaggerate.) It occurred to me that maybe the CIA *was* sending the Afghan freedom fighters weapons and finance. But clearly it was not what their courage deserved and not nearly enough to give them a chance of standing up to the Soviet army.

Ian Gilmour, deputy Foreign Secretary, wrote to me on 13 October 1980, obviously concerned that I was accepting what Gailani told me too much at face value. Gailani was only one of the Afghan leaders, he wrote. 'Your main worry is that we and other western countries are pursuing a policy of inactivity. I do not think that is true. Discretion is not the same as inactivity. Arms are getting through and the important fact is that they are reaching groups fighting inside Afghanistan.'

In the gentle but chilling tone of a Foreign Office warning, he continued his letter, 'I am sure that you would not want anything said that might prevent this . . . You will have read about recent [Soviet] attacks on [Pakistani] border posts . . . Publicity would not help . . . Not everything that happens can be a matter for public debate.' But I was not convinced. I still believed that we should help the *mujahedin* and announce proudly to the world that we were doing so.

Ronald Reagan was elected US President on 4 November and he let it be known that Richard Allen would be his National Security Adviser. This was encouraging and I felt that it was a good moment to push those close to the President-elect. So I wrote to *The Times* on 26 November suggesting that the West was doing well diplomatically over the Afghan war, but badly militarily. Gailani's NIFA had in the past year received, I wrote, only 1,000 rifles, 80 anti-tank weapons, 1,000 handgrenades, 400 mines and 200,000 rounds of ammunition. This was 'a tiny fraction of their needs'. They were simply not being given the tools they needed to do their job. I continued (on the basis of information that Gailani had given me) to suggest that most of the aid received was being directed to the Pakistan army, the black market and the pockets of various individuals. The only solution was to supply groups such as NIFA directly. The future not only of Afghanistan, but also of East–West relations as a whole depended on the new Administration's willingness to grasp this nettle.

Several governments picked up the letter and reacted to it angrily – though for different reasons. On 27 November the Soviet government's news agency TASS quoted from it as 'proof' of 'interference in the internal affairs of a sovereign country', of 'activities directed against the Democratic Republic of Afghanistan' by China, Egypt, Saudi Arabia and the CIA. My letter had touched on the West's constant fear, that the Soviet Union would exploit any outward sign of foreign help to the *jihad* as a pretext for attacks on Pakistan. Although General Zia was pro-Western, he did not govern his country according to Western values. He was a military dictator who believed in the extreme Islamic virtue of hanging murderers, in amputating thieves' hands and in the public flogging of adulterous women.

As the obvious source of my facts and figures, Gailani was therefore taken to task by his Pakistani sponsors and asked to 'clarify' them in public. He did this by obscuring the truth, in order to preserve his relationship with Pakistan. 'There is absolutely no question of the Pakistan army being in any way associated with the Afghan resistance . . .' he wrote.[8] Pakistan was helping the refugees with great generosity, he went on, but observing 'strict neutrality and non-interference' in the war inside Afghanistan.

The letter was disingenuous, but it was part of the mutual deceit essential to the 'great game' being played by East and West. Everyone knew that Pakistan was taking part in the *jihad*, if not its army then certainly its Inter-Services Intelligence. It was the only possible conduit for the *mujahedin*'s supplies. No one believed that Pakistan was neutral. But Gailani and his followers were guests in Pakistan and so his letter had to be written to protect Pakistan's official stance and allow them at least to keep up a show of neutrality.

A further blow to Gailani's claims, and to my efforts, was then delivered by *The Times*'s correspondent in Peshawar, Trevor Fishlock, in an article on 29 November (two days after the TASS report) describing the Afghan leader as 'a former Peugeot car dealer' in Kabul. The idea that Gailani controlled tens of thousands of fighting men was nonsense, he wrote. (He was correct.) Most of the fighting was being done by independent commanders, the 'men in the mountains' who operate in limited areas, owing perhaps no more than a vague loyalty to one of the Peshawar parties.

According to Fishlock and other critics, I was being too easily impressed by the *mujahedin* leaders, especially the 'moderates' who were then passing through western capitals in search of 'support'. (They wanted money.) Their liberal interpretation of Islam might be more to my personal taste than the harsh beliefs of Golbuddin Hikmatyar, I was being told, but I must accept that Golbuddin was the fiercer and more effective fighter, even if Gailani was the more convivial gentleman.

I was told that these were 'Gucci guerrillas' with an eye to their own self-enrichment, who wore gold Rolex watches and owned lavish houses in London, Paris and other expensive cities. It ill behoved well-fed men in smart suits, I was told, to plead the cause of penniless tribesmen. And I was wrong to be helping these 'fat cats' to grow fatter on the basis of an obviously hopeless battle against a superpower, an unequal conflict that would achieve nothing but useless bloodshed, and might even backfire by causing the collapse of Pakistan and a further Soviet advance southward.

This was the widely held view that I had to face. And it was well expressed in another Fishlock article:[9] 'The *mujahedin* are brave, fearless and patriotic. The familiar pictures of them, hawk-faced and unsmiling, bristling with beards and bandoliers, are the quintessence of defiance to authority. They are widely admired as symbols of resistance to tyranny. But they can never win. That is, they can never be instrumental in driving the Russians out. They can make life tough for the invaders from time to time, but never tough enough. They do not have the strength, weaponry and organization to do serious and lasting damage to a powerful and well-equipped foe with vast resources. They can never be much more than Geronimos.'

Among other points being made against me was the suggestion that the Soviet army was deriving useful training experience from this low-level military activity, its longest sustained campaign since the Second World War, and that the losses it was suffering were bearable, especially since it had absolute control of the media at home, which meant that there was no 'anti-war' clamour to 'bring the boys home'. Soviet control of the roads and airfields which they needed for their occupation seemed assured and unchallenged. The obvious failure of *mujahedin* groups to unite in the face of a common enemy was quoted as a further reason why 'they can never win'. It was a depressing scenario for those like myself who admired the *mujahedin* and wanted to help them.

Reagan became US President on 20 January 1981. At once the White House's rhetoric became sharper. Nine days later, at his first press conference, he said,[10] 'So far détente has been a one-way street that the Soviet Union has used to pursue its own ends.' He asked the American people to note that the Soviets had shown that their goal was world revolution and that they 'reserve the right to commit any crime, to lie, to cheat, in order to attain that'.

It was a moment not to be missed by anyone who felt strongly about Soviet behaviour in Afghanistan. In February 1981 I flew to Washington to support a *mujahedin* lobby of Congress organized by the Committee for a Free Afghanistan, a pressure group that had quickly arisen in the wake of Reagan's victory. 'Give us the tools and we will finish the job' was my appeal on the Afghans' behalf – the same appeal as that made by Winston Churchill on Britain's behalf in Washington forty years earlier.

Gailani's field commander, Hakim Aryobi, dressed for better effect in full Afghan combat outfit, made a fine impression on the Senators and Congressmen. They also met the new Deputy Secretary of State James Buckley and his deputy Nick Veliotes. I went with them during their week on Capitol Hill. In room after room we explained why it was in America's interest, in this particular case even if in no other, to help an Islamic cause. Our appeal was mainly to the right wing of Congress. I remember the pre-meeting prayers and the alcohol-free meals.

The Afghans were asked the usual questions. Was it America's business to give expensive weapons to 'rag-head' guerrilla fighters on the other side of the world? Did not America have enough problems on its own doorstep, in Guatemala and El Salvador? Might not any further involvement drag America into another 'Vietnam'? What guarantee was there that these weapons would not be sold to less friendly Islamic groups and turned against the West? How deep was the *mujahedin*'s commitment to the rule of law and pluralist democracy? The Afghans replied that the West appeared to be encouraging them to fight, while refusing to support them in any practical way. It was like cheering on a bull in a Spanish bullring, enjoying the spectacle of a contest while resigned to the fact that there was no real battle, that the bull, however brave, was going to die in the end whatever happened. This was not an honourable position for the West to take.

The Afghans told of the devastating effect of helicopter gunships. Aryobi said, 'They come seven or eight at a time. We have only one anti-aircraft machine-gun. They have up-to-date rocket launchers. We are defenceless against them.' They wanted ground-to-air missiles, if necessary the SAM-7 but preferably the American 'Red Eye' or 'Stinger', or the British 'Blowpipe'.

Daniel Graham, former Director of the Defense Intelligence Agency, told us, 'The "Red Eye" is a heat-seeking device, portable by one man. It takes about two hours to learn how to use it. You take the cap off it and point it in the general direction of the enemy aircraft.

The machine does the rest. You don't even have to pull the trigger. You have to be a very clever soldier to miss.'

We were shown samples of the Soviet 'butterfly mine', green propeller-shaped objects, almost like toys and each one the size of a large coin. They were being dropped by the million from Soviet aircraft on to Afghan territory where the *mujahedin* operated, fluttering down in such numbers as to make the whole terrain dangerous. Afghans who saw one would explode it by throwing a stone, but sometimes in the dark they would tread on one, in which case the result would be a mangled foot. Or a small child would pick one up because it looked pretty and, a second later, lose a hand.

It was a story of unresolved gloom and tragedy. In 1980 an average of 80,000 Afghans a month had crossed into Pakistan as refugees. The December 1980 figure was 118,000 and the January 1981 figure 143,000. There were 1.5 million Afghan refugees registered with the United Nations. The figure would soon reach 2 million. And that did not include the 'internal refugees', the ones who had fled from their villages, where the crops were being destroyed from the air and the people bombed, to the large Afghan towns, where there was at least a ration of food.

There was only one glimmer of light that we could find – the weakening morale of the Soviet occupying forces. It was beginning to emerge that this was not the Red Army of its heyday in 1945. The brave men who defended their motherland, drove Hitler back and raised the red flag over Berlin had been superseded by conscripts who felt little motivation for this dirty war in a faraway land.

They were subject to draconian discipline, but they still misbehaved. Vodka, the Soviet solider's traditional joy and recreation, was available only to officers. The rest were not deterred, however. They made their own brew out of various concoctions of antifreeze, eau-de-Cologne, brake fluid, aircraft de-icing fluid and an ingenious distillation of shoe polish toasted on slices of black bread. They also looted shops and sold military equipment, spending the money on hashish and pornography, anything to relieve the boredom and anxiety.

The American hostages were released from the Tehran embassy as the new President took over. Reagan was now anxious to prove his claim that his country had lost its self-confidence only because of his predecessor's weakness. 'I ask the CIA about Afghanistan and all I get is a nod and a wink and a nudge. I'll be glad when America decides to come out of the closet on this one,' said Congressman Doug Bereuter to our team of Afghan fighters and pro-Afghan enthusiasts. 'There is not a single person in Congress who opposes this idea in principle,' said Congressman Dorner. It was only a question of how it could be done without doing more harm than good. At the end of the visit I reported,[11] 'There is now a growing body of opinion on Capitol Hill that more must be done to help the Afghan fighters.'

Margaret Thatcher was an early recruit to the cause. She wrote to me,[12] 'I greatly admire the courage of those Afghans who are struggling against the Soviet troops who have invaded their country.' However, her reaction to my specific suggestion that we should help the *mujahedin* openly was more cautious: 'We have said publicly that it is important that the Resistance receives arms. The question of the supply of arms is complex . . . We are of course keeping in close touch with the Americans and the Pakistanis about Afghanistan.' She soon made it clear, though, that she was personally interested in helping the *mujahedin* in every possible way. And from then on, if ever the Foreign Office seemed to be showing signs of over-caution, she could be approached and relied upon to take a more vigorous attitude.

The reaction of Soviet and Afghan adversaries was even more encouraging. On 19 March the Kabul leader Babrak Karmal condemned[13] the American decision to supply arms to 'counter-revolutionary mercenaries' as if it had already been taken. No outside help would save this doomed cause, he told his Party plenum. It seemed that they were taking our efforts seriously.

And then I found myself personally attacked. *Izvestiya*[14] wrote about 'the anti-Soviet lord who came to Washington to meet up with various chiefs of Afghan bandit groups' and who planned to 'use his membership of this "All-Europe" parliament to internationalize the policy of interfering in Afghanistan's internal affairs'. It called on the United States and Western Europe to abandon their 'reactionary crusade' and 'dangerous illusions'. Soon there were demonstrations in Kabul, with large crowds bearing placards with the strange slogan, 'Death to the European Parliament!'

The Soviet government spokesman was exaggerating my influence. We were still a long way from a decision to provide the freedom fighters with the weaponry they needed. My conclusion, as I returned from America, was that in many respects our critics were right. The Soviet army had indeed achieved its objectives. True, most of the countryside was closed to them in the sense that they ventured there at their peril. In some areas *mujahedin* control was tight enough to set up a shadow administration and levy taxes. But the Soviets had what they essentially wanted – Kabul, Herat, Mazar-i-Sharif, the other main cities and the airfields and roads that connected them.

The *mujahedin* explained this and made it clear what they wanted from the Americans, but the decision whether or not to give them more sophisticated weapons was not easy. It involved the stability of Zia's government and various unwritten understandings between East and West. We knew too that, even when the money and material started to flow, much of it would be lost through corruption along the line of supply. Also, the only realistic supplier of such complicated material was the American government. There was no room for amateurs or loose cannons in this particular battlefield of the second cold war. Or so they kept telling me.

Undermining the Soviet Army's Morale

The question of the Soviet army's morale was rather different. Here there was room for non-government action. One way of attacking it was through the time-honoured method of using radio broadcasts as propaganda. The result was 'Radio Free Kabul', not the elaborate US-financed body, based in Munich, that broadcast to Eastern Europe, but a private enterprise, launched by the British MP Winston Churchill and the dissident Vladimir Bukovsky. It began to broadcast from small transmitters from inside Afghanistan to the occupying Soviet forces in the Russian language. Programmes were pre-recorded on to cassette by Russians who lived in the West and taken out into the field. They realized from the outset that any large transmitter would soon be located and bombed. The programmes were therefore put out on VHF from small portable sets a few miles from Soviet positions.

The broadcasters kept moving, since attacks could be expected as soon as they went on the air. Still, they attracted eager listeners from among the bored Soviet conscripts, especially at night. Radio Free Kabul adapted political propaganda to war conditions, using the experience of the British 'black radio' of the Second World War. Its aim was to sow discord between officers and other ranks, so producing a crisis of confidence in the army and eventually reducing Soviet morale to the point where the men were no longer prepared to carry on the struggle, where they feared the enemy less than they feared their own officers.

But would a few words on the radio induce Soviet soldiers to desert? They had been told by their officers, with some truth, that any man who fell into the hands of *mujahedin* would be chopped into small pieces. They may even have been told of of Rudyard Kipling's advice to the British soldiers who faced the same predicament a hundred years earlier. In 1981 Gailani had told me that Soviet soldiers who fell into his men's hands were killed immediately, because of 'our indignation at the suffering wrought upon our country by the alien invader'. Other group leaders shared his view and his policy. It would never have occurred to them to take Soviet soldiers prisoner. It was not the Afghan way.

Nor, indeed, was it the Western way in circumstances of guerrilla warfare. In Vietnam no quarter had been given to prisoners, on either side, except to Americans, whose lives the communist side had an interest in preserving. In 1943 German soldiers falling into the hands of the Greek resistance, for instance in the mountains of Crete, could expect to be killed after interrogation and British officers fighting with the Greeks did not protest. This was because guerrilla groups have no facilities for detaining the men they capture. It is exhausting and dangerous to guard them. Any lapse of concentration can allow the man to escape. Guerrillas are usually short of food. They have none to spare for prisoners. They are hardly ever able, except in the case of a 'VIP' prisoner, where special means may be made available, to transfer him to a camp or prison on territory that they hold.

A prisoner is a special danger to any guerrilla group that holds him. He attracts enemy activity. The enemy want to free him, if only to prevent him from giving away information, or even to kill him, for the same reason. In either case, his existence in the ranks of a fighting group draws unwelcome attention. It makes it more likely that the enemy will be taking pains to find them and dispose of the danger.

If he is freed, he becomes even more dangerous. He will then be a source of information about his captors – who they are, who their friends are, how they operate, what equipment they have, what are their weaknesses. Operations against the group will be made easier. A group that happens to hold a prisoner, if it falls under attack, will usually kill the prisoner at once, rather than risk the disaster of his being recaptured by, or escaping to, his own side.

Even so, we felt that the *mujahedin* stood to gain much by changing their policy. We appealed to them on humanitarian principle, and sometimes on Islamic principle, reminding them that any man may ask for Islam's protection and be given it – even an enemy. We told them that Soviet prisoners might one day be valuable. They could be exchanged for their own prisoners in Pul-e-Charki prison in Kabul, or for some political benefit, or even for ransom.

We told them that desertion had always been a problem in the Soviet army, especially in the Second World War, when whole armies surrendered and hundreds of thousands were willing to fight against their own country. We had every reason to believe that there were Soviet soldiers in Afghanistan who felt the same way, who had no stomach for the war and who would be happy to desert to the *mujahedin*, if only they thought that they would receive reasonable treatment. They would then be useful sources of information, for the West as well as for the Afghans, and their presence could be used to add to the pressure on the Soviet side.

We conceived the idea of an 'underground railway', a system of conveying these deserters to a new life in the West. We had in mind mainly the United States and Canada, where there were big Russian and Ukrainian communities who could support them psychologically in the difficult early days, then help them to learn English and find work. We wanted the *mujahedin* to agree, in future, to pass their prisoners after questioning across the border into Pakistan, where Western officials could interview them, establish their *bona fides* and arrange for their transfer to the West. We wanted them to be able to make the fact that this was happening well known throughout the Soviet army in Afghanistan, using Radio Free Kabul and other means of communication.

We believed that the effect of such amazing news on the Soviet Union, if it succeeded, would be devastating. Russians from Moscow to Kabul would be told, by Western radio stations if by no one else, that Soviet citizens were escaping to the West through the ranks of the Soviet army. We could imagine how Russians listening to Radio Liberty and the BBC would feel as they heard the voices of their 'boys' who had fallen into the hands of the 'bandits' describing the fine life they were now leading in New York and California.

This was the prospect to which deserters from the Soviet army and Soviet prisoners of war would now look forward. It would not be a slow death through every fabled refinement of oriental torture, as lovingly described to them in propaganda films and by their superior officers, and as had indeed been the case since the *jihad* began. Instead it would involve nothing worse than a flight on a fast Boeing to the other side of the world, where they would be welcomed as men who had 'chosen freedom', for the West and for the Afghan resistance as well as for themselves, and rewarded with all the glorious forbidden fruits of the capitalist world. They would describe for the benefit of Soviet listeners, in every lurid detail, the miseries of a soldier's life in Afghanistan and the miracle that had brought them to the wealth and safety of North America. This would bring home to the Soviet people, soldiers in their barracks and rank-and-file Party members in their flats, the unpopularity and absurdity of the Afghan war. The desertions would begin as a trickle. Soon they would be a flood.

We were delighted to find, towards the end of 1981, that some of the *mujahedin* groups had changed their policy, as we had suggested, and were keeping their prisoners alive, usually on condition that they embraced Islam.

It was then that I decided to go to Afghanistan myself – unofficially and with the help of my *mujahedin* friends. Leaders of several of the groups offered to take me north across the Pakistan border. They assured me that it was not dangerous. The distances were short – only sixty miles from Peshawar to Kabul. Much of it could be covered by jeep, the rest by donkey. I wanted to explain to the commanders in the field how they might combine a more humane policy towards their prisoners with a plan that might further their own armed struggle against the invader.

The opportunity came in December 1981. The European Parliament decided to ask three of its members to go to north-west Pakistan for a tour of the Afghan refugee camps. These camps were receiving substantial European money and it was quite understandable that the EP should make sure that this money was being wisely spent. The

MEPs eventually chosen were Carlo Ripa di Meana, Gérard Israel and myself. Carlo was a right-wing Italian socialist, formerly a communist, of noble family, well known in Italy for his and his wife's amorous adventures. Gérard was a French Gaullist, a lawyer, a specialist in human rights, a Jew but (belying his name) a less than fervent Zionist.

On 8 March 1982, Gérard Israel and I flew to Washington. We then attended President Reagan's 'Afghanistan Day' ceremony in the White House. It was a 'festival' recently designated by the European Parliament at my suggestion to coincide with the traditional Persian festival of 'Noruz', 21 March, the first day of spring. All this time we were making our preparations to fly to the North-West Frontier of Pakistan on 25 April. Much work was involved and it was done against the dramatic background of Argentina's invasion of the Falkland Islands on 2 April. I remember lunching with the Pakistani ambassador in London on 7 April. Our conversation at lunch was not so much about Afghanistan and the refugee camps, as it was supposed to be, as about whether 'the Empire' would succeed in 'striking back' against Argentina.

The ambassador, Ali Arshad, nevertheless had time to raise a very strange and disagreeable matter – the name of my French Gaullist colleague. It was unfortunate, said Mr Arshad, that one of the European Parliament's three delegates was called 'Israel'. Pakistan joined with all Arab countries and the rest of the Islamic world, he said, in opposing political Zionism. It would be hard for them to welcome a 'Mr Israel' as their guest, even if his aim was to help Pakistan's problems over 2 million Afghan refugees.

I told the ambassador that such a line of argument could not be serious. It would be one thing if Gérard were an ultra-Zionist, a supporter of Prime Minister Begin's policies, an advocate for Israeli annexation of Judaea and Samaria. Then they could well object to him on political grounds. This was, however, not the case. He was of Jewish origin, but his national orientation was towards France rather than to the land after which he was named. And his politics were not Zionist but Gaullist. There seemed no reason to slow down our preparations for the journey and, although deeply deplorable, it did not seem relevant to the trip when, on 11 April, I heard that a Jewish extremist had attacked worshippers at the al-Aqsa Mosque in

Jerusalem. During the morning of 19 April I was given injections against cholera and typhoid, and I started taking my malaria pills.

I was therefore already at a low and feverish ebb when the Pakistani embassy telephoned me that afternoon to say that Gérard Israel, because of his name, though not because of his race, was 'not acceptable' as a European Parliament delegate. Pakistan would be glad to welcome Carlo Ripa di Meana and me, said the spokesman, but not Gérard Israel, especially in view of the attack near the Jerusalem mosque the previous week.

Would Carlo Ripa and I, in that case, be flying out on 25 April as planned? I told Arshad with some feeling that we certainly would not. It would be impossible for us to accept a ban on a colleague based apparently on nothing more than a coincidence of name and an implication of racial prejudice. And, as for the attack on the mosque, I was sure that Gérard deplored it as much as we did.

I wrote to the Ambassador that same day pointing out that Islam orders its followers to respect 'the People of the Book', the Jews and the Christians who, like Moslems, revere the Holy Bible. I warned that the decision would cause great offence in Europe and damage Pakistan's reputation. I reminded him of Europe's aid to Pakistan in the joint task of supporting Afghan refugees and how our mission had hoped to plan how such aid could be increased.

In Strasbourg two days later Leo Tindemans, Belgium's Foreign Minister and president-in-office of the ten European Community countries, handed me a telegram in Dutch from Guy Copette, his ambassador in Islamabad. It explained that the Pakistani foreign ministry had told Copette on 15 April that Ripa di Meana and I were welcome, but Gérard Israel was unacceptable 'because of the name and origin of the said person'. In the debate that followed in Strasbourg I said that it was distressing to have to conclude that Pakistan, with which Britain had strong historical connections, was now ruled by an anti-semitic government. I was confident, I said, that the ten EC countries would make a vigorous protest. This was done on 26 April.

A senior Pakistani official told the British embassy, 'The only difficulty was Mr Israel's surname. Had he some other surname, the fact of his being Jewish would not have mattered. The problem for Pakistan was one of public attitudes, especially when feelings were running high because of the shootings in the al-Aqsa mosque. Afghan resistance leaders were likely to react badly and to refuse to see the group.' Ambassador Arshad wrote to me on 30 April also rejecting the charge of anti-semitism. Pakistan received many Jewish visitors, he said, but his government was afraid that the visit might cause 'complications' for Mr Israel. 'We in Pakistan intensely dislike situations which cause embarrassment to our guests.'

Our visit to Pakistan, and my unofficial foray into Afghanistan, were therefore postponed indefinitely. It was almost laughably depressing. Said Ahmad Gailani told me that, as far as he could say, the resistance leaders would have no objection to meeting Gérard Israel. Indeed, 'Israel' was a common Afghan surname borne by many of his friends. The pretexts thought up by Pakistan meant nothing to him, he said, although it would hardly be convenient for him to complain too much. After all, he was Pakistan's guest too.

On top of all the irritation, my arm was still hurting from the injections. It infuriated me that our plan to tackle the injustice of the Soviet presence in Afghanistan was aborted by such an absurdity as a man with the wrong surname. The matter had now become an international incident and it would be some time, I had to conclude, before it was resolved in a way that did not involve an unacceptable loss of face by either side. In the meantime I was effectively prevented, by loyalty to a colleague as well as by general principle, from entering Pakistan at all. My plan to subvert the Soviet army's loyalty and my way to the Khyber Pass were both blocked by an incident of the utmost foolishness.

11. *Two Lonely Soldiers*

It seemed that I would not, after all, succeed in crossing into Afghanistan. The racial slur imposed on my French colleague was too cruel. The rift would never be repaired. If Pakistan really found it necessary to ban a man from their country because of his name, there was no way of doing business with them. And Pakistan was essential to every aspect of our plan, indeed to every part of the *jihad* as a whole.

Still, I had not given up my idea of causing embarrassment to the Soviet government and its army by encouraging their soldiers to desert. Soviet imperialism was on the move and Afghanistan was the only country where Soviet interests were seriously under threat. It made sense to attack them at this weak point. We knew that morale was low in the army of occupation. Drugs were being widely consumed by the men and horrible alcoholic concoctions were being drunk. The Afghan countryside was still largely under *mujahedin* control. Four years of bitter war had done nothing to stem the freedom fighters' brave resistance, especially their capacity to ambush Soviet convoys. Only the helicopter gunships were free to roam the land with impunity, bombing and massacring at leisure.

Then in early 1983 Gérard Israel and I were given to understand that Pakistan regretted the April 1982 incident and was anxious to put matters right. Their urbane Foreign Minister, Muhammed Yaqub Khan, was a frequent visitor to Geneva, where he was holding 'indirect talks' with the Afghan government through United Nations intermediaries. He invited us to call on him to discuss how the idea of an EP visit to Pakistan might be revived and we flew to Geneva to meet him on 20 June.

It was obvious that Pakistan regretted its outburst of the previous year. Yaqub Khan was at pains to make clear that his country had no quarrel with the Jewish people, only with political Zionism and the State of Israel. It would have been impossible, he said, to welcome any 'Mr Israel' to Pakistan in the wake of the attack on the mosque in April 1982.

What he did not mention, though of course we knew about it, was that the European Community had given Pakistan large quantities of food and money for Afghan refugees. The dispute over 'Mr Israel' was therefore a small but irritating thorn in Pakistan's flesh. EC ministers had raised the issue regularly for more than a year, making it clear that they expected a solution to be found. The time had now come to make amends. Yaqub Khan assured us that Pakistan greatly regretted any insult. He would now like to invite us to visit Pakistan, to inspect the refugee camps and be briefed about the Afghan question. President Zia ul-Haq would invite us himself. In November 1983 there was the usual UN General Assembly vote on Afghanistan, with 116 calling for the withdrawal of all foreign troops and only sixteen against. By the end of the year it was agreed that the original three MEPs – Carlo Ripa, Gérard Israel and I – would fly to Pakistan on the Parliament's behalf. We arrived there on 29 January 1984.

The next day President Zia gave us a remarkable dinner. It was washed down with Coca Cola and it included a three-hour talk about Pakistan's role in the struggle against Soviet aggression. Zia spoke about Russia's historical role in the area, of its conquest of the Moslem areas of Central Asia and of its ruthless suppression of Moslem uprisings in the early years of Soviet rule. He mentioned Russia's nineteenth-century rivalry with British India, much of it involving the 'great game' for possession of Afghanistan, whereupon he was handed a large map of South Asia. Then, in a dramatic gesture, he covered the upper part of the map with a strip of red plastic cut into an irregular shape showing the extent of Russian penetration south towards the Indian Ocean.

'We are the front-line state, the "dam" against further Soviet expansion,' he said, explaining how the *mujahedin* were fighting not only for Afghanistan, but for the entire democratic world. And they had achieved some success, diplomatic as well as military. The Islamic and Western worlds supported them. So did a large majority in the United Nations. And they had won military successes. He agreed, as did everyone at that time, that it was inconceivable that they would ever beat the Soviet army on the ground. But they might succeed in forcing them to offer terms.

There was little here for Gérard or me to disagree with. We could see, however, that we were dealing with a man of tough religious conviction, far from the ideals of Western democracy. We made no progress, for instance, when we mentioned our distaste for judicial hanging and corporal punishment. These were penalties laid down by the Islamic religion, he replied, and was not possible for an outsider to question what was written in the Koran. He showed one flash of gentleness and humanity. Suddenly, with our discussions in full flow, his twelve-year-old daughter entered the room. She was mentally handicapped. Zia's eyes lit up as he saw her and he embraced her with a true father's love. He had been showing us the Islamic religion's harsh side. He was now reminding us of the Faith's humanity, its touching reverence for 'those whose minds it has pleased God to touch'.

In the following days we had our official tour of the government offices, the Red Cross and the refugee camps, accompanied by my friend John Ritch, a senior member of the staff of the United States Senate, who was by now an honorary member of our little delegation. I was very interested, though, in finding people to take me 'unofficially' into Afghanistan. My friend Ahmad Gailani took us to his training camp outside Peshawar, fifty miles from the Khyber Pass. We met his fighting men and were given a demonstration of their physical fitness. They showed us how to mix and throw a Molotov cocktail. They also showed us two former members of the Soviet army, both from Central Asia. I recall that we wanted to photograph them and we asked them to stand by a rock. They looked terrified, supposing that they were being lined up for an execution, staged for the benefit of the Western press.

On 3 February, at the headquarters of another group leader, Sibghatullah Mujadidi, who was to become President of Afghanistan in May 1992, we were given tea, cake and biscuits, and two more prisoners were produced. They were Igor Rykov and Oleg Khlan, both from the European part of the Soviet Union, one Russian, the second Ukrainian. Khlan was a gloomy character, unable to read or write and seldom willing to speak his mind. He sulked and brooded. He claimed to have deserted after being caught selling electric cable to an Afghan villager: 'This is how it's done. Several soldiers change into civilian clothing. Some steal some pistols or something else that can be hidden easily. Then we climb over the fence and go to the nearest tea-house to make the deal and exchange the pistols for what we need, hashish or fresh food.' It turned out that he had shot one of his comrades by accident and fled to avoid retribution.

Rykov was brighter and more articulate. And he used that first 'tea party' to give us a vivid account of how the Soviet army behaved in the field, telling me the terrible story of the Soviet lieutenant Anatoli Gevorkyan (see p. 130) who had run his bayonet through a sixteen-year-old Afghan boy's throat just to give a new recruit a 'taste for blood' and 'to show him how these things are done'. He mentioned another lieutenant who had massacred the women of an Afghan village, assembling them all in a small house and throwing hand grenades in after them. Rykov told us what we and the *mujahedin* wanted to hear, although I have little doubt that it was true, that large numbers of the Soviet army were on drugs, that several thousand had been killed in the Kandahar region alone, that he and Khlan would be imprisoned or shot if they went home. He even refused offers to send a message to his family, to tell them that he was alive: 'This would be very bad for my family. They could lose their jobs if it was known that they were related to a deserter.'

They wanted to live in a Western country, they said, and I was convinced that this should if possible be arranged, for humanitarian as well as for political reasons. I advised them to write letters to Prime Minister Thatcher, summarizing what he and Khlan had told us, on the basis of which I would try to persuade the British government to give them political asylum. Sure enough, the next morning one of Mujadidi's men brought Rykov's letter to me at the Khyber Pass Hotel in Peshawar.

He wrote to Mrs Thatcher: 'Soviet officers treat their men brutally. They beat them up often, treat them like cattle and humiliate one man in front of another. Often, during a battle, men will shoot their officers in the back. All this persuaded me and my friend Oleg Khlan to leave our unit and go to Pakistan to ask for asylum in another country, so as to explain about the illegal acts being carried out in Afghanistan by the communists. I ask you to grant me and my friend political asylum in your country, because any return to the Soviet Union now would be the equivalent of a death sentence for us. In England we will work like everyone else. I have several specialities. I am a qualified carpenter. I have driven trucks and light vehicles. The army trained me as a diesel mechanic. I hope this letter will receive your kind attention and I end my petition.'

The five-page letter was written grammatically and in a firm hand. Its argument seemed to me to make good sense and it persuaded me to make Rykov and his friend the first passengers on the 'underground railway' to the West. It was clear that they could not stay in Mujadidi's headquarters. They presented enormous problems. They had to be guarded night and day. They had already escaped once, and had wandered Peshawar looking for amusement before being recaptured.

Their presence near Peshawar was unwelcome to the Pakistani government and was calculated to attract the interest of Soviet agents. The Soviet embassy had protested about their citizens being held illegally on Pakistani territory. They had shown that they were ready to punish Pakistan. For instance, a week before our visit, on 27 January, two Afghan army MiGs had violated Pakistan's air space and bombed the border village of Angoor Adda, killing forty-two civilians and wounding sixty others.

The two Soviets were bored and irresponsible, Mujadidi explained. They had been on hashish and opium when they defected to his group and it had not been easy to get them off the habit. They claimed to have accepted Islam, but their background was Christian and it was impossible to say how genuine had been their conversion. Soviet agents might well kidnap them or entice them away, in which case they would give the KGB valuable information about his group and be used for Soviet propaganda. He would therefore gladly allow them to leave for a Western country, where they could start a new life.

We wanted to meet other Soviet prisoners, but were advised that there were no more in the Peshawar area. There were, however, an estimated 250 held at various points deep inside Afghanistan, at *mujahedin* bases attainable only on foot. The most accessible group, we were told, was to be found at Ala Jirga, 400 miles south-west of Peshawar, a base held by Hikmatyar's Hizb-i-Islami group. Hikmatyar's office in Peshawar gave us a letter of introduction to the camp commander.

On the morning of 4 February 1984 we therefore flew to Quetta, the main city of west Pakistan, and spent that day looking for a jeep to take us across the border into Soviet-occupied territory. The Hotel Nile, where we established ourselves, even though it was the best in town, was rudimentary, with no telephone, cell-like rooms, metal frame beds and oriental lavatories. Still, it proved surprisingly easy to find a driver, a vehicle and the necessary jerrycans full of petrol. By that evening everything was ready. We dined at the local Chinese restaurant and set off at five o'clock the next morning.

There were five of us in the jeep: John Ritch, the *Mail on Sunday* photographer Aidan Sullivan, our Hizb-i-Islami guide Ahmad, our Pakistani driver and myself. All three Westerners were in an unconvincing imitation of Afghan dress: white jacket, long scarf, flat hat and baggy trousers tied together with pyjama cord. This was necessary, we were told, because the Pakistan police were on the look-out for Westerners who crossed into Afghanistan and caused them trouble. However, if we had been stopped, the disguise would never have fooled them. Two of us were blue-eyed and all three were fair-haired and clean-shaven.

It looked an easy journey on the map, only 100 miles in a straight line north-east from Quetta to Ala Jirga, but in fact it was a bone-breaking ordeal in which we were jerked about by ruts and pot-holes along tracks and river beds, through an empty and harsh landscape. We covered half the distance in the first hour, fifty miles along the main road towards Chaman on the Afghan border, but then we turned right and thereafter our speed along the tracks and in and out of the ruts was seldom more than ten miles an hour and often down to walking pace. We bumped our way up the rough-hewn pass between the Khwaja Amran and Toba Kakar ranges, with their 10,000-foot peaks, until we were in among the snow and the track was a frozen sheet of ice. Three hours after leaving the main road our wheels began to spin and we stopped on the steep slope.

We were a mile from the top of the pass and unable to move forward, so we took to our feet, pushing the jeep and scattering under its wheels handfuls of earth collected and carried with us in the folds of our Afghan tunics. It helped the wheels to grip the frozen surface, but even so after an hour we had covered only a few hundred yards. The snow grew icier, the slope steeper, and the wheels simply would not grip. We pushed our hardest, but we feared that we would not be strong enough to get the jeep to the top of the pass before darkness fell.

We were saved by the appearance, from the opposite direction, of a

Pakistani bus containing thirty passengers, all of whom were mobilized by the kindly driver to push us up the final stretch. We rewarded the driver with a gift of money, enough to buy something for the passengers who had helped us at the next tea-house. Afraid we might get stuck again, he gave us the bus's statutory spade.

It was a moment of ecstatic relief when finally we lurched over the pass and slid down the mountain. Seven hours from Quetta we crossed the invisible 'Duran Line', the British-drawn frontier between Pakistan and Afghanistan. A large boulder marked with the words '*khush amadid*', Persian for 'welcome', told us that we were in Afghanistan, unofficially and illegally, at which point I got out of the jeep and changed out of Afghan clothes. I felt that it would make a better impression on the Afghan commander if I came to his door looking as I usually do, like an Englishman in dark suit and striped tie, rather than like an unconvincing Afghan.

Half an hour later, in the early afternoon, we turned a corner round a rock and came upon the Hizb-i-Islami control point. A green banner with the words 'WELCOME TO FREE AFGHANISTAN' hung across the track; its sides were well-manned with bearded *mujahedin*, all standing bolt upright with bandoliers and Kalashnikov machine-rifles across their chests, their fingers menacingly on the triggers, presumably alerted by the dust thrown up by our jeep. They made a fierce and brave impression. They asked us if we had anything to declare and we showed them our meagre luggage, overnight bags with a few packets of nuts and raisins, our cameras and tape recorders. It turned out that they were only worried about knives or firearms, none of which we had. Even John Ritch's bottle of vodka failed to upset them, Islamic fundamentalists though they were. It had been full when we set off from Quetta and it was now half-empty.

Ala Jirga was a village of mud huts turned by the *mujahedin* into a military camp, complete with anti-aircraft posts, training areas, a bakery, a hospital, even a guest-house where they accommodated us. It had no beds, just an area covered with mattresses where we were all expected to sit, eat and sleep. At the other end of the house there was a wood-burning stove and, through a doorway, a washing area with a tap but no basin. The lavatories were holes in the ground dug some distance away.

The commander, Abd ul-Rahman, was a former colonel in the Afghan army who had turned his coat, demonstrating this change of allegiance in dramatic fashion by spraying several dozen of his brother officers with machine-gun bullets as they sat eating and drinking in their canteen. He then fled to the *mujahedin* side. He was polite and hospitable, according to his Islamic duty. He was happy to let me meet his Soviet prisoners, as the note from his Peshawar headquarters ordered. Luckily for us, there was nothing against which we could properly complain. I was conscious, though, that we were stranded many hours from any hope of aid as guests of a man of ruthless determination, a fierce fighter and a senior commander in the extreme Hizb-i-Islami group, whose leader was an anti-western zealot. It would have been unwise for any of us to cause him annoyance, or to allow him to suspect our motives.

The food he gave us was the best his kitchen could provide, rice and a very liquid curry. By local custom, we were supposed to press the rice into a sticky ball, using only the right hand. The rice-ball is then an implement for soaking or scooping up the curry. It is a process that Westerners find difficult to master. We were therefore glad to find that the Afghans had a supply of spoons, kept only for foreign visitors. There was also bread, flat and round and baked in the camp oven, and a few sweet biscuits. All in all, we were grateful for the supplies we had brought with us, chocolate and raisins, although my happiest memory of the meals in Ala Jirga is of the tea. Strong and very sweet, it lifted the spirits like champagne.

There was nothing spirit-lifting about the Soviet prisoners. We met nine, five of them presented as Europeans, four as of Moslem background. They were brought to us one by one from the pits in the ground where they lived, dirty and depressed, anxious to make a show of gratitude to the *mujahedin* who had spared their lives, at least for the time being, in exchange for an affirmation of Islamic faith, and at the same time to make me aware of their desperation, in the vague hope that I might be able to help them out of their dire situation.

I asked one of the Moslems what he wanted to do. He replied, 'I want to live. Where? Anywhere, but not in the Soviet Union.' The others told me that they wanted to go to Turkey, first because it was a Moslem country, second because the Turkish language is similar to their own Uzbek or Tartar. They were confused and they told confusing stories. One of the 'Moslems', who gave me his name as 'Nasrulayev', turned out to be Sergei Tseluyevsky, a Russian from the town of Lomonosov, near Leningrad. Some claimed to be officers, thinking that this would make them valuable and encourage the *mujahedin* to spare them. Others minimized their role in the Soviet army, believing that their captors would be more merciful to junior men.

Most of them assured me that they would be executed if they returned home. Several seemed indifferent to their fate. One of these, who gave me his name as Sergei Andreyev, looked younger than the nineteen years he claimed, little more than a boy. He seemed to have given up the struggle for survival and, his friends said, he had not washed for several months. Everywhere about them there was the sweet stench of decay. Some of the prisoners, we were told, had been used by their captors as concubines.

There were two Russians being given especially bad treatment. This was because they had told the *mujahedin* that they wanted to return to the Soviet Union. One of them, Alexander Zhurakovsky, claimed to have been a sergeant in a tank unit. He deserted, he said, because he was going to be court-martialled for carelessness in the field, which had ruined an operation. He was confused, unsure whether to take a pro-Soviet or anti-Soviet line with the strange Westerners who had appeared from nowhere.

He said, 'If I go home, I think I'll be shot, or else jailed for a very long time. My parents are at home, though, and that's where I want to go. I was born in my motherland and that is where I want to die. I'll never be forgiven for what I did. I broke my oath and there is only one punishment for that.'

He was kept in a hole in the ground with Valeri Kisiliev, who was even more confused. He had run away from the army, he told us, into one of the Afghan villages, hoping to find some civilian clothes and then make his way home to Pyenza, 500 miles south-east of Moscow. Sometimes he claimed to be an officer, sometimes a private soldier. Sometimes he said he wanted to go home to Russia, sometimes to the West. His frequent changes of mood and story had made the *mujahedin* suspicious of him. He was dressed in rags and he wore rags wrapped round his feet. They were too swollen for shoes. He, Zhurakovsky and another prisoner, Sergey Myashcheryakov, who was too ill to be shown to us, lived in a cold cellar, seeing the light of day only two or three times a year. My visit was one of those occasions. Kisiliev did not know what month it was or that Brezhnev had died or that Yuri Andropov was now his country's leader. Their situation was pitiful, although I reminded myself that the state of Afghanistan was tragedy on a far greater scale. On my return, I wrote in my report for the European Parliament, 'I believe that Western governments should make it clear that in principle they are willing to give sanctuary to these people, a few hundred at the most, who were unwillingly sucked into the Soviet government's war in Afghanistan and made to pay the price for its adventurism.' John Ritch wrote in similar terms in a Report for the US Senate. (I am happy to say that a few months later Zhurakovsky and Iselnyevsky were transferred to the United States, although Kisiliev died in captivity.)

We spent that night on the floor of the camp 'guest-house', all of us on one large mattress, kept warm by our American sleeping-bags and by a stove in one corner. An old Afghan fighter stayed awake all night feeding it with wood. We were woken by our hosts' dawn prayers and soon there was black tea to revive us and prepare us for another day behind enemy lines. The old man fetched us cold water, which we used to wash and clean our teeth.

Those days in Ala Jirga were a brief and mild taste of discomfort, but enough to give us some small idea of what those who lived there, whether fighter or prisoner, were forced to endure. Yet, even as we thought about what it must be to spend months and years in this desolate place, we were forced also to understand the apparently harsh point of view of the Afghan *mujahedin*. Several thousand Soviets had so far been killed in the war. The figure was to rise to an estimated 25,000. A few hundred were enduring the sort of imprisonment we had just witnessed. But, compared to what the Soviet invaders had done to the Afghan people, this was a small burden of suffering. The number of Afghans killed, maimed or displaced from their homes amounted to 5 million. The population of Afghanistan was 14 million.

This was made clear to us by Abd ul-Rahman, the Afghan camp commander. He had no sympathy for the Soviets and he was only keeping them alive because he had been ordered to by his commander, Golbuddin, who was receiving Western supplies. They seemed to us worthy of pity. He had his doubts about them. He was not sure if he believed their conversions to the Islamic faith and to the Afghan side in the war. And he was not convinced of the wisdom of keeping them alive anyway. We asked if they could be released to the West, where they could undermine the Soviet war effort, but he saw no reason why his enemies should be set free to 'live like pigs', as he put it, in infidel lands. We were unable to persuade him and the more we pressed him, the harder it became for us to extricate ourselves from his hospitality.

He wanted us to stay longer as his 'guests' and it was some time before he let us go. Heavy clouds hung over the mountains and we knew that we would have to find another route home, since it would be dangerous to tackle the ice-covered pass in the dark. Luckily, we had a good guide and we made good progress, bumping our way back to Quetta along river beds and across fast-flowing streams. But then night fell and the going became more hazardous. Several times we were brought to a halt in mid-river by water thrown up by our wheels that drowned our engine. Each time we sat there patiently while the stream flowed by, as if the jeep was an island and we were marooned on it, waiting for the engine to dry. Our driver rolled up his trousers and paddled through the water around the car, wiping the engine with an oily rag, while we waited helplessly, hoping that it was going to start.

For several hours a snowstorm flung itself against the windscreen in the darkness. It was hard to see ahead, there was no sign of any other living thing and we were in the hands of a driver who, in John Ritch's view, 'would have driven us all off the edge of a cliff just for the hell of it'. The solution to Pakistan's problems, concluded Ritch, was more and better driving schools. Fate was kind to us, however, and we reached the Nile Hotel in Quetta in the small hours of the night. We flew to Karachi later that morning and by the afternoon I was drinking good Indian tea, with Carnation milk, and watching cricket on the Holiday Inn television.

We caught a flight to London the next day and, with the help of the six-hour time difference, I was on time for a European Parliament meeting, where I explained to euroconstituents in Willesden the effect of Europe's common agricultural policy on the price of groceries in British supermarkets. I told them that I had returned that day from Afghanistan, but their questions were about the price of butter.

Igor and Oleg

Yuri Andropov's death on 9 February made the story even more topical and on 12 February my report on the visit was printed with Aidan Sullivan's pictures. A few days later a fuller text was sent to the European Parliament. It was time, I suggested, to launch the 'underground railway' from Pakistan to the West, with Igor Rykov and Oleg Khlan as the first passengers. I wrote to Margaret Thatcher, sending her Rykov's letter and inviting her to arrange transfer of the two young men to Britain.

I wrote that Rykov was a mechanic, that he should eventually be able to earn his living in Britain, but that they might need medical treatment because of their drug problem: 'They admitted to me that they had smoked hashish in Afghanistan. Rykov said that more than 80 per cent of Soviet soldiers use it. Then, at one stage after his capture, he and Mr Khlan were given opium by their captors. This is quite a common practice and it is done to keep prisoners docile.' I advised her, however, that the drug problem ought to be containable. Mujadidi's son had assured me that drugs were no longer a compulsive habit for them. They were being weaned away from it in anticipation of release.

The Prime Minister replied on 21 February, 'As you say, this is a complicated matter. We are looking into it urgently . . .' On 27 March she wrote again, saying that Britain was ready 'on humanitarian grounds to look sympathetically on the particular applications of Mr Rykov and Mr Khlan', provided that they were sponsored by a private body and properly interviewed by the British embassy in Islamabad. The matter would take several months to arrange and, in the meantime, I should keep it confidential.

It therefore became my task, if I wanted to proceed, to make all the arrangements for the reception and accommodation of the two young men. Luckily, I could count on the support of loyal friends in the Russian community in Britain. I took a few of these into my confidence and they promised to help. So did the European Liaison Group, an umbrella body representing émigrés from central and eastern Europe. The *Mail on Sunday* offered several thousand pounds, enough to cover the boys' air fares from Pakistan as well as their early weeks' board and lodging, in exchange for the exclusive right to interview the boys and break the story.

Even so, it was a daunting prospect to make myself responsible for the future of two people, without one British relative or friend or word of English between them, both of whom had been taking drugs, though I knew not to what extent, on the basis of a one-hour conversation in an Afghan villa. It was a most unusual enterprise and I knew that, if it went wrong, at the very least my judgement would be called into question and I might also find myself saddled indefinitely with a heavy moral and financial burden. In the worst case, the *Private Eye* libel might even be revived. A kind friend reminded me, 'The memory of that allegation still hangs about like a bad smell in a telephone box.' I expressed these fears in a letter to Leon Brittan on 30 March 1984. In 1971 he had been my barrister in the libel case. Now he was Home Secretary. The project was going to be costly, I said. A five-figure sum would have to be spent before they were in a position to support themselves. And, because of the Prime Minister's understandable ban on premature publicity, it would be hard to raise funds before their arrival. The Russians in Britain would probably help with sponsorship, I wrote, but it was a small and not very rich community.

Brittan replied that sponsorship of an immigrant was not an open-ended commitment. It was designed to cover an initial period of not more than a year, during which there would be no restriction on work or residence: 'This would enable them to receive some social benefits, including access to the National Health Service . . . Much, of course, will depend on how able and willing Mr Rykov and Mr Khlan are to adapt to their new life . . .' This raised more questions than it answered, but I decided to proceed in spite of the risks, partly for the sake of the two men, whose chances of ever escaping from captivity must otherwise be limited, and partly so that we could use their story to proclaim the injustice of Soviet policy in Afghanistan, to the Soviet army as well as to the western public, in the hope of weakening Soviet morale.

Meanwhile Igor and Oleg were still held on the Afghan border and I was worried about their safety. Russian émigré activists, for instance the extravagant writer Nikolay Tolstoy and the 'NTS', an anti-Soviet body sponsored by the CIA, had begun to show interest in them. They were becoming objects of value to groups of many political views. It would not be long, I guessed, before Soviet intelligence found out what was afoot. However, Margaret Thatcher's approval of the scheme ensured that it was not neglected. On 6 April Geoffrey Howe, then Foreign Secretary, wrote to reassure me that things were moving: 'The Embassy have made discreet enquiries about the present whereabouts of the two prisoners. The Embassy have established that they are still living in Peshawar in fair comfort. They are not confined to the house, but can go out under escort and in disguise.'

Weeks passed, the formalities dragged on and I was standing for re-election to the European Parliament. I had kept my promise to say nothing, but others were visiting the boys in Peshawar, including Russian émigrés from 'NTS'. Soon many specialists in Soviet affairs had discovered what was being planned. On 16 May *The Times* wrote that Rykov and Khlan would soon be coming to Britain and accommodated by Nikolay Tolstoy at his country house. I wrote angrily to Charles Douglas-Home, editor of *The Times*, suggesting that his article might have put in jeopardy the lives of the two young men. If the Pakistan government read the item, they might well take fright and put a stop to the entire operation.

More and more 'experts' on the fringe of various secret services were visiting the boys and talking about our enterprise, often disappointed that they had not been involved in it at the outset. The danger of premature publicity was a serious one. There was only one way of getting these men out – through a Pakistani airport. All these Soviet prisoners had been moved across the Afghan–Pakistan border illegally by the *mujahedin*. They would now have to leave illegally for the West and Pakistan was going to be asked to turn a blind eye.

Soviet representatives in Pakistan, if they found out what was happening, could now intervene, either directly, by secret and violent action through their many agents in the Khyber Pass area, or else diplomatically. They would have good cause for complaint. Soviet citizens, soldiers from the Soviet army, were being moved in and out of foreign countries without proper documents. It was not the sort of behaviour that the local superpower would tolerate. The Soviet embassy in Islamabad might well threaten Pakistan with dire consequences for such hostile cloak-and-dagger treatment of its citizens, or at the very least demand the right to meet the soldiers, give them messages from their families, discuss their problems and try to persuade them to return to the motherland on the basis of false promises of immunity from prosecution.

The Times then printed a leading article on 18 May which began, 'Why are Western governments doing so little to save the lives of Soviet soldiers held prisoner by Afghan resistance groups?' No one seemed to be doing anything to help them. They fitted no category of people with special needs. Even the Red Cross in Geneva was unable to help. Their duty, they explained to me, was to care for prisoners of war and arrange for their repatriation. They could not be a channel for political defectors or deserters. The United Nations said that they looked after refugees, not soldiers. The problem of prisoners unwilling to return home at the end of a war had only been encountered in the context of the Soviet Union and other communist states. It had never been brought to international agreement. This was why it was now being left to the free enterprise of individuals like myself.

Geoffrey Howe wrote back on 23 May, 'I agree that publicity at this stage is unfortunate, particularly if it leads the Pakistani government to reconsider their position. However, we shall continue to press ahead . . .' A few days later, in mid-campaign for the Strasbourg parliament, I was advised that the interviews were done, that British travel papers of some sort had been put together and that the two boys were ready to be moved. The sponsors and I arranged for a Russian friend, Masha Slonim, to fly to Islamabad and escort the boys to London.

Early in the afternoon on European election day, 14 June, Igor, Oleg and Masha were met at Gatwick airport by *Mail on Sunday* reporters and taken to a 'safe house' nearby. I spent the day, meanwhile, from dawn to dusk in a last-minute effort to persuade the 518,365 voters of London North-West to send me back to Strasbourg for a further five years. At last I found a moment to call Masha at the *Mail*'s 'safe house'.

It was then that alarm bells started to ring. The boys were out of control. They had been given a goodbye 'fix' of opium by their captors shortly before being driven to the airport, enough to keep them in good spirits as they were smuggled past Pakistani immigration and on to the flight. But after a few hours they had become restless and jumpy. Masha then gave them some vodka from a private supply. (It was a 'dry' Islamic flight.) It was the first alcohol that they had touched for two years. It cheered them and calmed them. Oleg smoked a cigarette in the lavatory and nearly set the aircraft on fire.

Once they got to the *Mail*'s house their state deteriorated. They demanded opium, seemed surprised that there was none available and then demanded alcohol as an alternative. This was provided, but in a moderation that they found unsatisfactory. Masha and the reporters drank with them until they reached a state where they all needed a good night's rest. The boys, however, did not want to rest and, when the 'minders' insisted, they became aggressive. The 'safe house' became decidedly unsafe and no one slept much.

The next morning I hid all bottles of alcoholic drink from view and welcomed them to my home. They were excited and we greeted each other warmly enough, but they were also nervous and edgy and I found myself speaking to them like a father to rebellious teenage sons. Their future in the West, I told them, would depend on their readiness to fit in with Western ways. This would mean that vodka would have to be consumed in moderation – and drugs not at all. They would have to learn English and find jobs. Before this could happen, repair work was obviously necessary. They needed 'detoxification' and were admitted to the Charter Clinic off London's King's Road, where they were watched over by doctors and security men. They also needed elaborate dental work. Their moods varied between grateful euphoria and surly refusal to cooperate with our suggestions as to where their interests lay.

It took only a couple of days, amid the despair of withdrawal symptoms, for them to hint that they would like to contact the Soviet embassy. Our reaction was simple. They were free to go anywhere they wished. We did, however, point out the problems that they might then face as self-confessed deserters from the Soviet army. They had already been filmed by Western crews, attacking Soviet policy. It was, as Soviet history had shown, the ultimate crime, and Igor and Oleg seemed to understand this as soon as their black, angry moods subsided and they returned to reality.

In the clinic Oleg did little but listen to a Walkman that we gave him and watch the pictures of television programmes that he could not understand. We realized that he was quite illiterate, that it would be a formidable task to find him a niche in English life. Igor was more alert. Within a day or two he was reading our Russian books and puzzling his way through the English press reports of their arrival, which began on 17 June. We gave him a guitar, on which he at once began to play gloomy Russian songs with some skill. It was a tense day and an even more tense evening, as the European Parliament votes were counted in North-West London and I found my majority reduced to 7,422 – just 4.5 per cent more than my Labour opponent.

I knew now that Igor's and Oleg's arrival in Britain would not be an unmixed blessing. 'I want to speak English so I can get a job. I was a driver and mechanic in the army,' Igor told the *Daily Mail* the next day (18 June). However, his real state of mind was far from being so simple and helpful. Every few hours I received messages from the clinic about some new piece of erratic behaviour. There were security men at their doors, but the boys were not criminals and they were in the clinic voluntarily. If they insisted, they could leave any time, in which case they were capable of making a public scandal on the London streets. The opium had them in its grip far more firmly than I had been told at our brief meeting on the Afghan border. I was upset with Mujadidi's group for not telling me how addicted the boys were. Still, I did not want to discredit the people I was trying to support. I therefore told the *Daily Telegraph* that there was no malice in anything they had done: 'It is the traditional way of dealing with prisoners in Afghanistan, where there are no proper prison facilities . . .'

A week later, on 27 June, dressed in blue jeans and striped jackets donated by a kind Russian friend, they faced a press conference packed with journalists and television crews from many countries, including China. The Soviet bloc was not represented, but foreign Russian-language stations recorded everything, ready for onward transmission. In an opening statement they thanked their *mujahedin* captors for saving their lives and for freeing them. They had deserted, they said, because they found the war intolerable. 'We hope that other Soviet soldiers will follow our example. Perhaps in this way we shall help to put an end to this monstrous war that kills innocent people on both sides.' They then told their familiar story of massacres in Afghan villages, of handgrenades thrown into rooms filled with women and children. Morale in the Soviet army was poor, said Igor. Officers beat their men and kept them for days without food. And the pro–Soviet Afghan army was in an even worse state. It was 'a mess'.

Igor and Oleg were in fine form during the conference and the drinks afterwards. Newspapers then interviewed them, took pictures of them and bought them beer at the pub across the road. They were the heroes of the moment. They were getting the best medical attention. Their drugs problem, it seemed, would be overcome. Girls were flirting with them. Our plan seemed to be working and we were already looking for more soldiers in Afghan captivity for our 'underground train' to the West.

Their words appeared in the press the next day, 28 June. The Soviet embassy at once protested about our 'crude provocation', demanding the right to interview them. A Home Office official talked to them at my home and they both signed statements indicating that they did not need the help of the Soviet consulate. Masha Slonim invited them to stay at her house outside Henley, near Oxford. They rode her horses and made friends with her teenage son. It was when they moved back to London a month later, though, that trouble began in earnest. English lessons were arranged, and rooms with a Ukrainian family near Acton. Several members of London's small Russian community volunteered to help look after them. Girls from London's Ukrainian community were fascinated by them and fell in love with them. Even so, their autumn in London was not a success.

They were supposed to leave the house every morning for school, returning in the afternoon. All seemed well, but after two weeks the school reported that they had seen little of their two Russian pupils. Further inquiry showed that, instead of attending English lessons, they had been spending their days in the park, accompanied only by a full bottle of spirits, which they would empty during the course of the day. Their exposure to the world's media encouraged them to believe that they were people of importance, protected against the forces of the law. They therefore felt little need to spend energy on anything that did not involve vodka or women. Every few days I would hear of their latest 'scrape'.

One sultry evening, at a pub down by London's embankment, they were moved to take their clothes off and swim up the Thames, an escapade that was duly reported in *The Times* gossip column. They found a Ukrainian bar in Richmond, next to the police station, with an owner who thought it a kindness to give them drinks at low prices, the result being that they would pass out and spend nights on her floor. There was an incident outside a pub when, finding all the tables occupied, they tried to remove a group of peaceful drinkers by force. They took to shouting racial insults at black men in the street and, not surprisingly, were twice beaten up. On 29 September they quarrelled angrily and fought each other over the nature of Ukrainian nationalism. Trouble ensued and they spent the night in the cells next door.

These little stories were beginning to form a pattern, providing regular copy for editors of newspaper diaries. This was dangerous. If it continued, Western governments would not be encouraged to accept any more deserters from the Soviet army. The boys were cunning enough to understand why we were concerned and why people were reluctant to bring in the police, so they became bolder in their bad behaviour, less inclined to work or learn English, more insistent in their demands for money and alcohol. They realized that, by behaving badly, they had the power to embarrass us. They were using this power to extract favours from us from time to time.

And it was all of course aggravated by the genuine pain they were enduring as a result of loneliness, estrangement from Russian society and withdrawal from opium. They were lads from the country who were confused at having to live in a large foreign city, with a spotlight on them wherever they went in the Russian and Ukrainian communities. They were making no progress towards integration into British life. Their time was spent, at best, watching videos in the homes of Russian friends, at worst on the rampage.

The only hope seemed to be find them homes in the United States or Canada. In Britain they were condemned to living in the big city, in a goldfish bowl, in full view of the press, but across the Atlantic there were substantial Russian communities and wide areas of farmland. They had visited a Ukrainian festival in Manchester. They had enjoyed riding horses at Masha's house. But these were memories of home that could not easily be conjured up in Britain. The boys would feel far more at home in the spaces of North America.

I could see no way forward for them in London and on 4 October I wrote to Leon Brittan, Home Secretary, to express these worries. The decision not to place them under the care of the security services was correct, I said. They were not defectors or former KGB agents. They had not chosen Britain. They just wanted to escape from Afghan captivity and they had taken Britain only because I suggested the idea.

There was no good reason then for the British taxpayer to surround them with MI5 'minders' who would 'debrief' them and keep them out of harm's way in some 'safe house'. Their care had been left in the hands of private individuals. However, it now emerged that this care had become a heavy burden for the individuals in question. The boys needed round-the-clock nannying to keep them out of trouble in the big city. In Canada there would be fewer temptations. It seemed the only way of guaranteeing their future.

Meanwhile a series of seemingly unconnected incidents showed that the KGB was being more than usually active. In September 1983 Oleg Bitov, a staff member of the Moscow *Literary Gazette*, had defected to the West in Venice, then moved to Britain where he had spent the past year writing tough articles about the regime's destruction of Russian culture. Suddenly, on 10 September 1984, he disappeared from his flat in Cheam, near London, leaving £40,000 in a bank account and his new Toyota illegally parked.

A week later, in time-honoured fashion, he reappeared at a Moscow press conference to describe how he had been attacked by British agents in Venice a year earlier, then drugged and brought to Britain by force. He gave the names of several British intelligence agents and the addresses of MI5 safe houses. His anti-Soviet articles, he said, had been written as a result of the blackmail of the British secret services. He had been obliged to obey these orders while he waited for his chance to re-defect. His sudden return home has never been fully explained. His British friends suggested that he had become disillusioned with life in Britain and that he missed his fifteen-year-old daughter, Xenia, whom he once described as 'the dearest creature in all the world'. But there was no record of how he left Britain and why he should have done so suddenly, leaving behind his money and valuable possessions. KGB involvement seemed certain.

There were already indications, therefore, that KGB agents were in London, on the look-out for sheep who had strayed from the fold. Towards the end of October I heard rumours that Igor and Oleg were meeting strange men in strange places. A man from the Soviet trade delegation, it was said, was buying them drinks in bars and giving them recordings of sugary music, nostalgic Russian songs about a soldier who pines for his homeland: 'I long for home. I have not seen Mother for so long . . .' They were taking these songs back to Acton and playing them endlessly in their room.

We warned the boys about such meetings, but we could not watch over them night and day. They had reached the stage where they did not like being nursed by older people. Nor had we the right or power to tell them whom they might or might not see. They no longer respected well-meant advice of this sort. Then came more bad news. As part of their applications for entry into Canada they had been tested for drugs. The test showed traces of cannabis and LSD in their bloodstream. How had they got these drugs? They would not have had the money to buy them at street value. Had the 'trade delegate' given it to them? Could it have been slipped into their drinks without their knowledge? We looked for a conspiracy, but we could not be sure that there had ever been one. We did, however, now know that, as a result, there was no chance that Canada would accept them as immigrants.

There was a new cold-war disaster. On 2 November TASS announced that Joseph Stalin's daughter Svetlana had re-defected to Moscow with her thirteen-year-old American-born daughter Olga. It was as bad as the Bitov affair two months earlier. According to TASS Svetlana had become disillusioned with life in Britain. She had returned to the motherland. Soviet citizenship had been returned to her and granted to Olga, who had to leave her Quaker school north of London. Svetlana's seventeen years of anti-Soviet activity were forgiven, the Soviet authorities indicated. It paid them to be generous. The propaganda value of her return was so great.

It seemed therefore almost like the culminating point in a Greek tragedy when, on 9 November, Masha telephoned me with the news that the previous day Igor had received letters from his wife Galina and family in the Soviet Union. The letters had been mailed only a week earlier, which was high speed indeed for Soviet mail in those days of rigid censorship. We had to assume that the Soviet authorities had allowed the letters through for political reasons. Their timing was perfectly calculated to touch the young man's heart at a moment of emotional weakness and throw him into even deeper confusion.

The two boys had therefore set off for the Soviet embassy, as they told the Ukrainian family, to 'find out where we stand', and they had been gone some hours. I alerted the Home Office. We all knew though that, if the boys really wanted to contact the embassy and re-defect, for whatever reason, there was nothing that anyone in Britain could do to prevent them. The next day, Saturday, there was still no news. I went to Acton and spoke to the family. They could say only that the boys had gone the previous morning and not returned all night. They confirmed that they had vanished, although their things were still there, nothing was packed and Igor had left even his beloved guitar and Walkman, as well as a vivid account of his early months of army service. It was clear that they intended to return to Acton. Igor would never have left there without his guitar.

I also found the letters from Russia. Galina wrote, 'We are all longing to see you. We wait for you impatiently. Your little girl is growing up. She just had her third birthday. I kiss you again and again.' Enclosed was a colour photo of his daughter, Lenochka, a pretty little child on a tricycle, born after her father left to join the army. It was clear that they had intended to return to the house, if only to collect these precious objects. On the other hand, it seemed to me that the KGB, having once got them into the embassy, would not be keen to let them out again. They would now emerge, I thought, only for the drive to the airport and the flight home, suitably escorted.

That afternoon the Home Office made inquiries with the Soviet embassy, who at last confirmed what we had all suspected, that the two boys were inside it. Both sides then informed the press, the result being that I returned home to find an eager group of reporters and cameramen on my doorstep. Although in no mood to do so, I said something about my fear for the boys' future and my hope that, if they were indeed to return to Russia, the Home Office would first make sure that it was of their own free will.

Early the next morning, 11 November, Remembrance Sunday 1984, the Home Office called with the news that the boys would be flying out from Heathrow airport at noon, after being interviewed by British officials. I was invited to come to the Home Office while the interviews took place. Many central London streets were closed for ceremonies in and around Whitehall. Eventually, by a roundabout route, I reached St James's, where a bizarre scene awaited.

The Home Office had been opened specially for the occasion,

although it was Sunday, with me in one room and Igor and Oleg in another. A third room contained the officials. There was Foreign Office deputy under-secretary Derek Thomas and the head of the Foreign Office's Soviet department, Nigel Bloomfield, as well as a strong team of embassy men, including the Soviet Consul, Mikhail Ippolitov, and a young diplomat, Vladimir Ivanov, acting as interpreter.

I was shown statements signed by the boys. They reflected the new official Soviet version of events. They had agreed to come to Britain, wrote Igor, so as to find a way of going home to Russia and also to escape death, which awaited them if they remained in Afghan captivity. 'I do not wish to be in Britain, a country which is alien to me, and I do wish to go home and be of use to my people,' he wrote. Oleg wrote, 'I am a former Soviet soldier who served in Afghanistan and fell prisoner to the Afghans and spent a year in chains. Lord Bethell came there and suggested to us to come to Great Britain. We did not wish to, but thought that this is a way out, a way of getting home . . . Here we did not like it at all . . . Everything that I signed here I did under the influence of Lord Bethell, whom I do not want to see any more.'

Meanwhile the boys were telling British officials, with embassy staff present, that they were under no duress and that they expected no problems back in Russia, merely to be allowed home to their families. The British officials wanted Igor and Oleg to be allowed to repeat these sentiments to my face, so that there should be no danger of confusion. But Ippolitov would not allow it. He agreed nevertheless to see me. It was the coldest handshake I have ever received. 'They do not wish to see you,' he told me. He also refused to pass on the small Russian ikon that I had brought for them as a parting gift. 'They do not wish to receive it,' he said. What Igor had in fact said, I heard from Vladimir Ivanov later, was that he was not interested in the ikon, but that he would very much like to have his guitar.

I was out in the yard when they were brought down to the embassy car. Igor replied happily enough when I waved to them from a few yards away, but Ippolitov cut short the greeting. 'Get in,' he snapped. They got in and immediately the car moved off at some speed through the iron gates, up past Hyde Park Corner and towards Heathrow airport, leaving me with the problem of discussing it all with the journalists and camera crews who swarmed outside the building.

Ivanov says today, 'We naturally perceived that morning from different angles and not without emotions. I can testify that the boys really did not want to take a parting gift. They were already thinking about Moscow and their families and nothing else. Mikhail and I were nervous because we were already late and an aircraft was waiting. The behaviour of the press people outside was outrageous. Several times on our way to Heathrow, television cameramen put their motorcycles right in front of our car at high speed. It was like something from a James Bond film.'

I extricated myself from the press in time to watch the lunchtime television news, which showed the boys boarding their Aeroflot flight to Leningrad, guided towards the aircraft by a posse of 'heavy' Russian friends. 'I am sure that everything will be all right,' Igor told the cameras. I hoped fervently that he was right, but I thought it most unlikely. It was the height of the second cold war. The conflict between East and West was at its most acute. Igor and Oleg had given comfort to their country's enemies in Afghanistan and adversaries in Britain, and I saw no reason why the Soviet authorities would not impose on them the full force of their harshest laws. We all knew what the usual penalty was for desertion in the face of the enemy. I had read about it, and written about it in *The Last Secret*.

My words were then broadcast over film of the boys getting into the aircraft. I said that it would be a miracle if the boys were indeed allowed home, that in the 1941-5 war against Germany the usual punishment for Soviet soldiers who left their post, whether as deserters or as genuine prisoners, was to be brought back to the front line and shot in front of the comrades they had abandoned. The aircraft took off for Leningrad. Igor and Oleg, I then believed, even if they were not shot, would now be mixed among the millions of dots who lived in the Gulag archipelago and, at least to some extent, I must hold myself responsible for this tragic turn of events. It was one thing to reassure myself that we had done everything possible to help the two boys. It was another thing to contemplate the likelihood of their facing a Soviet firing squad and to ask myself whether I could not have done more. But what more could we have done? I never expected ever to see either man again, or even ever to find out what fate would be decreed for them by the overriding demands of Soviet national interest in the Afghan war.

The hate mail was substantial. 'What a bastard pig you are, Bethell,' began one letter, mailed as these letters so often are without stamp or signature. 'You son of a bitch, I knew they had taken a powder on you as soon as I heard the first news . . . What a laugh! It's no use trying to make anti-Soviet excuses. You exploited these young men for your own use to serve your political ego, and you've been double-crossed. Great!'

Nikolay Tolstoy, author of the sequel to *The Last Secret*, was quick to join in the attack.[1] He contributed several small articles to the press about the affair, all along the same lines, my foolishness in having brought about an important Soviet propaganda victory. It was indeed strange, I had to admit, that three such well-publicized re-defections from Britain could happen in two months. Was it coincidence? It was even being suggested that the whole episode had been planned by the KGB from the outset, that the boys' entire odyssey, from Afghanistan to Pakistan, then to London and then to Moscow, had been part of an elaborate KGB plot to embarrass the British government and all those who opposed the Afghan war, a plot that had succeeded only because of my recklessness, or worse.

In spite of my disagreements with her over Europe and other issues, I will always be grateful for the fact that it was Margaret Thatcher and not Edward Heath who was prime minister at that moment. He, I must assume, would have abandoned me to the tender mercies of the press, but she made no attempt to distance herself from what I had done. And I was not even one of her ministers. I was a mere member of the European Parliament, a body for which she felt scant respect. She nevertheless thought it right to support me at a very difficult time. 'We are all very grateful for the generous and honourable role which you played,' she wrote to me on 27 November. 'Like you I have grave fears for the fate of the two young men. But I believe that we all did our best for them.' This letter of support, which became known, helped me to survive the crisis. Vladimir Bukovsky also came to my support. He wrote to *The Times*,[2] 'We are deeply grateful to Lord Bethell and to the British government for saving the lives of two of our compatriots, who may be confused and unstable, but who nevertheless refused to become murderers.' These were two very powerful voices in the world of Soviet studies. They made sure that professional rivals from the world of Kremlinology would find it hard to revive the *Private Eye* campaign of the early 1970s.

We were now curious to know how the Soviet authorities would exploit the boys' return. They had two options, to present Igor and Oleg as traitors or as heroes. The first would be the traditional line. In Stalin's day a soldier committed a crime merely by letting himself be taken prisoner. Millions who fought bravely for their country in the Second World War, before falling into German captivity, spent years in Soviet labour camps after their 'liberation' from the enemy. And any hint of cowardice or self-mutilation in the face of the enemy, let alone desertion, made the culprit at once liable to the death sentence. This draconian approach was the Red Army's way of discouraging not only cowardice and desertion, but also any lack of enthusiasm for the battle.

Izvestiya's article of 2 December 1984 was therefore a surprise. Based on lengthy talks with Igor and Oleg, it told a tale not (as it might well have done) of desertion and disloyalty, but of two brave Soviet soldiers captured (or rather kidnapped) by Afghan bandits, ill-treated and threatened, dosed with narcotics and interrogated on military matters by cunning British agents, who had resisted every torment and temptation, staying faithful to their oath of allegiance to the Soviet army.

It told of our Peshawar meeting and described me as 'an imposing, sleek-faced man in a light suit', who was 'a career British intelligence man' and who offered to move them to Britain, and of how they decided to go, only because it would then be easier to get home. They were flown secretly to London and 'in a state of prostration' forced to appear before an anti-Soviet press conference: 'The special services approved the script of this political show. Lord Bethell presented it.'

'We weren't left alone with our thoughts for a minute,' Igor was quoted as saying. But eventually he came to realize, 'I could only live where I was born.' He remembered his Galina and 'our little Lenochka wrapped in a pink blanket'. And one day they had a stroke of luck. Their British secret service 'minders' seemed to have deserted them for a moment. They set out for the Soviet embassy, knowing that 'they could expect no mercy' from the British if their flight were discovered. They rang the bell and found themselves in the warm, welcoming arms of Soviet embassy staff.

It was lies, but it made us feel better. It suited the KGB to present the boys as clever Soviet patriots who had outwitted Lord Bethell and his accomplices, revealing us as the scoundrels we were. I was pleased about it. In that case, we hoped, if that was to be their official version, they might find it inconvenient to put Igor and Oleg on public trial. The boys could not be heroes and traitors at the same time. The thought that it might be in the Kremlin's interest to treat the boys leniently raised our spirits at a difficult time.

It meant that we had to absorb the Kremlin's insults in silence. If we had defended ourselves, pointing out that the boys had criticized Soviet policy willingly, without any improper pressure, we could have caused them further problems. Some time later a TASS report[3] spoke of Igor's 'bitter memories' of such men as Lord Bethell, 'who has sold himself out to Western intelligence services and Afghan bandit chieftains'. If TASS wanted to believe that, or to broadcast it, I was happy for them so to do, so long as they left Igor and Oleg in peace.

The correspondent quoted Igor thus: 'I was welcomed home warmly. My family and friends were waiting for me at the bus stop at my town in Krasnodar region. There was everything – hugs, kisses and tears of joy.' It was quite untrue, said TASS, that Soviet prisoners from Afghanistan who returned home were being tried and punished. We hoped that TASS was telling the truth.

Suddenly these hopes were shattered by a report in the French weekly *Le Point* that Igor had been shot by a Soviet firing squad. The *Daily Mail* telephoned me with the bad news. I had nothing to say other than that I was shocked. There was no official Soviet confirmation for the claim, but we knew that *Le Point* had good links with French intelligence and the *Daily Mail* clearly believed it. They printed it the next day (13 August 1985) under the heading 'Death of a Soviet Defector'.

Our hopes for Igor revived once again two weeks later. TASS reported that the *Daily Mail* was wrong, that the two boys were 'safe and doing well' after their ordeal of 'sophisticated brain-washing' and the 'far from humane methods' used by British intelligence. We now had no idea what to believe. And there was no way of checking. The telephone service into and out of Russia hardly worked. Mail into and out of the country was usually confiscated. And the movement of Westerners was restricted.

Igor was, in fact, alive and well, living with Galina and his family in Gulkevichi, a village near Krasnodar. And it can scarcely have been a coincidence that on 26 August, again two weeks after the *Daily Mail* report, he mailed a letter to the family in Acton that had sheltered him the previous year: 'Thank you for everything you did for us. It was you who told us how to find the embassy. And that was the last we saw of one another! Everything is all right with us. Oleg and I are in touch by letter. Everything is fine with him. . . And everything they frightened us with, how we were going to be shot or put in prison, has turned out to be untrue. We arrived in Moscow and then went home. You can imagine what sort of a meeting it was, how it was when I saw my little daughter. I did not think she would recognize me, but she took one look and immediately held out her arms . . .'

The letter reached London a month later, but for some reason the Acton family did not pass it on to the authorities, or to us, and for another six months we remained ignorant of the fact that Igor was alive. Then in March 1986 I was told that he was also sending messages through the family to his London friends. Typically, he seemed concerned most of all with the valuable objects that he had left behind in Acton. He asked us to mail him his jeans and Walkman, with a supply of spare tapes and batteries. He announced that Galina was expecting another child and in a subsequent letter asked us to mail him some condoms and contraceptive pills. He did not ask for his guitar, realizing presumably that it would be difficult to wrap and mail.

And so on 2 March 1986, the *Mail on Sunday* was able to give the happy news that Igor was alive and writing letters. There was no doubt in my mind that they were genuine. It was not only the handwriting, not only the fact that the writer knew much about Igor's stay in London and the friends he had made. This information could easily have been dragged out of him and exploited for the benefit of the Kremlin's reputation. The main evidence, in my mind, was their style, their carefree attitude of irresponsibility. It was quite unmistakable and it showed how Igor had been the despair as well as the admiration of the many British people who helped him. He was still thinking of little things that might brighten his life, not about the substantial ripples that he had stirred up in British–Soviet relations.

It still did not seem to have dawned on him what trouble he had brought on so many in Britain, from the Prime Minister down, as well as in Pakistan and among the *mujahedin* who had kept him alive, not to mention on his family and on others in his own country. It seems not to have occurred to him how luckily things had turned out and how close to self-destruction he had brought himself by behaving with such wild extravagance.

Although Igor and Oleg then left the forefront of my mind, I knew that I still had a duty towards them and must still try to trace them. Even after December 1986, when Sakharov was released and the Soviet system was becoming more liberal, there was still enough malice and violence in it for them to decide to do away with the two boys if ever they reached the conclusion that the West no longer cared.

Therefore, as soon as I was allowed back to Moscow in 1986, I inquired about the boys. I had no success. Afghanistan was still being fought as a patriotic war. No Soviet citizen was allowed to question this and there was as yet no sympathy for the purveyor of 'anti-Soviet propaganda'. I tried in 1987, again without success.

Then, in 1988, President Gorbachev took the political decision to pull Soviet troops out and re-evaluate Soviet involvement. Troops were withdrawn in February 1989 and, although political and logistic support for the Kabul communist regime remained, Edward Shevardnadze conceded that it had been a mistake ever to send troops south of the Oxus River in the first place. The 'liberal' press took the same view and in April 1989 I found myself being interviewed by Soviet journalists who appeared to disapprove of the Afghan war just as much as I did. They were from Moscow's *New Times*, a weekly journal that for many years was printed in many languages with serious KGB input, its main aim being to spread Soviet propaganda in the Third World. Its editorial line was now liberal and, although many of the KGB people remained, it now campaigned vigorously for a new society based on human rights and the rule of law. It was one of the many paradoxes of the Soviet system's dying days.

On 21 April they printed a four-page article about my Afghan experiences, but without any of the rudenesses so recently thrown by

TASS and *Izvestiya*. They asked me if I had used Igor and Oleg for propaganda purposes and quoted my reply: 'I opposed the Afghan war and they also opposed it. Regard that as propaganda if you wish.'

More importantly, *New Times* knew where both boys lived – Igor on his Caucasian farm, Oleg deep in the Ukraine. They put calls through to the one telephone that there was in each village and within a few days were able to confirm to me that both were well. I asked them to tell Igor that I still had his guitar and Walkman. Igor's reply, conveyed to me after I returned to London to fight the third European election campaign, was that he would be happy to meet me. And he would be happy too if I would bring him back his guitar.

New Times offered to arrange the meeting. It turned out that Igor had moved from the Krasnodar to the Leningrad region. After some discussion we agreed to meet him in the big city and on 22 June, four days after another touch-and-go European election victory, my son James and I flew to Moscow. The following night we took the Red Arrow to Leningrad. Russian sleeping compartments do not differentiate between men and women and the *New Times* reporter complained about my snoring.

I had no reason to feel any affection for Igor. He had caused us all much trouble. But I embraced him warmly and happily as soon as we met in Leningrad that midsummer morning. It was five years exactly since his arrival in London and I was just glad and very relieved to see him alive.

He was in good form but almost toothless. The Soviet Union's primitive dental service had simply extracted what remained from his mouth after years of neglect, in Afghanistan and elsewhere, leaving him with gums. He was with a young woman and a small child. Understandably, I called her Galina, but it turned out that he had moved on from the Gulkevichi village sweetheart who had beguiled him home, supposedly, in 1984. This was a new wife and child. He was living with them in Vologda province, 200 miles east of Leningrad, having left Galina with Lenochka and the baby down south near Krasnodar to fend for themselves on the farm.

He then answered the question that had concerned us for so long. How had he and Oleg been treated on the return to Russia in 1984? 'The KGB treated us quite well, by their standards,' he said. 'They picked us up at Moscow airport in a minibus on 11 November and took us straight to the Alyoshkin barracks. We were kept there for three weeks together in a cell while they interrogated us.

'No one told my parents that I was home. But they knew about it. They heard about it on the BBC. Then we had to write down every detail of our stay in Pakistan and England. And that is what I did, giving the whole truth and leaving out only the bits about the Richmond restaurant and the drinking problems. Then on 1 December we had this interview with the man from *Izvestiya*, with KGB men in the room. The *Izvestiya* man wrote it how they wanted him to write it, describing how we had escaped from British agents who would have showed us "no mercy" if they had caught us. It was rubbish. I said nothing of the kind. It meant though that, officially, we were heroes who had escaped from the enemy. You could say we were saved from the KGB by the KGB's own lies.'

His wayward behaviour in London, he explained to me, with perhaps some tiny trace of apology, was the result of more than a year of Afghan captivity, in a dark pit, relieved only by daily injections of opium. Then in the Charter Clinic in London he used to stand looking out of the window, from the fourth floor. 'There was a pub across the road and I used to watch young British people standing on the pavement there, glass in hand, having a good time. I longed to be with them. Then, when we were with the family, we did not want to learn English or work. We used to wake up and say, "What shall we do today? Where are we going to have a good time?"'

He said that they had gone to the Soviet embassy that November morning in 1984 only to find out their position if ever they decided to go home. This was why they had left their belongings. Then, once inside the embassy, they were not allowed to leave it. 'We sat there for three days, reading newspapers and watching Soviet television. They told us that if we went out we would be killed by the British secret service. It was sad, because I wanted to say goodbye – and collect my Walkman.'

The KGB's decision to let them go, said Igor, was influenced also by the fact they had given nothing of any value to British intelligence and that Soviet policy in Afghanistan was already being reassessed. And so on 5 December 1984 the army flew them to Tashkent for demobilization, which was completed on 26 December, and a day or two later, less than two months after leaving London, both men were home.

When I saw Igor in June 1989, he was earning 300 roubles a month, an above-average wage, driving a bulldozer in a chalk-pit. 'It is beautiful countryside, lakes and forests, but rather boring. Vodka is rationed to two bottles per person a month, with four bottles of wine as an alternative. No one drinks wine.'

I found it hard to believe, during Leningrad's 'white nights' of 1989, that glasnost had made such progress as to allow Igor to describe to me so frankly the strange end of his bizarre story. Neither of us felt any rancour for the dramas of November 1984. He even wrote a letter to Professor Mujadidi, the leader of the group that had held him in Afghanistan, thanking him for his 'Islamic generosity' in sparing his life. I quite understood that in 1984, in order to protect himself, he had had no alternative but to describe me as a spy and a kidnapper who had drugged him. 'It was what our politics needed,' he said. And he was in no way inclined, as some British as well as Soviet journalists had suggested, nor had he ever been, to blame me for any of his troubles.

I gave him his guitar and we walked with our friends to a small park on the River Neva embankment, where the *Aurora* steamboat is tied up, and we sat on the wall while he played his sad Russian songs. It occurred to me then that Igor was one of the lucky soldiers from the Afghan war. He was not one of the 25,000 that the Afghans killed. And they spared him when they had him at their mercy. He was lucky too, I suppose, that Margaret Thatcher and I decided to rescue him and luckiest of all that the KGB spared him on his return to Russia. Such thoughts consoled me as, the next day, complete with his new family and his guitar, his Walkman too and a quantity of spare batteries and tapes of our latest British recordings, he set off to catch the train back to his northern village.

12. My Friend Oleg

On 7 October 1982, during the Conservative Party's annual conference at Brighton, an apparently lonely and shy man in a shiny suit and with greyish hair came up to me at one of the many evening drinks parties being held in the Grand Hotel.

He introduced himself in poor English. He asked me, did I by any chance speak Danish, or Russian? The latter, it seemed, was our only common tongue. This was very strange. And it seemed even stranger when he told me that he was a member of the Soviet embassy, invited to Brighton that week as one of the Party's overseas guests. I remember how, at that time, with East–West relations at a very low ebb, I was shocked by the thought that such a blood-red cuckoo was being made welcome in our true blue nest.

He had just been transferred to the political section of the London embassy, he said, having served for some years in Copenhagen. It was now his job to build links with Britain's 'non-socialist parties', which meant in the Soviet embassy's judgement the Conservatives, the Liberals and the Social Democrats, with the Labour and Communist parties looked after by a colleague. He would like to invite me and some of my European Parliament friends to the embassy. He gave me his card and I saw that his name was Oleg Gordievsky.

His friendly tone surprised me, and an invitation to drinks at the embassy a month later surprised me even more. What did they want? My 'anti-Soviet activities on behalf of the British secret services' in Afghanistan and elsewhere were widely mentioned in the Soviet press and must be well known to him. What motive could he have for wanting to drink with an 'enemy of the people' like me?

I assumed, rightly, that Gordievsky was a KGB officer. Otherwise his superiors would never have allowed him to attend the Brighton conference. So I became more and more suspicious of him. What was his game? It more than annoyed me to think that the Conservative Party, always short of funds, should be spending money on hosting

1. Joseph Brodsky photographed by the author in his room at the Metropole Hotel, Moscow, January 1970.

2. The author by the Petrodvoryets fountains, near Leningrad (now St Petersburg), in August 1959.

3. Alexander Solzhenitsyn arriving in the West (*right*), walking with German writer Heinrich Böll.

4. The author visiting Afghan refugees near Peshawar, Pakistan, February 1984.

5. The author on his way north from Quetta into Afghanistan,
across the Toba Kakar pass, February 1984.

6. Margaret Thatcher and Avital Shcharansky, wife of the famous refusenik and dissident, with the author in the background.

7. The author with Lech Wałęsa, at lunch in the parish house of St Bridget's church, Gdańsk.

8. Ceremony for the dedication of the Yalta memorial, South Kensington, London, March 1982. *Top, right to left*: The author, Zoe Polanska, The Right Reverend Graham Leonard, Bishop of London, Sir Bernard Braine, MP, Nikolay Tolstoy (in tall hat), Angela Conner (sculptress) and (below in glasses) John Jolliffe. A Russian choir is singing in the foreground.

9. President Boris Yeltsin pays homage to the victims of the Katyń massacre at the memorial in Warsaw, August 1993.

10. The author with Soviet army defectors Oleg Khlan (*left*) and Igor Rykov (*right*), June 1984.

11. The author addressing an election rally in Tirana, March 1991, with Dr Sali Berisha, now President of Albania.

12. Oleg 'Super Spy' Gordievsky's wife, Leila, with daughters Masha and Anyuta, photographed by the author in Moscow, October 1990.

13. Pavel and Marta Ličko, organizers of the first translation of Alexander Solzhenitsyn's *Cancer Ward*.

14. Well-known dissident Larissa Bogoraz at her Moscow flat with her son, Pasha, in December 1986, a few days after the death in prison of her husband, Anatoli Marchenko.

15. Vladimir Bukovsky arriving in the West, December 1976.

16. Yuri Orlov and his wife, Irina, in New York a few days after their arrival in the West, October 1986.

17. Andrey Sakharov and his wife, Elena, with Lech Wałęsa in Paris, 1988.

the KGB, even if it was only to the extent of 'honest' red wine and cold sausage rolls.

I would have been more generous if I had known the truth. In fact Gordievsky had since 1974, at great personal risk, been working for my own country's Secret Intelligence Service (MI6). He was 'of a KGB background'. His father had been responsible for training NKVD officers. 'He was a conscientious Party member and he forced himself to believe that the Party was always right,' says Gordievsky today. His brother had a more colourful career in Soviet intelligence. He graduated from KGB Academy in 1957 and became an 'illegal', an agent working secretly in a foreign country under an assumed name. But, after serving in this dramatic capacity in several countries, he became ill and died in May 1972. Gordievsky himself joined 'the committee' as a young man, recklessly and unwisely, as he later conceded, largely because of these family connections and his interest in foreign literature and travel. He became a specialist in Germany and Scandinavia.

Then came the Soviet invasion of Czechoslovakia, which shocked him greatly. 'I decided that something had to be done against the system,' he says. 'I had become a convinced dissident and I wanted to do something practical.' British intelligence spotted these signs, he says, and with the help of Danish colleagues they watched him during his service in Copenhagen in the late 1960s and again in 1972–3. His first contact with the British was in 1973. By the end of 1974 he was a fully-fledged double agent, committed to the British side.

Of course, I knew none of this. If I had, I would not have begrudged him our sausage rolls. In fact, in all justice, the Conservative Party should have been rewarding him not with scarcely drinkable *vin ordinaire*, but with the best champagne that Brighton could provide.

Ill-disposed towards him as I was during that first meeting, I reacted to his strange overtures by making a request that I knew he would be in no position to grant. On 20 October 1982 I wrote him a letter. East–West relations were at their present poor state, I wrote disingenuously, because of the two sides' failure to communicate on matters of human rights. I would therefore be grateful if he would arrange for me to visit the well-known dissidents Orlov and Shcharansky in the camps where they were being held.

It was an outrageous idea. Soviet officials were then unwilling even
to discuss their penal system with foreigners. In their view, Orlov was
an ideological terrorist and Shcharansky a traitor who had given
information to the CIA. There were no 'dissidents' in the Soviet
Union, only freaks and criminals. In my letter I told him that I was
chairman of the European Parliament's human rights group and that I
was writing a report on human rights in the Soviet Union, due to be
debated in Strasbourg in a few months' time (May 1983). At present,
I said, trying my hardest to seem serious, the draft report lacked the
benefit of the Soviet government's point of view. It would, I suggested,
be preferable to settle such problems by discussion with the Soviet
authorities, or through the Helsinki Agreement procedure, now being
reviewed in Madrid, rather than by the 'megaphone' tactic of throwing
abuse at one another on public platforms and through the media.

I sent the Foreign Office a copy of the letter. There was a danger,
at the height of East–West conflict, confronting any Westerner who
maintained contact with any member of the KGB, on however trivial
a basis. It was essential to be 'covered'. They were a cunning and
ruthless adversary, quite capable of exploiting by blackmail or any
other means even the most casual contact with a British MP or writer.
Not only the reputations of Westerners, but also the liberty and lives
of Soviet citizens might be at risk. So I told the Foreign Office all
about it and they presumably passed the information on to MI6. I do
nevertheless see an irony in the fact that Gordievsky, as a good British
agent, must also have been keeping MI6 informed about his contacts
with me. I can only hope that the two versions of events coincided.

He did not write back, but he telephoned me. I was amazed. It was
more than ten years since I had been contacted by anyone from the
Soviet embassy. What mysterious reason could there be for it? I need
not have been so paranoid. The reason, he says today, was nothing
more than inter-service rivalry. The London KGB's aim was to build
up a circle of contacts in the Conservative Party and so to demonstrate
a deeper knowledge of the British scene than that submitted to
Moscow by the Ambassador and other non-KGB diplomats.

He informed his station chief, Arcadi Guk, I informed the Foreign
Office and on 10 January 1983 he arrived on my doorstep with a
bottle of vodka in a brown paper bag. He was polite, almost deferential,
in a way that I found deeply suspicious. 'Our Soviet government's

attitude to dissidents is too harsh,' he said. 'Anyone wishing to leave should be allowed to do so.' I smiled back at him, as far as I can remember, very cynically. 'That's what you would say, wouldn't you?' I wanted to say to him.

His reaction was equally strange when I told him that for the past twelve years I had been denied a Soviet visa, on account of my 'anti-socialist' activities. 'Of course you are anti-socialist. You are a Conservative. They should understand that in Moscow. They ought to hear the point of view of people like you. I would like to try to help you to get a visa.' Soviet officials did not usually see things in such simple and reasonable terms.

It was all very bewildering. 'I only ask one thing,' he went on. 'Please do not refer to any of our conversations publicly. I could be in serious trouble for talking to you like this.' 'Hypocrite!' I thought to myself. Did he seriously expect me to believe that every word of our talk was not being taken down, ready to be used in evidence at KGB Moscow Centre? He was probably wired for sound that very minute, with each nuance of our conversation being relayed to the Lubyanka by way of his embassy in Kensington Palace Gardens, London W8.

I saw no reason why the Soviets should suddenly feel well disposed towards me, at the height of the new cold war and a few months after their press had denounced me for my involvement with the Afghan opposition. What did it mean? If I went to Moscow and visited the survivors of the dissident movement, as I would have to, would I be safe? More importantly, would my Russian friends be safe? Was it all some great plan to lure me into an indiscretion, which could then be used against Mrs Thatcher's tough policies, or to provoke further arrests of dissidents, with the suggestion that they were agents of the British secret service?

Might I even be in physical danger? The feelings of the Soviet government towards me could only have changed for the worse. If they refused me a visa in 1972, they were not likely to give me one amid the horrors of early 1983, with East–West relations at their worst since Stalin's aggressions of the late 1940s and with the Kremlin ready to believe that the West was preparing a pre-emptive strike against them. As Gordievsky describes in his book *KGB: The Inside Story*,[1] the Soviet leaders believed that Reagan was actively planning for nuclear war against the Soviet bloc. And Gordievsky was one of the KGB team in London whose job it was to keep a special eye on activities in Whitehall and other corridors of British power, to inform the Kremlin when the strike was going to take place. This was Operation RYAN and, according to the then British Foreign Secretary, Geoffrey Howe, Soviet paranoia about it was at its height in 1983. Howe confirms that Gordievsky kept him secretly informed of the danger, especially during the 'Able Archer' military exercises that autumn, and Britain did what it could to allay Soviet fears. I am amazed that amid these crises Gordievsky had time to concern himself with such a small problem as my visa.

Still, I decided to follow the advice that Gordievsky was for some strange reason giving me and visit Russia for the first time in twelve years. I applied for a seven-day Thomson Tours holiday in Moscow. And at the end of February 1983, to my astonishment, he rang from the embassy to say that my visa was approved.

It was exciting, but I was conscious of the need to beware of the KGB, especially when they bear gifts. What weird game were the Soviets playing with me? Gordievsky told me that he had some 'friends' whom I might like to meet in Moscow. He says today, 'We were only anxious to show ourselves better informed than the ambassador was.' At the time, though, it was all very alarming. I thought of ending the meetings and cancelling the whole venture, but decided instead to sup with my longest spoon and to keep the Foreign Office in the picture at every stage.

I would have paid less attention to the Foreign Office's advice if I had known that they rather than the KGB were Gordievsky's true employers. They did not of course tell me that this was the case. They suggested caution, but not that I cancel the trip, so I collected all the addresses and pharmaceuticals needed for a Moscow week and agreed to see Gordievsky for coffee on 18 April, three days before scheduled departure.

On 10 March I set out with my two EP colleagues for the CSCE review in Madrid, where I met the notorious KGB colonel Sergei Kondryashov, whose job it was to defend Russia's treatment of dissidents (see p. 109). I came back and wrote about the Kremlin's 4-million-strong convict army, pointing out that the Soviet Union was the only country on earth that made a profit out of its penal system.

This was the bizarre background to what was going to be my first visit to Russia since 1971.

On 18 April, with thoughts such as these racing in my brain, I waited for Gordievsky's arrival. My bags were packed, the papers I needed were in my suitcase and my visa was in my passport. The telephone rang. It was an executive of Thomson Tours, very embarrassed. 'The Soviet embassy has cancelled your visa,' she said. 'They have told us that the aircraft will not be allowed to land in Moscow if you are on it. I have therefore cancelled your ticket. You will receive a refund.'

So much for Thomson Tours, I thought, and so much for Oleg Gordievsky. I did not expect him to appear that morning. If I had known how busy he was with Operation RYAN, monitoring Whitehall windows and the price of blood and Mrs Thatcher's visits to the Queen, I would have given him up for lost. He surely had enough problems. Still, he arrived on schedule, as polite as ever and very apologetic. 'You are right. This is not good diplomacy,' he said. I was in a bad mood and rather less polite. I invited him in, but did not offer him coffee.

There was confusion in Moscow because of a leadership struggle, he told me. We should keep in touch and soon I would get another visa. However, by this time I was fed up. I felt that he was playing cat and mouse with me, underestimating my intelligence by thinking he could fool me with another dose of hypocrisy. I told him that his government had behaved insultingly and that I would use the incident and the actual visa document, which I refused to surrender in spite of the Soviet Consul's and Thomson Tours's urgent plea, to embarrass the Soviet Union. Then I showed him the door. I never expected to see him again.

Where did this fit into the 'wilderness of mirrors' of the secret world? Had Mr Kondryashov taken offence at my rude article, which identified him as a KGB colonel, and asked his friends to take action against me? Or had they done it all just to tease, to test whether I might be 'bought' for a visa, a bottle of vodka and a little polite Soviet talk? Gordievsky was, as far as I was concerned, just another cog in this wicked machine, a devious Soviet apparatchik, a representative of the enemy whom I had no wish ever again to set eyes on. He passed out of my life.

Over the next two years his career flourished in the KGB's London station. In 1983 he was deputy KGB chief, under Arcadi Guk, and then, after Guk was expelled in May 1984, under Leonid Nikitenko. In June 1984 he secretly briefed Geoffrey Howe before the latter's visit to Moscow, where Howe spent seventy minutes being spoken to incoherently by the dying Soviet leader, Konstantin Chernenko. In December 1984 he was responsible for briefing Politburo member Mikhail Gorbachev during the latter's famous London visit, when Margaret Thatcher announced that here was a man with whom she could do business. In January 1985 he was recalled to KGB 'Centre' in Moscow to receive the good news that in May he would succeed Nikitenko as 'Resident', the top London job. The Resident's special codes were explained to him.

He returned to London to await this promotion to one of the KGB's most prestigious posts, living with his wife Leila and daughters Masha and Anyuta. Five-year-old Masha attended a Church of England school in Kensington. Leila worked as a typist, the same job that she had when Oleg first met her in Copenhagen. Soviet leader Chernenko died on 22 March 1985, and Mikhail Gorbachev, the Politburo's youngest member, succeeded him.

All seemed to be going smoothly for Gordievsky. In the early days of Gorbachev's rule the paranoia surrounding Operation RYAN came to an end, partly due to the advice Gordievsky had been supplying. No longer did the Soviets believe that the Americans were planning any pre-emptive nuclear attack on them. Then, quite suddenly, he was called back to Moscow for urgent talks with the top brass, including the then KGB chief Victor Chebrikov.

His sixth sense told him something was wrong. Sure enough, as soon as he arrived home, he found his senior colleagues ignoring him, or even treating him with hostility. His flat, he could tell, had been searched and books by Solzhenitsyn discovered under his bed. On 30 May he was told that his London mission was cancelled, that he was being assigned to home duties. 'We know that you have been deceiving us,' he was told. A bizarre evening took place, when he was drugged with Armenian brandy and questioned about alleged disloyalty.

The KGB, it seemed, had reason for suspicion but no proof. They did not know enough either to convict him or to be absolutely sure that their doubts were justified. This was his interpretation of the fact that they now let him go free, as a cat releases a bird, keeping him under close watch and hoping that he would panic and incriminate himself, perhaps by contacting the British embassy. For instance, he thought of contacting Leila in London to warn her not to return to Moscow, but decided that it would be suicide to make any such attempt. 'No telephone calls to London!' he had been warned by Viktor Grushko, his interrogator.

There was, however, I am presuming, a British plan ready for this eventuality. And, in those early days of June 1985, he thought about little else as he worked out how to put the plan into effect, all the time knowing that he was under such close observation that the slightest sign of guilt or panic would be known to the other side. He says, 'The flat was bugged very professionally. Leila confirmed this later. They played her my conversations and the quality of the recording was good, even though the record player had been at high volume at the time.'

The plan could not be implemented immediately. By the time it was ready Leila and the girls had been brought back to Moscow. This complicated his already meagre choice of options. Either he could confess and be shot for treason, or he could carry on with the plan, in which case he would have to take a terrible decision. He would have to escape without them, leaving his wife and daughters behind in the Soviet Union and hoping to recover them later.

On 30 June he saw Masha and Anyuta for what he thought might well be the last time. A few days later he kissed Leila goodbye. Their parting was made more poignant by the fact that she still had no idea of its significance, of his double life or of the imminent danger that he, and maybe she too, faced. He was later accused by the KGB and others of 'abandoning' his family. His answer to this is that the only alternative to separation that summer in 1985 was 'a few more weeks of freedom followed by execution as a traitor and even greater heartbreak for his family'.[2]

He went ahead with the plan and, I presume, found some way of explaining his predicament to the British secret service. Margaret Thatcher was informed. A difficult political decision then had to be taken. Should MI6 help him to escape from the Soviet Union? MI6 put it to the Prime Minister that it was vital, if only from the point of view of morale among other British agents in various countries, to rescue Gordievsky from the KGB's vengeance. It was important on moral grounds at least to attempt to save a man who had faced such dangers on Britain's behalf, and produced such good results. Also, a successful rescue operation would do wonders for MI6's credibility in the intelligence world and would leave Britain with a valuable 'property', a storehouse of priceless information which even the CIA would find useful. It would impress the Americans, and this is something that British intelligence always likes to do.

On the other hand, it was argued, it would be a 'James Bond' operation to take a Soviet citizen across his country's borders without proper documents, a violation of Soviet law and of the Vienna Convention on diplomatic behaviour, a most undiplomatic act and a most unusual way for Britain to behave in time of peace.

The Moscow ambassador, Bryan Cartledge, was aghast at the idea, as was the Foreign Office as a whole. But Margaret Thatcher was firm. Her robust approach to foreign policy and personal commitment to the aim of radical change in the Soviet Union overcame all objections. If Gordievsky was abandoned in Moscow, he would be arrested, interrogated, tortured and shot. He might be expected, under torture, to give away information that was vital to British security. At the very least, the great success of the 'Gordievsky operation' would be destroyed. She therefore decided that Gordievsky must be saved and gave orders to her secret services accordingly. This is what I presume.

Gordievsky gives me a partial account of his exploit: 'The second half of June 1985 I dedicated to planning, training and other preparations, like studying maps. The first days of July I devoted to specific acts of preparation, some of which turned out to be abortive. I made mistakes because I was so nervous. I also carried out certain manoeuvres designed to deceive the KGB and lead them along the wrong trail. They were listening to my telephone and I gave them false ideas about where to look for me after my disappearance. I began my journey at 3.30 p.m. on Friday, 19 July. I caught a train at 5.30 p.m. and the next morning I made my way to the border area, using a commuter train, buses and hitch-hiking. At about five o'clock that evening [July 20] I was on the other side of the border, very euphoric but also very sad. Some of my British friends were there.'

In a recent interview for a Russian magazine[3] he says, 'I got into a train going West, travelled all night, then during the course of the next half day made my way through forested country, reaching the border on foot.'

Gordievsky does not indicate which border he crossed. Nor does he confirm that he crossed with the help of British agents. However, on the basis of information from other sources, I am assuming that on 19 July he set out from his apartment on foot, pretending to be jogging, which he did at this time every day, carrying a few belongings including some light clothes in a plastic bag, and that the KGB surveillance team momentarily let him out of their sight, hardly imagining that he would be able to escape to London wearing only a vest and a pair of shorts.

I assume that he jogged to the railway station, changed into the light pair of trousers from the bag, and then caught an overnight train to Leningrad. I assume that the next morning he took a commuter train from Leningrad to Vyborg, eighty miles north-west of the city, and buses for some of the thirty miles between Vyborg and the Finnish border. I imagine that at some point between Leningrad and the Finnish border he met British agents and was packed into a secret compartment in a British diplomatic vehicle. This vehicle, protected by diplomatic immunity, then took him across the frontier. This was the 'hitch-hiking' element in the journey. A day or two later he was in England, in hiding in a very safe MI6 house.

The KGB were beside themselves with fury. The British, they were later to claim, had 'packed him like jam in a jam jar into a car with diplomatic plates and like criminals drove him across the frontier'.[4] They had three good reasons to be upset. First, they had suffered their most serious security leak in recent years, including the loss of agents in Britain, a total of thirty-one from the embassy and others less official. They had also, secondly, having at last uncovered the traitor, allowed him to slip through their fingers. Seldom in the KGB's history had there been such a series of humiliating lapses. Many heads in the Lubyanka, one must imagine, rolled as a result.

The third reason for the KGB's anger was that they had, in this particular case, the law on their side. If my presumption is correct, the escape involved violations of both international law and Soviet criminal law by British government agents. This at any rate is what the KGB believed. They accused Britain of flagrant illegalities and threatened an all-out war between the secret services. Assuming that he knew the names and whereabouts of all their illegal operators in Britain, they were forced to withdraw all these 'illegals', so losing the benefit of long years of careful secret planning.

The Soviet embassy described the expulsion of the thirty-one as 'an unwarranted act'. Their men never did anything illegal, said the embassy spokesman.[5] They retaliated by expelling British diplomats from Moscow and a lengthy 'tit for tat' conflict ensued. It was a small price for Britain to pay.

On 14 November the KGB sentenced Gordievsky to death *in absentia* and in this case, unusually, there was every reason to believe that they would try to carry out the sentence on foreign territory, so intense was their anger. They confiscated his property and vowed to the British and anyone else who cared to listen that *never*, under any circumstances, would Leila be allowed to leave the Soviet Union.

The details of this remarkable escape cannot be confirmed, but there is no doubt that they were repeated in confidence to senior spies in Washington, so lifting Britain's prestige in the secret world. It is said that Gordievsky has promised Margaret Thatcher personally never to reveal, without her permission, the secret of how she saved his life. 'Others may have to leave the Soviet Union by the same route,' he writes.[6] But the main reason is probably that he has been asked not to add to Britain's embarrassment by confirming that an organ of the British state did indeed act in violation of Soviet and international law.

My Astonishment

It was with total amazement that I opened my newspapers in London on 12 September 1985 to find that this apparently foolish fellow, whom I had met in Brighton nearly three years earlier and twice welcomed to my home, before dismissing him from my mind as a typical Soviet hypocrite, was in reality one of the greatest double agents in the history of world espionage and Britain's most valuable intelligence 'property'.

My first reaction, a selfish one, was of annoyance that I had never photographed him, either in Brighton or in London. The picture would have been syndicated all over the world and made me a fortune. I did, however, write an article[7] that was given the extravagant heading 'My Friend Oleg', about my regret at having nursed such dark thoughts on the man's character, at a time when he was risking his life on Britain's side in the battle against Soviet imperialism and against the paranoia that had given birth to the potentially cataclysmic Operation RYAN.

I had wasted nervous energy, I wrote, fencing with the spy who never was, with a presumed KGB man who was, in fact, exactly the opposite, and I looked forward to meeting him under different circumstances. Meanwhile I could only say how glad I was that he had neither been shot by the Soviet Union nor blown to pieces by the IRA bomb that exploded in that same Grand Hotel in 1984, exactly two years after our first meeting.

An even more bizarre question came to mind. Was it really the KGB who had cancelled my visa? Or could it have been the British? Maybe MI6 had sent their agent Gordievsky to see me to test my reaction to his ideas. Then maybe MI6 asked him to arrange for the visa's cancellation, to avoid the chance of yet another cold war incident through anything provocative that I might do, or to protect their man from falling under suspicion through helping such an incurable anti-Soviet propagandist as myself? It was all a fine illustration, I wrote, of the dangers that beset any mere individual so rash as to venture into this 'wilderness of mirrors', the 'great game' between East and West. The only guiding principle I could detect was a need never to believe anything that seemed obvious at first glance, indeed to believe the opposite.

The British secret services held Gordievsky under wraps for nearly five years. As a writer, I was sorry about this. I was understandably keen to renew our acquaintanceship. Also I wanted to apologize for my rudeness to him when he came to tell me about my visa on 18 April 1983. However, MI5 and MI6 were anxious to protect his security. It was assumed that he was living 'in a safe house somewhere in the South of England', but it was one of the Government's most closely guarded secrets where exactly the house was. I sent him a letter through the Foreign Office asking him to contact me whenever he felt so inclined.

For the first two or three years he saw no one outside a narrow circle of trusted officials. He went several times to the United States, where he talked to the CIA and helped British prestige by the amount of information that he gave. The quality of the material was 'pure gold' and, from Britain's point of view, it mended much of the damage inflicted on the special relationship by the treachery of Philby and others during the first cold war.

He, if anyone, was the one most qualified and entitled to tell his story and profit from it. He met Christopher Andrew, a Cambridge specialist, and they embarked on a book together, an academic history of the KGB and its predecessors, enriched by Gordievsky's own background knowledge and personal experience. But he was still tormented by the separation from his family, with whom he had no contact at all for more than two years. And all this time he was under advice from his British 'minders' to say and do nothing about it. He says, 'From 1985 to 1990 the people from the Foreign Office and the "friends" insisted that their secret diplomacy, designed to get my family to the West, demanded my discretion. I was not sure about this tactic and some of the "friends" [i.e. MI6] actually believed that publicity was the only way forward.' Leila was all this time under intense pressure, including the threat of being prosecuted herself, even though she had never known anything of her husband's double life.

She says, 'They made up their minds to take it out on me and our two little girls . . . I was in a state of shock after the death sentence in November 1985. That is why I agreed to divorce him. They told me, "Leila, you're not an idiot. He's a young man. Do you think he's spent all these months without a woman?" Then they said he was having an affair with an English secretary. Then they said that he had married her. I know that men fall out of love with their wives. It happens. But whatever he thought about me, I know that he would never abandon the girls. He worships them. I knew that he would be in touch, if only for their sake . . . There was one thing that they wanted out of me those first two years. They wanted me to write to Oleg, "I will not join you in England." Then, when the British asked them to release us, they could say, "She does not want to go." But they never got those words out of me.'

In December 1987 Margaret Thatcher raised the matter with Gorbachev personally at Brize Norton air force base, near Oxford, where he stopped briefly on his way to sign a defence treaty with

Reagan. She chose the best moment she could, just after Gorbachev had recited a Russian folk song beside the Christmas tree, to ask whether Gordievsky could now be reunited with his family: 'He pursed his lips and said nothing. The answer was all too clear.'[8]

That month, however, Leila did receive a long letter from her husband, after which she could tell that their marriage had a possible future, and from that time she did everything possible to join him. Again, it was something that the KGB could turn to their advantage. 'They came up with this strange proposal. "We will cancel the death sentence. The Soviet Union will pardon him. He can come back and join you and the girls in Moscow." I laughed at them. It was absurd. The KGB does not forgive a man for what Oleg did.'

The KGB saw it differently. Their press department announced in 1990: 'This compromise did not suit Gordievsky. Whether under pressure from his protectors or out of love for the "sweet life" he lives abroad, he turned it down. This means that he also turned down any possibility of being reunited with his family. So that is his affair.'[9]

They were now allowed to talk on the telephone. But their separation caused great distress. All Leila's friends deserted her. They could not bear being always questioned by the KGB after every meeting with her. Her mail was intercepted and she was unemployable. How could she work, accompanied as she had to be by a constant escort of KGB men? Her telephone was only left connected, in Oleg's view, because her conversations gave them useful intelligence.

Any relationship with another man was impossible, even if she had wanted it. 'If I so much as sneeze in the apartment, the whole KGB know about it immediately,' she said. She reverted to her maiden name, the common Turkic surname 'Aliyeva'. The name 'Gordievsky' would not have helped Masha and Anyuta at school. She lived a lonely life and told the girls that their father was 'working abroad'. But they were growing up and it would not be long before someone told them the truth, in which case they would be deeply upset and probably victimized.

On 26 February 1990, Gordievsky finally surfaced with a series of articles in *The Times* and an appearance on television in obvious disguise, a wig and false beard. 'The KGB has an appropriate service to deal with defectors . . . It is not nice to think that one's own death is being planned,' he said later.[10] Asked why he had changed sides so dramatically, he told *The Times*, 'Developments in the Soviet Union were so sad. It was impossible to save Russia from communism. It was lost, the beautiful old Russia, the beautiful eccentrics, the churches and sects, the variety of political parties, the fantastic art at the beginning of the century. It was all lost for ever.'

The KGB said, 'He did it because he wanted to earn money.' They also hint that he was blackmailed in Copenhagen over a sexual indiscretion and brought under British MI6 control. He analyses his motives differently. He did it, he told *The Times*, out of ethical conviction and in the hope that he could help at least to save *Western* civilization. His version is confirmed by a former CIA station chief in London, who told me, 'Until Gordievsky, I would have told you that there was no such thing as an ideological Soviet defector.'

Four months later he at last made contact and we agreed that, under strict supervision, he would come to my home for coffee. He would be without his wig and beard, so I was not allowed to photograph him. And so on 15 August 1990 we faced each other across the same glass table as we had in tenser times more than seven years earlier. We had been adversaries then, or so I thought, but now we were in the midst of Gorbachev's glasnost and perestroyka, allies in the fight against the KGB's remaining excesses. I was touched by his bravery and by the obvious suffering he endured through separation from his family. He gave me some extracts from my KGB file. They had me listed as 'a fierce anti-Soviet and anti-communist activist'. It was a description with which I could not quarrel. And he solved at last the mystery of my cancelled visa. It seems that I was wrong to have suspected any deep East–West conspiracy of 'the visa that never was'. It was nothing more than Soviet bureaucratic inefficiency.

When I applied in February 1983, he told me, the poor-quality embassy computer had not picked out my name, as a result of which visas had been issued, without distinction and in my case by mistake, to all those who had booked on the Thomson Tour. It was only when the lists of forthcoming tourists were sent to Moscow Centre, where the computers are better, that the error was detected and an order sent to London for my visa to be cancelled. Gordievsky remembers how Yuri Ivanov, one of the embassy's counter-intelligence officers, then working under cover in the consular department, came to him in

April 1983 'hiding his feelings of triumph' to tell him that the visa was cancelled.

Several interviews with Gordievsky had by now appeared in print, but his main revelations, he told me, were being kept for the publication of his book later that year. There was, however, one matter on which I might be able to help him. He knew that I had some experience and skill in causing public embarrassment to the Soviet authorities. Every violation of human rights, Andrey Sakharov had said, should be turned into a political problem for the violating government. Was I now prepared to use this technique to persuade the KGB to release his family?

He had come round to the view that secret diplomacy was not going to accomplish the aim: 'I decided to make the struggle for my family a public one. In 1990, and even more now, I came to the view that the policy of keeping me under wraps had been a great mistake. I am now very annoyed about the FO's misjudgement.'

There and then we cooked up the idea of my visiting Leila and the girls in Moscow. It was not going to be a simple task. True, the cold war was nearly over, but the KGB was still operating, albeit more gently than before, and one matter on which they felt strongly was the case of Oleg Gordievsky. Ever since mid 1985, Leila had been guarded night and day by KGB officers, a team of sixteen young men working shifts and equipped with every technical aid. They lurked outside the entrance to her apartment block on Davydkovskaya Street, on the outskirts of town, and followed her wherever she went, by car or on foot, with specific orders to prevent her from entering the British embassy or making contact with anyone from it. The plan used to extricate Oleg from the Soviet Union was not going to be allowed to work a second time.

In March 1990 a member of the embassy staff, Roderic Lyne, called on Leila with a message, a parcel of clothes and some money from her husband. He promised her regular help in the future. She was, after all, the wife of a naturalized British citizen, a person in distress and entitled to consular support. The Soviet authorities reacted with a furious aggression that was in no way in the spirit of perestroyka. Recalling the British embassy's 'illegal behaviour' in spiriting Oleg out of Russia in July 1985, they ordered Lyne out of the country and decreed that no British representative should contact her ever again.

Rodric Braithwaite, the ambassador, then faced long arguments with the Soviet foreign ministry. But he spent far more energy in trying to overturn the expulsion of Lyne than in insisting on the embassy's right to help Leila. Meanwhile he acquiesced in the KGB's edict, and all other parcels sent by Gordievsky to his wife remained undelivered. In short, the embassy made little of the problems of the destitute and persecuted wife of a British citizen, someone who had been subjected to considerable torment on Britain's behalf and to whom we all owed a debt of gratitude. Neither Lyne nor anyone from the embassy was ever permitted to get in touch with Leila in any way from March 1990 until after the August 1991 *coup d'état*. And in spite of Gordievsky's repeated entreaties, the parcels were never delivered and in the end they were returned to him.

Again and again Mikhail Gorbachev was appealing to the West to provide him with financial aid, to help him in his democratic reforms. It seemed nevertheless that in matters that closely touched the KGB's interest or self-esteem, such as the Gordievsky case, he was still in thrall to them and ready at their request to behave insultingly towards the British embassy. And Braithwaite's complaints to Chernyayev and Gorbachev's other senior aides produced no result.

Gorbachev was trying to survive by pleasing the West as well as the KGB. But, whenever it came to a conflict, he sided with the latter. He believed that he needed the support of the KGB head, Vladimir Kryuchkov, and that he could secure this support by doing the KGB favours. Richard Schifter, the US State Department's human rights chief, advised me that there was no hope of resolving the Gordievsky matter until the relationship between the President and the KGB fundamentally changed. Leila received no embassy support meanwhile and had nothing to live on but hand-outs from her father's pension.

My visit to her, it was hoped, would help turn the case from an espionage issue into a human rights issue, the clearest of all possible cases, a separation of a wife from a husband. And so I flew to Moscow on 29 September. Oleg had warned her by telephone to expect someone to call the following day, a Sunday, and I duly called her that morning from the Kosmos Hotel. So as not to give the KGB any pretext for suggesting that I was acting clandestinely, I at once told her my name and that I was a member of the European Parliament's human rights sub-committee. We agreed that I would come to her flat an hour later.

I assumed that the KGB would overhear our talk. They would then face a dilemma. Should they prevent us from meeting? Should they stop me entering the building? If they did, how were they to explain it to me? What should they do if I protested, or persisted? Should they be prepared, if necessary, to take me into custody? It was logical that they should, but they must have known that they would then face an ugly incident that would be made public and sound badly out of tune with Gorbachev's siren song of democratic reform.

Leila's 'boys', as she called them, the ones who hung about the entrance to her apartment block, were under orders to prevent any contact between her and any British official. Did this ban extend to MEPs and peers? The KGB had probably not taken the point into consideration and my Sunday morning call gave them little time in which to decide which was more important to the Soviet government, the appearance of glasnost at a time of economic difficulty or the need to keep Leila isolated from British contacts.

Glasnost prevailed. As I walked towards the front door, the 'boys' turned their backs and by the time I reached them they had lifted their car bonnet and dug their heads deep into its engine. I wished them good morning. They did not reply. 'They are frightened that I am going to photograph them,' I thought. I walked up the stairs, rang the bell, and the wife of 'the spy of the century' opened the door to me.

I handed her a letter from Oleg to prove my *bona fides*. She then gave me a spirited interview, which I had printed a week later in the form of an open letter to President Gorbachev: 'As far as I am concerned, Mr Gorbachev's reforms do not exist. I have done nothing against the Soviet Union. I have broken no law. But because of what my husband did in 1985, going over to the British side, I have for five years been treated like a criminal and am separated from the man I love.'

She talked about her round-the-clock surveillance. 'It must cost the Soviet government a fortune. So I protest. Not about the violation of my freedom, but as a taxpayer.' As for the KGB's offer to pardon her husband, her views were clear: 'Even if it's true, even if Gorbachev signs the pardon himself, what happens if Gorbachev dies and the head of the KGB takes his place? They would shoot him then and I would be the one who had lured him back here to be shot. I won't take such a sin upon my conscience.'

I finished my tea and we looked out of her living-room window. The 'boys' were no longer to be seen, although she assured me that they were still there, hiding in the trees. I left and my bewildered taxi driver took me back to the hotel. Two days later I called on her again and photographed her with the two girls, giving them each a polaroid as a souvenir. Masha hid hers, claiming that it did not make her look pretty.

After that first Sunday meeting, which the KGB had decided not to abort, I felt able to discuss the problem more openly with Russian friends and contacts. I told them that, whatever they might think about Gordievsky, who had undoubtedly committed a most serious crime under Soviet law, it was not in the spirit of the new East–West relationship for them to punish Leila and her daughters for what he had done. I pointed out that Britain had suffered more than enough through her secret agents defecting to the Soviet side. It was a catalogue of intelligence disasters – Philby, Burgess, Maclean, Blake, Blunt, Cairncross, Vassall, Prime and Bettaney. Each one had betrayed the most secret information and the first four had then succeeded in escaping to a privileged life in Moscow. Britain had been made to look amateurish and decadent. Our relations with the United States were seriously damaged.

I did not try to justify Gordievsky's decision to change sides. If I had, my Soviet colleagues' patriotic sentiment might have triumphed over their sense of common justice. I pointed out, though, that he had done what he did during the period of Brezhnev's 'stagnation', in the wake of the Soviet invasion of Czechoslovakia, at a time when dissidents were being arrested in Russia for non-violent political protest. He accepted that he had betrayed the Soviet system, but not that he had betrayed his country.

The British traitors, on the other hand, had rejected a democratic structure in favour of a false utopia, communism, which was supposed to be achieved by means of the brutal Stalinist tyranny. Blake had betrayed agents in Germany. Philby had betrayed British agents sent into Latvia and Albania. The agents they betrayed had been executed.

The KGB embassy officials betrayed by Gordievsky had merely been expelled from Britain. Gordievsky had given away the British KGB agent Michael Bettaney, who was sentenced to twenty-three years' imprisonment in 1984. He gave away a Norwegian KGB agent, Arne Treholt, who was sentenced to eighteen years in 1982. He gave away a Swedish KGB agent. That is all. Unlike Blake and Philby, he does not have blood on his hands.

But the main argument, I told Russian contacts, was that Britain had never punished the wives or families of these unmasked traitors. Blake's mother had visited Moscow many times, in spite of his boast of having denounced 600 British agents to the KGB, most of whom were executed. Burgess had had Christmas hampers mailed to him from Fortnum and Mason's London store – and a new Old Etonian tie every year. Maclean's wife Melinda had left Britain to join her husband in Moscow. Philby's son had visited his father in Moscow and sold photographs of him to the British press. Under English law, there was no way of preventing these people from going anywhere they wished to meet members of their families.

I put these arguments to Konstantin Lubenchenko, deputy chairman of the USSR Supreme Soviet's legal committee. It was a sign of how far Gorbachev's reform programme had gone that he reacted to my request not with anger but with interest. He was prepared to look at the problem as a lawyer rather than as a Soviet apparatchik. And he accepted our petition, translated into Russian by Oleg, as a source of information and a guide to our side of the case.

I showed the same paper to the editor of Moscow's *New Times* and he printed it in his next issue, together with one of my polaroid pictures of Leila taken the previous day. Moscow's *Niezavisimaya* (*Independent*) newspaper also promised to help.

The evening before I left Moscow, a long letter from Leila to her husband burning a hole in my pocket, I was mysteriously telephoned in my hotel room by Oleg Kalugin, the former KGB officer who had 'defected internally', making a political career out of attacking his former bosses publicly. 'Meet me at the corner of Gorky Street and Revolution Square,' he said. 'Don't worry. I will recognize you.' He told me, over coffee in the Savoy Hotel, that the KGB would never let the family out. If they did, they would be giving up a most important weapon of control over their agents abroad. Leila's release would be seen as a sign of KGB weakness and would send these agents exactly the wrong type of signal. Gorbachev might be a reformer, but the KGB still had enough influence over him to protect what they saw as vital.

Gordievsky was likewise pessimistic after I came back to London and told him of the various meetings. He told the *Sunday Express*, 'Its [The KGB's] members still represent the worst type of *homo sovieticus*, men with no compassion, no toleration. I can only see the KGB letting my family go as part of a package of agreements with Western intelligence.'

In spite of the glasnost of 1990, the Soviet embassy in London protested about my visit to the flat and Leila was summoned to the KGB office on Kuznyetsky Most in Moscow for a 'chat' about it with her KGB case officer. 'They told me that Lord Bethell was a very bad man, a British spy, an enemy of our country, that I should never have received him, and they asked me if I realized what I was doing,' she says. 'My case officer was irritated at what he saw as my foolish and impertinent behaviour. I answered that it made no difference whether or not Lord Bethell was a spy, since I knew no secrets and so would not have been able to tell him anything.'

It was then reported[11] that all foreign contact with Leila had been forbidden. On 26 November, her last day as Prime Minister, Margaret Thatcher wrote me a supportive letter, confirming that there was 'no justification' for the Soviet behaviour. It was one issue on which she and her 'nice Mr Gorbachev' seemed unable to agree. But still nothing was being achieved. All Britain seemed to be in love with Gorbachev and his government, but he still would not release Leila and her two little girls.

At the end of 1990 the British embassy in Moscow did not even send Leila a Christmas card. But at least the issue was now public and being highlighted as a British human rights issue. On 26 December *The Times* published my letter suggesting that it was 'pure Stalinism' to punish two small girls for a crime committed by their father. The Soviet government should not be allowed to get away with such behaviour, when 'their representatives come to London and ask for gifts of food, to be paid for by British taxpayers'.

More importantly, a debate on the issue had begun inside the

Soviet Union. On 31 January 1991, *Niezavisimaya* wrote to the KGB's new 'public relations department' to ask for their comment. On 28 February they printed my article about the case beside Lubenchenko's opinion, written as a reaction to the paper I had handed him the previous autumn. The Soviet tradition of holding hostage or punishing a traitor's family arose through the post-revolutionary fervour of the KGB's predecessor, the CHEKA, he wrote: 'This may be understandable from the moral point of view. The mark of shame, it is said, remains even to the third generation. But it has absolutely nothing in common with the rule of law.'

On 14 March *Niezavisimaya* printed the KGB's reply. 'Crocodile tears have already been shed on this same subject by Nicholas Bethell, a staff member of British intelligence and now a Lord, born in 1938 in London,' they began. It was the same form of words that they had used in their article about me and Igor Rykov in *Izvestiya* in the worst cold war days of December 1984. They claimed that Oleg had 'abandoned' his family by turning for help to his English protectors, so great was his terror. He had joined the British side in the early 1970s, they pointed out. So where was his sense of responsibility towards his wife and the daughters he was about to have? He must have known that matters would come to a head eventually. He had, in effect, condemned his daughters in advance to being without their father. And what could one now say about the motives of those (like me) who were pushing these children into the embrace of their traitor-father? How would they react, when they grew up, to the idea of having a father who had done such a thing? 'Traitors should consider such issues before they do what they do.'

We were making no progress. It was very sad, I wrote,[12] to see the Soviet authorities reduced to using harsh and old-fashioned language at a time when relations with Britain were otherwise good. On 21 March Congressman Bob McEwen raised the case in the US House of Representatives, at my request, reading the *Sunday Express* article into the record and urging colleagues to contact Gorbachev about it. Many of them did, but nothing came of it.

On 18 July, during a brief visit by Gorbachev to London, Prime Minister John Major again raised the case, again without result, the Soviet leader merely emphasizing how difficult it was, since Leila and

Oleg were divorced.[13] The whole story, I wrote that day (in the *Daily Telegraph*), was a throw-back to the bad old times when British students were not allowed to marry their Russian fiancées and Jewish refuseniks had to be bought out of the country with western money and technology. Oleg was 'the man perestroyka forgot'.

On 19 August John Major wrote to me, 'We are not being timid in our handling of this case.' He would continue to 'take action of a specific kind', since the case was 'an indicator of the Soviet Union's willingness to turn away from past practices'.

That same day Gorbachev was deposed, leaving government in the hands of communist hard-liners. Whereas it was a serious situation for the entire world, it was now a hopeless one for Gordievsky and his family. His arch-enemy Vladimir Kryuchkov was the strong man of the *coup d'état*. Clearly he was poised ready to rebuild the KGB's power and to inflict it on the Soviet people, Leila and her daughters foremost among them.

And then it happened, their first piece of luck. Two days later the coup was overthrown. Kryuchkov was arrested and hard-line Minister of Interior Boris Pugo committed suicide. The liberal Vadim Bakatin became KGB chairman and one of his first acts in office, in response to an approach by the British ambassador, was to lift the travel ban on Leila and the girls. One moment the 'boys' were there outside her flat, as usual, as they had been for years. The next they had melted away, never to return, without even saying goodbye. It is thought that Ambassador Braithwaite cleverly judged his moment. Whatever he may have done or not done in the past, he played his cards very well in August 1991 and achieved the objective.

The whole atmosphere changed. Leila was now invited to the embassy, even to tea with John Major, who visited Moscow briefly to give President Yeltsin his support. She took a few days to collect her belongings and then suddenly, on 6 September, my heart lighter than usual, I was sitting in the Spelthorne suite at Heathrow Airport's Terminal 4, sipping champagne and waiting for Leila, Masha and Anyuta to arrive by British Airways.

A junior minister, Lord Caithness, and other officials shook her hand. My wife Bryony gave her flowers. I was the first to embrace her. 'Where are we?' Anyuta kept asking. I gave her flowers and we all drank champagne. Leila gave a short statement to the press, thanking me and others who had helped her. And then she was driven away, with her two girls, to meet the husband she had not seen since his extraordinary disappearance from Moscow in July 1985.

13. Nelson Mandela

On 9 July 1983, at the new cold war's height, the Mayor of Moscow, Vladimir Promyslov, and nine of his top officials arrived in London for a 'fraternal visit' with like-minded municipal leaders of progressive views. His host was Harvey Hinds, Chairman of the Greater London Council, a bastion of what remained of British socialism after the Labour Party's massive defeat in the British general election a few days earlier, which had left them outnumbered by two to one in the House of Commons.

On the GLC therefore fell the task of spearheading Labour's opposition to Margaret Thatcher's flourishing government. Hinds was a British socialist of the old school, anxious wherever possible to see the pro-Soviet side of any situation or argument. So, whereas I thought of the Mayor of Moscow as no more than a Communist Party hack, a tormentor of the innocent, a man unworthy of London's respect, Hinds felt honoured by the Mayor of Moscow's visit and delight at the prospect of offering him the city's hospitality.

It irritated me and many other London ratepayers that a lavish nine-day programme for ten Soviet apparatchiks was being paid for out of our money. The 'junket' was ill-timed, coming as it did at a moment when the Mayor's comrades back home in Moscow were busy arresting Jewish refuseniks and arranging for the bombardment of Afghan villages.

I remembered too how Promyslov's name had come up in my talk with Elena Bonner in Florence in September 1975. It was Promyslov's personal decision, Andrey Sakharov's wife had then told me, that kept her and her husband from moving out of the cramped conditions in which they lived and into a larger apartment. He was the one responsible for the fact that their family of eight was forced to live together, with Elena and Andrey sleeping in the kitchen, trying to carry out their work for the community as well as their own daily needs, as a family of eight in two small living-rooms.

And this man was being received with honour by other mayors

from all over the world, she had complained. She wondered how such things could happen, and I shared her disgust. My personal feelings about Mayor Promyslov were therefore strong in 1975 and stronger still in 1983, when Sakharov and his wife were far away from home, condemned to exile by a decision which doubtless enjoyed the Mayor of Moscow's approval.

I was therefore delighted when Jewish groups obtained details of the Mayor's schedule and proceeded to disrupt his visit. Twenty protesters, shouting 'Free Soviet Jews' and demanding the release of Anatoli Shcharansky, encircled him and jostled him as he approached the Dickens Inn at St Katharine's Dock, where he was due to lunch on 10 July. I was glad to see it reported that a member of the Soviet embassy had broken one of the protesters' placards. It meant that the demonstrations were a success.

Promyslov made it clear that he supported the GLC and the Labour Party. Commenting on the banner hanging from the GLC offices at County Hall with the words '348,587 LONDON UNEMPLOYED', he said, 'There is much work to be had in Moscow and I would guarantee work to every one of these people.' I wondered what would happen if the GLC were so rash as to take the Mayor up on his offer, how many of London's unemployed would choose to live in Moscow and work for a municipal wage.

That evening I came to Harvey Hinds's reception ill-disposed towards the guest of honour and his entourage. I had with me a pocketful of metal pin-on badges, made to my order, to be given to any other guest who shared my view about the Mayor and his visit. They were circular and their text consisted of the three words 'ORLOV – SAKHAROV – SHCHARANSKY', printed one on top of the other and surrounded by a drawing of a ring of barbed wire.

Conservatives at the gathering accepted the badges with alacrity and helped me with my protest by pinning them to their lapels, but they were of course a minority and on one guest, I recall, the purpose of the message was completely lost. She came up to me, peering at my badge through her spectacles. 'I am happy to meet you, Mr Orlov,' she said. 'But I'm afraid I can't pronounce your other two names.'

There was therefore already a frisson in the air as Harvey Hinds called for silence and began his speech of welcome. I listened politely during the early formalities, until he began an intemperate attack on the Jewish groups that were protesting during the visit against the Soviet government's policies. He said something like, 'On behalf of the people of London I wish to say to the Mayor of Moscow how deeply sorry we are for the discourtesy shown to him by small, unrepresentative groups in our midst, who want to prevent the development of good British–Soviet relations . . .'

I was so shocked by the GLC Chairman's abject tone that I shouted across the room some words to the effect that I did not agree with him. It was bad manners. I was his guest and I was insulting his guest of honour, but at that moment it seemed more important to make a show of anger, and in such a way that the Soviets would be aware of it, than to be bound by the norms of cocktail-party behaviour. A few of those there thought the outburst appropriate, but it was a socialist function enriched by ten people from Moscow and a large contingent from the Soviet embassy. 'You are not very polite, Lord Bethell,' said one of the diplomats icily. If looks could kill, it would have been the end of my life. Anyway, I walked away down the corridor, Hinds and his friends shouting abuse at me. I forget the precise words used, but I recall his parting shot: 'What have you ever done to help Nelson Mandela?'

It was a valid point. Mandela was also a political prisoner, even though his gaolers were not communists but representatives of the white government of South Africa. So why was I not defending him? Hinds had brought to light the disagreeable side of the behaviour shown by many during those years of East–West conflict at its most acute. The West joined Soviet dissidents in attacking the Soviet government. The Soviet Union and its friends in the West attacked the South African government. But there was no 'common front' of Left and Right against both Soviet and South African oppression.

It was never an edifying spectacle when human rights issues were raised in the British parliament. Insults by Conservatives against the Soviet Union were hit back by Labour, like tennis balls, as insults against South Africa. Double standards were the norm. Motives were political rather than humanitarian, with both sides exploiting the sufferings of brave defenders of truth to attack foreign governments whose ideologies they found distasteful. This was my crime, according to my GLC hosts. I was keen enough to defend the Russian dissidents, anti-socialist trouble-makers whose extremism threatened the peace of the world, but I would never speak out for a black South African, a man close to the South African communist party, a socialist, even if he had been in jail for twenty-one years.

In 1983 Nelson Mandela was not the world figure that he is now. But I knew his case. He was one of the founders of Umkhonto wa Sizwe (Spear of the Nation), the African National Congress's armed resistance movement that had sprung up in the wake of the 1960 Sharpeville massacre in South Africa. Mandela said at his trial in April 1964, 'There were only two alternatives that they could see. One was to yield to the show of force, which carried within it an implied threat of similar reaction to any future campaign or strike on their part, or to fight it out. In the event of the latter alternative being adopted, the question then arose, how was this to be done?' They decided to amend the non-violent policy that had been the ANC's rule since its foundation in 1912. They did not at this stage embark on full-scale terrorism. They decided to mount low-key guerrilla operations, directed mainly at electricity stations and other public facilities.

He left South Africa illegally to visit Ethiopia and in June 1962 he came to Britain on a false Ethiopian passport. He met the Labour leader Hugh Gaitskell. He returned to South Africa. On 7 August he was arrested at a road block near Durban. Initially (7 November) he was sentenced to five years' imprisonment for incitement to strike and for leaving the country without proper documents. He was then re-tried on treason charges.

At the famous 'Rivonia Trial' in April 1964 it was pointed out on Mandela's behalf that no one had been killed at his instigation and that he had taken up the armed struggle only because all legal avenues were closed to him. He had never been allowed to stand for election, or even vote. He said in court, 'I planned it [sabotage] as a result of a calm and sober assessment of the political situation that had arisen after many years of tyranny, exploitation and oppression of my people by the whites.' Sentencing Mandela in June 1964, Judge de Wet rejected Mandela's complaint about the living standards of South Africa's blacks. They should not be compared with those of South Africa's whites, said the judge, but with those of black people in neighbouring African countries, and by this comparison black South Africans fared well and received high wages. He sentenced Mandela and other 'Rivonia' conspirators to life imprisonment. If any white person had been killed in the campaign, he implied, he would have imposed the death sentence. As it was, life in prison was the limit of the mercy that he could reasonably be expected to exercise in such a case.

Mandela and his friends were sent to Robben Island, a hunk of rock a few miles south of Cape Town, where about thirty political prisoners were put to hard labour in the lime quarry. They crushed stones, repaired roads and collected seaweed from the beaches. Mandela says, 'In the first ten years conditions were really very bad. We were physically assaulted, subjected to psychological persecution. We had to work every day in the lime quarry from 7 a.m. to 4 p.m. with a one-hour break, wearing shorts and sandals, with no socks or underwear and just a calico jacket. It was hard, boring, unproductive work and on rainy days in the winter it was very cold. The guards pushed us all the time to work harder, from dawn to sunset, and we could get solitary confinement if they thought we were slacking. The diet was maize porridge for breakfast with half a teaspoon of sugar, boiled grain for lunch with "puzamadla", a drink made out of maize that is, to put it mildly, an acquired taste, and porridge with vegetables in the evening. There was a lot of tension between guards and prisoners.' The anti-apartheid campaigner Helen Suzman, a Liberal MP and one of the few whites who ever visited the political prisoners, also remembers 'horrible conditions' on Robben Island, guards with Alsatian dogs on leads and one with a swastika tattooed on his hand. She recalls a prisoner complaining to her that he had been assaulted and the guard's reply, 'Ach, Mrs Suzman, it was nothing. It was only a kick up the arse!'

In the late 1970s conditions improved a little. Mandela and other older men were no longer required to work. They had sports facilities and they could study. Then, in April 1982, Mandela and five others were moved from the island to the high-security Pollsmoor prison, near Cape Town. It was not long before rumours began to circulate to the effect that conditions were now worse. At the time of my encounter with Harvey Hinds and his Labour friends in July 1983, it was widely believed that Mandela was being brutally treated in his new prison. A few days earlier (24 May) a letter had appeared in *The Times* over the signatures of the Duke of Devonshire, the Labour leader Denis

Healey and the Liberal leader David Steel accusing the South African authorities of having moved the black leaders so as 'to increase the severity of their punishment'. Their present conditions 'threaten their capacity to survive', they wrote, and the government's aim was 'to break the physical and mental health of these political leaders', who 'have not been allowed out of doors for a year' and 'are in effect entombed together for the rest of their lives'.

These words were inspired by a letter written by Winnie Mandela to the well-known South African dissident in London, Mary Benson. She painted a grim picture of a Mandela wrenched from his old friends Walter Sisulu and Ahmed Kathrada, with whom he had lived for the past twenty years, never allowed outside his cell, which was often flooded with rain and a danger to health. He had been forced to wear shoes that were too small for him, wrote Winnie, as a result of which he had undergone an operation.

Mandela could not be an Amnesty International prisoner of conscience. He was disqualified, since he supported the ANC's use of violence. He also admired the Soviet Union as the power that had done most to support the ANC and other 'liberation movements' against imperial rule. This made him a difficult person for a British Conservative to help. There were many in our party who supported South Africa and its apartheid system. He had nevertheless shown himself a man of iron conviction and, although his case attracted little attention during his first terrible decade on Robben Island, by the 1980s he had become the black man's folk hero in many lands, with streets in London named after him and the song 'Free Nelson Mandela' selling in large numbers. He symbolized the revulsion that many people, whether Conservative or not, felt for South Africa's racist policies. There was also the question of natural justice. The crime of which he had been convicted, damage to property and plotting to abolish apartheid, in no way merited a prison term of twenty-one years. Even if one were to take the view that he was guilty of the crimes of which he was charged, it was time he was offered parole.

I discussed the case with Helen Suzman, and in October 1984 I wrote to the South African government, assuring them that I did not support the use of violence, whether by the ANC or by anybody else, but asking whether I might be allowed to visit Mandela at his new place of confinement. It had been said in the European press, I told their embassy, that he was seriously ill and in pain as a result of ill-treatment. On the other hand, I had spoken to Nicolas de Rougemont of the Red Cross in Geneva, who had visited him recently, and heard from him that his conditions of imprisonment were satisfactory. I told the South Africans that I wanted to report to the European Parliament which version was correct.

It was a shot in the dark. A year earlier I had written to Oleg Gordievsky at the Soviet embassy, asking for permission to visit Soviet labour camps. My request had not even been considered. 'The camps are too far away. And the roads are bad,' Gordievsky told me. There seemed little reason why South Africa should be more helpful. Hardly anyone apart from Winnie Mandela and his close family were allowed to visit this most sensitive of 'security prisoners', as the South African government liked to call them. Senator Edward Kennedy, for instance, had gone to the prison gates, accompanied by the world's media, hoping to be allowed in to see him, only to be given the familiar Soviet-style reply that Mandela's imprisonment was in no way the business of foreigners.

It was therefore a surprise when Helen Suzman telephoned from Johannesburg towards the end of the year to say that a Cabinet meeting had approved my request. It was in their interest to set the record straight, I presumed, about how Mandela was being treated, and they must have thought that a Conservative from Britain, a member of the House of Lords, would be unlikely to take the side of a left-wing black revolutionary.

Arriving in Cape Town on 20 January 1985, I spent that Sunday afternoon being guided by Helen Suzman round 'Crossroads', the illegal slum township outside the city, frequently bulldozed, its 'houses' made of corrugated iron, patched with empty cardboard boxes and roofed with plastic sheeting. It was a wretched sprawl, a nightmare of a camp site and a disgrace to a rich country which claimed to be governed by the rule of law. Its merit was that it was only a short bus ride away from work in the big white city. Otherwise it was a horror, and I was surprised to encounter smiles and words of of courteous greeting from the black families as we walked down the alleyways between the shacks. Helen Suzman said, 'Why don't they throw stones at us? *I* would.'

The Minister of Justice, H.J. 'Kobie' Coetsee, explained to me the next morning that Mandela's only hope of release was by Presidential clemency. He was convicted of treason and his sentence meant what it said, imprisonment for the whole of his natural life. Coetsee conceded that twenty-one years was a very long time to spend in prison and that 'objectively speaking' he should be released, provided that a way could be found. But no way could be found until Mandela showed readiness to cooperate. 'He shows no sign of repentance for his crimes. He still supports the ANC, which is a proscribed organization, and its policy is to overthrow the state by violence. If he would renounce violence and join us in political debate, then maybe something could be done. The ball is in his court.'

Later that morning I was driven to Pollsmoor and given lunch – a very over-cooked steak and chips prepared by prison inmates. Pollsmoor consisted of a dozen long buildings, each one a separate unit, like the gloomy campus of a comprehensive school or red-brick university. There were separate sections for white, black and 'coloured' prisoners as well as for men and women. According to the Commissioner of Prisons, Lieutenant-General 'Willie' Willemse, each prisoner whether black or white enjoyed a minimum 10,571-kilojoule-per-day diet, decent clothes, family visits, recreation and the possibility of parole. His 'message' was familiar. South Africa, he said, followed North American or West European standards in its administration of law and order. The world judged South Africa far too harshly.

After lunch I was taken to the Governor's office in the maximum security block. Senior officers in yellow khaki uniforms with gold stars on their epaulettes, some with peaked caps pulled over their eyes like sergeants in the British army, scurried in and out talking excitedly in Afrikaans. The office furniture was clean and simple, dominated by a glass-topped desk and overlooked by a picture of State President P.W. Botha wearing a silver order and orange sash. After a few minutes a tall man with silvering hair, in impeccable olive-green shirt and well-creased navy blue trousers, came into the room, shook my hand and greeted me in precise, educated English. He was anxious to put me at my ease and he invited me to sit at the desk, where I would be more comfortable and could take notes. For a few seconds I almost believed that he was yet another general or colonel in the South African prison service. His manner was self-assured and he stood out as obviously the senior man in the room. He was, however, black. And it was only then that I realized that here was the man I had come half-way round the world to meet.

Mandela and I sat down and talked for rather more than two hours under the alert gaze of his personal guard, Major Fritz van Sittert, although the latter did not interrupt any subject in our talk or intervene, except when books or papers passed between us. Mandela, it soon became clear, had no serious complaint about his prison conditions in recent years. The issue was not how they were treating him. It was whether or not they were entitled to keep him in gaol, denying him the right to live in his own house, to vote, to stand for parliament, to be elected president.

He said, 'I am in good health. It is not true that I have cancer. It is not true that I had a toe amputated. I get up at 3.30 every morning, do two hours physical exercise, work up a good sweat, then read and study during the day. I get South African newspapers as well as the *Guardian Weekly* and *Time*. I am with five other prisoners, all senior ANC men, in one big cell. We have a radio, VHF only unfortunately, so that we can only get South African stations. We have a little garden, large pots out of which we grow tomatoes, broccoli, beans, cucumber and strawberries. Things could only be made really better here if they were ready to dismantle the whole system, for instance by appointing a black senior prison officer, but of course this cannot happen under apartheid.'

He referred to the prison officers, including the Governor, Brigadier F.C. Munro, with an understanding bordering on kindly condescension. 'Poor Mr Munro, he has very little authority. Everything that touches the six of us he has to refer to Pretoria. They restrict my visitors. They block my letters. It's not the poor Brigadier's fault. It's the politicians. It means that things can get exaggerated. One time, for instance, my shoes were too small. I mentioned it to my wife, she was upset and there was a fuss in the press. It was even quoted in the song "Free Nelson Mandela". Meanwhile they gave me size nine shoes and everything was fine, but I had no way of telling her.'

Prison conditions were not the problem. The point was the apartheid system. And the other question was whether Mandela should have been in prison at all. Even by the harsh standards of South African law, he had by 1985 long ago atoned for his few symbolic acts against government property in 1962. He was being kept in prison, as the government made no attempt to hide, not for anything that he had done, but for fear of what he might do, or what might happen, if he was released.

Even on the vexed question of the armed struggle, it emerged that what he had to offer differed not so much from what 'Kobie' Coetsee had suggested to me earlier that day: 'The armed struggle was forced on us by the government. And if they want us now to give it up, the ball is in their court. They must legalize us, treat us as a political party and negotiate with us. Until they do, we will have to live with the armed struggle. Of course, if they legalize us, I am sure that the ANC would declare a truce, but we cannot talk under present conditions. The government have tightened the screws too far. We cannot be the first to lay down our arms. After all that has happened, it would be humiliating. So we are forced to continue – though within certain limits. We only go for hard targets, like military installations and the symbols of apartheid, government buildings and property. We do not touch civilians. It may happen that someone is killed in a fight, in the heat of battle, but we do not believe in assassination, except perhaps in the case of an informer who is a danger to our lives.

'For instance, I deeply regret what happened in Pretoria on May 23rd, 1983. A bomb went off and more than a dozen people were killed. It was a tragic accident. Something must have gone wrong with the timing. On the other hand the incident that took place in Vryheid [Natal] a few weeks ago was quite justified. Some ANC men were in a house and the security forces were looking for them. We have reason to believe that their policy is to shoot our men rather than arrest them. So they opened fire in self-defence and a Lieutenant was killed, as were several of our soldiers.'

Mandela told me that he had several times been offered release if he would give up political activity and go abroad. He had rejected every temptation to sell his mission in life for a ticket to freedom. 'My place is in South Africa and my home is in Johannesburg. If I was released, I would never obey any restriction. If they confined me for instance to the Cape area, I would break the order and walk to my home in Soweto to be with my wife and daughter.'

Our talk ended and I was invited to visit Mandela's cell. And so we walked in slow procession, Mandela leading the way, asking me about recent world developments, his hopes for Mr Gorbachev as a new type of Soviet leader, his ideas about nuclear disarmament, up several flights of stairs and round corners. What did I think about the Schultz–Gromyko disarmament talks? Would the Liberals at last make a breakthrough in British politics? What was Mrs Thatcher's secret of success? Who was now the leader of the Labour Party? (Neil Kinnock had recently taken over from Michael Foot.) Brigadier Munro and his men followed behind us. Every few seconds he asked for a door to be opened and this was done, after much saluting and clanking, by a sergeant with heavy keys. It was as if he was showing me round his stately home.

Eventually we reached Mandela's 'private penthouse' and I could see at once that it was not what Winnie Mandela had described in her letters to London and elsewhere. It was not a room in a five-star hotel, but it was not a dank dungeon either. It was more like a school dormitory, a large room with six beds set widely apart, many books, and adequate washing and toilet facilities in a separate area. Most of the day the six prisoners had access to a long L-shaped yard surrounded by high white walls. There was a volleyball court and a ping-pong table. The six prisoners were allowed into the yard most of the time. Mandela showed me his famous pots of fruit and vegetables, like a landowner showing me his farm.

I talked briefly with the other prisoners. His friends Walter Sisulu and Ahmed Kathrada, it emerged, had not been 'wrenched from him', but were with him in the six-man cell. I listened to their complaints. There was indeed a damp patch on one wall. They also complained, although Brigadier Munro tried to intervene, about over-zealous censorship of their mail and showed me several examples of letters with holes in them cut by the censor, looking as if they had been through a shredder. They apologized for being in pyjamas. They politely overrode Munro's objections as they listed these problems, but Mandela retained the initiative as master of the conversation, joking as we prepared to leave him, 'Aren't there any other complaints? Doesn't anyone want to go home?'

We walked the last few yards towards the end of the enclosure. A sergeant opened the heavy steel door. Mandela said, 'Well, Lord Bethell, this is my frontier and this is where I must say goodbye.' We shook hands and I told him that I would write to him. It was a sad moment as I walked back through all those doors and down the stone staircases, until finally we reached fresh air and the fine Cape summer. I felt poorer at being so suddenly deprived of the man's exhilarating company and I hoped very much to meet him again under happier circumstances.

The main political fact that emerged from the meetings that day was that both sides were keen for talks to begin between the government and the ANC, but each one wanted the other to make the first move. Mandela and his followers wanted to be legalized without condition, in which case he would recommend a truce in the struggle. This was the realistic policy that the government eventually adopted five years later. But in January 1985 they insisted that Mandela must 'repent'. The precondition was for him to express regret for past actions and end all fighting. Then they might speak to him. This was unrealistic. Mandela was never going to repent. If he had, he would have done so twenty years earlier.

I met Louis Le Grange, Minister of Law and Order, and he told me, 'We are not so weak as to agree to talks with the ANC now, but if they lay down their arms we will talk to them. As for Mandela, if you ask me to recommend his release so that he can carry on where he left off, I say no. We cannot help him until he gives us some indication by his attitude. As things are now, his release would only invite a lot of trouble and problems.'

The next item on my agenda was meant to be a meeting at Helen Suzman's home near Johannesburg with Winnie Mandela and their lawyer Ismail Ayob. It emerged, though, to my shocked surprise, that Winnie was not in the least interested in talking to me about what her husband had told me the previous day. I was soon to discover that she and those in the ANC leadership who shared her very vigorous views were suspicious of my motives. They did not trust British Conservatives, especially Conservatives who for unknown reasons were favoured by the South African government with permission to visit Pollsmoor prison – a privilege denied to almost everyone else, including, a few days earlier, Senator Edward Kennedy. Something must be wrong with me, they thought.

Ayob reluctantly agreed to take me to the Mandela home in Soweto in his vintage car, but when we arrived Winnie was 'not at home' and 'not feeling well' and she even hinted to Ayob that I must be in the pocket of the notorious Bureau of State Security. Restraining my anger and disappointment, I told Ayob that I was, allegedly, on the payroll of so many secret services that one more or less would make little difference to an already very complicated career. But Winnie had been, until then, virtually the only one with access to her famous husband. It was through her and her alone that his views were given to the outside world. It was not in her interest, any more than it was in the South African government's interest, for Mandela to be portrayed to the world as a man of moderation. She therefore maintained her hostility, issuing a press release that denounced my interference in a matter over which she felt entitled to claim monopoly control.

I flew home and wrote[1] about Mandela's life and opinions. *The Times* wrote,[2] 'There is speculation that the Government wanted to sound out Mr Mandela's views without talking to him directly, and when Lord Bethell applied for an interview some months ago it decided that his Conservative credentials and specialist interest in human rights made him a suitable intermediary.'

The South African government had a card up its sleeve. Speaking in the Cape Town parliament on 31 January, President P.W. Botha gave his MPs a lengthy explanation of why the visit had been allowed. It had been widely referred to in the South African press, although the law prevented any quotation of Mandela's own words. Botha said that South Africa had benefited through my assurance that conditions in Pollsmoor were up to the highest standards. I had given the lie to the false allegation 'that Mr Mandela's health has deteriorated in prison, that he has been ill-treated and that he continues to be held under terrible and inhuman conditions'. He then recalled the offers of sanctuary to Mandela made by various black leaders, observing 'that Mr Mandela and his associates prefer to stay in prison rather than be released to their country of origin'. (He was emphasizing, by this last remark, his claim that Transkei and other 'Bantustans' were not part of South Africa.)

He went on to say that he was 'not insensitive' to the fact that Mandela and others had spent a long time in prison. He then made a most surprising announcement. He was prepared, he said, to consider the release of the ANC leaders if they renounced the use of violence and undertook to obey South African law. This condition, he said, was one that 'even Lord Bethell' could hardly object to, since I had assured him in my original letter[3] in which I asked for the visit that I opposed the use of violence for political ends. He read my letter out loud in parliament.

It was now suggested by some, including Winnie Mandela, that I had been used by President Botha to expose Mandela as a man of violence, a terrorist who was keeping himself and his friends in prison through a stubborn refusal to choose the path of peace and debate. But this was not the way that Mandela himself saw my efforts. Helen Suzman wrote to me after visiting him in July 1985 that he had seen my articles and liked them. He was pleased to have had the chance to explain his views in detail and have them conveyed accurately to a world-wide public.

It was also suggested that I had served the government's interests by refuting Winnie Mandela's version of her husband's conditions of detention. For instance, my statement that Mandela was generally content with his conditions was mentioned by Foreign Minister 'Pik' Botha in a BBC Radio 4 phone-in: 'A very eminent British personality . . . quoted Mandela as saying that he was very very well treated . . .' To this extent, my report had given Pretoria what it wanted. But I had merely confirmed the facts observed by others, such as Helen Suzman and Nicolas de Rougement of the Red Cross as well as by Mandela himself. It helped no one to tell horror stories of inhuman treatment, as the three signatories to the letter in *The Times* had unwittingly done, when they were quite untrue.

The episode did not have the effect desired by the South African government. Mandela came across from the resulting publicity not as an extremist or killer, but as a man of moderation. My report written for the European Parliament was circulated to various political leaders and in it he emerged, bearing in mind the extent of his personal sacrifice, as a man amazingly lacking in bitterness. His lawyer, Himan Bernadt, wrote to me later,[4] 'He and his colleagues in Pollsmoor like it [the report] very much and think you have done a good job.'

There was little more that I could do as an initiator of South African dialogue. The government now knew where my sympathies lay. It was their policy still to discredit Mandela, not to give him a platform and have him portrayed as a statesman, and they were no longer inclined to do me favours. Still, I felt by now that Mandela was the only hope for any peaceful resolution of the conflict. Whenever I could, during the years 1985-90, I therefore promoted Mandela as a man with whom the government and the Western world would eventually have to deal, in spite of his links with communists and his belief in the need for armed struggle. I tried my best to stay in touch with him and he, although I did not know it, also wanted to maintain our acquaintance, maybe so as to use me as a link with Britain and other parts of the outside world.

In March 1985, two months after Mandela and I met, the ailing Konstantin Chernenko died, to no one's surprise, and Mikhail Gorbachev assumed the Soviet leadership. Mandela wrote to me asking me to compliment Margaret Thatcher on her attitude to the new leader, in particular on her conclusion that he was a man with whom she could do business. He wrote in his Pollsmoor cell that this was the sort of positive move that could reduce world tension. 'And then I thanked you for coming to see me and for the constructive article that you wrote about our visit.'

The letter never reached me. It was specially frustrating, since I was told by 'Kobie' Coetsee that Mandela was writing me letters. 'In terms of the general policy relating to outgoing mail, a response from Mr Mandela could possibly experience delay,' he wrote. He also told me that my letters, or at least some of them, were being passed to Mandela and that he was replying to the points made by me. I wrote to him every few months about how we in Western Europe viewed South Africa's problems. Every 18 July I wrote to him with birthday good wishes and he stayed on my Christmas card list, although I never got one back.

Mandela was later to tell me that, every time he wrote me a letter, he was asked to rewrite it, but without any indication as to the part of the letter that was causing the problem. The result was that none of his letters ever left the country and they remain, years later, still in ministry files, in spite of my efforts to recover what I regard as my property. I presume that Coetsee thought that I might make the contents of any letter public – as indeed I would have, since I had given no undertaking not to. And he saw no reason why a political prisoner in Cape Town should be allowed to use a foreigner in London as a conduit for his pronouncements on world affairs.

I tried to explain meanwhile the nuances of Mandela's political views and the extent to which they differed from those of more bellicose ANC colleagues. There was, for instance, his attitude to the Zulu leader Chief Gatsha Buthelezi. The ANC generally and its Radio Freedom in Addis Ababa were in the habit of dismissing him as 'a Bantustan puppet' and calling for his 'liquidation', either political or physical. In fact, the two leaders were on good personal terms. They exchanged letters and in 1985 Buthelezi wrote to President Botha with queries about Mandela's state of health, as usual asking the government to release him.

Secondly, Mandela was at odds with the ANC's basic political line, which was to demand an immediate and total transfer of power to them from the apartheid government. Mandela favoured negotiations on power sharing. He told the American lawyer Samuel Dash, 'Unlike white people anywhere else in Africa, whites in South Africa belong here. This is their home. We want them to live here with us and share power with us.'[5]

Thirdly, as he had explained when we met, he wanted to limit the armed struggle to attacks on buildings and 'symbols of apartheid', and he deplored such loss of civilian life as that caused by the 1983 Pretoria bomb. ANC radio on the other hand made it clear[6] that they wanted 'the whole country to go up in flames'. Their radio in Addis Ababa announced, 'We have got to take the battle right into [the whites'] homes, into their kitchens and bedrooms. Police and soldiers must be killed even when they are in their homes.' All this time random killings of innocent civilians were being carried out by ANC members (though not always under ANC orders) and their then leader, Oliver Tambo, did not normally feel the need to apologize for them. Winnie Mandela supported this policy of total war against the South African establishment, calling for the 'necklacing' of anyone who 'sold out' to the regime. Such fiery statements were of great help to the South African government, being used by them to discredit her husband.

Fourthly, whereas Mandela favoured a truce as soon as the ANC was recognized and brought into political debate, the ANC mainstream's policy was to continue the armed struggle right up to the transfer of power. I was in the House of Commons in October 1985 when ANC information officer Thabo Mbeki told a group of British MPs, 'We are following the example set by liberation movements in Vietnam and Rhodesia. If there was a truce, both sides would have to end their violence, and it is difficult to see how this could be done while apartheid remains in force.'

In the late 1980s, however, the South African government did not find it convenient to emphasize such distinctions, preferring instead to portray their stubborn adversary as an unrepentant terrorist, a believer in the use of violence of the crudest sort – an image that his wife's oratory did much to encourage. They no longer felt that I could be useful to them. Therefore, when in February 1986 I wrote to Coetsee asking for permission to meet Mandela again, he replied curtly[7] that 'a visit is not considered opportune at this stage'. After that, Coetsee stopped replying at all, although I kept up my side of the correspondence, sending Mandela letters on various subjects, political and personal, some of which reached him, mainly about the ANC's two-track policy of fomenting unrest in the townships and demanding pressure from the outside world through sanctions. Some of these letters reached him, but his replies were always 'delayed' *sine die*.

Margaret Thatcher was one of the few leaders who opposed sanctions. At the outset she had kept away from the Mandela issue, referring all my letters on the subject to Foreign Secretary Geoffrey Howe, but she was firm in her opposition to apartheid and after 1987 she began promoting Mandela's cause. On 9 February 1988 she wrote to me, 'The humanitarian and political case for Mandela's release is compelling.' Mandela always admired the British Prime Minister, in spite of the differences in their views.

Keeping up the campaign to explain Mandela's views to the Western world, we awarded him the European Parliament's Sakharov Prize and at the end of 1988 I arranged for his fourteen-year-old grandson Mandla to travel from school in Swaziland to receive it – a scroll, a medal and a cheque – from our then president, Lord Plumb. I wrote to Mandela to tell him what had happened, but the letter never reached him and he only heard of it during the Easter holiday in 1989 when Mandla took the Strasbourg trophies to him in a warder's house in Victor Verster prison farm, his latest place of confinement.

He was finally released on 11 February 1990, five years and a month after our meeting. I watched the historic moment that Sunday afternoon on British television. At first the cameras picked him up as a dot in the distance, then as a tiny figure seemingly walking on air through a ghostly mist. Finally the zoom lenses made him recognizable and hundreds of millions of people saw for the first time the man who had been hidden away for twenty-seven years. Having met him more recently, I was one of the first to pick out his tall figure from the throng of people that gathered round him as he walked, quite firmly and with a lighter step than one would have expected in a man of seventy-one, until he reached his car and his ANC friends, who took him immediately to a rally in Cape Town, an hour away.

A month later I flew to Johannesburg and we met for the second time, in different circumstances, in the offices of the newly legalized ANC. Walter Sisulu and other released prisoners came to shake hands and recall January 1985, again apologizing for having received me in pyjamas in their Pollsmoor 'dormitory'. A young ANC secretary brought us tea and I remember Mandela's horror when he realized that he had been so careless and discourteous as to help himself to sugar without offering me, his guest, the bowl first. After twenty-seven years in gaol, it was gentlemanly behaviour almost to excess.

We talked about his plans for new electoral and taxation systems, about the need to give South African blacks a share of the economy as well as a share of power. He spoke of the 'need to address the concerns of the whites' and of the problems he would face in finding a way that might satisfy most of the present ruling minority as well as the strident demands of the ANC's left wing and its Communist allies. He had been invited to address the Labour Party's annual conference in Blackpool in October 1990, he told me, and he hoped to do so, but he hoped also to address the Conservative conference a week later. Back in London, I reported this offer to our then chairman, Kenneth Baker. He was very surprised to hear it.

Privatization was under way in Poland. The Berlin Wall was being demolished. The cold war was nearly over. The ANC's struggle was no longer part of it. The Soviet Union was no longer keen to embarrass the West by fomenting South African revolution. Mandela talked with admiration of the Gorbachev reforms. He wanted to see the same spirit of reassessment, he went on, in the West's attitude to past empires in Africa and elsewhere. Britain in particular should admit and apologize for its historic role as an oppressor of black peoples. 'I would like to see Western spokesmen admitting that with imperialism they brought untold suffering to millions of people in what is now the developing world. Mr Gorbachev has at least had the courage to admit his system's faults. Like you, I was brought up to be proud of the British empire, on which the sun never set, and even now we appreciate the British love of democracy. In colonial times, when the British were putting pressure on you, the best place to run away to was Britain itself. Generally though we now have to say that British imperialism was bad and we would like Britain to accept this. It would increase our admiration for British institutions.'[8]

In 1985 we would both have had time to pursue such historical themes, but in 1990 he was needed for more important duties. He visited foreign countries, received awards, met heads of state. Then he came to Strasbourg, where he made a speech and 're-received' the Sakharov Prize which fourteen-year-old Mandla had accepted on his behalf a year earlier. The ANC kept their hero moving from place to place, to the point of exhaustion, but in the end they had to concede that his true work lay at home. In the short term, security was going to deteriorate. There would be upheavals. Bloodshed was unavoidable. Mandela's job was to stop the riots from becoming civil war and mass carnage. His twenty-seven years in prison were but a preparation, it seemed, for the monumental task that he now faced.

My meeting with him in January 1985 was only an episode. But it generated publicity about an injustice and promoted Mandela in his future role as a conciliator between black and white. It played a small part in rescuing the man from the fake roles into which both Right and Left had cast him. My summary of his political views showed that he was no demonic killer, anxious only to destroy. On the contrary, he was South Africa's only hope. And, when I looked at what he had endured from 1962 to 1990, I had to be amazed at the moderation with which he planned to embark on his political task.

He was no martyred weakling either, as the Left sometimes liked to portray him, condemned to everlasting entombment as a symbol of South Africa's evil system. I tried to explain that he was not so much a victim of past injustices as a man of his country's future, a man who prefers to build rather than to destroy. This was the gist of everything that he told me and that I reported.

These pages provide, I hope, an answer to the taunts of Harvey Hinds and the other Labour activists from the Greater London

Council in July 1983. Their suggestion that I am indifferent to the human rights of socialists, or of black people or of those who are not my political allies, was shown to be incorrect.

14. The Katyń Murder Mystery, 1940-92

The horror of Katyń is thrust upon anyone who knows Poland and its people. It encapsulates the nation's feeling of outrage at fifty years of cruel foreign occupation, Nazi German and Soviet Russian. The story was told to me in every detail during my visits there in the 1960s, researching my biography of Władysław Gomułka. It was Russia's great crime against Poland, something that could never be forgotten.

Katyń, I was soon made aware, was no mere item of wartime history, no mere episode in the destruction of 6 million of Poland's 30-million population between 1939 and 1945. It was the touchstone of the Polish predicament, the most vivid example of their ill-treatment at the hands of their eastern neighbour. It symbolized their long service as Russia's satellite and their betrayals by Britain during and after the war. It showed how Soviet Russia had decapitated and subjugated their entire nation – and how no one, not even their British allies who had guaranteed their integrity in March 1939, had seemed anxious to care about it.

On 17 September 1939, Stalin invaded Poland by agreement with Hitler, as set out in the Molotov–Ribbentrop pact of a few days earlier. The Red Army took many Polish prisoners, by the end of the year an estimated 180,000, and they kept them in camps in conditions of great hardship. It was noted at the time that about 15,000 prisoners, those whom the Soviet Union might be assumed to dislike most, mostly army officers but also landowners, policemen and others from the forces of law and order, including junior employees of the civil service, postmen for instance, were being kept in three special camps: at Ostashkov near Kalinin, at Starobielsk near Kharkov and at Kozielsk near Smolensk, just by the settlement known as Katyń.

Although no one outside the Kremlin knew it, these 15,000 leaders of Poland's pre-war society were doomed to be massacred. They were seen by Stalin and his men as the core of Polish hatred of the Soviet Union, and of Russia, the depth of which he had discovered himself during visits to Poland before the Revolution. These Poles, in his view, were enemies with whom he could never become reconciled. It was a problem for which there was only one solution, the physical elimination of all the men in all three camps.

On 5 March 1940, the Soviet secret police (NKVD) chief, Lavrenti Beria, signed a TOP SECRET letter, beginning, 'TO COMRADE STALIN – The prisoner-of-war camps of the NKVD of the USSR and the prisons of the western districts of Ukraine and Byelorussia today contain a large quantity of former officers of the Polish army, former members of the Polish police and intelligence organs, members of Polish nationalist counter-revolutionary parties, participants in secret counter-revolutionary rebel organizations, escaped personnel and others. All of these are ferocious enemies of Soviet power, filled to the brim with hatred for the Soviet system.

'These prisoners of war who are officers and police are trying to continue their counter-revolutionary work in the camps, carrying out anti-Soviet agitation. Each one of them only waits to be set free, so as to have the opportunity to join actively in the struggle against Soviet power. Organs of the NKVD in western districts of Ukraine and Byelorussia have unearthed a series of counter-revolutionary rebel organizations. The role of active leadership in these counter-revolutionary bodies was played by former officers of the former Polish army as well as by former police and gendarmes.

'Among the escaped personnel and violators of our state frontier, whom we now hold, a significant number of people have also been found who are participants in counter-revolutionary espionage and rebel organizations. The prisoner-of-war camps contain altogether, not counting warrant officers and other ranks, 14,736 former officers, civil servants, landowners, policemen, gendarmes, prison guards, settlers and intelligence officers. More than 90 per cent are of Polish nationality.'

Beria went on to list these 'enemies of the people' by rank and profession, after which he advised Stalin that all 14,700 files should be transferred to the NKVD 'in order that they may be specially dealt with by the use in each case of the highest measure of punishment – death by shooting'. The cases, he suggests, should be dealt with collectively by a three-man court or *'troyka'* of senior NKVD men without the prisoner being brought to trial or informed of the accusation against him. Approval of Beria's suggestion is shown by the signatures on page one of the March 1940 paper. It was signed not only by Stalin himself, but also by his key Politburo members Vyacheslav Molotov, Anastas Mikoyan and Kliment Voroshilov, with the names of Kalinin and Kaganovich added to show that they agreed orally. The paper, which was found in the Presidential Archive and came into my hands fifty-two years after it was signed, indicates that the matter was then handed over to Beria's deputy, Bogdan Kobulov, for implementation.

A few days later, knowing nothing of this scheme, the Poles in the three camps were told that they were to be moved to camps where conditions were better, from which they might soon be released. Survivors from the camps recall how cheered they all were by this announcement. Any change, they thought, must be a change for the better. And so day by day, throughout April 1940, they were entrained from the camps in groups of from 50 to 350 and taken away for what they hoped would be happier destinations. Each man went through the usual formalities before departure. Names were re-checked and registered. They were finger-printed and inoculated afresh and given certificates to prove that this had been done. They were given sandwiches for their journey and it was noted that some of these were wrapped in clean white paper, something almost unknown in the Soviet Union in 1940.[1] They were never seen again. In the course of that month, April 1940, all 14,700 Poles were murdered and buried in mass graves.

No one outside the narrowest of NKVD circles knew of these terrible events. But people began to guess that something was wrong. After April 1940 letters from the men to their families in Poland stopped arriving. The families were concerned and the Polish Red Cross sent several hundred inquiries to Moscow, but nothing was heard back and nothing could be done. The Polish government was moved to London after the fall of France. Britain was fighting alone, with only a small number of Poles as its allies, and the Soviet Union was an unfriendly neutral which had joined Hitler in occupying Polish territory. The NKVD was at this stage cooperating with Hitler's Gestapo against any signs of Polish political activity.

Hitler's attack on Russia in June 1941 from one day to the next turned these adversaries into allies. Stalin wasted no time in releasing Poles from camps, including their commander, General Władysław

Anders, hoping to turn them into an army that would fight the invader from Soviet territory. However, after these massive releases were at an end, the Polish government were alarmed to find that 15,000 of their prisoners could not be traced. They made more inquiries, but the Russians produced no officers, only evasive and self-contradictory answers. In October 1941 Molotov told the Polish ambassador in Moscow, Stanislaw Kot, that he had 'no information' about them. The Poles found this incredible, since the NKVD were well known for the careful account they kept of all their prisoners. They began to fear the worst, but in the atmosphere of the time, with the Red Army and the Soviet people bearing the brunt of Hitler's aggression, with Leningrad and Moscow under siege, they felt unable to push Stalin too hard.

The blow fell on 13 April 1943. Radio Berlin announced that German occupation forces at Katyń, twenty miles from Smolensk in western Russia, had unearthed the bodies of several thousand Polish officers. Berlin claimed that they had been murdered in the spring of 1940 by the Soviet security police, the NKVD. The Soviet authorities at once denied Germany's accusation. A day or two later the Polish Prime Minister in London, Władysław Sikorski, lunched with Churchill and told him what a serious problem had arisen. He had a 'wealth of evidence', he said, demonstrating that the Soviets were responsible. Churchill's immediate concern was over this threat to the wartime alliance with Russia, without which the war could not be won. He told Sikorski, 'If they are dead, nothing you can do will bring them back.'

On 19 April Anthony Eden told the Cabinet that 'he had done all he could to persuade the Poles to treat this as a German propaganda move designed to sow discord between the allies'. He was in a quandary and anxious to gloss over the question of which government was responsible. Sikorski faced an even more fearful dilemma. He too wanted to avoid an open breach with Russia, but he was outraged by Moscow's refusal to reply coherently to his many telegrams about the missing men, many of whom were relations of his close colleagues. He could not simply accept without protest the probability that they had all been massacred. Emotion ran high, and he was persuaded to invite the Red Cross to conduct an inquiry.

Stalin and his men took this request correctly as a suggestion of

Soviet guilt. Their reply was to defend themselves not by evidence but by abusing their accusers. Ivan Maisky, Soviet ambassador in London, told Churchill, 'The Poles were a brave but foolish race who had always mismanaged their affairs. Their feckless government could not understand the folly of a nation of 20 million provoking one of nearly 200 million ... Russia's patience was not inexhaustible ...'[2]

The British government was now bombarded with anti-Polish advice and resolutions from various British bodies. The Snowdown miners from Dover wrote, 'Tell the reactionary landlord clique of the Polish government to stop playing Goebbels's game and act "ally" to the Soviet Union or be branded Hitler's friends in Britain.' The Hampstead Garden Suburb branch of the Communist Party attacked the Poles for 'so readily falling prey to the lying and fantastic allegations of the Nazi enemy'. A cartoon by Low in the *Evening Standard*[3] showed a Polish officer hammering an iron wedge into the tree of British–Soviet–American accord. Several trade union branches asked London to stop the Polish government's allocation of newsprint and transfer it to the *Daily Worker*.[4]

'Hitler's Polish accomplices' was the heading on an article in *Pravda* on 20 April, which claimed that the Poles had fallen into German hands after the Red Army's withdrawal in 1941, and then been murdered by the Nazis. The barrage of abuse continued and on 26 April came the disaster that Britain and the United States had dreaded. Stalin and his government were so disgusted by the cruel Polish accusations, they said, that they would now break off relations with the Polish government in London.

Stalin told the British ambassador in Moscow, Archibald Clark-Kerr, on 8 May, 'Its [the Polish government's] present members did not want to live in peace with this country. They had shifted to the Soviet government all the old hatred that they had felt for the Tsarist government. They did not understand the changes that had taken place. They persisted in trying to play one ally off against another, complaining today to us and the Americans about the Russians, tomorrow to the Russians about us. They thought that this was clever, but in fact God had given them no brains.'[5] Stalin was himself the man who had given orders for the mass-murder. He was nevertheless capable, without shame, of using the Poles' correct allegation as a pretext for breaking diplomatic ties.

On 4 May Eden told the House of Commons, choosing his words carefully, that Britain 'has no wish to attribute blame for these events to anyone except the common enemy'. He deplored 'the cynicism which permits the Nazi murderers of hundreds of thousands of innocent Poles and Russians to make use of a story of mass murder in an attempt to disturb the unity of the Allies'. Eden did not actually state that Germany was responsible for the murders, but speaking in the British government's name, he gave the clear impression that this was the case. As for what should be done about it, his only advice was 'least said, soonest mended'.

Eden's statement of 4 May 1943 was to remain as a stain on Britain's conscience for nearly fifty years. It was not exactly a lie. It was an attempt to avoid admitting what he and his Foreign Office friends then knew to be an extremely inconvenient fact. It was what is known in official circles nowadays as 'being economical with the truth'. At the time, with Stalin bearing the brunt of the war against Hitler, the deceit may have been forgivable. But it was to be allowed to continue by Eden's successors, in the face of many changes of government and of Foreign Secretaries, for half a century after any good reason for the deceit had disappeared.

British ministers and officials were repeating Eden's line for public consumption, but in their secret memoranda they were writing the opposite. They pointed out that the case raised many difficult questions. Why did all the letters home from the Poles in the three camps cease in April or May 1940? Why had not a single missing Pole ever been seen anywhere after that date? Why did all the diaries found on the bodies have their final entries in March or April 1940? Why were the Soviets being so evasive, giving contradictory answers to Polish inquiries? It all seemed to show that they must have been shot in the spring of 1940, when Katyń was under Soviet control. Owen O'Malley, British ambassador to the Polish government in exile, wrote in his emotional and disturbing paper on the affair: 'The Germans overran Smolensk in July 1941 and there is no easy answer to the question why, if any of the 10,000 had been alive between the end of May 1940 and July 1941, none of them ever succeeded in getting any word through to their families.'

He reconstructed the last moments of the Polish victims in sentences that many in Whitehall found deeply shocking: 'If a man struggled, it seems that the executioner threw his coat over his head, tying it round his neck and leading him hooded to the pit's edge, for in many cases a man was found to be thus hooded and the coat to have been pierced by a bullet where it covered the base of the skull. But those who went quietly to their deaths must have seen a most monstrous sight. In the broad pit their comrades lay, packed closely around the edge, head to feet, like sardines in a tin, but in the middle of the grave disposed of less orderly. Up and down on the bodies the executioners trampled, hauling the bodies about and treading in the blood like butchers in a stockyard. When it was all over and the last shot had been fired and the last Polish head punctured, the butchers, perhaps trained in youth to husbandry, turned their hands to the most innocent of occupations – smoothing the clods and planting little conifers all over what had been a shambles.'

Frank Roberts and Denis Allen, then middle-rank FO officials, agreed with O'Malley that there must be a 'presumption of guilt' against the NKVD. 'This is very disturbing,' wrote Alexander Cadogan, permanent secretary at the Foreign Office. Certain moral principles lay behind Britain's war effort. How could they be reconciled to an alliance with a government capable of such a crime? How would Britain, after the war, be able to punish Nazi war criminals if she condoned this Soviet atrocity? But everyone agreed that it had to be done. The alliance had to be preserved. And so the British government went along with the Soviet version. They lied to the British people, in the British people's best interest.

But they did so not without misgivings. In his report O'Malley invited the government not to fall under St Paul's curse on those 'who see evil and burn not', to remember that by lying they were making themselves an accessory after the crime. He wrote: 'We have been obliged to appear to distort the normal and healthy operation of our intellectual and moral judgements. We have been obliged to give undue prominence to the tactlessness and impulsiveness of Poles, to restrain the Poles from putting their case clearly before the public, to discourage any attempt by the public and the press to probe the ugly story to the bottom. In general we have been obliged to deflect attention from possibilities which in the ordinary affairs of life would cry to high heaven for elucidation, and to withhold the full measure of solicitude which, in other circumstances, would be shown to acquaintances situated as a large number of Poles now are. We have in fact perforce used the good name of England like the murderers used the little conifers to cover up a massacre . . .'

And so the matter was left until the war was over and Poland passed under Soviet control. At the Nuremberg trials the Soviets tried to blame Nazi Germany for the Katyń massacre, but they did not press the accusation. The matter was glossed over. The February 1945 Yalta agreement was violated by Stalin and the grand alliance dissolved into cold war. In 1952 the Madden Commission of the U S House of Representatives declared the Soviet Union guilty of the crime. Western historians of the period universally supported this verdict. But the British authorities, even though there was no longer any overriding need to preserve British–Soviet relations, refused to move from the 'neutral' position taken at the end of the war. Eden's suggestion of German responsibility, pronounced in 1943, was allowed to remain as Britain's final word.

Examples of the Foreign Office's very cautious attitude emerged in a debate about Katyń in the House of Lords on 17 June 1971, when the minister Lord Aberdare said, 'Governments are not at liberty to voice half-formed views, speculations or suspicions.' The British government, he said, 'has absolutely no standing in the matter'. It had never been involved in any inquiry into Katyń and the inquiry at Nuremberg had been inconclusive. The Polish government, 'whose wishes should surely be respected', saw the matter as closed. Any British pronouncement now would open old wounds and lead to 'pain, disagreement and ill-will'. These comments by a British minister, presumably drafted by the Foreign Office, caused great offence among Poles at home and abroad. Katyń was the crime that had not only deprived Poland of many thousands of their finest men, but also brought abuse from East and West alike raining down on Poland's head. The crime had been committed against Poland, and Poland had been made to appear the guilty party. The victim had become the person accused. Also, the crime had caused a breach between the Soviet and Polish governments. And it was that breach that had led to the recognition by Moscow of its alternative regime, the communists based on Soviet territory, who were eventually to supplant the London government of Poland and, in the spring of 1945, be recognized as

Poland's legitimate regime.

It was absurd for Lord Aberdare, as a British minister, to suggest in 1971 that the Polish communist government's view of Katyń ought to be respected. Warsaw operated under Soviet control and was bound to support the Soviet version. It was wrong to suggest that Britain had no standing. In 1943 Anthony Eden had supported the Soviet version. Did he and his successor still support it? In 1943, according to a British ambassador, England's good name had been used to cover up a massacre. Was this still the case? And as for pain or ill-will, the pain felt by the Poles over the mass murder of friends and betrayals by allies was not going to be lessened by evasive answers from British ministers. Foreign Office men like Cadogan and Roberts had made it clear in 1943, albeit in their private memoranda, that Stalin was guilty. Why could they not say the same publicly now that the war was over, now that there was no longer any reason to lie?

It was a prime demonstration of how Poland had endured so much and been rewarded with so little. In six years of war, 20 per cent of her population, including 90 per cent of her 3 million Jews, perished at Nazi hands. Victory came in 1945, but the sufferings were only just beginning. Stalin decided that he needed a Poland 'friendly to the Soviet Union' as part of his ring of buffer zones that surrounded his territory. He therefore maintained a strong army garrison in the 'liberated' land, forcing upon it a communist-dominated government that he had himself previously created on Soviet soil. Poland was thus 'given away' to Soviet control in the February 1945 Yalta Agreement. It passed, not without more bloodshed, from one foreign occupation to another.

Poland's sad predicament affected me not only because of its essential injustice, but also because Britain and the United States had allowed it to happen with so little protest. Poland was Britain's gallant ally from the first day of the war. Her government-in-exile was set up in London. Polish soldiers fought alongside ours at Monte Cassino in Italy. Polish airmen fought with the Royal Air Force over Britain's skies. They received no reward other than to be allowed to stay in Britain, if they wished, as refugees. Stalin promised at Yalta to hold 'free and unfettered elections' in Poland. Elections took place in January 1947, but they were organized by the communists and guaranteed to produce a pro-communist result.

Władysław Gomułka took power in Poland amid a wave of anti-

Stalinist revulsion in 1956. Although still one of Poland's few believing communists, he gave his people certain concessions that those in other satellite countries did not enjoy. The power of the secret police was curbed. Private ownership of land was tolerated. There was some freedom of speech, though not of written expression. And Poles with access to foreign currency, for instance through a relative, could usually travel abroad. But it was not much and even he, the so-called 'Pole first and communist second', was ready to follow the Moscow line by describing the Katyń massacre as 'a provocation organized by Joseph Goebbels'.

After the 1956 events, Stalin's statues were removed from Polish cities. The secret police were tamed. A limited freedom of speech was allowed. But still no Polish or Soviet authority seemed ready to admit Stalin's crime against the Polish nation in 1940. Only in Moscow, and at the highest and most intimate level, was the truth consigned to paper. On 3 March 1959, the then KGB chief Alexander Shelepin summarized the problem in chilling terms: 'TOP SECRET – TO COMRADE KHRUSHCHEV, N.S. – In the KGB we hold personal files and other materials, dated 1940, referring to the shooting that same year of imprisoned or interned officers, gendarmes, police, settlers, landowners and other such persons from the former bourgeois Poland. In all, by decision of a special "troyka" of the Soviet NKVD 21,857 people were shot: 4,421 in Katyń forest (Smolensk district), 3,820 from Starobielsk camp near Kharkov, 6,311 from Ostashkov camp near Kalinin and 7,305 from other camps and prisons of the Western Ukraine and Western Byelorussia . . .'

The letter went on to refer to Stalin's order of March 1940 that had ordered the massacre, as quoted above, and to raise the question of what was to be done with the 21,857 personal files. They were of no operational or historical interest to the KGB, he observed, nor were 'our Polish friends' ever likely to need them: 'On the contrary, some unforeseen circumstance might lead to the discovery (literally 'deconspiracy') of the truth about the operation, with undesirable consequences for our state, especially since there already exists our "official version" of the Katyń forest events . . .'[6] He asked Khrushchev's permission to destroy the individual files. And this was done.

By 1959 I was already aware of Katyń's importance. It infuriated me that the Soviets would not admit what they had done in 1940, that the British seemed still to be backing the Soviet version of events. It was yet another burden that the Poles were being forced to bear. Why should the murderers of their young men go undetected? And why was the Foreign Office of Britain, decades after the war was over, still taking part in the cover-up? I vowed then that I would do what I could to unearth the truth.

In 1972, shortly after being banned from the Soviet bloc, I found O'Malley's report and the main 1943 Katyń documents in the Public Record Office in Chancery Lane, London, and my long article based on these papers for the *Sunday Times*[7] was the first airing of the idea that the British government had all along, ever since 1943, been convinced of Soviet guilt. It called for 'a liberal application of facts', which might 'shock the patient momentarily' but would 'disinfect the wound'. There could be no hope that Poles and Russians would be reconciled, I believed, until the truth was admitted on the Russian side. It was also, since we had backed the Soviet version in 1943, Britain's duty to set the record straight.

While preparing this article in April 1972, I wrote to Anthony Eden (Lord Avon), reminding him of what he had said in the House of Commons in 1943, how he had said one thing while believing another, and asking him if he now might like to comment further. His reply (1 May) was short and evasive, merely referring me to the House of Lords debate a year earlier: 'It seems to me that however strong one's feelings about the horror of Katyń, Lord Aberdare's conclusion is inescapable and I accept it.' His simple belief in the idea 'least said, soonest mended' had apparently not changed since 1943. My own view, which I wrote in the *Sunday Times*, was that so long as the truth remained concealed the wound of Katyń would continue to fester, growing ever more filled with poison.

The Memorial

The Polish community in London were outraged by the Public Record Office revelations. They began raising money to commemorate the massacre's victims and by 1974 the funds were ready and a site agreed – St Luke's churchyard in London's Chelsea. But it was only the beginning of the organizers' problems. They then found themselves in a bureaucratic imbroglio which was to cause further grief to all those whose families had been killed by the NKVD.

A bizarre alliance emerged of worthy British bodies determined not to allow the Poles to honour the memory of their relatives. The Church of England lodged an objection to the St Luke's site and a number of local residents also protested. In the Court of Arches, the Church's highest tribunal, the Bishop of London's representative George Newsom ruled against giving the site to the Poles for their memorial. It was, his verdict proclaimed, likely to perpetuate bitter feelings and was 'not consistent with the Church's ministry of reconciliation'. He was disturbed that the memorial would carry the date 1940. This would be an assertion of Soviet guilt 'without giving those who are accused the chance to defend themselves'.

The Church of England was at once accused by the Poles' colourful spokesman Louis Fitzgibbon of 'acting like Pontius Pilate', but their objection was supported by the Chelsea Society and the Victorian Society. Local people living near the church protested that St Luke's was 'a sunny little garden bright with flowers, much used and enjoyed by people of all ages'. An obelisk, they said, would cast a shadow over it in more than one sense. The Archdeacon of Middlesex, John Hayward, also objected to an obelisk, since it would seem like 'a finger pointing to the sky asking for justice'. Frequent visits to the memorial by Polish pilgrims 'would entail the removal of flower beds and much wear and tear of the turf'.

Again, the Poles had good reason to feel that scant account was being taken of the theft of their country, of their unique contribution to victory over Hitler or of their predicament as exiles. The British authorities had decided, it seemed to them, that problems of flower beds were more important than the memory of their 21,000 murdered friends and relatives. The St Luke's site was taken from them and eventually Kensington and Chelsea Council agreed to provide an alternative site at Gunnersbury on London's western outskirts.

It was now the turn of the Soviet government, helped by their Polish comrades, to enter the picture. In 1972, according to the then Foreign Office minister Julian Amery,[8] they had asked him 'as an extremely important request' to stop the Katyń project. He then demanded to see all available documents and concluded, 'It was perfectly clear that the Russians were responsible for the massacre.'

The project therefore continued, running past the Labour Party's victory in 1974, after which no fewer than ten protests were made by the two embassies to Foreign Secretary Anthony Crosland and Defence Secretary Roy Mason. Polish ambassador Artur Starewicz protested personally to the Mayor of Kensington and Chelsea, Joselyn Sundius-Smith. Vladimir Semyonov, Counsellor at the Soviet embassy, wrote her a threatening letter accusing the Council of 'following in the footsteps of the Goebbels lie against Britain's ally in the Second World War' and ordering her 'to prevent' the memorial.

The monument was nevertheless erected at the alternative site near Chiswick, but by the time the moment came for the unveiling, Britain's Labour government felt yet again inclined to surrender to the communists' crude bullying. In spite of what Julian Amery had concluded four years earlier, Crosland wrote to the Katyń committee repeating the Foreign Office's ancient theory that the evidence was not firm enough to allow him to reach a conclusion on who was guilty. Airey Neave, Margaret Thatcher's friend, criticized Crosland's 'craven attitude',[9] but this did not prevent the government from taking a number of decisions calculated to fudge the issue and insult Britain's murdered allies. They could not, or would not, ban the project altogether, but they would distance the government from it in an attempt to minimize Soviet anger.

Roy Mason explained that the proposed inscription on the obelisk, 'KATYN 1940', was a clear attribution of guilt to the NKVD, a charge which the Soviet government denied. It would therefore be wrong for the government 'to endorse one particular view by being represented at the unveiling ceremony'. He cancelled the British regimental band that was booked to play funeral music and gave orders that no British serviceman could attend in uniform, even in a personal capacity.

No British minister was present at the ceremony on 18 September, 1976, the day after the thirty-sixth anniversary of Stalin's invasion. 'Who are they afraid of? The big bad wolf?' remarked Emmanuel Shinwell, the only Labour politician who attended, of his government's decision to boycott the event and impose their boycott on others. A few Conservative opposition MPs were there, happy to criticize the government for its rudeness and timidity but, of course, unable to speak in the nation's name.

It was typical of the defeatism of those days, I wrote,[10] that British ministers were so cowed by their fear of Soviet reaction that they were unwilling to honour the memory of murdered wartime allies, that they were ready even thirty-six years after the event to allow the truth about the massacres to be covered up by the good name of Britain, like the conifers planted in 1940 to cover up the mass graves by the murderers themselves.

On my return home from the ceremony I telephoned James Callaghan's office, begging him as Prime Minister to make at least some expression of sympathy with the families of the Polish victims. A week later I received a low-level reply from a junior Foreign Office minister, Goronwy Roberts, emphasizing the 'deep sense of repugnance which the tragic crime of Katyń engenders in all those who know of it'. The letter was an attempt to be sympathetic, and as such it was printed in London's daily Polish newspaper,[11] even though it totally ignored the question of which government was guilty of the crime.

The Katyń affair was therefore allowed to fester for more years as a shocking example not only of Soviet brutality, but also of British cowardice and ingratitude. After Margaret Thatcher came to power in 1979 British ministers were allowed to attend the annual ceremony at the Katyń memorial. In May 1980 a number of Soviet dissidents outside Russia, including Vladimir Bukovsky, expressed their regret at what their country's police had done to Poles forty years earlier. The issue nevertheless remained stagnant until Mikhail Gorbachev and his glasnost campaign started to consider it.

In July 1987, visiting Poland for the first time since 1969, I was told about the Soviet–Polish historical commission, newly set up to investigate the 'blank spots' in past relations between the two countries. They had in mind Stalin's pact with Hitler, the partition of Poland in 1939, the mass deportations of Poles to the East in 1940, the Red Army's failure to help Polish forces in the 1944 Warsaw uprising, the faked 1947 elections and, of course, the Katyń affair. It seemed doubtful whether they would find anything of value. Włodzimierz Kowalski, a Polish member of the commission and a charmingly drunken pro-Soviet manipulator, told me first that all documents on Katyń had been destroyed, second that all those involved in the massacres were dead. He was wrong on both counts.

On 28 May 1988 came a sign of a breakthrough. Moscow Radio referred to Katyń as a historical 'blank spot' and questioned the 'accepted view' that the Nazis were responsible. It seemed as if they were on the point of admitting the truth. I wrote that the admission, if it came, would be 'the most striking example of glasnost to have emerged from the Gorbachev era so far'. Meanwhile the British remained unmoved. On 11 July the Foreign Office minister Lord Glenarthur repeated the old story that there was 'no conclusive evidence'. I complained to Margaret Thatcher, advising her that anyone who believed that would believe anything, and on 27 July the Foreign Office at last reversed itself, partially, and took a step forward, admitting that there was 'substantial circumstantial evidence pointing to Soviet responsibility'.

In Moscow glasnost was gathering momentum and making more progress on the Katyń issue than London was. In April 1990 the moment of truth finally arrived. Gorbachev gave President Jaruzelski of Poland a file of documents, including lists of the names and dates of birth of more than 15,000 murdered men, together with a formal apology for what his predeccessor had done exactly fifty years earlier.

Was this to be the end of our long quest? Could the Katyń affair now be laid to rest? Was Polish honour satisfied? It seemed that there were many in Poland who felt that a mere apology from Gorbachev was not enough. What about the men who had done it? An NKVD officer aged thirty in 1940 might well be alive, a sprightly eighty, in 1990. Germans suspected of war crimes were still being pursued in many countries, including Britain, even half a century after the event. Moscow was insisting that such prosecutions continue.

I went to Moscow in June 1990 and found Soviet officials apparently keen to tell more about their country's past crimes, including Katyń. Defenders of the old system were under attack at home and, in terms of foreign policy, there was a feeling that Russia should purge itself of past horrors by confessing them and repenting. I made some inquiries at various archives and in the end, rather surprisingly, found myself invited on 11 June to meet archivists from the Central Committee of the Communist Party, just down the hill from KGB headquarters. It was there that I discovered that there was at least one man still alive who was closely involved in the mass murder.

I was shown documents, some of them initialled by Stalin's secret police chief Lavrenti Beria himself, consigning quantities of Polish prisoners to their deaths. There were other papers describing the detail of the operation, some of them drafted by a NKVD officer, a Major of State Security then aged thirty-two, who in spite of his youth had been placed in charge of all Polish prisoners of war and interned persons in 1939–40. His name was Pyotr Karpovich Soprunenko.

I saw a document that Soprunenko had signed on 20 February 1940, asking for a group of 400 Polish officers, landowners and frontier guards to be 'handed over to the NKVD Special Commission'. The papers were marked with Beria's initials to show agreement. It was the equivalent of a mass death sentence. The NKVD Special Commission, it was explained to me by Central Committee official Valentin Alexandrov, was a three-man tribunal that considered political cases in Stalin's time. Neither the accused nor any lawyers needed to be present. The 'judges' acted on the basis only of a list of names with short biographical notes. Sentence of death was then passed by a stroke of the pen without the accused being informed.

No photocopying was allowed, but I made notes from the few documents shown to me by Alexandrov that day, including Soprunenko's report, and I summarized them in the British press.[12] The evidence showed that 15,131 Poles had been 'placed at the disposal of the 1st Special Detachment of the NKVD in April/May 1940', in other words, shot. Another Soprunenko paper confirmed that he had destroyed by burning all their records – card indexes, photographs and files. So where was this Soprunenko now? Alexandrov told me that he was still alive. He was living in Moscow, in a large apartment off Sadovoye Koltso, on his pension as a retired army major-general. I telephoned the flat and his daughter Elena answered. The general was too old and ill to talk, she said. 'These stories are very upsetting for him. He cannot discuss them. He is very ill. I can tell you one thing. The order about the Polish officers came from Stalin himself. My father says he saw the actual paper with Stalin's signature on it. So what was he to do? Get himself arrested? Or shoot himself? My father is being made a scapegoat for things that were done by other people.'

I had little time for her excuses. The same pleas were being made on behalf of eighty-year-old Latvians who had murdered Jews in 1943. I was interested, though, to hear this eye-witness confirmation, albeit at second hand, that such a document signed by Stalin had once existed. It was important to find it so as to prove that the massacres had been no capricious act, ordered by some local commander. They were authorized at the highest level as an act of policy. Gorbachev now regretted what was done, but many in the Soviet Union disagreed with him. The chief archivist, Valentin Alexandrov, told me, 'We in the Central Committee receive many letters from veterans' organizations, asking us why we besmirch the names of men who were only doing their duty against the enemies of socialism.'

It was clear that Soprunenko was a war criminal of the first degree. And the question now arose, would he be brought to trial for murder, either in Poland or in his own country? On 17 July I was told in the House of Lords that 'in view of the long-standing concern in this country over the Katyń massacre' the British embassy in Moscow would inquire what was to be done in the case. Quite apart from such a case's legal merits, it was convenient for London to do this, since Moscow was pressing for the extradition of a handful of suspected Nazi war criminals still alive in Britain. It was useful to be able to point out that there were Soviet war criminals too.

I continued my investigations in Warsaw and on 14 September Poland's deputy Minister of Defence, the former Solidarity spokesman Janusz Onyszkiewicz, gave me copies of all the papers that Gorbachev had given Jaruzelski in April. They were mostly lists of thousands of Polish names and dates of birth, probably the same lists that the NKVD Special Commission had considered as the basis for its mass death sentences.

A typical document, headed TOP SECRET and FOR YOUR EYES ONLY and dated 1 April 1940, was addressed to Major Borisovyets at Ostashkov camp near Kalinin (now renamed Tver), north of Moscow. It began, 'On receipt of this order you will dispatch to Kalinin the under-mentioned prisoners of war now held in Ostashkov camp. They will be placed at the disposal of the NKVD commander of Kalinin district . . .' There follow forty-nine Polish surnames, first names and patronymics and the man's date of birth. The paper is signed 'SOPRUNENKO'.

The documents Onyszkiewicz gave me indicate that throughout

April 1940 a total of about 500 Poles a day were shot in three separate Soviet localities – near Kalinin in the north, near Kharkov in the south and near Smolensk in the west. Many of these mass death warrants bear Soprunenko's signature. The 14,552 murdered Poles mentioned in Alexander Shelepin's memorandum of March 1959 were thus accounted for, although no news of the other 7,305 ever emerged. By now the Polish Ministry of Justice was asking the Russians for permission to question Soprunenko. The British ambassador in Moscow, Rodric Braithwaite, made two inquiries but received no reply and let the matter drop. Nothing much more was done by the Foreign Office or by the Moscow embassy.

Returning from Warsaw, I reported[13] that the net was tightening around the former NKVD commander and, sure enough, in April 1991 he was interrogated for several hours on videotape by officers of the Military Prosecutor's office in Moscow, under the command of Major-General Vladimir Kupiets, at his apartment and in the presence of his two daughters. They made good progress and in September 1991, a few days after the failed *coup d'état* against Gorbachev, I was told that the military prosecutor in Moscow was ready to discuss with me the progress that he had made in his investigations.

The Soprunenko video, a copy of which I later obtained, explained how Stalin's order of 5 March 1940 for the murder of the Poles had been put into effect. And it gave us our first pictures of the war criminal, who was by then in hiding. It showed a gaunt old man trying without success to show himself as innocent of the terrible charge. His behaviour was shifty and evasive. At first he denied knowing anything of any massacre of Polish prisoners and claimed to have spent all April 1940 at Vyborg on the Finnish border. But then video testimony by another witness, eighty-nine-year-old Vladimir Tokaryev, who had been the NKVD chief in Kalinin district in 1940 and the recipient of many of his death warrants, was played to him to jog his memory.

Although weak and blind, Tokaryev spoke firmly. His memory seemed clear and what he said corresponded entirely with the documents. 'In March 1940 we were taken to the office of Beria's deputy, Bogdan Kobulov, about fifteen or twenty of us, and told that 14,000 Poles were to be shot "on orders of higher authority". I later learnt that "higher authority" meant the Politburo. When I learnt of the scale of the operation, I asked Kobulov if I could stay behind after the meeting for a word, just the two of us. I told him that I had never taken part in any such operation, especially on such a scale ... Soprunenko knew about everything. He was in charge of all the Polish prisoners of war and he prepared everything. He addressed us at that March 1940 meeting with Kobulov.'

At last Soprunenko admitted that he was 'probably' at the meeting. Then, under pressure from interrogator Lieutenant-Colonel Anatoli Yablokov, he said that he recalled being handed the actual Politburo order, signed by Stalin himself and that he 'felt bad' about it. He was then shown lists of executed Poles, each paper with his signature on it. Again and again the interrogators asked him, 'Is this your signature?' Again and again, in spite of expert evidence to the contrary, he denied that the writing was his.

Viewing the three-hour tape, I was left with a feeling of disgust at the old NKVD man's pathetic attempts to distance himself from the murders. There was no doubt that he was guilty. If he had been a German, if he had carried out such a duty on Hitler's behalf rather than on Stalin's, he would certainly have been hanged after the end of the war. He seemed to me to symbolize all that was rotten about Soviet society.

Tokaryev gave a different impression. He seemed to speak frankly and he gave his interrogators a chilling description of what happened in April 1940 at his Kalinin headquarters. The actual killings, he said, were done by three trained executioners specially sent from Moscow – Blokhin, Sinyegrubov and Krivenko: 'They took the Poles along the corridor one by one, turned left and took them into the Red Corner, the rest room for prison staff. Each man was asked his surname, first name and date of birth – just enough to identify him. Then he was taken to the room next door, which was sound-proofed, and shot in the back of the head.

'Nothing was read to them, no decision of any court or Special Commission. They were just handcuffed and taken to the execution room. There was a rule then that a prosecutor must be present at all executions, but in this case there was no prosecutor, again for the reason that Kobulov mentioned, that there must be no witness who was not himself involved. Otherwise he might give away the truth.

'There were 300 shot that first night. I remember Sukharev, my driver, boasting about what a hard night's work it had been. But it was too many, because it was light by the time they had finished and they had a rule that everything must be done in darkness. So they reduced the number to 250 a night. How many nights did it last? Work it out for yourself: 6,000 men at 250 a night. Allowing for holidays, that makes about a month, the whole of April 1940.

'I remember a few individual Poles, for instance a young man. I asked him his age. He said he was eighteen. He smiled like a young boy. I asked him how long he had been in the frontier police. He counted on his fingers. Six months. What had he done there? He had been a telephone operator.

'Blokhin made sure that everyone in the execution team got a supply of vodka after each night's work. Every evening he brought it into the prison in boxes. They drank nothing before the shooting or during the shooting, but afterwards they all had a few glasses before going home to bed.

'I asked Blokhin and the other two: "Won't it take a lot of men to dig 6,000 graves?" They laughed at me. Blokhin said that he had brought an excavator from Moscow and two NKVD men to work it. So the dead Poles were taken out through the far door of the execution room, loaded into covered trucks and taken to the burial place . . . When it was all over, the three men from Moscow organized a big banquet to celebrate . . .'[14]

In September 1991, shortly after the *coup d'état*, I discussed this terrible confession with the Moscow military prosecutors. We viewed the tapes of the interrogations and I congratulated them on the work they had done to bring the crime of Katyń to light. General Kupiets and his officers, showing me the tapes in September 1991, in those brief days of Russian 'freedom of information' that followed the *coup*'s collapse, were as moved to horror as I was by these bloody revelations. They seemed determined to bring the matter to court for the sake of Russia's good name and they were sure that there was a case to answer–against Soprunenko, Tokaryev and several others involved in the Katyń murders. Neither their age nor the fact that they operated under Stalin's and Beria's orders would exonerate them, they said, any more than German defendants at the Nuremberg trials were forgiven because they obeyed orders and were now close to death. It was unlikely, said Kupiets, that anyone would want to lock the killers away for the last months of their sad lives. He did, however, believe that the truth ought to be made public at a public tribunal: 'The system of NKVD special commissions was completely outside the Soviet constitution. It had no basis in law, even in those days. An execution carried out under their authority was, quite simply, a murder.'

Major Sergei Shalamayev, another interrogator, said, 'I am not saying that Tokaryev and Soprunenko should be dragged out of their apartments and shot. But we do want to see the truth established in all its detail, and where we believe that guilt exists for crimes of such unspeakable horror, a proper verdict passed by an appropriate court of law.'

The military prosecutors did not get their wish. Russia's post-communist government was ready to put Stalinist or Brezhnevite criminals on trial in the flush of liberalism that followed the August 1991 coup. The mood did not last, though, and Yeltsin's government needed the new KGB to keep order amid the crime wave that Russia now endures. He found it hard to select the few murdering monsters who most deserved to be put on trial. Russia after the Soviet Union was not like Germany after Hitler. The system changed, but the same people remained in positions of power and no one relished the strife that would accompany any search for the 'guilty men' of the Stalin or Brezhnev period.

Lech Wałesa's new Polish government also seemed content. In their view, the confessions of the Soviet and Russian governments had purged the offence by their apology and national honour was satisfied. Economic progress was now their priority and the great sin of half a century ago could be left on one side. A political decision was therefore taken in Warsaw, once the truth about Katyń and other horrors had been fully made known, to put the file back in its drawer and leave the criminals alone.

Finally, on 11 November 1991, the Foreign Office minister Lord Caithness admitted the truth that his Department had known from the very outset in 1943, 'The Soviet authorities' admission in April 1990 that the NKVD (forerunner of the KGB) was responsible for the massacre was very welcome.' And then in October 1992 a telefax arrived from Moscow and I held in my hand the long-awaited document,[15] the last piece of the bloody jigsaw, the paper ordering the massacre with Stalin's actual signature on it, sent to me by a Moscow friend. At last, fifty years too late, it could reasonably be said that the story was told.[16]

15. Poland as a Russian Colony

I became fond of Poland during my many visits there in the 1960s, but in 1968 it went mad, not only its communist government but its people too, and I temporarily lost this feeling of special warmth. There were four reasons for this. The first was the 'anti-Zionist campaign' against the Jewish community that followed the 1967 Six Day War between Israel and the Arabs. The second was the brutal repression of writers' protest and student riots in March 1968. The third was Polish participation in the invasion of Czechoslovakia on 21 August 1968. The fourth was the government's massacre of workers in Gdańsk in December 1970.

It was irritating as well as sad. For several years I had been writing a biography of Poland's then leader, Władysław Gomułka, and every time I finished it I felt the need to go back and re-write the last chapters. Gomułka was an ambivalent political figure. He had spent several years under arrest in gaol in Stalin's time and was then thrust into power on a wave of anti-Stalinist reform and patriotic fervour in October 1956. Unlike the Hungarians, whose bid for autonomy had been crushed by Soviet tanks, the Poles had managed to acquire a measure of self-government and freedom of speech in the post-Stalin years. Gomułka epitomized this achievement.

Any Czech, East German or Russian who criticized the communist system in open conversation with foreigners was likely to find himself in serious trouble. The Poles, though, were in a better position. They were not as rich as the Czechs or East Germans, but they could usually say what they liked, thanks to Gomułka, even if they could not write it, and if they owned land they could usually till it. They could run a small business, or visit friends or family in Western countries. They only got into trouble if they expressed their opposition through active politics, for instance by having their views printed abroad or by unofficial, uncensored means at home.

This was Gomułka's positive side. He was a communist, but he had stopped the killing and the torturing of the Stalin years and, many thought, he had made the best of his country's unhappy geographical situation, wedged between two great countries that were its traditional enemies.

In the 1960s I was impressed by the ease with which I was allowed to travel into and out of Poland, at least once a year, sometimes more often, and to talk openly about politics to a range of lively characters, usually with the help of alcohol in large quantities. I would be offered books and plays for translation into English for the BBC, sometimes even interviews with literary and political figures. I would never have been able to do this in Moscow or Prague or East Berlin.

Then it fell apart. Israel won the Six Day War, much to the Soviet Union's regret, but to the delight of many in Poland who applauded the Zionist state's David-over-Goliath military achievement. Some of those expressing pro-Israeli sentiments were Jewish officers in the Polish army or Jewish Party officials. Prayers for Israel were even being said in Polish churches. Israel's supporters in Poland, even the nation as a whole, were now subjected to a classic anti-semitic witch-hunt.

Hitler had massacred 90 per cent of Poland's Jews. In 1945 only 300,000 had survived out of a pre-war community of 3 million, and by the end of the decade only a tenth of these survivors remained in Poland, most of the rest having emigrated to the new Zionist state that in 1948 opened its doors to every Jew in the world, wherever he or she lived. They seized the opportunity to escape, since it made little sense for them to stay in the land where their friends and families had been gassed. If they were communists, keen to play a part in the new Poland under Soviet guidance, they might wish to remain. And 10 per cent of the original 10 per cent (no more than 30,000) did remain, some rising to high positions in the Party, the army and the secret police. However, most of Poland's Jewish survivors were keen to take advantage of immigration opportunities. Some left to start life anew in the new state of Israel, others in the New World.

In 1967 these few remaining Jews of Poland were put under pressure and accused of responsibility for the nation's troubles. 'Zionist elements' were alleged to be subverting the socialist state. Gomułka, whose wife Zofia was Jewish, said in a speech during the Six Day War that a Pole should only have one motherland. A well-known writer,

Antoni Słonimski, replied that he understood the point, but why did this motherland have to be Egypt?

Jews were summoned by their superiors and asked their attitude to the war. Any reply short of outright condemnation of Israel was then interpreted as Zionism and the result was demotion or dismissal. A press campaign, mounted by the secret police, portrayed Poland's Jews in the familiar role of greedy schemers, masters of disloyal propaganda and manipulators of world finance.

In early 1968 a political crisis arose because of the production of a play, *Forefathers*, by the national poet Adam Mickiewicz. It is a drama of the early nineteenth century that pinpoints Polish resentment against the rule of Tsarist Russia. The producer had highlighted every anti-Russian line and, every time such a line was uttered from the stage, the audience reacted with loud applause. The play became a matter of internal security. Gomułka closed it and issued a personal statement condemning the style of the production.

Then in March 1968 young Poles began to show interest in their southern neighbour. This was a new departure. The usual Polish attitude to the Czechs and Slovaks was one not of hatred, as with Germans and Russians, but of condescension. They were '*pepiczki*', which meant that they were more interested in middle-class values than in fighting for freedom against any foreign invader, whether Russian or German. But in 1968 the Czechs *were* enticed by the possibility of reform within the communist system. Alexander Dubček, the new Czechoslovak leader, had launched the idea of 'socialism with a human face'. Like Gomułka, he was a convinced communist, but he believed that such views could be reconciled with national independence, pluralism and a free press. In many large towns Polish students took to the streets to support the Dubček experiment. But they had not made their alliances with workers in the factories. They had no economic muscle. Units of shock troops, flying from town to town, were able to disperse them and crush their initiative.

One might have thought that, in the light of his 'liberal' background, Gomułka would show sympathy with what Dubček was trying to achieve and that, as an internationalist married to a Jewish woman, he would be appalled by the anti-Zionist campaign. It seems that he did not. The days of toleration were long gone. He allowed the campaign to endure for more than a year. He was ruthless in his treatment of the student demonstrators. And he was one of the toughest when the question arose whether or not to crack down on the Czechoslovak heresy.

When I came to Poland in March 1969, it was not the Poland that I remembered from earlier visits. Earlier in the decade I had been struck by the humour and gaiety that existed amid the poverty and anger. Now the atmosphere was full of small-minded menace. Most of the country's leading Jewish intellectuals, including the theatre producers Jan Kott and Ida Kamińska, had left for Israel or the United States. Some fifty writers had been expelled from the Communist Party and others, such as the author of *Ashes and Diamonds*, Jerzy Andrzejewski, were on a black list of those whose work could not be published. Young people were in jail for having taken to the streets against censorship. A rival communist, Mieczysław Moczar, was challenging Gomułka for the leadership on a platform of good discipline and national pride. The London ambassador, Jerzy Morawski, had been dismissed for lack of vigilance. Books were on sale suggesting that Jews had spearheaded Stalin's excesses and collaborated with Hitler in organizing the Holocaust.[1] Polish armies had just helped the Soviets to stamp out freedom in a neighbouring country. There was no great terror, no widespread fear of violent death, but there was a feeling of moral unease as the Poles came to realize how little they had reacted against this national anti-Jewish campaign, how bad the whole thing looked from any outside standpoint, bearing in mind what had happened to the Jews in Polish places with the terrible names Auschwitz (Oświęcim), Majdanek and Treblinka.

I had with me proof copies of my Gomułka book. When I gave them to Polish officials, they at last realized that it was a serious project. They had refused all help in my research, but now, at the final stage, they arranged interviews, for instance with Party Secretariat member Artur Starewicz and with another grey eminence in the leadership, Jerzy Putrament. A rising star in the Party, Mieczysław Rakowski, then editor of the 'liberal' weekly *Polytyka*, was kind enough to read a proof copy and give me his thoughts over lunch at the Hotel Europejski. They helped me with last-minute improvements, but I was still sad about it. Gomułka, my chosen subject, was never a hero but now he was now emerging as little better than a Russian stooge. His achievement in giving his country a measure of autonomy within the Soviet empire was besmirched. And it was not just the communists who had 'let me down'. The Polish people as a whole had not protested against the anti-Jewish campaign, nor had there been any great outcry against their army's involvement south of the border. My book's first edition, published in July 1969, reflected this disappointment.

In December 1969 I was invited to a conference organized by the British and Polish foreign offices in Cracow. I spoke about recent events with some emotion. As a friend of Poland, I said, I was shocked by the outbreaks of chauvinism and intolerance, not to mention military aggression. Reaction to my remarks from the Polish side was fierce. My views were those of the 'White Guard', or of West German revanchism, they told me, and I was provoking the Polish people to rebellion against Russia, in other words to mass suicide. Our chairman on the British side, Eric Berthoud, a former ambassador in Warsaw, was angry with me for 'rocking the boat'. By my rash outburst, he advised me, I had embarrassed him and deprived myself of the opportunity of dialogue with influential representatives of the Polish government. Sure enough, a mark was put against my name, not only by the Poles but by the British too. It was nineteen years before the British side asked me again to join their Round Table team. And it was nearly eighteen years before I was allowed back into Poland.

In fact it was by my own decision that I stopped speaking to these people, whose behaviour in 1968 shocked the world so deeply. It is true that I was soon on the Soviet Union's black list too, banned from all the Soviet bloc, but even if I had not been I would probably not have gone to Poland. I was no longer enthusiastic to help it towards a more gentle form of government. What they had done, or not done, was abominable. I reassured myself with the thought that the Polish communist side fully shared my view that it would be better for all concerned if I stayed away from their shores.

Gomułka enjoyed one last moment of glory. Willi Brandt, the German Chancellor, came to Warsaw on 7 December 1970 and signed a treaty abandoning German claims to the eastern borders of 1937. The way was now open to full German–Polish diplomatic relations. Brandt also used the visit to apologize on Germany's behalf for the wartime massacres of Poland's Jews. In a famous gesture, which I later recommended to the Soviet government over the Katyń massacre and to the British over the forcible repatriations to the Soviet Union of 1945, he went down on his knees before the memorial to the Warsaw Ghetto fighters.

Five days later Gomułka announced rises of 15 per cent or more in the prices of basic foodstuffs: 16 per cent on flour, 14 per cent on sugar, 17 per cent on meat, 92 per cent on coffee. It was a wretched Christmas present for a tired and deprived nation. Two days later several thousand workers from the Lenin shipyard in Gdańsk marched against Party headquarters. They were met by police who fired into the crowd. Gomułka himself, it turned out, had given orders to use force against the protestors. He was a very different man from the Gomułka who had described the riots in Poznań in 1956 as justified, defended the workers who took part in them and vowed to his people that the methods of Stalin belonged to the irrevocable past. On 17 December the morning shift at the Gdynia shipyard was met with gunfire, killing seventeen as the men got off their train. Many others were killed in Szczecin. Thousands were arrested, including a young Gdańsk shipyard worker, Lech Wałęsa. The official death toll was given as forty-five, but it was certainly much higher.

At this point the Minister of Defence, Wojciech Jaruzelski, told Gomułka that he would not use the army to crush Polish workers. The crisis had brought the Polish leader to the edge of a nervous breakdown. He had been in power for fourteen years and had become blind to criticism, unable any longer to tolerate dissent, any word of which he now believed must be born of malice or disloyalty. He was famous for throwing his telephone at visitors across his office table and for no longer knowing the value of an average Polish monthly pay packet. There was no sympathy for him at his hour of collapse, only a deep sadness that he had failed to fulfil the high expectations that had brought him to power in the heady days of October 1956.

On 20 December the Central Committee met in emergency session and voted Gomułka out of office, together with his friends Zenon Kliszko and Marian Spychalski. He died in September 1982 and, a few days after his burial, some witty fellow wrote on his tombstone, 'Welcome to the Underground!'

I took less interest than I might have in these violent events, being involved in my own political troubles, including my resignation from my own lowly government post. I left office, as it happens, fifteen days after Gomułka did and, like him, I gave up hope of any return, although I did write[2] about Gomułka's fall afterwards on the basis of information provided by Polish friends and, of course, I found myself once again obliged to change the biography. The first edition, finished in 1968 and published by Longmans in July 1969, ended with the words, '. . . it will be many years before such a man as Gomułka can be fairly judged. His achievements, both good and bad, have been so momentous. There is as yet no scale of values capacious enough to weigh him and work out his balance.' The second edition, printed as a Penguin paperback in 1972, takes into account the events of 1968-70 and ends with a tougher verdict: '. . . beaten and humiliated, he can do no more than draw his pension and ponder uncomprehendingly on what went wrong, while Poland, recovering from her latest bloody wounds, judges him very harshly indeed.'

Edward Gierek took over the leadership on the basis of his popularity in Poland's industrial south-west, the Katowice region, known as 'Katanga', after the copper-rich province of Zaïre, because of its mineral wealth. He spent the 1970s in the vain task of trying to build a socialist economy on the basis of joint ventures with western firms and loans from Western banks. It did not work. Poland became massively indebted to Western banks and the money helped the Polish working man and woman only in the very short term. Their living standard was by now one of the worst in Europe, worse than in many developing countries. Eventually rationing was introduced for some food items – meat, sugar and chocolate.

Ten years passed and in the summer of 1980 unrest erupted once again in the Gdańsk shipyards, the nursery of Polish political change. Workers began a strike which was soon an out-and-out rebellion. They barricaded themselves inside the gates, demanding the right to form a trade union free of communist control. The police, conscious of the memory of the shipyard workers who were killed in December 1970, surrounded them but did not attack them. Western television highlighted the events for many days, emphasizing the great risk Poland ran. It was an incongruous picture, a vast crowd of working men standing at the shipyard gates, surrounded by images of the Virgin Mary, whom they knew as 'Queen of Poland', with banners and red and white carnations, to mark Poland's national colours. Much of the time they were on their knees, either praying or singing their national anthem 'Poland is not yet lost, so long as we are alive ...' We were told that they had a leader, Lech Wałęsa, a shipyard electrician, who had been active in the 1970 rebellion and arrested briefly.

The strikes showed no sign of ending. On the contrary, they began spreading to other industrial centres. In August 1980 the deputy prime minister, Mieczysław Jagielski, went to Gdańsk to negotiate with Wałęsa and the strike leaders, as usual ready to offer material benefits, higher pay which everyone knew would soon be wiped out by inflation, but not to concede the basic political demand for the right to choose their representatives by secret ballot, as opposed to having them imposed by the management in the form of the Communist Party.

The crisis moved quickly towards victory for the strikers, at least in the short term, and by the end of August the negotiators sent by communist leader Edward Gierek were ready to concede most of Wałęsa's demands. It was proposed to set up a nationwide trade union movement, to be known as Solidarity, with a membership many millions strong and with the legal right to take part, albeit as an opposition, in the decision-making process.

My letter in the *Daily Telegraph* on 27 August 1980, written at the request of leaders of the Polish community in London, pointed out the moral debt owed by Britain to Poland – our failure to carry out the guarantee of Poland's integrity in 1939, our cover-up in 1943 of Stalin's massacres of Polish officers, our decision at Yalta in 1945 to leave Poland under Soviet control by recognizing Stalin's protégés as the new government and our acquiescence in the rigged Polish elections of 1947, which Stalin had promised at Yalta would be 'free and unfettered'. I might have added Britain's refusal to allow Poles to take part in the Victory Parade in London in 1946, or our general failure to acknowledge Poland's part in the war.

It would be wrong for Britain now to provoke the Poles to armed rebellion and disaster, I wrote. (This is what the CIA-financed Radio Free Europe had done during the Hungarian uprising in 1956.) Poland was lumbered with communism for the foreseeable future. There was, however, a chance that the Poles might obtain some limited benefit from the present crisis, especially trade unions that truly represented the workers' interests.

I wrote that there was meanwhile an urgent need for funds to provide the men on strike with the means to present their case, to communicate with the rest of the country, including writers and other well-educated supporters, and with the outside world. Some of this task was fulfilled by western radio, which was not jammed and was widely heard, but the printed word was a separate problem. No criticism of the socialist system was allowed in the censored press. The alternative view could only be brought to the people through unofficial printing and secret distribution. I therefore invited readers to send money to Count Edward Raczyński, the leader of Polish communities abroad. He had been Polish ambassador in London in 1939 and then President of the government-in-exile, the one de-recognized by Britain after the 1945 Yalta agreement. He and his friends had contacts in Poland who would put the money to its proper use.

Within a few days several thousand people had replied to the appeal. A total of £25,000 was collected and spent on the sort of equipment that the new movement craved, mainly printing presses and duplicators. As in all communist countries, it was a crime to possess such machines, which by Leninist tradition were more danger-ous to public order than machine-guns, more calculated to subvert the people and lead them away from socialism. They had to be smuggled into the country, often piece by piece, then re-assembled and used to produce the printed propaganda that is the life-blood of opposition to authoritarian rule.

Others, however, reacted not with money but with guffaws of sceptical laughter. For instance, the 'This England' column of the *New Statesman* on 19 September quoted my letter as a caricature of the Thatcher era, whereby a Conservative peer, a supporter of the new 'anti-trade-union' laws, was cooperating with a Polish count, a reactionary element if ever there was one, to assist a foreign trade union of shipyard workers. Why would I support a trade union only when it was in conflict with a communist government? They saw only the superficial paradox and cynicism of my gesture and they made up their minds that Conservative criticism of the Soviet system was no more than a covert attack on socialism at home. Labour colleagues assured me that I was hypocritically exploiting the Polish issue so as to bolster Thatcher's 'war against the working classes'. They did not know the extent to which Count Raczyński and his friends in London were accepted in Poland, by workers as well as 'aristocrats', as part of the struggle of the masses against foreign-imposed communist rule.

In December 1980, at a debate with representatives of the Transport and General Workers' Union in Kilburn, north-west London, I tried to explain that the Polish People's Republic, governed by a single party, where the expression of anti-communist views was forbidden by law, could not be compared with the problems faced by left-wing groups in Britain under Mrs Thatcher. At least the latter were permitted to put their socialist point of view, I said, without interference from the police. In Poland the public expression of anti-socialist opinions was a criminal offence. Jack Dromey, speaking on behalf of the TGWU, was not convinced. My efforts on behalf of his Polish brothers were a smoke-screen, he told me. Others in the audience suggested that Lech Wałęsa and his strikers were 'an anti-socialist movement' and any Conservative supporting them did so merely to serve his own class interest.[3]

The outburst put Soviet policies under strain, threatening them with a conflict on two fronts, Poland as well as Afghanistan. It was a Soviet problem, but it re-emphasized western weakness. It showed the West unable to help its friends. Once again the Russian bear was on the point of gobbling up a weaker neighbour, while America did nothing but stand on the sideline and cheer on the little country that was being so brave. I remember being telephoned from Warsaw in the evening of 24 August 1980. Gierek had just appeared on television 'looking older than he had the previous week', promising that the Communist Party 'would honestly change its policy' and in future allow free trade union elections by secret ballot. He announced the dismissal of Prime Minister Edward Babiuch and other leading figures. I then spoke to the well-known academic and former communist Leszek Kolakowski, who was then representing in Britain the strikers' body known as 'KOR', the 'Workers' Defence Committee'. It was a great step towards pluralism, he told me, but 'similar promises have been made before, by Gomułka and others'.[4]

The communists were thus induced to negotiate seriously and, on 30 August, they accepted the Gdańsk Agreement, which Wałęsa proudly signed with a pen bearing an image of Pope John Paul II, his fellow-countryman and mentor. His Solidarity union was now legal, a movement that spanned all Poland. It would enjoy the rights of association – to recruit members, and take part, in a limited way, in political debate.

The agreement was hailed in the West as a triumph for détente. However, most Poles saw it from the outset as too good to be true. I forecast[5] that it would go the same way as Poland's other agreements with the Soviet Union, into an already-full bin of signed and disregarded documents, in particular the Yalta Agreement, in which Stalin had promised that Poland would enjoy 'free and unfettered elections'. I pointed out that the present struggle between Russians and Poles should be seen against a background of hundreds of years of wars. Russian leaders, when they hear the word Poland, tend to reach for their revolvers. The Soviet Union might be the most progressive of nations, but it had an alarming tendency to go back into Poland.

I had in mind Stalin's promise of neutrality when Hitler invaded Poland on 1 September 1939, his promise to help the underground Home Army if they rose up against German rule in Warsaw in 1944, and his promise of safe conduct to Leopold Okulicki and other Polish underground leaders in March 1945. All had been broken. The January 1947 Polish elections had been followed by widespread arrests of those who criticized Stalin's line.

More recent examples of Soviet unreliability included their army's promise to withdraw from Hungary in October 1956 and their savage counter-attack on Budapest a few days later with a consequent loss of 60,000 Hungarian lives. Then there were the agreements signed by Brezhnev in July and August 1968 with Czechoslovak reformist leader Alexander Dubček. They too had been merely a prologue to armed attack.

Maybe Gierek could accept the Gdańsk agreement, but in the long term Brezhnev would never allow it – for two reasons. First, the Kremlin's view was that the defence of Moscow began at the gates of Warsaw, that Poland was essential to the policy of defence through imperial conquest. The Soviet Union 'defended' itself by attacking and occupying a ring of buffer states, whose governments it controlled. The main Soviet armies were in East Germany and Poland was the main channel of communication to them.

Also, the Kremlin would not tolerate a further concession to Polish semi-independence in internal policy. In the other countries of the empire almost all means of production belonged to the public sector. In Poland agriculture was largely in private hands and there was a significant private sector in light industry and retail business. In other countries the churches were dominated by the state. Priests were recruited by the police and, if they forged contacts with fellow-believers abroad, they were liable to arrest for treason. In Poland the Catholic Church enjoyed independence and power and close links with Rome.

The Polish people's freedom to express dissident views and to travel abroad could be allowed only up to a certain limit. If Moscow allowed Poland a second privilege, free trade unions, the result would be an unacceptable dilution of the purity of communist domination, an encouragement to further demands from the largely anti-communist population, and the risk that the 'plague bacillus' of pluralist thinking would spread to other central European nations, then to the Ukraine, so putting the empire in peril, and then perhaps even to Russia itself.

The Polish communists might have signed the Gdańsk agreement, but it was clear from their public statements that the Soviet Union did not support it. On 2 September, three days after the agreement was signed, TASS accused Wałęsa of taking money from Western trade unions who wanted 'to undermine socialism'. On 17 November Leonid Zamyatin, a hard-line ideologist who was later to be Soviet ambassador in London and support the August 1991 *coup d'état*, accused the West on television of pouring 'millions of dollars' into Poland to finance anti-communism. He attacked Wałęsa for leading a campaign to 'undermine the public's faith in the system'.

The question of Gierek's removal had become one of 'when' rather than 'whether' and on 6 September 1980 a Party nonentity, Stanisław Kania, took his place. 'We prefer Kania to Vania,' the Poles joked, 'Vania' being the diminutive of 'Ivan', a common first name for Russian soldiers. The people's mood nevertheless remained deeply pessimistic. An invasion from the East, followed by much Polish bravery and bloodshed and the eventual disaster of military defeat and mass deportation of civilians, seemed as inevitable as the last act of a Shakespeare tragedy.

It was a conflict for which there was no clear way out for either side. The Poles were determined to find an alternative to their position as a Soviet satellite, their foreign policy dictated from Moscow and their economy crippled by the Marxist strait-jacket. A few months earlier colonial Rhodesia had become independent Zimbabwe. The obvious question for the Poles was why Poland should be any less entitled to the same level of independence. Why should European countries be the only ones in the world which were not given the right to rid themselves of colonial rule? Why should the Soviet bloc be the only empire in the world that was being allowed to survive?

It was equally obvious, though, that the Soviet Union would never grant the Poles any such thing. Their military position, in their view, depended on their control of Polish territory and, if they could not enjoy this control with the Polish people's consent, they would have it without it. That was the 'Brezhnev Doctrine'. And they would insist on it, even if this meant using their armed might. Our memories of 1956 and 1968 convinced us that in such matters the Soviet Union does not bluff. Poland would never have full independence. It was a question only of finding out how far the Poles could go without provoking Brezhnev to invoke the doctrine that bore his name. That is the way I thought in those days.

President Reagan assumed office in January 1981, with Lech Wałęsa's Solidarity a legal trade union, and was quick to establish his position as the scourge of the 'evil empire'. On 29 January he said in his first press conference, 'So far détente has been a one-way street that the Soviet Union has used to pursue its own ends.' This was true, I thought at the time, especially in Afghanistan and in Poland. But what was the US President proposing to do about it?

The Soviet government replied not with apologies but with threats. On 30 January TASS reported that the Polish crisis was deepening and the country was being reduced to anarchy, with mass absenteeism, strikes, disruption and the seizing of state property. 'Forces hostile to the socialist state are becoming ever more active.' The same day *Pravda* carried a report from Warsaw accusing Wałęsa and the Solidarity leaders of using blackmail and physical force, of planning the eventual overthrow of communism.

In Poland meanwhile there was a golden age of cooperation between workers' leaders like Wałęsa and the writers who helped them to express their political views. Western visitors found in Solidarity an impressive equality and comradeship. The educated opposition whose job it was to spread the word, abroad as well as at home, worked easily with the working men who organized the new trade unions and therefore controlled the real political power in the movement. Poland's intellectuals did not want to make the mistake of isolating themselves from working people, as they had in 1968. Unity among the opposition was all 'a wonderful dream', said the veteran dissident Adam Michnik, arrested more than a dozen times since 1968 and now able to express his views in print for the first time.[6]

On 16 February, Kania appointed yet another new Prime Minister. It was a fateful choice – Wojciech Jaruzelski, a general and Poland's Minister of Defence. He spoke Russian, having been deported with his family to Russia when war broke out, and had then fought with the Red Army against Germany. He had also been Minister of Defence during the 1970 crisis and he enjoyed the Kremlin's trust. He and his new deputy, the 'liberal' Mieczysław Rakowski, opened further talks with Wałęsa's unions, which were in the awkward position of demanding more pay for less work. Jaruzelski tried to reassure the Kremlin by telling the Sejm (Parliament) that 'evil, hostile forces' were 'expanding their activities against socialism' and vowing that 'Poland will remain forever a member of the Warsaw Pact'.

The Soviet invasion of Poland was turning into the great story that never happened. 'For the fourth time in eight months, the Russians did not invade Poland last week,' said an article in the *Economist*.[7] It seemed that every few days there was some incident, a warlike speech or a government change, apparently suggesting that something drastic would now be done to solve the riddle. Every month the journalists poured into Poland, wrote their apocalyptic stories, waited a few days, doubtless hoping that the doom they had predicted would this time come to pass and provide them with good material, and then withdrew until the next time the mixture started to boil.

On 4 March 1981, Brezhnev addressed his allies, including Kania and Jaruzelski, at a Moscow meeting: 'The socialist community is inseparable. Defence of it is the cause not only of each state, but also of the entire socialist coalition.' It was a clear reference to the supposed danger that the Polish developments posed to his bloc and his famous doctrine.

On 26 March Reagan told reporters that the Polish situation was 'very serious and very tense'. If Soviet troops moved, added his adviser Edwin Meese, it would be a serious threat to world peace and retaliatory measures might be taken, such as a naval blockade of Cuba. The European Community threatened trade sanctions.

It seemed therefore too much of a coincidence on 13 May when Pope John Paul II was shot in St Peter's Square, Rome. Many of us thought, as we heard the news, that it had to be the ultimate example of world communism's alliance with evil. The Turkish attacker, Mehmet Ali Agça, confirmed this, telling the Italian police that the plot was conceived in a hotel room in Sofia, Bulgaria, where another Turk had offered him $1.7 million to shoot the Pope. Agça named three Bulgarian officials who, he said, were involved, one of them being the Bulgarian airlines man in Rome, Sergei Antonov. Western intelligence unearthed disturbing facts to support this theory. There was an undoubted 'spill-over' of the Soviet training of ANC and PLO armed groups into the various left-wing terrorist movements of Western Europe. It emerged that the famous German terrorists Andreas Baader and Ulrike Meinhof had received training at a PLO camp in Jordan. The KGB's indirect involvement in European terrorism was therefore established, since the KGB took pride in their links with the PLO. They may not have carried out acts of murder in Western countries themselves, although of course they had in the 1950s, but their Bulgarian friends were steeped in terrorism, as we knew from the attack on Georgi Markov and others in 1977. Bulgarian assassins might therefore have been operating in Rome at the request of the KGB, or of certain sections of it.

It was clear who stood to gain by the Pope's death. He was an inspiration to the Solidarity movement. Therefore, although nothing was ever proved, it seemed that Brezhnev may well have followed Henry II's example in asking to be rid of the 'turbulent priest' Archbishop Thomas à Becket. After all, the Pope was causing him great inconvenience and on 7 April he had denounced the Pope's Solidarity friends as 'enemies of the socialist system'.

Two weeks after the attempted murder another tragedy hit the Church with the death of Cardinal Stefan Wyszyński, Primate of Poland and hero of the bad years under Stalin. At the same time President Reagan told students at West Point academy that they would soon 'be holding back an evil force that would extinguish the light we have been tending for 3,000 years'. His words reflected the feeling of the time that the Soviet government was now dangerous and wicked. Not content with imprisoning non-violent dissenters at home, launching military aggression in Afghanistan and threatening it in Poland, it was now engaged in a campaign of terrorism against the West's most revered figures.

One could, on the other hand, appreciate the deep anxiety of the Kremlin in 1981, as Solidarity grew in strength, the hostility of the Reagan administration became fiercer and the Soviet army proved themselves unable to destroy armed resistance in Afghanistan. Within a few months Solidarity had acquired 9 million paid-up members and by September they were holding their first Congress in a sports hall in Gdańsk and calling for free elections to the Sejm (Parliament). The Church was by now integrated into state structures. Mass was broadcast on state radio and crucifixes were to be seen hanging on office walls. It was against the principles of Marx and Lenin, against 'democratic centralism', to have two substantial bodies acting independently of the Communist Party's rule in a socialist state.

It would not have been difficult for the Soviet leaders to form the view that the Pope and Lech Wałęsa were key figures in a political process that might prise Poland from the Soviet bloc. In October both East Germany and Czechoslovakia closed their borders with Poland and, once again, the West explained loudly how serious would be the consequences if the Soviet Army did in Poland what it had done in Czechoslovakia in 1968.

When tanks appeared in the streets on 13 December 1981, it was therefore hardly a surprise in itself, although it was Soviet tanks that we had all been expecting, not those of the Poles themselves. In the course of one night the Polish police and army under General Jaruzelski declared martial law and transferred power to a 'military council of national salvation', arresting Wałęsa and 10,000 Solidarity activists. The Polish generals had plotted well and caught the opposition unawares. They set up road blocks and cut all telephones, train services and other means of communication before the Solidarity leaders realized what was afoot. Opposition was therefore possible only on a local basis, without coordination. Even so, nearly 100 Poles were killed in anti-police riots and protests.

The Polish people's resistance had once again been crushed by armed force, inspired from the Russian side of the border. This was expected, in view of the Kremlin's belief in its right to rule neighbouring lands. What was *not* expected, though, was that the deed was this time done not by the 'big brothers' in the East, as it was in September 1939 and in the civil strife of 1944-7, but by the 10 per cent of the Polish nation who over the years had pledged themselves to the Soviet side. Jaruzelski was later to say that he acted out of patriotic duty, to keep the Soviet army from invading and so preserve Polish sovereignty, but at the time not many Poles believed him.

Solidarity's leaders were in jail, with Wałęsa a 'prisoner of the state' hidden in the island castle of Otwock, twenty miles south-east of Warsaw. The army patrolled the streets. Telephone calls and mail, until then monitored by the police secretly and illegally, were now subject to open and official censorship. The Communist Party was back in full control, the official 'communist only' trade unions were given back their monopoly and their relieved Soviet comrades were waiting in the wings. It could hardly be foreseen at this, Solidarity's darkest hour, that they would ever reappear as a political force. The official trade union was allowed to become a fountain of privilege, a distributor of subsidized holidays and cars. It built up its numbers, whereas the illegal Solidarity was reduced to a few thousand active 'underground' members.

Solidarity was in fact merely scotched, not killed. Seeds of the movement remained in the work force. The free trade union was ready to rise from the ashes of December 1981. Solidarity leaders were gradually released and Wałęsa was given his job back as an electrician in the Lenin shipyard. He was soon back in the political arena, though, and the money we had collected for Solidarity in 1980–81, already converted into printing equipment, was being put to good use. Typewriters and printing presses, smuggled into Poland in the days of trade union freedom in 1980–81, were taken from their hiding places. Illegal printing became an important industry. Once again the Solidarity line was proclaimed through secretly printed leaflets passed from hand to hand in factories.

They were no longer, it seemed, the mass movement that they had been in 1980–81. Their numbers in the work place were small and their demonstrations were not the mass rallies of their period of legality. The adrenalin of crisis could not be maintained year after year. The Polish people needed more than that to keep their families alive. A certain 'government by exhaustion' was therefore available to the communist minority. But their banners were still to be seen in public gatherings, for instance at football matches, even though the police fought them, identifying the banner-carriers with binoculars and sending 'snatch squads' to grab them. Solidarity was semi-paralysed, but the police could not stop the movement's existence. And the Church supported them, even though the Primate of Poland, Cardinal Józef Glemp, felt it necessary to maintain a position of neutrality.

In 1984 one priest, Father Jerzy Popiełuszko, became well known for especially defiant behaviour. His 'Mass for the Fatherland', held on the last Sunday of every month, was relayed by loudspeaker to the streets and squares around his church, St Stanisław's in Żoliborz in northern Warsaw. He attracted congregations of up to 10,000 and his fame spread through the country. His oratory appealed not only to men from the steel works near by, but also to workers from other cities. They would come to Warsaw by train, attend his service, tape record the sermon and take it back home for others to hear.

The authorities did not like him. Like John Paul II, he was a turbulent priest, a danger to the state's monopoly of power and a thorn in their side. In the first months of 1984 his house was attacked, his car was vandalized and a tear gas grenade was thrown through his window. The police were trying to warn him off, but he was undeterred and carried on with his sermons.

In October 1984 members of the secret police, the Służba Bezpieczeństwa or 'SB', decided that Popiełuszko was a public menace whose disappearance would in no way be regretted by the government. A number of SB officers led by Captain Grzegorz Piotrowski, whose job it was to curb the Church's political activities, already annoyed by the amnesty of 600 political prisoners that President Jaruzelski had declared three months earlier in an attempt to end the trappings of martial law and rehabilitate his country internationally, decided to take the hint from above seriously and act upon it with appropriate zeal.

On 18 October they waylaid Popiełuszko in his car near Bydgoszcz, dragged him to the side of the road, beat him unconscious and threw him into the boot of their car. They then drove him to the edge of a forest near Toruń, beat him even more ferociously and threw him dead into a reservoir. They planned that he would never be discovered, but his driver had escaped from the police trap and raised the alarm. Soon the whole country knew that the much-loved priest had been kidnapped by police. But there was no sign of him and, as the days passed, his millions of admirers grew ever more fearful as they waited for the inevitable discovery. On 28 October the Pope said public prayers for his safety in St Peter's Square, Rome.

On 30 October frogmen found his body, his hands tied, his mouth gagged, his body bruised, his face lacerated. The news was quickly passed to the highest levels of government and, by them, to the Church hierarchy. When it was announced in St Stanisław's church that evening, there was a moment of shocked silence followed by piercing cries of grief, lasting many minutes, a shout of anguish that soon engulfed the whole nation and beyond. Once again, for a moment, it seemed that Poland's cause was doomed. *The Times* pointed out on 2 November, 'Even in the darkest period of Stalinism, Polish policemen did not resort to the kidnapping and assassination of Catholic priests.'

Piotrowski's excuse when brought to trial was that he had acted in what he perceived to be the interest of the state as communicated to him by his superiors from the highest level. Asked about the ferocity of the attack on Popiełuszko, which amounted to sustained torture, he replied: 'If only he had done what we told him to, we wouldn't have had to hit him so hard.'

On 3 November some 250,000 people attended Popiełuszko's funeral, crowding into the same streets and squares that had previously resounded to the tones of his fiery sermons. 'Solidarity lives because you, Father Popiełuszko, died for it,' said Wałęsa at the graveside. St Stanisław's church at once became, and remains, a place of pilgrimage.

British Foreign Office minister Malcolm Rifkind, whose family originate in Poland, happened to be in Warsaw on a mission planned to heal the breach in Poland's relations with the western world. He found himself caught up in the drama of the mass funeral. On 5 November he visited the grave to lay a wreath – one of the first foreigners to do so – after which he met several Solidarity leaders, in between meetings with communist leaders, explaining that the people of Britain wished to share in Poland's grief. Although it was his decision, taken on the spot in the midst of crisis, he was also acting in line with Margaret Thatcher's policy of backing responsible anti-communist movements in Poland and the Soviet Union in ways that did not always coincide with the strict rules of diplomacy. His example was to be followed by other western foreign ministers. Apart from the socialist Greek government of Andreas Papandreou, which gave comfort to the Polish junta, western ministers visiting Warsaw after 1984 always insisted on meeting Solidarity leaders and on visiting Popiełuszko's grave.

The murder gave new impetus to the Solidarity movement. Their activity in the factories increased, even though anyone caught conducting unofficial trade union activity was liable to instant dismissal. Illegal printers worked even harder. Only a shortage of paper, and police vigilance in shops where paper was sold in large quantities, kept the industry from growing. Money appeared from Poles in the West, enabling ordinary typewriters to be replaced with new 'golf ball' machines. Official printing shops did 'moonlight' work for Solidarity, sometimes for money, sometimes out of a sense of duty, always at considerable risk. By the end of the 1980s Solidarity was beginning seriously to re-emerge.

In August 1987 the Poles finally took me off their black list and I returned to find the country in a worse state than I remembered from my last visit eighteen years earlier. I wrote on my return[8] that there was enough poverty to make nine out of ten Poles weep, while the tenth, the one with access to foreign currency, laughed all the way home from the *bureau de change*. I stayed in the Victoria Hotel, then the best in Warsaw, which meant that there was hardly a Pole to be seen among the guests. I remember dining on smoked salmon, fillet steak and wild strawberries and cream, washed down by a good bottle of Hungarian wine, and paying the waiter with a $20 bill, whereupon he gave me an amount of Polish złotys in change that was the wages of a skilled worker for two weeks.

I met Janusz Onyszkiewicz, then Solidarity's main spokesman. He said, 'We have mineral resources and fertile land. This should be a land flowing with milk and honey. But instead we have farmers ploughing fifteen-acre holdings, drawing their water from a well, with no telephone or electricity, not allowed to rationalize their land holdings, starved of seed and fertilizer, and *still* their productivity is higher than in the public sector of farming.' As we travelled by train from Warsaw to Gdańsk I could see what he meant. There were cows in tiny fields, never more than one or two of them, each one tethered to a post in the ground with a metal chain, slowly walking round and round, turning the pasture into six-yard-diameter circles of new mown lawn, their only change from this routine being when their owners came to milk them by hand into buckets.

We walked from Gdańsk railway station to St Bridget's church. The substantial house belonging to its priest, Father Henryk Jańkowski, was Solidarity's unofficial headquarters, well known for the quality of the refreshments served to sympathetic visitors. We were drinking our coffee when a member of staff came to tell us that security men had surrounded the building. We looked out of the window and there were indeed about twenty of them, mostly in plain clothes. I was honoured to be told that their commander was a full SB colonel. All the SB men outside, it emerged, were known by name and by rank to the Solidarity people inside. They had obviously known of my arrival and had moved into their positions as soon as I went through the door.

We decided nevertheless to set off for Wałęsa's holiday cottage an hour from town. Eleven SB men followed us in three unmarked cars. The cost of the elaborate surveillance must have been huge and I felt obliged to apologize for the burden that I was placing on the shoulders of the already hard-pressed Polish taxpayer. Just outside town a marked police car drew in front of us, forcing us to stop. A man in uniform demanded our documents and took them to the SB in the cars behind, who then spent thirty minutes examining and explaining them, three Polish identity cards and one European Parliament *laissez-passer*. We could see the colonel leafing through them and talking on the radio to his superiors. The policeman then came back to our car, documents in hand, and asked us where we were going. 'We're going on a picnic,' said Onyszkiewicz. The policeman scowled, but he gave us back our papers and allowed us to proceed.

Wałęsa was living with his wife and eight children, four girls and four boys, in a tiny steep-roofed pine chalet in a village reached only by a bumpy track. It had no telephone, which meant that we could not warn him and our arrival was unexpected. He had obviously been enjoying a siesta and he greeted us sleepily in his baggy tracksuit. His wife offered us tea to drink, it being the 'month of sobriety', a Solidarity policy designed to wean the Polish people away from the mass alcoholism that for years had helped to keep them politically docile. He was plumper than I remembered him from television in the great days of 1980-81 and he wore round his wrist a silver bracelet with the Polish word '*Solidarność*' engraved in red.

His quick-fire oratory and frequent movement from subject to subject strained my rusty Polish. He was fed up with the Poles being the paupers of Europe, he told me, and he believed that the 'absurd abstract system' would soon vanish. 'It may have meant something once, when land and factories were being taken over by the people who worked them, but it divided and destroyed and now it has become a labyrinth of the absurd and we have to escape from it.' We talked for about an hour, while the police cars waited for us at the end of the road, not risking the bumps. They then escorted us back to the priest's house in Gdańsk and from there to the station, and they watched through the window, checking that we were aboard, as the train set off back to Warsaw, taking us out of the jurisdiction of their particular branch of the security police.

The next day I met one of Solidarity's illegal printers. He joined us at a café on Nowy Świat, one of Warsaw's main streets. Introducing himself as 'Jacek', he was happy to talk about his work, but not to give his surname or be photographed. He had already served several prison terms and he lived a nomadic life. Once a month he visited his family, but it was a complicated process leaving them. The police had his home 'staked' and, every time he went into it, they would spot him and follow him when he left, hoping to be led to the secret place where he produced his newspaper. They would then confiscate the machinery and arrest everyone they found there. It might take him three days to make sure that he had thrown them all off and was 'clean'. I asked him how many toothbrushes he had. 'One!' he replied, producing it from his top pocket and waving it in the air triumphantly.

I flew home feeling very sad about Poland's predicament. They were 'back to square one'. There was no hope for them. And the most dismal aspect of the story was the ironic fact that in the Soviet Union, their oppressor, there *was* hope. Glasnost and perestroyka had moved into a higher gear after Sakharov's release in December 1986, eight months earlier. In the Soviet Union there was the beginning of dialogue between the communists and the democrats. In Poland there was none. The government and Solidarity's underground opposition had nothing to say to one another. It was weird to see Soviet communism less paralysed than its Polish 'liberal' variety. I wrote about this[9] and was duly attacked by the Polish government's spokesman, Jerzy Urban, in one of his famous press conferences.[10]

Poland's only ray of light, I kept being told, was Margaret Thatcher. They called her 'our iron lady' and had a touching faith in her ability to show the way forward out of the disaster. Even communists seemed to admire her resolution and they often used her argument that short-term sacrifices were essential for long-term progress. I wrote to her on 14 August that she had many 'votes' in Poland and congratulated her on what Malcolm Rifkind had done after Father Popiełuszko's funeral in November 1984. His action, based on her policy, had paved the way for expressions of the same feeling by other Western leaders, including Italy's Giulio Andreotti and Spain's Francisco Ordoñez, and of course Britain's Geoffrey Howe, everyone except the Greeks. She wrote back on 19 August in her own hand from holiday in Cornwall, 'We are always eager for news of Poland and her brave people.'

It was time to exploit her unique position in Polish opinion. In February 1988, helped by a Polish friend, Gustaw Gottesman, a well-known writer, editor and political *éminence grise*, I sent her a ten-page analysis of Poland's situation and a request for her help in easing the pain. Poland was reduced to the status of a Third World country in Europe, I wrote. The average industrial wage, 30,000 złotys a month, had a purchasing power of $60. Many foodstuffs were not available for long periods or were rationed. The rationing system was irregular, depending on which item was scarce at any given time. In February 1988, for instance, meat and chocolate were rationed. The meat ration was two and a half kilos a month, including sausage. The chocolate ration was 200 grammes a month for children under sixteen, with none for adults unless they had access to foreign currency. The shortage of anaesthetics meant that hospitals could not carry out essential operations. Toilet paper was so scarce that people were forced instead to use waste paper or leaves. Basic pharmacy items were seldom available.

Shops would be pestered by disappointed shoppers and they would post signs saying 'no razor blades, no cotton wool, no tampons' to keep away the customers.

On 30 November the government's economic plans were put to a referendum. Less than two-thirds of the electorate voted and, of these, less than two-thirds voted in favour of the measures. It was, in terms of Soviet-bloc elections, a crushing defeat. It then emerged, according to a December 1987 public opinion poll, that 60 per cent of Polish young people wanted to live abroad for a long period or for ever. The reasons they gave were low wages, poor housing and lack of prospects. It was absurd as well as tragic to find such feelings of despair in a land of rich resources and 37 million people, many of them highly qualified in science and technology.

I asked what the West should do about it. In many people's view, the West should do nothing. Poland was after all the Soviet Union's largest ally. Was it the West's fault if the imposed Soviet system had proved unable to satisfy the people's basic economic needs? It made sense in terms of the ideological battle to leave Poland to stew in its own juice as a terrible example to the outside world of the meaning of Marxist–Leninist socialism in practice.

On the other hand, an imaginative policy of 'Marshall Aid' to Poland could be used to loosen communism's grip on the country by showing its inability to operate without western help. It would lessen the chance of unrest in Poland. Any such unrest would have a bad impact on East–West détente and Mikhail Gorbachev's reform process. It would have to be 'sold' to the Polish government on the understanding that it was not an attempt to undermine its sovereign rights or detach it from the Soviet bloc and it would also have to be 'sold' to the 'non-existent' Solidarity movement.

On 8 February the Prime Minister replied to me that, whereas it would be wrong to envisage large grants to the Polish economy, not least because of the $40,000 million owed by Poland to western governments and banks, the West might be ready in due course to make new long-term credits and reschedule Poland's debts. The key to any such policy was that 'the Polish authorities must first show a clear commitment to appropriate reforms'. It was implied, though not spelled out, that this would involve political as well as economic reforms. In other words, if the economy was to be helped, the workforce would have to be placated. How could this be done? The authorities had no way of improving living standards, certainly not in the short term. The money was not there. They could only satisfy workers' demands by resuming their dialogue with Lech Wałęsa and the Solidarity movement. It was an economic necessity, even though its implications were highly political and liable to strain Poland's entire system. This was the bitter pill that the Polish government was being invited to swallow.

If 'Marshall Aid' was to be forthcoming, the country's economy would have to be brought under discipline. The principle of sacrifice in the short term in the hope of prosperity in the future, although rejected in the referendum, would be reinstated. Prices would have to be increased and wages held down. Food subsidies would be phased out and the złoty held at its present level. Wage differentials would be increased and over-manning reduced in such heavy industries and 'centres of working-class achievement' as mining and shipbuilding. The conditions to be set by the West were, in short, a Marxist's nightmare.

In early 1988 I was asked by the Foreign Office to join the Anglo-Polish Round Table, to be held at Rozalin outside Warsaw. I had not been invited since 1969, when the Polish side denounced me as a 'white guard'. We arrived on 6 May to find the Gdańsk shipyard and the mines in Nowa Huta again on strike. Wałęsa and several of his leading supporters were occupying the premises, while the police formed a cordon round the wall, hoping to starve them out. Several leaders of Solidarity, including Onyszkiewicz, were under arrest. Others, for instance Adam Michnik, had taken sanctuary on Church property. Other large factories were coming out in sympathy. Our Round Table team consisting of seventeen MPs, journalists, diplomats, academics and business people were driven to Rozalin and accommodated in a dilapidated country house, with no telephone or hot water.

My 'friend' who had 'helped' me with my Gomułka book in 1969, Mieczysław Rakowski, by then deputy prime minister, came to dinner and told us of his admiration for Margaret Thatcher, whose trade union laws were the basis for his own, and his confidence in the wide generosity of the World Bank. Poland was only poor and in need of loans today, he went on, because it had never had any colonies to exploit and because Britain betrayed it by not providing support at the beginning of the Second World War.[11]

When Rakowski came to discuss Solidarity, his attitude was even tougher. He would neither talk to Wałęsa or re-legalize his movement, he told us. He pointed out that it makes no sense for workers to demand 50 per cent pay increases when a country's productivity is 7 per cent less than it was ten years ago, even in the face of 70 per cent inflation. He referred to the strikers' indiscipline and ventured to suggest how the British Prime Minister would react in the same case. He made no suggestion as to how the workers' anger was to be tackled in the long term. Nor did he explain why the World Bank or Western business might see fit to invest in an economy that was in such disarray. Rakowski sat down and our British chairman, Mark Bonham-Carter, then asked us all to raise a glass to 'the Polish People's Republic'. I could not bring myself to join him.

Meanwhile word reached us that Solidarity leaders, both in and out of jail, were unhappy that we had come to Poland, so sharp was the conflict, especially since the chairman of the Polish side was a top man in the official communist trade union. We slept that night, several to a room, reeling from the deputy Prime Minister's tactless speech and feeling that maybe we were making a mistake in being there at all.

Our talks had hardly begun the next morning when the writer Neal Ascherson arrived from Warsaw with alarming news. Onyszkiewicz, Solidarity's spokesman, had been sentenced to three months in gaol for 'slandering the state' by giving inaccurate information to the BBC. The trial had been held at seven o'clock that morning and had lasted twenty minutes. The authorities hoped in this way to minimize publicity, but the shabby pretence at justice attracted attention to the case out of all proportion to the severity of the sentence. Janusz's wife Joasia had been born in Britain. The family were well known to many of us and the timing of his trial, in the first hours of a bilateral meeting with British experts, could hardly have been worse. It was worse than a crime. It was a mistake.

The news was whispered round the meeting. As soon as I heard it, I suggested that we suspend our talks to discuss the fate of this man whom so many of us knew. He had in fact, not so many years earlier, attended a Round Table meeting as a Polish delegate. I said that his proper place was with us at Rozalin, not in a Warsaw jail.

The British team then retired to another room to discuss it. The MPs and the journalists were for suspending the meeting. Our chairman, Mark Bonham-Carter, and the academics wanted to carry on talking. So did a leading British businessman, who spoke of the need to build up trading links over a long period, whatever difficulties might appear. 'A week may be a long time in politics, but ten years is a very short time in business,' he pointed out. Norman Reddaway, a former British ambassador in Poland, argued weirdly that the government could not be blamed for a decision taken by the Polish courts, which were a fully independent body. A Labour MP, Frank Field, then said that he had been in favour of maintaining the meeting, but now, having heard the ex-ambassador's arguments, he wanted to break it off.

I urged suspension. It was unthinkable for us to stay as guests of the men who had just put our friend in jail for no good reason. If we did, we would pay a heavy political price for abandoning at its hour of need a movement that looked set to become the next Polish government. And I made it clear that I would leave Rozalin whatever was decided, even if my view was the minority. After some debate, the majority accepted this point of view and Bonham-Carter was given the unenviable task of informing the Polish team that we no longer wished to sit around the table with them. We walked round the courtyard in small groups, waiting for him to emerge from the encounter, which he finally did, pale with embarrassment, deeply worried about how our rudeness would affect his future meetings and, as I later learnt, blaming me personally for having initiated the scandal. He made sure that I was never invited to a Round Table again.

Polish communist delegates, who had nailed me as the 'main initiator' of the rupture, joined the mêlée in the courtyard and showered me with abuse. I was called a warmonger and a hooligan. We packed our things, some of us found cars, the British embassy sent a bus and we made our way back to Warsaw. The next morning, 8 May, some of us went to Mass at St Stanisław's church in Żoliborz to pay our respects at Father Popiełuszko's grave. Most then flew home.

I took the 6.07 express to Gdańsk the next morning and was invited to another good lunch by Father Henryk Jańkowski, who had just been to the police station to return a truncheon dropped during a recent police attack on St Bridget's church. We discussed the 'Marshall Aid' idea and Adam Michnik, a fugitive from justice enjoying asylum in the priest's house, said that it was in Gorbachev's interest to have dialogue between the Polish government and Solidarity. It was the only way of averting a breakdown of the economy of a substantial ally. I then sat in on a long telephone talk between the Bishop of Gdańsk and the local chief of police over how to end the strike. It is a bizarre industrial dispute, I thought, where the management is represented by the police, the workers by the Church.

Jańkowski's house was a centre of supply for Wałęsa and his men on the other side of the shipyard wall. Every few minutes packets of food, clothes and letters were taken from the house by groups of young local boys or 'urchins' ('*kajtki*' in Polish), like Gavroche and the Artful Dodger, who ran with them towards gaps through the wall or over it ('*przez płot*' in Polish). I was keen to go with them. It was the only way of talking to Wałęsa, but Jańkowski advised me that if I tried and failed, or even succeeded, too much embarrassment would result. Instead he asked a young man to guide me on a walk round the perimeter.

A few hundred yards from Jańkowski's house I began to feel that we were not alone. Then suddenly men in light-blue fatigues moved in on us, their hands reaching into my pockets for my camera and passport, bundling me in the wrong direction. A few seconds later I was made to get into the back of a police van which was also being used as a rest area for policemen guarding the shipyard. They had been up all night, it seemed. Some were reading comics. Others were slumped in various ungainly positions, snoring loudly, their riot gear hanging on hooks, their machine-guns and tear-gas launchers scattered everywhere. It was a very strange feeling, the only time that I had ever been arrested anywhere, although I was indeed worried about my young Polish guide. They were not going to do anything to me, I was confident of that, but he had a job and a family. I would be flying home to London the next day, but he would be staying in Gdańsk.

After about twenty minutes in the back of the van we were taken in a decrepit police car to a police station on the edge of the city and handed over to a Security Service (SB) interrogation team. They wore civilian clothes and they were not polite and, when I asked to be questioned in my own language, they refused. They wanted to know why I was in Gdańsk, why I spoke Polish, why I was taking photographs. My explanation that I was vice-chairman of the European Parliament's human rights sub-committee made little impression. I was by now becoming bored and I told them that Poland badly needed a perestroyka campaign. The Soviet Union had much to teach the Polish police, I said, and they should take lessons in courtesy from the KGB at Moscow airport, who had asked me questions in much gentler fashion two months earlier. It made the Polish policemen very angry. The suggestion that the Russian police were more polite or civilized than they were caused deep resentment. At this point the officer in charge felt the need to check with Warsaw. I waited for fifteen minutes, standing in the corridor outside his office, while he applied himself to the telephone, explaining to his superiors what his men had done and inviting suggestions as to what he should now do.

I do not know what Warsaw said, but it put my SB men in a more flexible frame of mind. It was all a mistake, they said, smiling mirthlessly and handing me back my camera and passport. They assured me that the young Pole was already released and they bowed me out through the main door. I hailed a taxi and arrived back at St Bridget's some two hours after leaving it, to find Michnik and the other hardened jailbirds of the Solidarity leadership there to greet me with approval and merriment. At last I was 'one of them', it seemed, since I too had been a guest of the Polish taxpayer, albeit for rather less than one hour, whereas they had amassed many decades in various prisons. There was time only to drink a quick toast to Poland's future before I caught the early evening express back to Warsaw. Radio and television people were waiting at the Victoria Hotel, keen to know how I had survived my few minutes in a communist prison and (yet again) by what right I, a supporter of Margaret Thatcher's trade union laws, was at such pains to defend a foreign trade union.

Flying back to London the following afternoon, I turned to *The Times*'s back page. 'Lord Bethell Detained' was the alarming headline that caught my eye. It was a long article for such a brief incarceration, but it illustrated the sensitive balance of Polish politics, how easily it could be disturbed, and it gave me the chance to write about the need to help the Solidarity movement.[12] The Polish press, informed by the SB that I had actually crawled into the shipyard through a hole in the fence, was also moved to cover the little story. I was accused of 'a blatant criminal act' and it was suggested that 'even a non-aristocratic guest, used to a minimum of good manners, does not behave towards his hosts like some loutish hooligan'. A Pole who sneaked into a British coal-mine during a miners' strike, they said, would also have found himself in trouble with the police.[13] This was true, but the comparison was unfair, since I had never entered the shipyard.

The strike ended a few days later. Wałęsa and his friend Tadeusz Mazowiecki marched out of the shipyard arm-in-arm, apparently defeated again. But there was a limit to the number of blows of this type that communist power could take at a time of radical change in Moscow. Western journalists wrote Solidarity off as a spent force, just as they had in 1981, and once again there was an uneasy calm as both sides took stock and tried to mend their fences. I complained to Zbigniew Gertych, Polish ambassador in London, about the rude articles. His reply was to invite me to lunch at his home, where he apologized and asked me not to worry. They were written by 'little dogs' (*piaski* in Polish), he told me, meaning by journalists under SB control.

The Polish government wanted nothing that might obstruct Margaret Thatcher's visit to Warsaw, scheduled for later in 1988, which they hoped to use to instil into the Polish people a sense of Thatcherite discipline and belief in long-term benefits. The communist government had seized on her, an unlikely ally indeed, as a figure trusted by the Polish nation who might help to persuade them to make short-term sacrifices in the hope of long-term gains. Articles by Norman Tebbit began to appear in the Polish press.

Wałęsa's request was now, on the face of things, modest. He wanted the rights of a 'legal opposition', access to the press and media and to decision-makers in their capacity as representatives of a section of society. They were asking, in other words, for pluralism. The government indicated in reply that they were ready for allow 'socialist pluralism', open debate between groups of different Marxist interpretation. However, non-socialist bodies like Solidarity would still remain banned. The outside world would not accept this. Western embassies in Warsaw were in close touch with Solidarity leaders, following the example set by Malcolm Rifkind in 1984. Vice-President Bush had received Wałęsa at the American embassy. The government's insistence that Solidarity no longer existed and could not be allowed to exist became less and less credible.

Some of us now hoped to make the Thatcher visit, by which the Polish government set so much store, a catalyst for further change in their attitude. I advised her, instead of inviting Wałęsa down to Warsaw, to call on him at St Bridget's in Gdańsk, his headquarters, in other words to give him the status of Leader of the Opposition and to pay special honour to his movement. This idea was put forward by the British side and the Poles had little alternative but to agree. If they had not, there would have been no Thatcher visit.

In late August 1988 strikes began again, only this time the government indicated their willingness to bring Wałęsa and his people into the negotiations. 'The Polish economic puzzle consists of three essential pieces: the communist government, the unofficial trade unions and the sources of financial help,' I wrote.[14] None of these pieces could achieve anything, unless it fitted in with the other two. On 19 September, after a long Sejm debate in which Prime Minister Zbigniew Messner was made the scapegoat for failure to implement economic reform, the Polish government resigned *en masse*. New people were needed, said Jaruzelski, to implement the reforms. A few days later Mieczysław Rakowski, whom I knew from 1969 and the May 1988 Round Table dinner, won the dubious honour of being made Prime Minister of another beleaguered communist government.

It was a dangerous moment for Europe as a whole.[15] Whatever happened, whether there was another military takeover, or a Soviet invasion, or even a hand-over of power to Solidarity, hard-liners in Moscow would blame it on Gorbachev and his reformers. If Poland went badly from Moscow's point of view, which seemed inevitable, the clock would be put back. Perestroyka and East–West relations would be at risk. On 29 September I took Onyszkiewicz to 10 Downing Street, where he explained to Charles Powell, the Prime Minister's assistant, his hope that the Thatcher visit would pull together all the strands needed for progress, economic as well as political. I talked to Powell about his boss's visit several times in the course of the following month. On 19 October I wrote to her, asking her to tell Jaruzelski and the others 'that, if Solidarity is brought on board, Britain and the West will see more sense in encouraging the rescheduling of existing debts, the offering of new credits and the setting-up of joint ventures'.

Rakowski replied with an act of aggression. He closed the Gdańsk shipyard, Wałęsa's workplace and Solidarity's cradle, explaining that it was done 'for purely economic reasons' and on the basis of sound Thatcherite principle. It was a trap, writes Margaret Thatcher, one no less dangerous for being clumsy.[16] On 2 November she arrived in Poland, the first British Prime Minister ever to visit the country. 'She is, after all, a Polish heroine,' I wrote.[17] She met Rakowski that evening and found him 'not an impressive or persuasive advocate' for closing the shipyard. He had timed the closure only so that she would feel obliged to approve it, but she told him that, since 90 per cent of its work was done for the Soviet Union, its viability depended only on the exchange between the rouble and the złoty. 'Where there is no real market, there can be no real estimate of profit or loss.'

The next afternoon she visited Jerzy Popiełuszko's grave at St Stanisław's church and spoke to the murdered priest's mother. 'He will always live in your heart,' she told her. She then spoke to Jaruzelski for nearly two hours, telling him that trade unions were less important in Britain than in Poland, since Britain had free elections. She expanded on this theme that evening at a dinner for Jaruzelski and his ministers: 'History teaches us that you only achieve higher growth, only release enterprise . . . when people have freedom of expression, freedom of association, the right to form free and independent trade unions . . .' She used the same speech to tell the Poles that in ten days time, 13 November, a contingent of Poles who had fought during the war in British uniform would for the first time take part in the Remembrance Day march past the Cenotaph in London. The fact that the Poles, uniquely of Britain's wartime allies, were not allowed to march in this parade had been a running sore in the Polish people's feelings towards Britain since the June 1946 Victory Day parade.[18]

The next day she flew to Gdańsk for the long-awaited visit to St Bridget's church. Father Jańkowski gave her a specially good lunch, including pheasant stew, and Onyszkiewicz did the translating. It was then suggested that she might like to see the church. She and Wałęsa walked together the few steps across the yard and through the great door, to find the building full of supporters, all of whom rose to their feet as she entered and sang the hymn 'Lord, give us back our free Poland'. She could not keep the tears from her eyes.[19] Even larger crowds welcomed her as she walked through the city in her green outfit, the Polish colour of hope, waving to the crowds but not returning their V-for-Victory salutes. When the great day of Polish freedom came, she told them, they would find Britain ready not only to stand and cheer, but also to help in practical ways. She can hardly have imagined how quickly she would be called upon to redeem this promise.

She helped them, I suppose, as best she could, making known her sympathies while being careful not to insult her communist host. And Jaruzelski had the last word. She was already in her seat in the Royal Air Force machine, about to take off for London, when he arrived in his car unexpectedly on the tarmac and jumped out with a large bunch of flowers. And so, in spite of their fierce arguments, she was in the end charmed and impressed by the military ruler and his gallant Polish gesture. 'He allowed me to visit his opponents. It was generous of him,' she told me at 10 Downing Street the following Monday, 7 November. She also said that, although she had been deeply moved by her reception at the church in Gdańsk, she was disturbed by Solidarity's lack of detailed knowledge in matters of politics and economics.

In fact, the general was not being generous but merely facing reality, which was that the days of communist rule were numbered. The picture had changed since the arrogant communist behaviour during the strikes a few months earlier. Wałęsa had shown that he could paralyse the nation at will. And the government no longer had the strength to use punitive measures against him. The word from Moscow was that Poland's problems must be solved without bloodshed. The Soviets were not prepared to embark on another 'Hungary' or 'Czechoslovakia'. And the word from the west was that no help could be expected for Poland's battered economy until Solidarity was brought into the political arena.

The government therefore set Solidarity another trap, inviting it to join them in new Sejm elections on a joint list, prepared in advance, on which they would be allowed to put forward up to 40 per cent of the names. Then, after the elections, they would be asked to join a coalition government. Solidarity MPs would become ministers in certain economic areas, though of course a communist would be prime minister and communists would retain such key departments as defence, internal and foreign affairs. Solidarity would then be part of the 'establishment' and they would have influence. Government would no longer be an exclusive communist preserve.

The difficulty was that in any conflict they would be a minority and liable to be outvoted. Then, being part of the coalition, they would have to go along with the policies with which they disagreed. They would have responsibility with influence but without power, unable to criticize without criticizing themselves. Their political popularity depended on their readiness to point out the disasters that were the unavoidable consequence of the socialist system. They would be blamed for events over which they had no control and they would lose this popularity.

They agreed instead to take part in 'round table' talks with the government and as a result of these talks, in early 1989, agreement was finally reached for Solidarity to take part in elections to both houses of parliament. The elections would be determined in advance in the sense that in the more powerful Lower House (Sejm) communists and their allies would have a guaranteed majority. Solidarity would then be a legal opposition, operating legally from their minority parliamentary base. Elections duly took place on 4 June 1989, and Solidarity swept the board at every level where they were allowed to compete. Jaruzelski was forced to admit that his party had lost the election, even though he and it still ran the government.

It was an artificial state of affairs that could not long continue. By the summer it was clear that the Communist Party's allies were uneasy about the impossible position in which they were placed by the round table agreement. Sejm members began to think about their futures. Thousands of East Germans were finding their way to the West through Hungary. Rioting broke out in East Berlin and, again, Gorbachev refused to allow the use of force. Rakowski, who had by now reached the less-than-dizzy height of Communist Party leader, opened talks with Solidarity, asking them to suggest a new prime minister, on the understanding that Jaruzelski would retain the presidency, that communists would retain the ministries of defence and internal affairs, and that Poland would remain within the Warsaw Pact. Wałęsa put forward Tadeusz Mazowiecki as his candidate. 'For the first time relations with the Soviet Union will be based on relations between peoples rather than between parties,' he told the Sejm. They duly elected him Prime Minister on 24 August 1989, by 378 votes to four, with forty-one abstentions.

Three days later I was once again at Father Jańkowski's house in Gdańsk. We could hardly believe what had happened. Would Moscow tolerate a Poland under non-communist rule? Would the Solidarity leaders, mostly writers and academics, be able to run the country without running into bankruptcy and a communist backlash? The economy was in a worse state than ever. Many in the towns were going hungry and meat was almost unobtainable. We went across to St Bridget's church for midday Mass and, when Father Jańkowski read out the message I had brought from Margaret Thatcher, the congregation burst into loud applause at the mere mention of her name. Was it not all happening too quickly? When I had last lunched in that house, fifteen months earlier, Wałęsa had been under siege in the shipyard, Michnik had taken sanctuary on church property and I had been arrested for getting too close to the shipyard wall.

Lunch was unreal. Wałęsa told me why he had chosen Mazowiecki to be Prime Minister and advised me that it was in the West's interest to build up the Polish economy. If we succeeded, we would have a market of another 40 million people for the goods we produce. 'This week our farmers are gathering in the harvest, loading it with pitchforks. It would be better for both of us if they used British tractors.' On a less serious note another guest at the lunch, the Polish-American heiress Barbara Johnson, told us of her plans to buy the shipyard for $100 million and turn it into a profitable private company.

The next morning (28 August) Prime Minister Mazowiecki saw me briefly to make a similar plea for economic help. 'We must act fast, because only at this precise moment will I be able to count on overwhelming public approval,' he told me. Most of the civil service and the armed forces had pledged him their support, he said. Solidarity would not act like the Afghan opposition, vowing a fearful vengeance against those who had backed the previous regime. Their devotion to communist ideas had never been more than superficial, he pointed out. 'And if they cannot support us, we will replace them.' True Marxists would always find a welcoming home for their talents in East

Berlin or Prague, he added, not foreseeing that within a few weeks the communist system would be gone there too. But it was up to the West meanwhile to prop up this strange and fragile non-communist structure, isolated as it was inside the Soviet bloc. We drank in grapefruit juice to the non-return of communism and I wished him well in his dangerous experiment.

We had no idea what was going to happen, that within ten weeks Berliners would be dancing on the Berlin Wall, that within three months the communists in Czechoslovakia would be overthrown, that before the end of the year the dictator of Romania would be shot dead and that soon the Soviet Union would no longer exist. By the time I next visited Poland, in 1990, it was all different. Terrible problems remained, but they were not the ones that I had fought with such emotion since the early 1960s. The 'Polish People's Republic' was the 'Republic of Poland'. Dzierżyński Square was Bank Square and the 'militia' were the 'police', as they had been in 1939. Gorbachev had admitted Stalin's responsibility for the Katyń massacre and Mieczysław Rakowski had retired from the political scene. It was almost as if those fifty years of foreign rule had never happened.

16. The Fall of 'Sir Dracula'

Romania was a Balkan tragedy that for several years stayed untouched by the liberalism that came with Gorbachev's reforms. A relic of the past, buried at the outskirts of Europe, clouded in many western minds by the myth of the Transylvanian vampire, the so-called 'Conducator' of Romania, Nicolae Ceauşescu, had ruled the country since the death of Stalin's friend Gheorghe Gheorghiu-Dej in 1965. He ran an old-fashioned dictatorship, as if Stalin was still half-alive, as if no one had yet had the courage to drive a stake through his heart.

He gave many of the nation's top jobs to members of his substantial family. His wife Elena was a member of the Politburo, as well as being put forward as Romania's leading scientist. Dissent from the Communist Party's line was brutally repressed and permission to travel abroad or emigrate virtually impossible. Romania had once been the granary of Europe, but the inefficiency that comes with central control of agriculture was reducing it to near starvation.

Ceauşescu's most successful export was his population. Rich Romanians could buy their relatives out of the country. The 250,000 Germans were especially keen to make use of this facility, since they all had somewhere to go, a country ready to accept them. In the late 1980s the Federal Republic was buying 12,000 Germans a year from Romania for £4,000 each. Educated Germans cost more, and even higher prices were demanded for anyone in prison. At the same time, while exporting his Germans for large sums, Ceauşescu was keen to increase his population as a whole. He made abortion punishable by ten years in jail, and every married woman was expected to have at least five children. If she did not, money was deducted from her husband's pay packet.

When it came to foreign policy, however, we found the dictator's policies more interesting. Romania was the only member of the Soviet bloc that did not break with Israel after the Six Day War in 1967. And its armed forces did not take part in the invasion of Czechoslovakia the following year. As a result, he received the highest rank of the Légion d'Honneur from the hands of General de Gaulle personally and was honoured by many other Western leaders. He was even made an Honorary Citizen of Disneyland. They knew about his internal policies, but they preferred to turn a blind eye to them, so as to encourage him along the path of greater independence from the Soviet Union.

He thus became the West's favourite communist leader and, some years later, the British government of the time, led by James Callaghan and David Owen, decided to invite him too. There was nothing strange about that. Many communist leaders had come to Britain since Stalin's death, at the government's invitation. Some of them had even been invited by the Queen to lunch at Buckingham Palace. The surprise was that the Romanian leader and his wife were to arrive in Britain on 13 June 1978 not on a government-to-government basis but on a *state* visit. It meant that Nicolae and Elena would be the Queen's personal guests. It is not of course known what the Queen thought about having to play host to this controversial person who sold his citizens for money. She acted on ministerial advice. And so they arrived at Gatwick airport and were taken from there in the royal train to Victoria station, where they were met by the Queen and driven to Buckingham Palace in a horse-drawn open carriage. In her speech after dinner at Claridge's hotel that evening she spoke of his 'heroic struggle' for Romania's independence, adding how much Britain was 'impressed by the resolute stand you have taken to sustain that independence'.

Ceauşescu spent much of the next few days in talks with Owen and Callaghan, while his wife received honorary degrees from the Royal Institute of Chemistry and the Polytechnic of Central London. The Romanian embassy had previously explained the need for a long red carpet for Elena Ceauşescu to walk down on her way to the platform, and for all those involved to be clothed in full academic dress. These were unusual items to be used at ceremonies sponsored by the scientific bodies in question and they were only obtained with difficulty.

The high point of the visit was the exchange of gifts and honours. The Queen gave Ceauşescu a rifle with a telescopic sight and his wife a gold brooch, receiving in return two hand-woven carpets. She made him a Knight Grand Cross of the Order of the Bath. He gave her the

Star of Romania and took the lavish 'GCB' collar back to Bucharest, where it was displayed in a special pavilion open to the public and dedicated to the dictator's glory, a demonstration to the Romanian people of the esteem in which their leader was held by rulers of great nations.

Only one small incident marred the state occasion. In the early evening before the Claridge's dinner one of London's best-known Romanian émigrés, Ion Ratiu, arrived with a small group of fellow-Romanians and a few placards outside the hotel entrance, ready to show their displeasure at the presence in Britain of the man who was causing such suffering in the country they had been obliged to leave. However, as the motorcade arrived, the Metropolitan Police moved in on the demonstrators, fenced them in with crowd-control barriers, asked them to move into another street and drove a long truck between them and the point where Ceauşescu was due to arrive. The police had received orders that the Queen's guest must not be embarrassed by the sight of these people who so much disliked him.

Ion Ratiu argued with the police, demanding the right to express his point of view in a peaceful demonstration. His words fell on deaf ears. He and his friends could still not see the hotel entrance. He then climbed over the barrier, as a result of which he was immediately arrested, taken in a van to Savile Row police station, charged with obstruction and fined £50. He therefore wrote to me to express his shock at what had happened. He had always believed, he wrote, that in Britain every person is entitled to express a legitimate point of view. He had been prevented from doing this and now, because he had insisted, he was left with a criminal record.

At this point I had little concern for Romania. I had never been there and, if anything, I understood the government's wish to court Romania's dictator as a means of embarrassing the Soviet Union. I understood what a valuable tactic it can be to drive a wedge between adversaries and I recalled Winston Churchill's classic decision in 1941 to support his old enemy Stalin in order to win the war against Hitler. I nevertheless felt uneasy about the hypocrisy involved. We were pandering to the vanity of a brutal oppressor, in peacetime, allowing our country's good name and the prestige of our Queen to be used to prop him up, so discouraging the Romanians in exile who believed in democracy. It was wrong, I thought, that they had not been allowed to make their protest outside Claridge's hotel.

The police had behaved heavy-handedly, I thought. If anyone deserved to be arrested it was the Queen's guest, not the harmless émigré, Ion Ratiu. I therefore wrote to the Home Office and told them so. And in May 1979 the new Conservative minister, Leon Brittan, wrote back to say that he agreed. New instructions had been given to the police, he said, not to prevent anti-dictator protests of this sort in the future.

The Papusoiu Case

The Home Office had still not learnt enough about the Romanian regime. On 14 March 1983, the Romanian citizen Stancu Papusoiu, who had smuggled himself into Britain on a truck, asking to stay as a refugee on the basis that he 'did not like communism', was served with Home Office form IS 92 ordering him to report to Heathrow airport for a flight to Bucharest. It was the beginning of an alarming episode that put in question a large area of government policy towards Eastern Europe and threatened the political career of at least one Home Office minister.

A British friend of Papusoiu, Shan Rees, went with him to Isis House, an immigration office in London, to argue the point that Romania, in spite of its independent foreign policy, was one of the most brutal regimes in Europe. After a few minutes two policemen came into the waiting-room, took away Papusoiu's cigarette, handcuffed him and took him down to the cells. As they dragged him away, he screamed for her to help him.

They told Shan that, although this was not the usual procedure, they were afraid that he might kill himself or 'go to ground'. This was why his deportation to Romania was being brought forward: 'He's got to go back, so he might as well be put out of his agony.' She was allowed to visit him for a few minutes on the eve of his removal. On a blackboard outside his cell were written the words 'Escaper – Suicidal'.

Only after he had been put on the Romanian Airways direct flight to Bucharest on 16 March, by Securicor guards, did the enormity of the affair become public. It was the first forcible removal of any individual to Romania or the Soviet Union since the last Russian soldiers had been repatriated on the basis of the Yalta Agreement in May 1947, shortly before the onset of the first cold war. The press also noted the very strange behaviour of the Labour Party in the matter. They behaved strangely inasmuch as they did nothing.

The Times pointed out[1] that Papusoiu was an unfashionable Home Office victim. If he had been a Chilean or an Irish Republican or the Pakistani fiancé of a British woman, Roy Hattersley would have been quick to attack. Still, the press made up for this inactivity. A half-page in the *Sunday Express*[2] featured a photograph of David Waddington, the Home Office minister responsible, under the heading 'Britain's Day of Shame', describing the deportation as 'this wicked act' and rejecting Waddington's explanation that 'any punishment he receives will be a direct result of his illegal departure from Romania, and not based on his political or religious beliefs'. In the Home Office's view, Romania's laws forbidding foreign travel were deplorable, but they did not amount to persecution.

The press was quick to compare Papusoiu's removal to the much larger affair of the forcible repatriation of Soviet citizens in 1945. This is why they telephoned me. *The Times* wrote, 'The spectacle of a young Romanian being frogmarched, handcuffed and protesting, on to a 'plane bound for Bucharest does little for British pride in its traditions.' The Home Office kept pointing out that our laws on asylum protected those facing persecution, not prosecution. I kept replying that in a country where it was a serious crime to go abroad without permission the two words mean much the same.[3]

On 28 March I pointed out in *The Times* that it was nonsense for the Home Office to expect a flood of immigrants from Romania or the Soviet Union. In 1982 the total number of applications from those two countries had been thirty-two. Later that day I initiated a House of Lords debate, in which Lord St Oswald suggested that 'something pretty foul was done' and the future Master of the Rolls, Lord Donaldson, used especially blistering language. 'To send someone innocent of anything that we can admit to be a crime, and in breach of Article 13 of the United Nations Universal Declaration of Human Rights, to certain imprisonment behind the Iron Curtain seems to be almost impossible to defend,' he said. He also wanted to know why the 'uncriminal' Papusoiu had been handcuffed in an immigration office. Handcuffs should only be used in serious criminal cases. And why was he arrested at all, when he had committed no crime, before he had even failed to obey the Home Secretary's order to leave the country?

And if it was untrue, as the Home Office assured us, that Papusoiu had been frogmarched on to the aircraft, was he nevertheless led there reluctantly and in handcuffs? 'If so, what is the difference? To whom was he presented in this sad condition? To the Romanian secret police? Did they give back the handcuffs to Securicor and put their own on, as happened to Bakunin's fetters at the frontier when he was transferred from a Habsburg to a Tsarist jail?' I then asked why the man had been deported without anyone even collecting his few pitiful belongings for him – a pair of trousers, a pair of shoes, some postcards and a mouth organ. These were questions that the Home Office minister, Lord Elton, was able to answer only with difficulty and amid widespread objection from all sides of the House.

The fact that Papusoiu was an eccentric and wayward character, liable to contradict himself in the statements he made to officials, and a man with no special claim on British hospitality, could not conceal the deep concern felt in the country at the idea of handing over any man, whatever his faults, whatever rights he may or may not have had under the international convention on refugees, to the tender mercies of a man like Ceauşescu and his police.[4] The Home Office insisted, though, that from the legal point of view Papusoiu's case had no merit. And Margaret Thatcher backed her minister. She wrote to me on 18 April, 'Having studied the facts myself, I am satisfied that the correct decision was reached . . .' She then, typically, let it be known in private that in her view a mistake had been made, that her own Government's decision had been wrong.

The public debate lasted several weeks, then died away. The Home Office had tried to put down their 'marker' for the principle that no man, even a citizen of one of the world's worst dictatorships, can automatically claim asylum in Britain and be immune from deportation. But they had picked the wrong time to make their point. This was March 1983, the high point of the second cold war and of East–West hostility. Many thousands of Poles had been given temporary shelter in Britain as a result of the imposition of martial law in December 1981. Papusoiu's removal caused them great alarm. It later emerged that the Romanians were happy to be rid of such an eccentric citizen, but this did not excuse the Home Office's high-handed and fear-provoking action. It was, I think, in part as a result of our very loud protest in press and parliament that no such case of deportation to a communist country was to recur while the second cold war lasted.

Systematization

Ceauşescu's behaviour grew worse as the 1980s drew towards their close. As Poland had, he developed vast foreign debts and he tried to pay them off by squeezing more work out of his people, exporting everything of value that they produced. In 1987 he sold the European Community £1,500-million worth of oil products, textiles, tableware and furniture, buying a mere £400-million of EC goods in return. The country's life expectancy decreased and infant mortality grew, partly because of almost daily electricity cuts which affected hospital equipment, especially the care of premature babies. The elderly were also phased out of society. Ambulances were ordered not to answer emergency calls if the patient was over seventy years of age. Milk was hardly ever available, even in powdered form. Typical ration allowances were seven ounces of bread a day, one ounce of sugar a day and ten eggs a year. Such luxuries as butter or chocolate were sold only for foreign currency.

His final madness was his 'systematization' programme, an attempt to close down Romania's picturesque villages and move the people into cities. The country's 13,500 villages were to be reduced by half. Those that remained would be transformed through concentrated density, with no building more than ten metres from another. Villagers' private plots, on which they relied to feed themselves, were being abolished. He dreamt of abolishing the difference between town and country, of creating a single working people, of concentrating them in a socialist metropolis, in rows of identical box-like buildings in which they could be more conveniently kept under control.

Villagers were receiving orders to leave the houses in which they had raised families and lived all their lives. Notice was short, seldom more than three days and sometimes only a few hours, after which the bulldozers simply arrived and flattened the building. It was done whether or not the owner had removed his belongings and whether or not he was still inside the building. The burden was on him to move all he owned to the stark and cramped alternative accommodation made available by the 'systematization' authorities, usually a single room in a barrack-like block with communal washing and cooking.

At a hearing on Romania held by the European Parliament's human rights sub-committee on 20 February 1989, the daughter of playwright Eugene Ionesco read out a message from her father begging the Western world not to accept 'the genocide of our traditions' by remaining silent, while villages and villagers' lives were destroyed. Although two British Labour MEPs, Stan Newens and European socialism's 'terrible child' Richard Balfe, spoke well of Ceauşescu, the rest felt that something must be done, if not to stop him in his tracks, at least to weaken his resolve. We suggested cancelling our trade agreement with Romania. We checked how the United Nations and the Helsinki process might be mobilized against him. It was hard to think of anything that might have any effect on the man.

His Order of the Bath

His only weak point, I decided, was his Order of the Bath and Légion d'Honneur. They were important ingredients of his prestige at home, presents made for reasons of foreign policy, now being used by him as supposed proof of how much Queen Elizabeth and General de Gaulle had admired him. If they were taken away, people in Romania would hear about it and opponents of his rule would be greatly encouraged.

I asked the government[5] how many foreign heads of state held British honours or decorations. The answer was forty-five, of which fourteen held the GCB. I then wrote[6] outlining the horrors of his government and suggesting that the removal of his foreign honours would be a blow to his vanity, his prestige and ultimately his power. There were several recent cases where British citizens had been stripped of honours. Anthony Blunt had lost his KCVO after being revealed as a Soviet agent. John Profumo's privy councillorship was forfeited because of a sexual scandal. The jockey Lester Piggott was stripped of his OBE for tax evasion. Emperor Hirohito was no longer a Knight of the Garter when Japan and Britain were at war. Why should Ceauşescu the mass-murderer retain his GCB?

I thought that the Foreign Office would agree with me. Our ambassador in Bucharest, Hugh Arbuthnott, had recently been ill-treated by Ceauşescu's police. While attempting to visit the well-known dissident Doina Cornea in Cluj, he had found every street leading to her house blocked off with 'No Entry' signs. He had driven on into the street he wanted and been angrily accused of violating Cluj's traffic laws. He was then, according to Lord Trefgarne, the FCO minister, 'manhandled and subjected to some abuse'. It is a serious matter when the police of a foreign country show disrespect to one of Her Majesty's ambassadors.

On 10 April, therefore, I asked in the House of Lords if the government would advise the Queen to take away Ceauşescu's GCB. But Lord Trefgarne's answer was defensive. 'It would be inappropriate to involve Her Majesty in a political gesture of the kind proposed . . .' he said. And a chorus of 'Hear! Hear!' from my 'noble friends' followed him in support. Trefgarne then confirmed that Romania had still not apologized for beating up the British ambassador. The House was showing its wish not so much to address Ceauşescu's human rights record as to invoke a constitutional truism, that the Monarchy must be kept free of all political involvement. They feared perhaps a long list of demands for the cancellation of British honours. President Banda of Malawi and President Mobutu of Zaïre, for instance, were also holders of the GCB.

My idea was therefore scotched. If there had been the chance, I would have observed that the Foreign Office had already involved the Queen in Romanian politics by advising her to invite the Ceauşescu couple to Buckingham Palace in 1978. I would also have claimed that I was proposing not a 'gesture' but an act of politics that would have an effect on Romanian internal affairs. And I was frustrated that the government would not support me. Still, the episode gave me the chance to protest again: 'The whole British honours system, not to mention the Palace's credibility, is put in disrepute while the Order of the Bath remains around the neck of this despot.' I suggested that the 'Order of the Bloodbath' would be a more appropriate award.

Two weeks later support for my line suddenly appeared from a strange source – the Queen's eldest son. In an unusual foray into foreign policy, the Prince of Wales attacked Ceauşescu for 'the wholesale destruction of his country's cultural and human heritage'. Among thousands of other memorials, he said, the tomb of his great-great-great-grandmother was threatened with demolition. Again, it was the constitutionality of the Prince's speech that aroused most interest,[7] but I wrote to congratulate him, restating my view that the Queen had been badly advised over the 1978 visit, and he replied on 4 May, 'The pressure must be kept up somehow. I think you've got a good point about the GCB, by the way.'

Ceauşescu retained his GCB meanwhile, although it was clear to all by these exchanges that Romania had declined a long way from its semi-respectable status of 1978. During 1989, 500 Romanian citizens were crossing the border into Hungary every month. If they were of Hungarian origin, they were usually allowed to stay. Otherwise, they were sent back to an uncertain fate. The United Nations appointed a special rapporteur to look into Romania's human rights record.

The appalling state of Romania was in stark contrast to events in other East European countries. In the rest of the region the sun was peeping through the clouds. There were the anti-communist rebellions in Poland, East Germany, Czechoslovakia and Hungary. Even Bulgaria was moving towards pluralism and the Soviet Union was on the point of abolishing the Communist Party's monopoly of power. Only in Romania and Albania, it seemed, were the old dictators still firmly in control.

It seemed that only Ceauşescu's family still supported him: his wife Elena and her sister Alexandrina and his brother-in-law Manea Manescu, who were all still in the Politburo, his brother Florea, who edited the Party newspaper, his brother Ilie, who was in charge of the army, and his son Nicu, who was chief of the Young Communist League. In November 1989, as communist rulers elsewhere were falling one by one, he received sixty-seven standing ovations in a five-hour speech about his achievements as the nation's ruler.

On 16 December police tried to arrest and deport a Protestant clergyman, Laszlo Tokes, from the city of Timisoara, where he served the large Hungarian community. Large crowds rioted in Tokes's defence. Troops fired on the unarmed demonstrators and a bloody rampage ensued, in which 2,000 people were killed. On this occasion the rioters were not cowed. The killing encouraged people in Timisoara to further action and within two days the whole area was in open revolt. Still, on 18 December Ceauşescu decided to go ahead with a state visit to Iran as scheduled.

Returning from Iran on 20 December, Ceauşescu claimed on television that fascists, hooligans and Hungarian mercenaries were responsible for the violence. He declared a state of emergency and banned foreigners from entering the country, but his speech was unconvincing, it seems, because that evening tens of thousands of people in many Romanian cities took to the streets in protest. Workmen downed tools to join the opposition and, in some places, the army joined them too. Western diplomats in Bucharest reported large numbers of Securitate roaming the streets. Securitate men, it was said, were executing army officers who refused to fire on demonstrators and the death toll had reached 5,000. Women and children had been crushed by tanks or skewered on Securitate bayonets.

That day I returned to London from Andrey Sakharov's funeral in Moscow to find Romania in flames and Ceauşescu being attacked everywhere, even in the House of Commons. Once again, albeit very late in the day, people were wondering why Ceauşescu was still allowed to enjoy one of Britain's highest honours. Nicholas Fairbairn said, 'How many people does this frightful tyrant have to kill before the Foreign Office will . . . advise the Sovereign to remove from him the inappropriate honour?'

The next day (21 December) Ceauşescu made a final attempt to sustain his regime, addressing a crowd of 100,000 in Bucharest's University Square. They were meant to be a selected audience, loyal to the dictator, but many students and others had infiltrated them and Ceauşescu was howled down. He understood that he would not be able to finish his speech and with a petulant wave of his hand he left the presidential balcony for the last time. Armed clashes, resulting in many deaths, continued for the rest of that day in Bucharest and long into the night. By the next morning (22 December) it was clear that the army had gone over to the opposition and a 'Committee of National Salvation' was being formed.

Ceauşescu and his wife knew that their power was gone, that their only hope of saving their lives was to escape. In mid-morning he was taken from his palace roof by helicopter to Titu air base outside the city, presumably intending to flee the country. But he could find neither a suitable aircraft to take him nor a suitable country to receive him. The word was flashed around the world. The Ceauşescu dynasty had fallen and the deposed couple were driving through the countryside, like Bonnie and Clyde, looking for someone who would shelter them. At noon Radio Bucharest announced that Romania, after more than forty years of communist rule, was free.

It was at this point, on 22 December, with the dictator finally deposed, that the Foreign Office at last advised the Queen to take away his GCB. It was done, according to a Foreign Office spokesman, 'as a mark of revulsion at abuses of human rights in Romania'. A senior FO official, Sir John Fretwell, told the Romanian ambassador, 'We welcome this end of a treacherous, primitive and aggressive dictatorship.' Strong words were finally being used and strong action taken. The *Daily Express* announced the next day: 'Queen Strips Dracula of his Knighthood.' She would also be returning the Star of Romania that he had given her eleven years earlier. I was happy to hear this, but I recalled how my advice in this sense nine months earlier had been spurned as 'inappropriate', since it 'involved Her Majesty in a political gesture'. And I remembered the 'Hear! Hears!' from my own benches.

I wondered why what was inappropriate nine months ago could be appropriate now. Was it merely because he no longer enjoyed power that the Foreign Office was prepared to act against him? Would it not have been more brave, principled and effective to have hit him while his oppressive regime was still on the attack? I could not help asking myself whether, if we and our allies had acted sooner, showing thereby how we in the West despised him, Ceauşescu's opponents might have been emboldened to get rid of him sooner, in which case many lives would have been saved.

Ceauşescu had more worries that day than the loss of his GCB. He and his wife were caught in their car. Then somehow they escaped. Every day that he survived gave encouragement to his dwindling band of supporters, especially the Securitate, who were happy to carry on shooting, since they had no future once Ceauşescu was no more. The issue remained in doubt for two more days, until at last on Christmas Day he and his wife were caught, subjected to a summary trial and shot. I am no supporter of the death penalty, but on this occasion I was encouraged to think that the dictator's disappearance would result in the end of the civil war, which indeed proved to be the case.

Britain's reputation in the matter was thus to some extent repaired. The honour that Ceauşescu had put to shame was cancelled in the nick of time, in the dying minutes of the dictator's cruel reign and in the dying hours of his life. There was, however, a final quirk of fate. The GCB was cancelled, but the actual bejewelled GCB gold collar, worth about £25,000, was lost. It had disappeared amid the chaos of revolution.

Various theories were put about. It was rumoured that the chain and badge had been acquired by an eccentric American millionaire, presumably for him to wear in his bath. The most likely suggestion was that it had been grabbed by a thief and melted down for the value of its metal. In 1990 I inquired about it, but was told by the Foreign Office that it would be wrong to press the Romanians on such a matter while their entire country was in such confusion.

In March 1994 I inquired again. This time, to my great surprise, action was taken through diplomatic channels and the GCB was found, intact in all its elements, in two black boxes in the Museum of National History in Bucharest. It was flown to London and subjected to a good cleaning before being restored to the care of James McGurk, custodian of the Grand Chancery at St James's Palace.

17. Albania – The Last Domino to Fall

All through the second half of 1989 the red dominoes were knocked over: Poland in August, East Germany and Czechoslovakia in November, Romania in December. The intensification of the second cold war, marked by the attacks on dissidents in the late 1970s, then by the invasion of Afghanistan and Sakharov's arrest in early 1980, seemed a century ago. The Soviet Union still had a year and a half of formal existence left as a communist state, but it was obvious to all that Marx's and Lenin's political heirs were mortally wounded as a force in world affairs.

By early 1990 there was only one European country where communism still had a few months left. This was Albania, a small land of 3 million people, a rough rectangle 120 miles long and fifty miles wide, squashed between Greece and Yugoslavia, fifty miles to the east of Italy's heel.

I remember well the effect of it all on Keith Toms, my Labour opponent in the June 1989 European election, a lover of all things of the far Left, allegedly the owner of a dog named Lenin and a cat named Trotsky. We were at a civic function in Harrow in May 1990, commemorating the forty-fifth anniversary of the end of the Second World War and honouring the 'New Europe'. Toms felt unable to raise his glass to a Europe that had so recently and entirely rejected his faith. He therefore toasted the only Continental land that still gave him ground for political optimism. He drank to Albania.

Throughout those years of 'war' with Russia, Albania was the country whose name no one bothered to speak. It was as if it did not really exist. It was like Ruritania. Even the name of its pre-war ruler, King Zog, sounded like something out of a fairy story. We could see Albania while on holiday, from restaurants at the north-east corner of Corfu, but we never went there. We knew only that their dictator, Enver Hoxha, ran a police state that made the Soviet Union seem a paradise of liberality and lavish living.

In Albania under Hoxha permission was needed to mail a letter, or to travel by bus from town to town. No private citizen was allowed to own a car. Travel abroad, except on official business, was unthinkable. When soldiers on patrol boats found swimmers trying to escape from Albania across the three-mile strait, they would shoot them and claim a substantial reward. Escapers caught on the Greek border were dragged behind tractors through the streets of their home town, as an example to the rest. There was no private market in home-grown food. Even artists and poets worked for a salary, producing pictures and verses as the state's plan required. Only the state could indulge in economic activity. In 1967 the practice of religion was banned and priests were executed for baptizing children. Amnesty International confessed at one stage that they could not report on the Albanian human rights record. It was so bad that there was no way in which their people could collect information about it.

We did not realize the extent to which it was Britain's and the United States's fault. Hoxha's cruelties were sharpened by the fact that from 1949 to 1953 the West had sent its agents into Albania to remove the communist system. It was the failure of this half-hearted and very secret operation that was used by the communists to justify their country's isolation from all Western influences.

During the Second World War famous guerrilla fighters from Special Operations Executive (SOE) in London fought with Albanian partisans against Italian and German occupying forces. There were the famous Balkan 'musketeers' – Julian Amery, David Smiley and Billy McLean – and other legendary figures – Alan Hare and Peter Kemp. They all resented the way British policy was mishandled, or even betrayed, by left-wing influence in SOE headquarters, which had seemed all too happy to allow pro-Soviet governments to emerge in Albania and other Balkan lands. They believed that Britain should have backed the traditional rulers in these countries, as was done in Greece. Amery writes, 'We armed the communist partisans. We denied arms to the nationalist resistance movements. Had we supported both, we might have been able to bring them together as we did in Greece. Our failure to do so helped to bring Hoxha to power.'[1]

Most of SOE were persuaded that communist groups were more worthy of British support, since they were killing more Germans. It was commonly suggested that, whereas the nationalists were the better gentlemen, the partisans were the better fighters. Many in SOE even believed that communism was the ideology of the future and should therefore be supported on its merits. In Yugoslavia and elsewhere such men were content to allow communist groups to triumph in the civil war that followed victory over Hitler's Germany. Enver Hoxha, a graduate of a French university, was the partisan leader and as such he used the equipment given him by the British to take over the government, having kicked out the 'musketeers' and other British anti-communists, so remaining Albania's absolute ruler from 1944 until his death forty-one years later.

After the war, Western representatives were no longer welcome in Albania. The SOE men who had parachuted into the country and risked their lives for it, who had arranged parachute drops of equipment and gold for the resistance and fought with them against Italian or German rule, were reviled as 'imperialists' and 'fascists'. It infuriated SOE that their efforts and the bravery of their agents were rewarded in this way. And the final straw came in October 1946. Two British destroyers, the *Saumarez* and the *Volage*, were badly damaged by mines while sailing though the Corfu Channel, and forty-three British sailors were killed. The International Court in The Hague awarded Britain damages for the incident, which Albania refused to pay. In reprisal, Britain retained a quantity of Albanian gold, lodged in the Bank of England during the war.

Adding injury to insult, Hoxha's government then began supporting the Greek communists, under Marcos Vafiades, who were fighting the King and his pro-Western government. Albania was a safe haven for these men, who operated out of the mountains of north-west Greece and enjoyed the Soviet Union's support, contrary to the agreement reached between Churchill and Stalin that post-war Greece would be part of the Western sphere of influence.

By 1948 Greece was only one area where Stalin was behaving dangerously. On 10 March the Czechoslovak foreign minister Jan Masaryk was found dead in the courtyard of his house, apparently having been thrown out of a window. Communists then took over the government, establishing a one-party state. On 24 June Soviet forces cut off all surface links between Berlin and western Germany, forcing the United States to supply the city by air for the next year, at huge cost. Stalin was also consolidating his empire by purging political leaders of independent thought from neighbouring countries – Laszlo

Rajk from Hungary, Władysław Gomułka from Poland – and trying to bend Yugoslavia's leader, Jozip Broz Tito, to his will. Most dangerous of all, the West discovered that Stalin's scientists had exploded Russia's first atomic bomb. It was against this background, at the height of the first cold war, that Britain and the United States embarked on a secret plan to 'detach Albania from the Soviet orbit'.

The plan made political sense. Cold war had broken out between East and West. And Stalin was not fighting by Marquess of Queensberry rules. Therefore the West was entitled to retaliate, using Britain's expertise in guerrilla warfare, acquired in many anti-Nazi resistance movements, and exploiting the fact that Albania was now, because of Yugoslavia's defiance, geographically cut off from the rest of the Soviet bloc, a weak and isolated land, purporting to be part of Stalin's chain but no longer linked to it.

Unfortunately, the scheme was doomed from the outset. The tactics used in the wartime anti-Nazi underground, it turned out, were not suitable for use in a tightly controlled communist society. The Albanian government also proved themselves skilful in infiltrating the groups of young men, as they underwent training in various British and American localities, in West Germany, Greece and Malta. Most terrible of all, the man sent by the British secret service to Washington as MI6 station chief and joint commander of the entire operation, Kim Philby, was a Soviet double agent. As a result, the armed Albanians whom the British and Americans sent in to foment anti-communist rebellion – some by parachute, others by boat, others overland from Greece – found Hoxha's security forces waiting for them at every point of entry and apparently well informed as to the purpose of their arrival. Most were killed or captured. The rest staggered across the Greek or Yugoslav borders. Philby writes in his own memoirs, 'A few members of the party did succeed in struggling through to Greece, where they were extricated, with immense difficulty, from the clutches of the Greek security authorities who would have shot them for tuppence. The information they brought was almost wholly negative. It was clear, at least, that they had nowhere found arms open to welcome them.'[2]

Philby might have added that he was himself one of the main reasons why the operation failed so ignominiously. The captured Albanians were tortured and either executed or imprisoned, some for more than forty years. Members of their families too were arrested in large numbers. And the West was forced to conclude that communism would never be overthrown by armed subversion. The plan to 'roll back' communist rule in the Soviet orbit had fallen on its face at the first hurdle.

I began researching this bizarre episode in 1980 and was shocked to find that the West had treated so many brave but ill-trained men, anxious to free their country, in such cavalier fashion. It was not that I objected to secret operations or to the use of violence in reply to communist violence. On the contrary, I was happy that we had been bold enough to strike back at Stalin's excesses. But this was the secret service at its worst – patronizing, inefficient and irresponsible. I could understand their ruthlessness in a ruthless conflict, but not when it was backed up by such dismal lack of professionalism and disregard for the lives of the Albanians (known by MI6 as 'pixies') whom they were sending into the field, not to mention their families, innocents who were also condemned to endure Hoxha's revenge.

The British secret service was living off the fat of its Second World War successes. Former MI6 officer Rodney Dennys told me,[3] 'It was the dying twitches of the SOE. For a moment, years after it had been disbanded, SOE came back into its own, with agents in the field, and in the Balkans, SOE's favourite area.' But in 1948 there was none of the surgical skill that had made SOE the world's experts in guerrilla warfare a few years earlier. The operation was shot through with leakages and its main detail was passed across the traitor Philby's desk in Washington. We must presume that he passed it on to his Soviet friends. Dick White, who became head of MI6 in 1956 and was then a senior officer in MI5 (counter-intelligence), told me,[4] 'No doubt Philby betrayed the Albanian operation, but overshadowing this is the fact that all émigré organizations are hopelessly infiltrated from the outset.'

Adem Gjura, one of the leaders of a group sent in by American intelligence from a training school near Heidelberg in November 1950, was one of the few to escape with his life. In 1983 he told me that he was sent into the field with no plan of action and no idea of where he might find friends. His men had been selected with little regard for any physical or mental aptitude they might have for such a daunting task. They were scrawny and unfit, not the 'commando' type. And their training was rudimentary. They were, for instance, parachuted into Albania without ever having done a practice jump. Their parachute 'training' consisted of jumping off tables on to the floor. Then, when the aircraft took them over Albanian territory, the noise of its engines alerted any police who were in the area. Dennys confirms, 'It was a mistake to use parachute drops. An aircraft in a deserted area sticks out a mile. Small boats were better.'

In short, the 'pixies' were used by Britain, and even more so by America, as guinea-pigs. They were sent in to risk their lives on the cheap, in the face of hopeless odds and in the hope of discovering whether more ambitious operations might be mounted against Stalin's other satellites. Two days before he landed in Albania, Gjura was later told, a 200-strong contingent of Albanian police came to the area where he was due to drop, telling local people that Adem Gjura was about to arrive by parachute. It was only because they missed the dropping zone and landed some miles away that they escaped the trap that awaited them.[5]

There was one lapse more unforgivable than all the rest. The Albanian operation was in full swing when disaster struck its British organizers. On 25 May 1951, two senior diplomats with secret service links, Guy Burgess and Donald Maclean, defected to the Soviet Union. It soon emerged that they had been Soviet agents since long before the war. Kim Philby, who had befriended Burgess and offered him the hospitality of his Washington home, was at once under suspicion. He was called back to London and interrogated by a well-known Queen's Counsel, Helenus Milmo, as well as by Dick White of MI5. White told me in 1983, 'I was by that time totally convinced that Philby was the culprit. Why had he built up this cover life, joining the Anglo-German fellowship and having himself accredited as a journalist to the Franco side in Spain? But I was rather alone in my suspicions. His own service supported him. The idea of his being a traitor was too incredible for them to hoist on board. He had such a good record.' Philby was asked to leave the secret service later that year. According to Dick White, this was done mainly to satisfy American feeling, which was then in the grip of McCarthyist hysteria, in spite of advice given by most of his friends, including George Jellicoe, who thought that he had been badly treated.

And yet, knowing though they did that the Albanian operation was fatally flawed, that one of its main organizers was in the service of the enemy, that for nearly two years he had presumably passed on all information given to him to the men against whom he was supposed to be fighting, British and American intelligence nevertheless carried on sending Albanians into a field of battle where they had no hope of survival.

For instance, Muhamed Zeqir Hoxha (no relation to the dictator) was trained by American intelligence near Heidelberg, then taken to Greece and parachuted into Albania during the night of 23 July 1951, two months after Burgess's and Maclean's defection. He says, 'About midnight we dropped on Vergoi plain, which ought to have been a safe place. Instead, we found ourselves surrounded by the forces of Albanian security assisted by armed civilians. We started fighting and two of our group were killed, leaving the other two of us trying to escape. We wandered through the mountains and in the evening of 28 July we met more security forces. I was wounded in the elbow and captured.' Hoxha was sentenced to twenty years in prison. He served more than twenty-four years, much of it in the infamous Burrel work camp.[6]

The final collapse of the Albanian operation, two years after Philby's dismissal, led to a widespread purge of real and imagined enemies by the Albanian police. Many thousands were arrested. Large numbers were killed for their involvement in this ill-judged British and American attempt to 'roll back' communist rule.

I remember thinking, as I researched this dismal story in the early 1980s, while Hoxha was still in power, that these were the same men, the 'spooks' from the MI6/CIA 'wilderness of mirrors', who had queried my behaviour and loyalty in 1970, and cut short my career, with at least one man in their pay, the editor of *Survey*, Leo Labedz, feeding lies about my work to columnists on a scurrilous magazine, frightening my House of Lords boss, George Jellicoe, with insinuations that could not but remind him of the difficulties he had himself faced as Burgess's and Philby's close colleague in Washington in 1951, in the wake of Burgess's defection and Philby's dismissal. And it was these same 'guardians of the nation's security', according to my Chief Whip, Michael St Aldwyn, who advised Edward Heath that he would be running a risk of scandal if he retained me as a minister in 1970, or reinstated me after I won my libel action in 1972, or even if he sent me to the European Parliament in January 1973.

Still, this was not why I wrote *The Great Betrayal*. I was anxious not to refight battles of the early 1970s, but to find out why these feckless guardians had taken it upon themselves on the basis of such a flimsy and ill-conceived plan to send men to certain death by ambush in hostile territory. I had great respect for the men of action, like Amery and Smiley, who had initiated the plan, but not for those in MI6 who had supervised the operation of it and allowed it to continue beyond any sensible limit. They should have seen how it was going wrong. They should have aborted it and saved the lives of those involved. And even in 1994, in spite of their protestations about their commitment to 'open government', the British and American authorities were still refusing to allow access to the official documents that described and explained this mad escapade.

Why had they carried on with the operation in July 1951, knowing that a traitor had been at its centre? Parliament was not informed of the policy of 'roll back', or allowed to supervise its instruments. The Prime Minister and his two senior colleagues had not the time to exercise their powers of supervision or control. The press were kept at arm's length. Unlike the Americans, we in Britain had no Privacy Act, no Freedom of Information Act. A special section of the Official Information Act of 1988 bound all present and former MI5 and MI6 officers to a lifelong duty of confidentiality. The very existence of the service MI6 was not admitted. So it had been allowed to carry on creating mayhem in a small Balkan country. In fact, they were a dangerously loose cannon in the British government's armoury, as I had good reason to know.

The Great Betrayal was published in 1984, serialized in the Sunday press, made into a BBC film and then printed in many other countries, including eventually (in 1994) in Albania. Although it was widely read, the impact it made was limited, partly because of Albania's obscurity and seeming irrelevance to the East–West conflict, partly because the whole story was so weird as to be unbelievable. It was described as 'surreal' by many reviewers. Hardly anyone in the main stream of modern history knew where to start in checking my facts. It seemed to many almost like a work of fiction, a tale of a made-up plot against the unimaginable government of a non-existent country.

Enver Hoxha died in 1985 and a few tiny openings to Albania began to emerge. Ministers from Europe visited the country. Trade with the West increased slightly. Britain still had no relations, because of the dispute about the Corfu Channel and the gold dating from 1946, but a few companies were allowed to send charter flights of brave tourists, who were fed with British boarding-school food at its worst and shown as many landmarks of the nation as could be fitted into a long weekend. I decided to enrol in one of these tours, and arrived in Tirana on 18 November 1988.

It was only two hours from Gatwick airport, but as if we had flown to the other side of the moon. We filled in our customs forms, confirming that we had no explosives or religious propaganda, waited while our luggage was searched and got into the Albturist bus. Our guide, a well-known secret policeman, Ilie Zhulati, told us all his good news. There was no traffic problem, since there were no private cars. There were no exhaust fumes, muggings or drugs. Local people kept well away from foreigners. Cooking was done on wood-burning stoves. There was equality. Everyone's wages were tiny. The walls of buildings were free of graffiti and the fertilizer on the fields had no chemicals. Women picking fruit or vegetables in the fields by hand made a pretty picture as we drove by. The ecologists among us in the bus – and there were many – were full of admiration.

The problem of this rustic idyll was that it was based on repression and poverty. 'It is not true that we arrest people for going to church,' said our guide. 'How can we? There are no churches. And it is not true that strikes are illegal in Albania. It just so happens that since 1944 there have been no strikes.' At the last parliament elections, he went on, there had been a 100 per cent turn-out, of which 100 per cent had opted for the communist Party of Labour. It meant that on election day there was not one single person ill, abroad, away from home or otherwise unable to vote. We were shown 'the Home Office museum', built in honour of 'our brave secret police', who had foiled the plots of half a dozen invading countries, forcing foreign agents to leave behind 'their equipment and their bones'. Amery, Smiley and other former SOE agents from the Second World War were featured in it as the worst fascists, war criminals and enemies of the Albanian people.

We were told during our stay by deputy Foreign Minister Mahomet Kaplani and others that Stalin had been too kind to critics of the Soviet system, that perestroyka was a vicious heresy, that Gorbachev was a traitor, that Yugoslavia was a capitalist country, that religion is a plague bacillus and that 'one day you will all choose the Albanian way'.[7] All in all, it was a bite from a very unpleasant apple. As we walked back towards our aircraft, at the end of our four days, we saw the secret police getting off, having made sure that there was no poor Albanian hiding in any of the luggage racks or lavatories.

I could now well understand why Albanians risked their lives trying to swim the Corfu strait. It was only three miles from near the southern port of Sarande to the Greek island. Many succeeded, with the aid of rubber rings, although many others were shot in the water.

It lasted two more years. By the end of 1990 influence from the outside world, especially from Italian television, was beginning to infect the purity of Albania's Leninism. The repeal of Article Six of the Soviet Constitution earlier in the year had allowed anti-communist parties in Russia to emerge and take part in public life. Central Europe was well embarked on private enterprise. At last some part of Albania's small political class, most of them Communist Party members themselves, began to question the strange 'religion' that had mesmerized them for forty-five years. Sali Berisha, a well-known heart surgeon, emerged as the main critic of Party policy. The people then took over. On 14 December 1990, riots were in full spate in Tirana and other large cities. Statues of Hoxha and Stalin were pulled down, although Lenin was briefly allowed to remain.

One such incident took place in Elbasan, fifty miles inland from Tirana. Several thousand people took to the streets shaking their fists. A few of them attacked public buildings. Midhat Haveri, a young critic of the regime, got hold of a loud-hailer and took control of a section of the crowd, leading them in a chant of the opposition slogan 'Freedom and Democracy' and making the all-Europe anti-communist V-for-Victory Churchillian gesture. He assured them that they had won the day and that they need not cause damage. Eventually the crowd dispersed. Late that night police arrived at Haveri's flat and dragged him away from his wife and two young daughters to the local prison. There, under the command of Chief of Police Vladimir Hysi, they tortured him mercilessly as the supposed ringleader of the riot. Five days later he was brought before a military court, accused of trying to overthrow the state, convicted and sentenced to twenty-five years.

The government under President Ramiz Alia realized, though, that their days in power were numbered. By the end of that year, 1990, they were forced to announce fundamental changes. Albania was in future to enjoy a mixed economy and pluralist democracy. The first multi-party elections would take place on 31 March 1991. A 'Democratic Party' led by Sali Berisha emerged in opposition to the communists. A hasty pre-election campaign began in the early weeks of 1991 and I was one of those invited to observe it. A centre was erected to receive foreign parliamentarians and journalists for the great experiment in democracy. I flew to Tirana on 29 March.

It was very different from the Albania of thirty months earlier. Ramiz Alia's people were resigned to the idea of building an economy on the basis of Western help. It meant that they were keen to show that they were democratic and ready to respect Western norms of human rights. But they had a long way to go. Some political prisoners had been released, but others were newly arrested as a result of the events of recent weeks, some for violence, others merely for the loud expression of a point of view. The president of the electoral commission, Rexheb Maidani, was himself a candidate. The opposition Democratic Party (DP) was starved of the tools needed to win votes: telephones, cars, fax machines, word processors, printers. Their candidates were moving from village to village by donkey or bicycle or on foot. The communists were richer and better trained in the manipulation of people and, most importantly, they controlled the radio and television output.

It was at Elbasan on 30 March that we first heard about Midhat Haveri's case. DP headquarters told us that he was in the local police station, in solitary confinement and on a starvation diet, battered by the torturers and without medical attention. On an impulse, my friends and I set off for the police station, followed by a small crowd of DP supporters. We knocked at the door and asked the chief of police to receive us. After ten confused minutes, we were shown into Vladimir Hysi's office, clearly one of the best equipped in all Albania.

We asked if we could see Haveri. The answer was no. We asked if he was in the building. 'Yes,' he said. 'He is serving twenty-five years for vandalism.' My EP colleague Edward McMillan Scott asked about his health. 'He is in good health.' In that case, we asked, can we see him to make sure that he is in good health? 'No.' The Chief of Police was adamant but very nervous. He must have found it strange being interrogated by foreigners in his own police station.

The next day, Easter Day, we set off on a tour of polling stations to watch the votes being cast and, making a slight detour, we called in at Bardhor labour camp, near Kavaja. We had been told in Elbasan that many other DP political prisoners were being held there. It looked from afar like a shabby version of a prisoner of war camp from the Second World War, complete with a 'death strip' between two lines of barbed wire, and with armed guards both inside and out. On closer inspection it emerged that conditions were much worse. The guards used live ammunition and their orders were to open fire at the slightest sign of resistance or attempt to escape. I met Edmond Pojani, serving a long sentence for 'offending against Enver Hoxha's memory', and several other 'politicals' mixed in with thieves and violent criminals. One of the latter tried to climb the wire as soon as our group arrived. If we had not been there, he would have been shot. Another gave me a vicious-looking knife as a souvenir. Another gave me a written account of a recent riot in which several of his friends had been shot dead. Bardhor was from the inner circles of hell.

The communists won the election that day, but it was a short-lived victory. The DP won massively in the towns. Even Ramiz Alia lost his Tirana seat. The communists won in the country, where 75 per cent of Albania's people live. The DP had simply not been able to get their candidates into the villages.[8] But the towns were the centres of politics and resistance to communist rule was resumed almost at once, on the basis that the March 1991 election had been unfairly conducted, and Sali Berisha's supporters were prevailed upon to join a coalition government.

Two weeks after our return to London, I was telephoned from Albania with the happy news that Midhat Haveri's twenty-five-year sentence had been quashed. Maybe our visit to his gaolers had helped. He was free and being treated for his injuries. A few weeks later all those in prison for political offences were released.

Another unjustice, the slur on Britain's wartime intelligence effort, was about to be righted. On 21 September 1991, the SOE 'war criminals' Amery and Smiley returned to Albania as Sali Berisha's guests. Smiley writes, 'As we crossed the coast of Albania, my thoughts went back forty-eight years to the time we left in the dead of night by motor torpedo boat, with a price on our heads, the relief of going tinged with sadness at leaving our loyal friends behind.'[9] A few days later 'emotions ran high', Smiley recalls, when they met their interpreter from 1944, Sheqir Trimi, 'whom we had been compelled to abandon to what we feared would be certain death when we left Albania'. He had survived and spent seventeen years at hard labour, five of them in solitary confinement. Amery then addressed the DP Congress, already preparing itself for an inevitable second round of elections, recalling how Hoxha had put a price on his head in 1944. 'I have to remind you, though, that the offer no longer stands,' he told the 1,300 people in the audience.[10]

Berisha was by now a friend of Britain, and the Conservative Party was backing him in his bid for power. On 10 October 1991, I gave him lunch in a fish restaurant at the Party Conference in Blackpool. He later came as our guest to the EP in Strasbourg, and I gave him dinner, a better dinner than lunch had been in Blackpool. On 12 March 1992, his party won the new elections and he was elected President of Albania.

A few days later a letter arrived with even more satisfying news. Midhat Haveri had taken several steps forward since his twenty-five-year term had been cancelled on 10 April 1991. He was now chief of police of Elbasan, in charge of the building where he had so recently been kept. And, in this capacity, one of his duties was to guard a new prisoner, Vladimir Hysi, the ex-chief of police who had tormented him so cruelly during the night of 14 December 1990.

18. Andrey Sakharov's Arrest

In January 1980 Brezhnev's men, conquerors of Afghanistan, felt strong enough to neutralize the leading figure of the dissident movement. In the afternoon of 22 January they arrested Andrey Sakharov in a car on his way to the Academy of Sciences, took him to the prosecutor's office and told him that he was exiled by decree to Gorky, a closed city 250 miles east of Moscow on the River Volga, where he would not be able to speak to foreign journalists and 'other criminal elements'. He was also stripped of his awards, his 'Hero of Socialist Labour' medal and other prizes.

At the same time, police descended on his wife Elena in their flat at 48b Chkalov Street, cut off the telephone and placed guards on the door. Western journalists, alerted by a TASS announcement, dashed to the flat, but were turned back as they turned right from the lift towards Apartment 68 on the sixth floor. Meanwhile Elena was told that she would be allowed to travel with her husband to Gorky, but she would have to pack at once to catch an aircraft leaving in two hours, at 6 p.m.

Husband and wife were taken separately to the airport. On arrival in Gorky, they were met by a section of local KGB and escorted to an apartment at 214 Gagarin Prospect in Shcherpinki, a dreary housing estate eight miles from the city centre. 'It is a normal flat,' Elena told me later. 'Four rooms with a bathroom, television and gas, about forty-two square metres in all. Everything was there waiting for us, including furniture and food in the 'fridge, but no telephone. It was a KGB service flat, what they call a 'secret hotel', used for meeting people confidentially.'

I recall the reaction evoked by news of the arrest when I announced it to the European Parliament's political committee that Tuesday afternoon. Apart from one British Labour colleague, Alf Lomas, who defended the KGB's action, Left and Right were for once united in their outrage and concern, not only for the Sakharov family, but also for the world's physical future. It seemed to us not only a most brazen act of repression, but also an aggression against Western opinion as a whole, all the more so in view of our own helplessness. There was nothing we could do, it seemed, any more than there had been a month earlier during the invasion of Afghanistan. The Soviets had calculated well. The West was powerless in the face of a calculated snub to Western opinion and to the U S President personally.

It marked the end of the West's theory that Sakharov belonged to the small 'untorturable class' of Soviet dissident. Until 1980 it was believed that a great Soviet scientist would never be severely punished, since scientists were more important to the Soviet government than members of any other profession. 'There are no untouchables now,' wrote *Le Monde*. 'It marks the end of a certain coexistence between the two superpowers.'

The Sakharovs were nevertheless, by the standards of the early 1980s, reasonably free in their flat in Gorky (now Nizhni-Novgorod). They could even carry on their dissident activities. Elena says, 'Don't forget that up to 1984 I could travel between Gorky and Moscow, talk to people and write to people. For instance, I helped Shcharansky's mother whenever she wanted to say anything to the press. And it irritated them. But, as the months passed, I became more and more isolated. Some of our friends went abroad, others were arrested, others were simply afraid to stay in contact.'[1] Andrey carried on his scientific work, writing letters to colleagues abroad, even publishing papers, all of which was presented by the Soviet media to suggest that he was not being significantly punished. 'It is no worse than for a British scientist to be required to live in Manchester,' one Soviet commentator wrote.

Communication with the outside world remained possible, although restricted. In November 1981 they even won a battle against the KGB, on behalf of Lisa Alekseyeva, the fiancée of Aleksey Semyonov, Elena's son by her previous marriage. Aleksey had emigrated in 1978 and for three years Lisa had been trying to join him in the United States. Andrey and Elena went on hunger strike and after sixteen days, to the surprise of many, Lisa received her passport. It was clear to everyone concerned that the Politburo had reversed the KGB's decision for political reasons. The KGB was humiliated by this rare defeat and they made up their minds that Sakharov's hunger-strike 'weapon' would never again be allowed to succeed.

On 25 April 1983, Elena suffered a severe heart attack. Six months later Sakharov wrote, 'My wife's condition is still not stabilized and remains life-threatening.' She needed complicated heart surgery – she eventually underwent a sextuple by-pass operation – and it seemed that such treatment was not available in the Soviet Union, especially not to her. She already had experience of Soviet hospitals, in 1975, when no competent doctors could be found ready to face KGB reprisal by giving her the treatment she required.

Sakharov then made a political mistake. He sent the famous Stanford University physicist Sidney Drell a letter, printed in the July 1983 number of the American journal *Foreign Affairs*, suggesting that the Soviet Union's massive silo-based strategic missiles, designed for a first strike against the United States, were destabilizing. It might help, he said, towards reducing 'these most destructive weapons' if the United States 'were to have MX missiles, albeit only potentially'.

The KGB seized on this cautious idea to stir up a public campaign. *Izvestiya* printed a letter from four members of the Academy of Sciences accusing Sakharov of wanting 'to compel our country to capitulate before an American ultimatum'. He received about 2,500 abusive letters from those who had accepted this distorted version of Sakharov's support for multilateral disarmament. There was even a withdrawal of support from the Western liberal scientific community.

Elena's medical condition was still serious and Andrey was insisting that she be allowed to visit the United States, for medical treatment and to see her family. He wrote to Yuri Andropov and then, when Andropov died on 9 February 1984, to his successor Konstantin Chernenko: 'Her visit has become a matter of life or death for us.' On 30 March he was summoned to the Gorky visa office and told that there would be a reply to his request in a month.

However, the KGB had no intention of showing leniency at this crucial political period, with a stop-gap leader in the Kremlin and amid war in Afghanistan as well as rumours that Reagan was preparing a nuclear first strike. On 2 May Andrey was seeing Elena off for one of her periodic trips to Moscow. He watched her through the airport window walking towards the aircraft. A car drew up alongside and police arrested her. 'My first interrogation, and body search, took place right there, at the airport. They told me that I would be charged under Article 190, with disseminating anti-Soviet material known to be false.'

Andrey went back to the flat. Two hours later Elena was brought there by the local KGB chief, who gave them both a threatening speech, accusing her of being a CIA agent and making her promise not to leave the city. On 4 May TASS accused her of contacts with American diplomats and of planning to go to the United States to seek asylum. Andrey decided that he had no alternative but to begin yet another hunger strike.

On 4 May their friend Irina Kristi flew to Gorky. The Sakharovs' flat was now heavily guarded, but Irina, standing in the street, was able to exchange a few words with Elena, who was on the balcony of the flat. Irina flew back to Moscow to find plain-clothes guards at her front door and her telephone cut off. Still, she was able to give Western journalists the vital news that Andrey had begun his hunger strike two days earlier.[2]

The Sakharovs' isolation was now complete. They were quite cut off, not only from the West and from Moscow, but also from the people of Gorky. Elena told me, 'He goes out for walks sometimes. People notice him, but they don't talk to him because he always has the KGB with him, as do I. If we go into a shop, they come in after us. Anyone who goes up to us is stopped physically. How many are there? Maybe 100. Don't laugh when I say 100. No one knows.'

The Tormentors of Semashko Hospital

On 7 May 1984, while on hunger strike and walking with Elena to the police station for her next interrogation, Andrey was seized by KGB men disguised as doctors and taken to Semashko hospital, where for four months he was subjected to a level of forced feeding of such ferocity that it amounted to physical torture. First they fed him through a vein. He was tied hand and foot, thrown on to a bed and held down by orderlies, while a needle was inserted into his arm. As a result he passed out, then suffered a brain spasm or mild stroke, which caused him to slur his speech in later years.

The West knew nothing of this. The family's isolation was too thorough. Still, we suspected something disagreeable. 'Is Andrey

Sakharov dying?' asked the *Washington Post*,[3] pointing out that the Kremlin's behaviour was 'pure malice and vindictiveness, the policy of a petty, frightened power lacking in both decency and self-confidence'.

We relied for our information on such unreliable sources as Georges Marchais, the French communist leader, who was happy to support the KGB over the Sakharov case in every possible way. He claimed in a radio interview on 20 May to know from 'the highest Soviet officials' that Andrey's and Elena's health was 'satisfactory'. Her heart problem was 'stable', he added, and her eye problem could easily be treated in a Soviet hospital. There was therefore no reason why she should need to travel abroad.

On 25 May the KGB doctors tried another method. They fixed a clamp on Andrey's nose and, whenever he opened his mouth to breathe, they prised it open more with a lever, then spooned food between his teeth and held his mouth tight shut, so that he could not spit anything out, until at last he was forced to swallow in order to be allowed to breathe. He felt a constant feeling of suffocation, the veins on his forehead bulging to bursting point. The effect of this treatment on an elderly man with a heart condition, who had already suffered a stroke, can well be imagined.

He suspended his hunger strike, but was kept in the hospital, unable to speak to Elena, who was still under investigation. In June 1984 he became subject to fits of trembling and doctors told him that this was a sign of Parkinson's disease. They said, 'We won't allow you to die. We'll get the women out with the clamp to make sure of that. But you will turn into a helpless invalid, unable to pull up your own trousers.'

Andrey felt that this was more terrifying than death. It was Orwellian, he recalls in the long letter describing his ordeal that he wrote to Anatoli P. Alexandrov, President of the Soviet Academy of Sciences, on 15 October. The threat of the onset of Parkinson's disease was as terrifying to Sakharov as the cage of rats in Room 101 was to Winston Smith in Orwell's novel, all the more so for the fact that it was all happening in 1984.

Andrey and Elena were out of touch all this time. On 1 August he wrote to the public prosecutor, asking to be joined as a defendant in her case. But there was no reply and on 10 August her trial began.

The next day she was convicted of slandering the Soviet state and sentenced to five years' exile, to be spent in Gorky. Andrey then summoned up the resolve to resume his hunger strike and on 7 September he did so.

The KGB doctors had by now had enough of their annoying 'patient'. They discharged him on 8 September. He and Elena were reunited that day, and it was only then that he learnt for the first time about her conviction in court and sentence to five years of exile. He ended the hunger strike so as to help her at a difficult time. 'Her death would be mine as well,' he said. Shortly afterwards he drafted his letter to Alexandrov, which began, 'I appeal to you at this most tragic moment in my life . . .' It was the traditional route that any eminent Soviet scientist would take, asking the President of his Academy of Sciences for help. However, Alexandrov did not reply and did nothing of any use in answer to his colleague's urgent plea.

The Sakharovs passed a dismal winter. Their flat was searched again, and Andrey's radio, typewriter, tape recorder and all his writings were taken away, so that he was starved of scientific stimulation. Only a handful of visitors, all authorized by the KGB, called on them. Elena said, 'We bought another radio, but it works badly because they have set up a special personal jamming station opposite the flat. It affects the television too. We can't even get Radio Moscow.'

The KGB had filmed Andrey in Semashko hospital. Now they were filming the couple walking in the street and giving the footage to their 'journalist' Victor Louis to sell to television stations. Extracts were shown, for instance, before Mikhail Gorbachev's famous visit to London in December 1984. Elena said, 'They must have a range of different scenes by now. Therefore, if we die, they can keep the outside world happy by sending a film every now and then.' It annoyed her that Western television firms were boosting KGB funds by paying large sums to Louis for such invidious material.

On 31 January 1985, Elena's appeal was turned down. Her five-year sentence was thus confirmed, making it even less likely than ever that she could travel abroad. Andrey therefore braced himself for yet another hunger strike, which he began on 15 April, a month after Chernenko's death and the beginning of the Gorbachev era. But Gorbachev's arrival to power was of no immediate benefit to either of them. A week later Andrey was being forcibly fed in a way that he describes as 'excruciating', although sometimes he offered only symbolic resistance. Again he was tied up and held down, his nose was clamped and food was forced into his mouth with a spoon.

On 31 May the senior KGB officer attached to his case, S. I. Sokolov, visited him in hospital and spoke to him threateningly, insisting that the idea of Elena travelling abroad was impossible. He also asked Andrey to withdraw several of his past statements, such as the letter to Sidney Drell and the suggestion that the bomb in the Moscow metro on 10 January 1977 might be a KGB provocation.

Sakharov's only hope now was to appeal to President Gorbachev directly. On 29 June 1985, he wrote explaining why Elena's visit to the United States was so important. He was ready to bear responsibility for his own actions, he explained, but it was 'intolerable' that his wife should be made to suffer for what he was doing.

By now, more than a year after Gorbachev's takeover of power, both sides were looking for a compromise that could extract them from an impossible situation. Sakharov wrote that he was ready 'to cease entirely making political statements and instead concentrate on my scientific work'. He soon learnt that Gorbachev had 'been made aware' of the letter and had asked a group of trusted advisers to prepare a reply. But he still seemed no nearer achieving his main objective. He wrote, 'On 4 July, not being able to bear any longer my separation from Lyusya [Elena] and not knowing anything about her, I wrote a statement ending my hunger strike. The same day I was let out of hospital.'

At the end of July 1985 there was to be a top-level East–West meeting to 'celebrate' the tenth anniversary of the Helsinki agreement. Sakharov thought that his quick release from hospital might be linked with this event. Again, film of the Sakharovs walking in the street was released to the West by Victor Louis, the aim being to convince the West that the couple were leading a normal life.

Sakharov's story continues, 'Lyusya and I were together for two weeks. It was a good time to be alive and it gave me strength to endure another hunger strike.' On 25 July, for the fourth time since 1981, he again stopped eating and within two days he was back in the hospital. On 13 August a new and especially vicious form of forced feeding was begun. 'They started administering drips containing glucose and protein preparations into both thighs, 15 subcutaneous and 10 intravenous. The sheer quantity of the drip was enormous. My legs blew up like pillows and were painful.'

Meanwhile the matter was being considered at the highest Soviet level and affairs were beginning to move in his direction. Gorbachev digested the 29 June letter and on 29 August it was discussed at a meeting of the Politburo. Fourteen senior comrades – among them KGB Chairman Viktor Chebrikov, well known for his participation in KGB murders and in the manufacture of KGB poisons, Edward Shevardnadze and Boris Yeltsin, both of whom were then orthodox members of the Soviet leadership – were there with S.I. Sokolov, the top KGB officer who had visited Sakharov in June and was the KGB's direct contact with him.

Gorbachev began, 'At the end of July [sic] I received a letter from a certain Mr Sakharov, whose name will not be unknown to you. He asks us to allow his wife Bonner to go abroad for medical treatment and visit relatives.' Gorbachev wanted his comrades to decide 'which decision will give us more problems, letting her go abroad, or not letting her go'. A decision had to be taken immediately. He was soon to meet President Reagan and, if permission for her travel were to be given just before the meeting or just after, it would look as if the Soviet Union had backed down. 'And this would be undesirable,' the Soviet leader observed.

As the Politburo member responsible for KGB matters, Chebrikov was then invited to sum up the position: 'Sakharov is sixty-five. Bonner is sixty-three. He does not enjoy good health. He has lost weight lately and is undergoing tests for possible cancer. He has largely lost his position as a political figure and recently we have heard nothing new from him. So perhaps Bonner ought to be allowed to go abroad for three months. As you know, she is in exile, but under the law we can interrupt her sentence for a specific period. Of course, once she reaches the West she will be in a position to make statements, receive prizes and suchlike, and it is possible that after undergoing treatment in Italy she may go to the United States . . .'

His worry was that Elena might then move in with her daughter Tatyana in Boston and start agitating for her husband to be allowed to join her, in which case many protests would be expected from Western countries, including communist parties. 'The trouble is that we cannot let Sakharov go abroad,' he explained. 'The ministry is against it, since he knows in detail the whole course of development of our atomic weaponry. Specialists have told us that he could be put in charge of a laboratory and then carry on the military research with which he is still familiar.'

The Politburo's hatred for Elena now emerged: 'We must not forget that he acts very much under Bonner's influence . . . She has one hundred per cent influence over him,' said Chebrikov. 'That's what Zionism does for you!' remarked Gorbachev. 'She is now under our control, but she has become more and more malicious as the years pass, and as soon as she is in the West it will boil over. Bourgeois propaganda will have a concrete person on which to base all sorts of press conferences and other anti-Soviet activity,' said G.A. Aliyev. 'We can expect no sort of decency from Elena Bonner. She is a devil in skirts, a paid-up supporter of imperialism,' added M.V. Zimyanin.

Chebrikov nevertheless cherished the bizarre hope that, with Elena safely out of the way, Sakharov might perhaps be brought back into the Soviet fold. 'That's why he ran off into hospital, where he could feel more free,' suggested Nikolai Ryzhkov, strangely. Gorbachev then mentioned the concessions that Sakharov might be expected to give, some of which he had already agreed with Sokolov and included in his 29 June letter. He would state that he understood the reasons why he was not allowed to travel abroad. He would ask his wife to 'behave well' while in the West. And he would refrain from political statements. On this basis the Politburo agreed to yield to the request which Sakharov had fought for and suffered for all those months.[4]

A week later therefore, on 5 September, Sokolov called on Sakharov again in the Gorky hospital, hoping to be able to implement the Politburo's decision. Again he was asked to renounce past statements: about the Drell letter and the bomb in the Moscow metro. He refused. He was, however, ready for his wife's sake to make the other three above-mentioned concessions.

He told Sokolov that he would not be making any more political statements himself. He was also prepared to sign a paper accepting the Soviet government's right not to allow him to travel abroad, for reasons of national security, since he had in the 1960s had access to military secrets, some of which might still be significant. Thirdly, he agreed to ask Elena, if she went to America, not to make any statements to the press or mass media. 'I was allowed three hours with Lyusya and we carried out Sokolov's requests.'

There followed 'forty-eight tiring days and nights of waiting' before Elena finally went to the Gorky visa office and was told, on 21 October, that she would be allowed to go to America. Two days later Andrey was out of hospital and they were together again in the Gorky flat. On 10 November they spoke to their family in Boston and a week later Gorbachev's meeting with Reagan took place.

On 27 November Elena flew from Gorky to Moscow. Over the next five days she was carefully watched, knowing that any false step would mean the cancellation of her exit permit. For several years I presumed that somehow she was able to provide the American embassy with copies of the papers on which this story is based – his letters to Alexandrov and Gorbachev, and his appeal to 'friends' for his wife's release – and that the material reached the West in a diplomatic bag. In fact, according to her daughter Tatyana, the papers were taken to the West 'by brave and loyal friends', not by any government agency. Without their help the story might never have been told, since on 2 December she was carefully searched at Moscow airport before being allowed to board her flight to Rome.

The world's hunger for news of the Sakharov family could still not be satisfied. Elena was in Western Europe, besieged by journalists, but she could speak to them only by breaking her agreement with the Soviet authorities, in which case she would not be allowed back to Moscow and Andrey would be left on his own. She was pictured in Western magazines with one finger across her lips to illustrate this vow of silence that had been forced upon her.

On 15 December she flew to Boston, where she was met by her children, Tatyana and Aleksey, and by her mother, Ruth Bonner. They drove to their home in Maplewood Avenue, Newton, an hour's drive from Boston. American doctors then descended on her with a range of complicated treatments for her many medical problems, including a necrosis of the heart muscle and spasms of the coronary arteries, necessitating a sextuple heart by-pass, and secondary glaucoma with progressive narrowing of the field of vision.

For some years I had been in touch with Yefrem Yankelevich, Tatyana's husband, but I knew that Elena lived in very strained circumstances, even in America. It seemed unlikely that she had been able to bring documents to the West and even more unlikely that we would be able to meet since she was banned from giving interviews and she was observing the ban. Then, in early February 1986, came a telegram from the Boston 'headquarters'. There *were* some papers that might be of interest. Would I like to come and see them? It was an exciting offer.

I invited the *Observer* to sponsor me, which they did with alacrity, and flew to Boston the next day, 6 February 1986. I had not seen Elena since December 1975 in Rome. 'You have put on weight,' was her only comment to me as I walked in through the door. We spent the next two days working feverishly on the papers. I could see at once that they were formidable. They showed not only the depth of the torment to which Sakharov had been subjected in hospital during his hunger strikes, but also the bravery that both husband and wife had shown, alone and defenceless as they were, in the face of the KGB's assembled army of brutality.

Frustratingly, I could not quote Elena, because of what she had promised, but she talked to me off the record about her husband's bizarre life. 'Andrey is now in the flat on his own. He sees no one, except sometimes a scientist approved by the government. He does everything for himself – shopping, cooking, cleaning. The only chance he gets to talk to anyone is with us here in Boston, over the telephone, about twice a month. Sometimes he goes out for walks. People notice him, but they keep away from him, because he is always accompanied by the KGB. If he goes into a shop, the KGB go in after him.

'We get mail sometimes, mostly magazines and newspapers. It has to be left with the policeman who sits outside our door. He hands it to us over his shoulder. We say thank you and he says nothing. It is a strange way to behave. Is life boring? No, it is too terrifying to be boring. I had six by-passes. And now there are complications. I also have pericarditis and pleuritis, and very low blood pressure. And that is without even mentioning such trifling matters as my teeth.'

Elena then learnt for the first time that the KGB had filmed them and sold the film in the West as proof of the fact that their lives were normal. She tried to warn Andrey from Boston over the telephone. 'They are taking pictures of us,' she told him several times. But he never heard her. The telephone link was connected to a delay system and her voice was cut short every time she said something that the KGB disliked.

On 8 February Mikhail Gorbachev, visiting France, unwittingly helped us by informing Western journalists that the Sakharovs lived in Gorky 'under normal conditions'. Sakharov was only not allowed to travel abroad, he said, because he had worked on the Soviet H–bomb and knew state secrets. Everywhere he went, it must have seemed to him, he was being asked about the Sakharov family. The problem was bad for his image as the new 'nice' Soviet leader. But at least, when he said that Sakharov was leading a normal life, no one could tell him what a liar he was. There was no proof. I was about to provide this proof.

The next day, the *Observer* led its front page with my story, 'Sakharov Tells of KGB Torture'. Over the two following Sundays people in several dozen countries could read 'the Gorky papers', as they came to be known, with their detail of Andrey's 'normal conditions' of life and of the brutal methods used on him in hospital, as described in these past few pages. The embarrassment caused to Gorbachev was immense. This was the object of the exercise. I was following Sakharov's own advice: 'Every violation of human rights must be made into a political problem for the violating government.'

The *Observer* paid a fee for the use of the papers, which were then sold to more than twenty journals in as many countries, so generating funds that were used to help Dr Sakharov and to promote human rights in the Soviet Union. The American press deplored this arrangement. First, they had been 'scooped' by a British newspaper on their own doorstep. Second, it ran contrary to the ethics of American journalism to provide payment to a source of information, or for an interview. The material was of public interest, they thought, and should have been available to all. The British press felt no such inhibition. Also we knew that newspapers would give the material more prominence if they had to pay for it. The agreement with the *Observer* enabled the Sakharov family to control this very sensitive material, with my help, making sure that its publication did Andrey and Elena no harm. And the main aim was achieved. Serious pressure was brought to bear on the new Soviet president, at a time when he was considering whether or not to take the plunge and order Sakharov's release.

It cannot have pleased Gorbachev that the worldwide publication of the 'Gorky papers' made him and his government look like crude bullies of the old Soviet school, tormenting an old and sick man for the non-violent expression of his political views. Never again, he must have thought, at any meeting with any Western leader, even with a foriegn communist, would he be able to brush the Sakharov case aside. Gorbachev had it in his power to solve the Sakharov case by letting him return to Moscow. Elena's fear, though, was that the KGB might take it upon themselves to solve it in another way. Andrey was in poor health. He had heart problems. She told me that day in Boston, 'They could creep into our flat during the night, smother him with a pillow and simply announce that he had died of a heart attack. No one would be able to say that they were lying.'

The Last Days in Gorky

The terrible thought that Andrey might die, or be murdered, while she was away made her all the more anxious to return to him. And she was afraid that the KGB might use the publicity surrounding 'the papers' as a pretext for keeping her out of the country. We had been careful not to quote her directly in any of the articles, but it seemed likely that she was the channel through which the papers had reached the West, presumably with American help. The KGB assumed, although it was not true, that the papers had reached the West through the United States diplomatic bag.

The KGB could be forgiven for claiming that Elena was keeping the letter of her vow of silence, but not the spirit of it. Still, in view of the importance of the papers as a lever on the Soviet government, it was a risk that had to be taken. The whole operation, I believe, had a deep effect on Sakharov's future life and on the Soviet Union, and I am happy to have played a part in it.

The announcement that Elena would pass through London on her way home and be received by Margaret Thatcher provided the KGB with a pretext for rearguard action. Victor Louis was sent in to put the KGB's point of view. *She* was the obstacle, he said, to Andrey's return to Moscow:[5] 'It is not his behaviour. It is hers. He wants a quiet life, but she would start calling press conferences.' How many politicians had she seen, and how many doctors? She was, Louis suggested, using the typical hackneyed phrase, 'helping forces hostile to the Soviet Union'.

Again, it was all Elena's fault, Louis was suggesting. She was the sinister and evil force that had achieved some weird hold over the great man and enticed him from the true path of Soviet patriotism. She was not deterred, however, and on 30 May she spent an hour with the British Prime Minister, after which both ladies told the press that Louis's 'blackmail' would not succeed. Margaret Thatcher said, 'We will keep faith with Dr Sakharov.'

Meanwhile in Gorky the KGB were trying hard to make the best of their impossible position. Various journals, including *Novoye Vremya* and *Literaturnaya Gazeta*, asked Andrey to write for them. He replied, 'So long as I have a noose round my neck, I will write nothing.' The KGB were by now under pressure from Gorbachev and other political leaders to 'resolve the matter'. It was unclear, though, how the matter could ever be resolved without one party or the other emerging as thoroughly dissatisfied.

In February 1986 Sakharov sent Gorbachev another letter asking for the release of fourteen political prisoners. Top of the list was the veteran dissident Anatoli Marchenko, author of *My Testimony*, known to be seriously ill in prison. In March he went to Gorky hospital for work on his teeth and was met by Dr Obukhov, his old tormentor, who insisted on talking to him about politics and then confronted him with a series of demands. 'He used the occasion to try to get some apology out of me for my letter to Academician Alexandrov and the articles in *The Observer*. He began by asking me to write a letter of thanks to the hospital dentists and then argued that they had fed me by force not so as to torture me, but to save my life. This was his cunning way of approaching the problem.'[6]

I saw Elena as she passed through London on 30 May, but only briefly, surrounded as she was by journalists, celebrities and Russian friends. It was amazing, I thought to myself, how dramatically her life was now going to change. Today she was a queen among an admiring and adoring public. In a few days she would be returning to the crude hostility that covered every aspect of their lonely life in Gorky together. I could in no way predict how soon they would emerge from this dismal half-world.

In early June they resumed life in the Gorky flat, guarded night and day by teams of KGB people. And so it was for almost all the rest of 1986. There were rumours of freedom, but nothing definite, suggestions that 'something might be done' as soon as the couple 'learnt how to behave themselves'. Attempts were made to entice Andrey into print. Tempting offers were made and, all the time, film of the couple was still being shot secretly and offered to the West by Victor Louis, to suggest that they were living under 'normal conditions'. There were grounds for optimism, but nothing of any significance was emerging. Obviously a serious battle over internal policy was being fought at the highest Soviet level.

Elena's book appeared in the United States and, again, it was suggested that her desire to be famous was damaging her husband's interest. Still, Gorbachev was under growing pressure at home and abroad to show whether or not his glasnost and perestroyka really meant anything more than the usual appeals to work harder and drink less.

It was in September 1986, the family believe, that the decision to release the Sakharovs was taken in principle, not only by Gorbachev, but also by the Politburo and the army general staff, who hoped to profit from Andrey's known opposition to America's Strategic Defence Initiative, known as 'Star Wars'. But it did not mean that the KGB were going to release him in practice. They had spent most of that year trying to mitigate the embarrassment that was to come by squeezing concessions out of the stubborn pair. If they then released them 'free of charge' and for no good reason, it would be the beginning of further appeals on behalf of other 'anti-Soviet agitators'. Sakharov and his 'evil' wife were trouble-makers, even in Gorky. What would they be like in Moscow?

The world was in two minds. Did glasnost and perestroyka mean anything? Was the Soviet government ready to embark on its more conciliatory approach to Western opinion? Gorbachev was full of talk about liberalization, but did it mean anything, or was it merely '*klyukva*', the Russian for 'puffball'? Presumably there was a struggle for power. Gorbachev's realistic approach to economic difficulty demanded friendly East–West relations. This would not be possible without releasing Sakharov and other important cases. However, the KGB were presumed to be opposed to any such releases.

I had not been to the Soviet Union since July 1971. Again and again they had made it clear that I was unwelcome. But now signals of liberality emerging from Moscow encouraged me to think that I might, after a gap of fifteen years, be granted a Soviet visa. I made inquiries from the Foreign Office. Geoffrey Howe promised to help. But then came an incident that put all thoughts of a visit to Moscow to one side, as the KGB committed one of the most provocative acts of the entire decade.

The Daniloff Case

On 30 August 1986, an American journalist in Moscow, Nicholas Daniloff, was, in his own words, sandbagged by eight KGB men on a Moscow street and bundled into a van, his hands tightly and painfully handcuffed behind his back. It was the first time for many years that a Western journalist in the Soviet Union had been so mistreated.

The KGB's purpose was soon clear. One of their spies, Gennadi Zakharov, had been arrested in the United States and was about to be charged. They would use Daniloff to 'buy' their spy out of an American prison. Or they would charge and sentence him. They claimed that he had been caught red-handed receiving written material from a Russian friend, Misha, about the Soviet army in Afghanistan. 'I knew this man Misha for several years,' Daniloff said a few days later.[7] 'He is a very charming fellow. Our relationship grew over a period of time. I trusted him.' It was a familiar story. Misha was of course under KGB control and he had trapped his friend into an incident which now threatened to disrupt the forthcoming summit meeting between Reagan and Gorbachev in Reykjavik, Iceland.

Westerners could hardly remember a similar case, where a Western journalist had been lifted from a Moscow street, handcuffed, thrown into a cell and charged with espionage. It was a throw-back to the behaviour of the Soviet police during the first cold war in Stalin's day. How did it hang together with Gorbachev's claims that he wanted warmer East–West relations? Either he was being duplicitous, or he was being undermined by strong forces within his own government. The atmosphere in Moscow's foreign community was icy. Western journalists huddled together for comfort, afraid of more arrests. Many westerners cancelled their visits to Moscow. The thaw in East–West relations was apparently at an end.

The crisis lasted for two weeks before being defused. In mid-September, Daniloff and Zakharov were given into the custody of their respective ambassadors and, a few days later, flown home. Inevitably, though, this raised the question whether any summit meeting could achieve anything useful so long as the Soviet Union still insisted on equating investigative journalism with espionage, resorting to hostage-taking whenever they wanted to cover up their dubious behaviour or liberate one of their spies. If this was to be Soviet policy in the future, glasnost and perestroyka were without meaning, and East–West summit meetings were without purpose.

19. *Orlov's Release and Marchenko's Death*

Meanwhile there were mysterious goings-on in Kobyay, a tiny settlement near Yakutsk, 3,000 miles east of Moscow, where the veteran dissident and former chairman of the Helsinki group, Yuri Orlov, was serving five years in exile. He had completed his full seven years in the labour camps in February 1984 and been moved to an icy and marshy wilderness, reachable only by aircraft, where he lived in a small wooden house rented for him by his wife Irina and some Moscow friends.

He was now sixty-two and he received a tiny pension – 67 roubles a month. His Yakutian neighbours had been told that he was an enemy of the people and were wary of him. He was confined to an area two miles from the village centre and spent much of his time walking in the woods and picking mushrooms. Vegetables will not grow in the frozen earth, but friends helped him to build a greenhouse, where he grew cucumbers and potatoes. During the summer, when the lakes and rivers briefly unfreeze, he fished for carp.

On 28 September the local KGB boss arrived at his hut on a motor-cycle and ordered him to pack. He was then taken on the back of the 'bike', his suitcase in his hand, to the earth runway of Kobyay airport, flown 220 miles south to Yakutsk and from there by a roundabout route to Moscow. He had meanwhile heard about the Daniloff case on his radio and, hoping for the best, he wondered whether he might be linked with it. But his heart sank when he found himself taken straight from the airport to Lefortovo prison, where he was told that he was under investigation for yet another crime against the state.

He says, 'I stayed in Lefortovo for three days, not knowing if I was going to be set free or sent back to prison for another term. I was under great stress. The idea of more years in a labour camp was unbearable. I would have risked death rather than endure it. Finally on 2 October the investigator told me that, by decree of the USSR Supreme Soviet, I was deprived of my citizenship and sentenced to be

325

sent into exile abroad. I stayed in prison until Sunday morning, 5 October, when they put me on a flight to New York.'

The Kremlin had released Orlov as a 'sweetener' for the American side in the Daniloff–Zakharov 'swap'. It was a concession to sugar the pill that the American public was being asked to swallow. It was after all by any standard an unequal deal. Zakharov was a professional spy. Daniloff was a professional journalist, an American citizen of Russian origin, arrested for legitimate journalistic activity. It was absurd to put the two men in the same category. The American government was nevertheless enticed by the idea of rescuing Yuri Orlov, one of the great heroes of the Soviet democratic movement. We remembered the outrage caused by his arrest in February 1977 (see p. 94). As soon as I heard that he was on his way to the West, I flew to meet him in New York and on 5 October joined the welcoming throng of his admirers waiting to shake his hand.

Orlov at once flew to Washington to meet President Reagan, who was due to meet Gorbachev in Reykjavik a few days later, his plan being to talk to Reagan about certain named political prisoners and ask him to raise their cases with Gorbachev in Iceland. 'It would be no threat to the Soviet Union to release these people. There are not so many of them,' Orlov told me later. There were now no more than an estimated 200 to 300 convicted of anti-Soviet agitation under Article 70. Like Sakharov, he believed that the most urgent case was that of Anatoli Marchenko, known to be seriously ill in Chistopol prison. Sakharov had already mentioned it in a letter to Gorbachev eight months earlier.

There were also around 3,000 convicted of lesser offences, under Article 190, most of the cases linked with religion, for instance conscientious objectors and 'speculators' arrested for selling Bibles or religious objects. Although this total was well down on the '10,000 or more' prisoners of conscience estimated by Sakharov in his interview with the BBC in 1975, it still included some dissidents and Jewish 'refuseniks' whose names were well known in the Western world.

The day after he flew from Washington back to New York, Orlov spoke to me for several hours about his hopes for Russia's future, as well as about his ill-treatment in Perm No. 35 labour camp and of his nightmare journey from Perm to exile in Kobyay, after his seven-year term expired on 10 February 1984, seven years to the day after his arrest: 'They took me in those "Stolypin" prison wagons, 20 to 25 men crammed into a cell the size of an ordinary compartment, about 120 in each car. It was chaos and confusion, and we were the ones who suffered. Salt herring was part of our diet, but it made us thirsty and the guards had no time to give us water. Eventually we got the water, but then they had no time to take us to the lavatory. The windows were broken and it was very cold, although we did have warm clothes. At stops along the way they took us from the train to a transit prison, making us march at the double with all our things and 'encouraging' anyone who could not make it. It took a whole month, from 10 February to 6 March 1984.'

I asked him about his hopes and expectations for his country. Probably Gorbachev wanted to build a freer Soviet Union, he said, while keeping the socialist system. But the bureaucrats and, of course, the KGB would deeply oppose such changes. He certainly did not predict that the whole Soviet system and empire were going to collapse. Khrushchev had lifted the 'iron curtain' a bit, he said, and with luck Gorbachev would lift it a bit more. Prisoners would be released and foreign travel would be made easier and censorship might be eased. There was talk, for instance, of large-scale releases of political prisoners like Anatoli Marchenko. Measures of confidence would thus be built between East and West. And confidence was a better guarantee of peace than disarmament.

It is interesting to recall how modest Orlov's hopes were, as he spoke in October 1986. 'I would not support a move from a socialist to a capitalist society. Each country has its history and this creates limits for any programme of reform . . . If we were now to renounce socialism, it would be a national humiliation, leading to cynicism and disintegration of morale . . . So let us keep socialism, but a democratic socialism with an opposition, free trade unions and so-called "bourgeois freedom", but without private industry on any great scale . . .'[1]

Orlov's optimism was limited, but in October 1986 I saw little reason to share it. There seemed so little evidence of improvement. Jewish emigration, that barometer of the East–West climate, was at a disastrous level. In the whole of 1986 only 914 were allowed to leave, the lowest number since figures began to be kept. Washington's resolve to develop SDI ('Star Wars') was still seen by the Kremlin as part of an aggressive policy on the West's part. Concessions over human rights seemed unlikely in such circumstances. The Marchenko case, for instance, was still dragging on, in spite of Sakharov's and Orlov's interest in it, and there was no prospect of its being solved.

On 11 October Reagan and Gorbachev arrived in Reykjavik. The atmosphere between the two teams mirrored the chill of an Icelandic autumn, noted the *Guardian*. But the next morning the two met face to face, with only note-takers and interpreters. Leaving Hofdi House at midday, Reagan shouted to reporters, 'We're not through yet.' They returned for a second session after lunch. Then the meeting ended. Little had apparently been achieved. Reagan confirmed that he had raised the Marchenko case, but had received little assurance of movement on this or any other human rights issue.

The Marchenko Tragedy

Gorbachev had, it emerged, several weeks earlier given the order to 'sort the Marchenko matter out', in other words to release him. But it was an equivocal order and officials on a lower level in the KGB took it as a licence to try to force some concession out of him, or out of his wife Larissa Bogoraz, as a condition of release. It was a classic KGB pattern.

A brutal cat-and-mouse game ensued. Larissa, a dissident famous for having been one of the seven who demonstrated in Red Square against the invasion of Czechoslovakia in August 1968, was told on 13 November that her husband could be released – under certain conditions. He would have to apologize, admit his guilt and ask for mercy. Then a few days later she was told that, since she was Jewish, the whole family might be allowed to emigrate to Israel.[2]

Larissa knew that this was impossible. Marchenko had been offered this way out in the past; he had not agreed then and would not agree now. He was not Jewish and his aim was to build a democratic Russia. But in 1983 he had been badly beaten up in prison by warders. He was being punished for small offences – for not wearing his cap, for lying on the bed during the day and for reading a book after lights out. These offences were used as a pretext for cancelling his family visits. She had not seen him for more than two years: 'I knew that in 1984 he was firmly resolved to stay. But I also knew that three years had passed since then, three terrible years. He might have changed his mind. I told the KGB that, if they let me visit him, I would put their offer to him.'

She never got the chance. Since 4 August Marchenko had been on hunger strike. She assumed that he was forcibly fed and that he had then ended the strike, or was about to end it. On 28 November she received her last letter from him, in which he asked for a food parcel. Her next piece of news was on 8 December, a telegram from Chistopol prison telling her that her husband had died.

'I do not say that they killed him outright,' she told me. 'On the contrary, I think that they did not want him to die. They wanted to make him better and force him to emigrate, to put him in a false position, since again and again he had said that he would never leave for Israel. They wanted to be able to say, "You see, he was ready to go all the time." It is undeniable, though, that he did not get the treatment he needed. This was not because they did not want to, but because the doctors did not know how to handle his illness. Soviet prison doctors are useless in any serious situation.'

The KGB would not even give Larissa a death certificate. She never discovered the cause of his death. In fact, they made only one concession, a very unusual one. They allowed Marchenko's family and friends, nine of whom made the exhausting journey to the prison, to give him a Christian burial. They were lucky to find a nearby church that was open and a priest who was prepared to carry out the ceremony. Larissa says, 'We were afraid that he would have a very emaciated look about him, but it turned out that there was no sign of weariness in his face. He seemed peaceful and serious, like a man who has finished the work he has to do. And at that point things became a little easier for me.'

It was the democratic movement's time of deepest despair. Nothing seemed to move the Kremlin bosses, even the imminent prospect of outright defeat through American scientific achievement in the arms race. Jewish emigration was at its lowest level for years and the rule still prevailed that political prisoners should be broken in prison, beaten up and mentally crushed, before their release could be contemplated.

Black Propaganda

It was a year and a half since Gorbachev had assumed power. There had been talk of change, but in spite of Sakharov's release still no evidence to suggest that he planned to curb the most brutal features of the KGB's power. He had just allowed a famous dissident to die of ill-treatment and neglect in prison and had arrested an American journalist in a Moscow street on a trumped-up charge. He was proclaiming glasnost, but showing little sign of it. And he was allowing the KGB to intensify 'active measures', especially black propaganda, against the West.

For instance, in February 1986 Radio Moscow invented the theory that germ weapons were being made in South Africa, with American help, having the power to kill black and Arab people while leaving whites and Jews unharmed. The charge was then bounced to and fro between the press of the Soviet Union and the Third World, even receiving the support of left-wing activists in the London Borough of Brent.

A cartoon appeared in *Pravda*, on 31 October 1986, showing the AIDS virus, encased in a great test tube, being handed to a senior US Army officer by a proud American scientist, who was supposed to have invented it for use in America's arsenal of germ warfare. The Soviet press then fed this idea to newspapers in some eighty countries, again mainly in the Third World, claiming that prisoners in American jails had been offered early release if they allowed themselves to be injected with the AIDS virus. The prisoners were then 'released into New York' where they could spread the disease.

Other Soviet publications accused American intelligence of arranging for the murder of Olaf Palme, Indira Gandhi, Aldo Moro and Martin Luther King. The aim, it appears, was to present the United States as a pariah nation, especially in the eyes of the Third World, as had been done with some success against Israel and South Africa. It was an aggressive KGB conspiracy that contrasted badly with Gorbachev's protestations that he sought East–West détente and a more open Soviet society.

Pravda cartoon depicting AIDS as an invention of the Pentagon: a late example of anti-American propaganda (*Pravda*, 31 October 1986)

Amazing Events in Gorky

On 1 December 1986, the Politburo met finally to discuss the Sakharov issue. Gorbachev, in the chair, told his comrades that Sakharov was 'moving towards a patriotic position' and that maybe the time had come to allow him back to Moscow. 'If there is any movement in his heart, we must make use of it,' said Gorbachev. 'We can say to him, "The whole country is now energetically working. You must join them."'

Politburo members agreed that it was now in their interest to allow Sakharov's return. And so KGB chief Victor Chebrikov was invited to enlist the new President of the Academy of Sciences, Guri Marchuk, to help them by calling on Sakharov and preparing him for the news.

And so two weeks later, a week after Marchenko's death, at about 10.30 p.m. on 15 December, the doorbell rang at the Sakharovs' apartment in Gorky. The late-night visitors, it turned out, were telephone engineers who had been called out from their homes a few minutes earlier to do an emergency job. Over the next twenty minutes, watched by a KGB man, they installed a telephone in the flat. The work was done on a temporary basis, without nailing the wire to the wall, and without a single word of explanation. Elena says, 'It was typical KGB behaviour. They never tell you anything unless they have to. They were afraid we might have said we don't want any telephone.' As they left, the KGB man told the Sakharovs, 'You will be receiving a call tomorrow morning at ten o'clock.'

In fact, the only call that came through the next morning was from the operator, telling them their number. Andrey told me, 'We waited and nothing happened and I had it in mind to go out and do some shopping. But there was an interesting programme on television, which is the only reason why we were there at 3 p.m. when it finally rang, five hours after it was supposed to. I picked up the receiver and a voice said that "Mikhail Sergeyevich" wanted to speak to me.' In this dramatic conversation, which I first reported,[3] Gorbachev told Andrey that Elena was 'pardoned' from her conviction under Article 190 and that the Supreme Soviet decree exiling him to Gorky was 'varied' to enable him to 'return to patriotic work'. Andrey then expressed his doubts over whether the decree had even existed.

Elena says, 'I can tell you that almost the entire conversation from Andrey's side was about the Marchenko tragedy and the fate of other prisoners of conscience, with nothing about himself.' Andrey asked Gorbachev about the human rights cases he had raised in his letter to him in February. Gorbachev replied that not all the cases deserved sympathy. Andrey's riposte was that Marchenko had been 'murdered' in prison and that the release of prisoners was important for justice, for the country, for international trust and for the success of Gorbachev's personal efforts. 'It was clear too that Sakharov was the one who brought the conversation to a close, and perhaps not as politely as one might have expected in the circumstances.'

Two days later the President of the Academy of Sciences came to Gorky at Gorbachev's request. Anatoli Alexandrov, to whom Andrey had appealed in vain two years earlier, at the most tragic moment of his life, had by now disappeared from his high post in the wake of the Chernobyl disaster eight months earlier, on 26 April 1986. A car was sent to collect Sakharov from his flat and take him to an office where the two scientists discussed the future. They agreed that Sakharov would return to research at the Lebedev Institute in Moscow and that he would abide by his promise to avoid political activity 'except in extraordinary circumstances when, to quote Tolstoy's words, one cannot stay silent'.

Marchuk, it turned out, was hardly more sympathetic to the Sakharov cause than his predecessor had been. He complained of Sakharov's 'nihilism', to which Sakharov replied that it was no crime in the Soviet Union today to speak out honestly along the lines of a policy of glasnost. Sakharov said, 'Marchuk then told me that he had spoken to many members of the Academy of Sciences and that, if I continued to emphasize "negative aspects" of society, I would find myself in a vacuum. This was a message not from Gorbachev, but from certain other organs. They were trying to frighten me, to warn me that things might get bad for me again.' Even at his moment of triumph, it appeared, he was being threatened by the leaders of Soviet Science, under orders from the KGB.

The next day Andrey went to the police station where, after some delay, Elena's identity document as an exile was exchanged for a regular passport. Two days later, on 22 December, they both caught the train, arriving in Moscow at seven o'clock the next morning, where they were greeted by a large and enthusiastic crowd. They found the Chkalov Street flat in a poor state and still without a telephone. It had been empty since Elena's daughter-in-law Lisa had left for America five years earlier. Gorbachev would be embarrassed, she said, if he knew what sort of flat he was sending them back to.

Back to Moscow

I had been banned from the Soviet Union since July 1971 and it was around this time, in the autumn of 1986, that I heard that my application for a Soviet visa had been granted. My complaint had been added to Geoffrey Howe's list of small issues and handed to the new foreign minister, Edward Shevardnadze, during a recent meeting. I was now booked to fly to Moscow with my two sons for five nights at the Kosmos Hotel in Moscow, one night on the train and one night in Leningrad. I looked forward to the prospect with a mixture of delight and apprehension. I was going to the Soviet Union on a tourist visa, but it was not only tourism that I had in mind. I did not want to be picked up in the street by the KGB, as Nicholas Daniloff had been only a few weeks earlier. On the other hand, it was a great stroke of luck that I was due to land in Moscow four days after Andrey and Elena had arrived there by train from Gorky. It meant that I had a real chance of meeting Dr Sakharov, one of my great heroes.

In November 1985 Gorbachev had promised to solve ten cases of divided USA/USSR families. In May 1986 he promised to solve another seventy. But today, at the end of 1986, nearly half of these cases were still blocked in the bureaucratic pipeline. Was he deceiving the West, or was he simply not in control of his own government machine? These were the questions foremost in my mind as I arrived at Moscow Airport on 27 December 1986. It was more than fifteen years since I had last been in the Soviet Union, at the height of the *Private Eye* problem, and after that all my requests for a visa had been met by silence from the Consulate in London. 'You must understand that "no reply" is also a reply,' one consular official was kind enough to tell me, adding with a typical air of Russian mystery, 'When we hear about your case from Moscow, *you* call *us*.'

But it was too soon to assume that I would succeed in seeing anyone in particular. It was one thing to be issued with a Soviet visa, but quite another thing (as I knew from my experience in April 1983) to be allowed into the Soviet Union. Those Christmas days were therefore anxious. Every time the telephone rang, I feared that it was Thomson Tours to tell me, yet again, that they were obliged to cancel my ticket. The prospect was nevertheless exciting, and the Sakharovs' release added to my excitement, although I had no idea what it might mean. Soviet policy was as it had been fifty years earlier, in Churchill's words, 'a riddle wrapped in a mystery inside an enigma'. I wrote, 'Was it a further step in the programme of reform, designed to make his country freer, richer and less aggressive? Or was it an act of cynical showmanship, designed to delude and divide Western opinion in the hope of easy profit?'[4] And yet there were some hopeful signs. There had just been a long talk between Gorbachev and the British ambassador, Bryan Cartledge. Recent unrest in Kazakhstan had been, unusually, shown on Soviet television. Brezhnev had been criticized in *Pravda*. The poet Irina Ratushinskaya had been suddenly released half-way into her seven-year sentence for 'distorting history'. Margaret Thatcher was to visit Moscow in the spring.

And so we set off from Gatwick airport, our luggage full of gifts for prisoners of conscience, my notebook full of interesting telephone numbers, very wary of how we would be received at the other end. Two years earlier the Soviet government newspaper had branded me as 'a staff member of British intelligence' and only four months earlier an American journalist had been arrested in the street and charged with espionage. I had no wish to have Soviet 'customs officers' going through my address book, finding the presents that I had brought for the families of imprisoned dissidents or the Christmas card for the Sakharovs signed by Margaret Thatcher. I wondered what tactic I should adopt if the KGB started going through my things item by item and page by page, as they had at Brest on the Polish border in July 1966. Should I resist? Would they use force? I need not have worried. The customs check was uneventful. And so, after an uneatable dinner in the Kosmos Hotel we made our way through a shoal of gaudy prostitutes out into the Moscow winter night. The temperature was minus 20°C and we were dressed in fur, with several layers of undergarments. There were no taxis, but we found a car ready to take us to Red Square and back for fifty roubles – a large sum in those days.

It was a moment of great excitement for me as my son James and I walked into Red Square around midnight. The square's floodlights shone dazzlingly against the snow. It seemed almost like day and I felt a sense of triumph even to have been physically allowed back into the country for which in spite of my harsh criticisms of its political system, I felt such warm affection. I had no idea whether or not things were now going to improve, but I was resolved to enjoy an exciting week and to give the democratic process, if any such process existed, if possible another tiny push forward.

The next morning I called on Larissa Bogoraz, Marchenko's widow. It seemed an endless cab ride, but I was kept on edge by the cutting cold and by the fact that it was my first day in Russia. We drove from the Kosmos Hotel to where she lived on Leninsky Prospekt, with my broken-legged son William on crutches and with James and their friend Simon Wolfson carrying the presents, suit-cases full of warm clothing for those still in the labour camps. Larissa received us with great warmth, but it was only that month that her husband had died in Chistopol prison and she seemed very frail, of spirit as well as of body. Her twelve-year-old son Pavel was even more gloomy. 'I think that things are going to improve now,' she said. 'Pavel thinks they won't. It should be the other way around.'

We had dinner with the poet Bella Akhmadulina at the Film Club. William's leg was in plaster after a rugby accident and his toes froze during a walk in the park on hard icy snow at a temperature of minus 20 degrees. We rushed him into a nearby shop, where his circulation was rubbed back to activity by a kindly Russian matron and we wrapped his foot in a copy of *Pravda* to give the broken bone insulation and inner warmth.

The British ambassador gave me tea from a silver pot, whereas a more junior American diplomat took me to a transparent plastic cubicle in the basement of his embassy for a full debriefing about the fluid situation in Moscow. We talked in what looked like a space capsule, or like the gas chamber in San Quentin prison, a sound-proofed box designed to thwart KGB microphones. And so we discussed, endlessly, what it all meant. Was there any chance of a freer Soviet Union? Or was it all pretence? This was the debate at the turn of the year 1986-7.

Sakharov's release was a reason for optimism, Marchenko's death for the opposite. There were rumours that political prisoners would be released, that dissent would be tolerated, that Gorbachev looked for real reform of the system. We hoped that this was the case, but we had been so often disappointed in the past.

My First Visit to Chkalov Street

As a member of an Intourist group, I was expected to follow their programme. For the evening of 28 December a visit to the circus was on the schedule. I decided instead to try to fulfil one of my great ambitions, to meet Andrey Sakharov. The problem was that I could not warn them. They had been back in the flat less than a week and they had no telephone. They were bound to be tired and nervous. And I would have to take the risk of turning up as an uninvited guest, who is 'worse than a Tartar' according to the Russian proverb.

Swaddled and fur-hatted against the cold, I was dropped by taxi in the street outside the apartment block. I had no idea how things would be. Would the entrance be guarded, as it had been so often in the past? Would there be KGB men in the street outside, in the entrance hallway, or on the seventh-floor landing, outside the flat? Would they take me away, or would they merely send me to join the rest of the group at the circus? The hall was pitch dark, the inside of the lift even darker. I was looking for Apartment 68. Where would it be? There was no light and nothing written to indicate the way. So I went up, striking a match every couple of floors to check the apartment numbers. Eventually I came to the right number and pressed the doorbell. I had no idea who might answer, whether or not the Sakharov family was at home, still less whether they would be in fit state to welcome me after such an amazing few days.

The door opened an inch or two, and through the chink I could just make out the kindly face and professorial wispy-haired head of Andrey Sakharov. His expression told me that he had answered that door far too many times already that day. Timidly, I told him my name. His kindly face began to smile. He shouted for Elena to come to the door to confirm that I was who I claimed to be and not some intruder. This done, I was allowed to cross the threshold, and a few moments later, relieved of my fur hat, rubber boots and three layers of overcoat, I was sitting in the famous Sakharov kitchen, warmed against the biting cold by all four of the gas stove's burners and by the bowl of steaming purple *borshch* (beetroot soup) that Elena immediately put before me.

I could see at once that here was a man weakened by the violence and pressure of recent years. He slurred his speech. His sibilants were confused. His jaw sometimes hung open and, if asked a question, there might be a several-second delay before he began to answer. He had suffered a stroke, I was later told, during the attacks on his body by the 'feeding team' in Semashko hospital. The stroke had damaged his powers of speech slightly, but not his powers of thought.

He thanked me for the March 1986 articles in the *Observer* and other newspapers. They had, he confirmed, put pressure on the Gorbachev government and maybe hastened his release. It was a great happiness and privilege to be with Andrey that icy Sunday evening and to be told by him that I had helped him.

I returned the next morning (29 December) and was allowed to talk to him for three hours, all of it on tape. Harold Macmillan's death was distracting senior editors, but after several cryptic telephone calls the *Observer* agreed to print the salient points of what was to be the first substantial interview with Sakharov since his arrest seven years earlier.

His message was one of guarded optimism: 'Those in the new leadership who share Mr Gorbachev's ideas believe that economic progress can only be achieved by serious reform, by creating an open society. This means releasing prisoners of conscience, freedom to move both inside the country and abroad, freedom to distribute information and religious freedom. This would be a great step forward, both for the Soviet Union and for the world. The world can sleep peacefully only if we become more open. There are some in the West who want the oppression to continue. They want to keep us weak. In their view, the worse it is for us, the better it is for the West. This is a mistake. It is safer to have a strong, healthy neighbour than a weak, sick neighbour. And these days a neighbour is a country that can be reached by a ballistic missile.'

Freedom to emigrate, he said, provides a regulatory mechanism against oppression, in which context he mentioned the case of Serafim Yevsyukov, whose wife had called to see him the previous day: 'He is in Stolbovaya mental hospital. They say that his desire to leave the Soviet Union is a symptom of his illness and that therefore he must stay in hospital until he is cured of this desire. We know that he has been beaten and also given harmful insulin injections.'

He wanted the West to keep up the pressure on Gorbachev so as to help him carry out his internal reforms. Less oppression in the Soviet Union was a better confidence-building measure, a better guarantee of peace than arms reduction. The next step would be for Gorbachev to pull his country out of regional conflicts in Angola, Ethiopia and especially Afghanistan.

Andrey's proposals, like Orlov's three months earlier, seem modest in retrospect. He said nothing, for instance, of any challenge to the Communist Party or socialist system, nothing about the privatization of agriculture or about independence for Poland, let alone for the Ukraine. But in the context of the Marchenko tragedy, the Daniloff provocation and the Reykjavik failure, they seemed utopian. The Soviet Union was a superpower, an imperial nation, in which the Party enjoyed a monopoly of power. In 1986 I could see no chance of their ever giving up what the Constitution guaranteed them.

I heard a rumour in Moscow that Sakharov would in future be *allowed* to criticize the government, that Gorbachev was convinced of the need for loyal opposition, not of course in order to challenge communist rule or replace it, but to make it more efficient. This apparently was why he had been brought home from Gorky. I thought the rumour absurdly over-optimistic. There might in future, I thought, be licensed criticism of the detail of administration, but never of the system itself. If there were, the system would be under threat. Liberalization would become revolution, and this was something that Gorbachev would never risk. There were still, as Sakharov conceded, several thousand political and religious prisoners in Soviet jails. Would they all be released and allowed to criticize too? These were ideas beyond the wildest liberal dream.

I took photographs of Andrey as he wrote a note to Margaret Thatcher on the back of a postcard showing the statue of Alexander Pushkin: 'Deeply respected Prime Minister! We are touched by the

New Year greeting from you and your husband. We are deeply grateful for your many years of concern for our family, Happy New Year! With hope! 29 December 1986. Elena Bonner. Andrey Sakharov.' We said goodbye and I walked out into the cold, my notes, cassettes and other precious objects stuffed into the bottom of my trouser pockets.

I saw no evidence of the KGB, but I was not looking for them and I had to presume that they were there. I had no reason to be sure that they would not seize me in the street, as they had seized Daniloff four months earlier. Alternatively, they might wait until I flew out of Leningrad airport four days later and confiscate the tapes at the customs check, on the grounds that they were 'anti-Soviet material'. The thought of losing them filled me with terror.

Laboriously, therefore, I spent the afternoon back at the Kosmos Hotel re-recording the tapes from my younger son's Walkman. What was I to do with the duplicates? The British embassy was my obvious ally, but the Foreign Office had already made their position clear. Under the Vienna Convention, they told me, non-diplomats cannot use diplomatic mailing facilities. And no exception could be made in my case, even over such a deserving matter as tapes of a Sakharov interview. They would rather that I did not skate along the edges of Soviet law, they told me, but if I wanted to run the gauntlet of the KGB at Leningrad airport and risk going to jail, that was entirely my own affair. It was only just over a year after the Oleg Gordievsky affair, which involved (I presume) a far more serious violation of the Vienna Convention by the British embassy in Moscow. I suppose that this was why they were in such a cautious mood.

The Americans were not so squeamish. I hurried to their embassy, where a member of their political staff welcomed me and took me down again to his transparent plastic bubble, where I handed him the duplicates on the understanding that he would send them to me by diplomatic mail if my originals were confiscated.

It seemed strange to be begging this simple service from a foreign government, but I was once again the victim of British diplomatic timidity. Alone of Western embassies, the British were anxious in every way to minimize their interference in the Soviet Union's internal affairs. The embassy was there to maintain good relations with the

Kremlin and its great might, which enjoyed international legitimacy, not to help Sakharov and his small band of dissidents, still less to assist a 'loose cannon' like myself. The Americans, on the other hand, saw it as part of their ideology to take the occasional risk and, sure enough, my duplicate tapes, mailed in Finland, arrived at my home in London a few days later.

In the event, the KGB made no attempt to steal my precious material and we enjoyed the rest of our wintry week without interference, visiting Jewish refuseniks and other outcasts but also enjoying the good things of Moscow and Leningrad, including the black caviar, which was then available in abundance for a small number of roubles. We flew home safely on 3 January 1987. My articles duly appeared in the *Observer* for three weeks, and the full Russian text of what Andrey and Elena had said to me took up seventeen pages in the Paris magazine *Kontinent*. I gave Margaret Thatcher the card that Andrey had written her and told her that Andrey and Elena would be glad to meet her during her forthcoming Moscow visit, scheduled for March 1987.

Anatoly Koryagin

My doubts about Soviet liberalization continued. In 1987 prisoners of conscience did indeed begin to trickle out of the camps and back to the big cities. But it was no great act of liberation. It was done with lack of grace and amid much confusion. The KGB achieved this by relaxing the conditions of release. The rule had been that any dissident might be 'pardoned' by admitting his guilt and 'repenting'. The KGB might then release the person, their honour being satisfied, their faces saved and a 'positive result' achieved. By the end of 1986 some dissidents had achieved release on this basis, but not many, since the KGB's conditions were seen as humiliating.

In 1987 the dissidents were invited not to express regret for past actions, which they usually refused to do, but merely to promise to obey Soviet law in future. This was a less onerous compromise with authority. Many were now able to sign with a clear conscience, claiming that they had never broken the law in the first place. The year's early weeks thus produced the release of many who agreed to this condition and for the first time, after two years in office, Gorbachev's popularity in the West began to soar.

The path to the edges of democracy did not run smoothly, though. On 26 April 1987, I went to Lucerne to meet Anatoly Koryagin and his wife, Galina. His was a truly abominable story. He had been in jail since 1981 for diagnosing as sane dissidents in the Ukraine whom the KGB wanted to be confined in mental hospitals. Galina told me,[5] 'In those years every one of our family was beaten up in the streets of Kharkov, our home town, some of us several times. My sons were attacked. So was my mother and so was I. In 1982, after Alexander was severely concussed by an attack when he was nine, I took the matter to court. The judge ruled that it was quite "natural" for public opinion to express itself against an anti-Soviet family like ours.'

Their other son, Ivan, was treated even worse. 'He would come home from school in tears. The other pupils, egged on by their teachers, were calling his father a traitor and a fascist.' When Ivan was fourteen, he was called to the front of school assembly and told to speak out against his father's behaviour. He protested and was expelled from school. Two years later he was attacked in the street, then charged with hooliganism and sentenced to three years in prison, to be released only a few days before the whole family flew to Switzerland.

Koryagin did not share Sakharov's view that it was now a dissident's duty to stay in the Soviet Union and take part in the process of reform. 'I do not for the moment see any sign of the sort of changes that would allow me to carry on my work.' One day Russia would be a democratic country, he told me, but it would not happen as a result of anything that Mr Gorbachev was doing. 'They released me only because the West kept pestering them about me,' he insisted. He was just happy to be in the West, away from his Soviet tormentors, and he would not risk spending another day in the country that had so misused him.

A Meeting with 'Mr Niet'

Some pieces of good news were nevertheless emerging. Before the end of 1987 I was able to report[6] that of the 754 Soviet political prisoners listed by the émigré academic Kronid Lubarsky, 233 had been released. At the same time Keston College in Kent knew the names of 180 people in prison for the practice of Christianity, against 333 a year previously. Cases of British–Soviet divided families numbered thirteen at the start of the year, nine when Margaret Thatcher was in Moscow in April 1987 and four in November 1987. Jewish emigration rose to 787 for the month of August and 721 for September 1987, against 914 for the whole of 1986.

In late October 1987 I set off with two EP colleagues to Vienna for the usual four-year review of the Helsinki Agreement. In April 1983 I had been horrified by the aggressive talk of the KGB colonel Sergei Kondryashov, who spoke for the Soviet delegation. In 1987 the leading Soviets were Yuri Kashlev and Yuri Kolosov. We expected something of the new gentle Soviet approach, but we were gravely disappointed. Kolosov spent more than an hour explaining his theme. 'We will fight against you as we fought against you in 1917,' he told us. When I protested that 1917 was twenty-one years before I was born, he replied, 'Well then, as we fought against your grand-father.'

The appointment of Edward Shevardnadze in July 1985 meant that fresh air was blowing through the Soviet foreign ministry. But the ghost of his predecessor Andrey Gromyko, known as 'grim Grom', still haunted its corridors. In 1986 Gorbachev, apparently aware of this, observed that national interests were not served when a Soviet diplomat was known as 'Mr Niet'. In 1987 Yuri Kolosov, although a young man, was the embodiment of this mythical figure from the past. His view was that the emigration of Jews amounted to a brain drain which had to be strictly controlled. 'You in the West limit the export of your technology. We limit the export of our Jewish scientists.' He added, 'Our Constitution was put together by a process involving every one of our 280 million people. We are not going to change it because of Mr Orlov, Mr Shcharansky, Mrs Bonner and a couple of hundred dissidents.' In his country, he said, everyone enjoyed the most vital human rights, the right to housing and the right to a job, rights which Soviet citizens lost as soon as they emigrated, since they could not be guaranteed in the capitalist world. This, he explained improbably, was why his government was receiving requests from unemployed British workers who wanted to emigrate to the Soviet Union.

In 1987–8 there were many such Soviet officials fighting a rearguard action against the wave of reform that Gorbachev had ordered. They believed, correctly, that the system of human rights suggested to them

343

by the West would inevitably lead to the collapse of the Soviet empire. And they were determined to prevent this. Sakharov's return to Moscow had been a signal for change, but for more than a year it was impossible to say whether any such change would be fundamental, or who was going to win the bureaucratic battle.

Sakharov's Battle for Reform

This is why we doubted whether Sakharov would be able to achieve anything of substance in the face of hard-line KGB opposition to his every move. The fear was that Gorbachev might delude the West with a façade of reform, a Potyomkin village, and lull us into a sense of false security simply so as to acquire western technology and credits. Intense debate surrounded this question, with the traditional 'anti-Soviet' groups claiming that Gorbachev was trying to 'con' us into helping him to rebuild his failing economy. Glasnost and perestroyka, they said, were all one gigantic deception. The Soviet Union was 'playing possum', pretending to be weak and helpless, whereas in fact it was as savage as ever. The signals were indeed confusing. The Soviet economy's failures were harming the interests of large sections of the population, who were then quick to blame Gorbachev's 'liberal' policies for the failures. Would these hard-liners launch a counter-attack, on the basis of the dissatisfaction felt by so many who remembered better days?

I did not think so. It seemed to me more likely that Gorbachev was persuaded of the need to move away from Brezhnev's stagnant policies. It may not have been any liberal conviction that motivated him, still less any weakening in his commitment to the communist ideal. His hope was merely to bring about a more prosperous Soviet Union through a fundamental change of policy, part of which entailed a better East–West climate and more freedom for the individual to express initiative. This was the cause in which he had enlisted Sakharov's help, and Sakharov was ready to cooperate. Who was I to disagree?

But another question arose. Would Gorbachev ever be able to tackle such Herculean labours? It was not just a question of fulfilling the West's basic demands, which he could do by releasing the prisoners, ending the regional conflicts and relaxing censorship. He would also have to correct his country's decrepit health service, unjust legal system, old-fashioned industry, inefficient agriculture, the cripplingly high military budget, the high level of pollution and the dangerous conflict between the nationalities as well as the drunken fecklessness of large sections of the work force.

If Sakharov was ready to help, he could indeed be Gorbachev's valuable ally. There was, for instance, his opposition to 'Star Wars' (SDI). He was qualified to speak about SDI politically as well as scientifically, and he to some extent supported Soviet policy on it. He was convinced that it was not a viable defence system. He told me, for instance, that no one knew what SDI was trying to achieve, whether it would defend the West as a whole or only North America, and it could too easily be beaten by the technology of the other side. Any system of defence against a missile attack was expensive and cumbersome, he said. He estimated that the cost of building SDI would be ten times the cost of penetrating it: 'We know that the United States has more industrial resources than we do, but not ten times as many.' In the first weeks of 1987 he was allowed to repeat these arguments, and these alone, on Soviet television. In February he attended a Moscow 'peace forum' of experts opposed to Reagan's defence policies. Meanwhile he persisted in his efforts to have prisoners of conscience set free, but Gorbachev did not reply to his messages and the two men did not meet.

In March 1987 Margaret Thatcher visited Moscow. At the beginning of the year I had advised her to meet the Sakharovs and I was determined that she should do so, although the Moscow embassy and the Foreign Office were instinctively against it. There is a clear convention on such matters, they told me. A British leader on an official visit to a democratic country may meet members of the *legal* opposition. In a dictatorship, though, the opposition is *illegal* and must be boycotted by embassies and visiting ministers for fear of damaging government-to-government links. Margaret Thatcher did not accept this argument. She invited the couple to lunch with her at the embassy on 31 March, although the event was not announced in advance and not included in the programme. Afterwards Andrey spoke to the press on the embassy steps about perestroyka and the review of political cases: 'A few years ago, not even very long ago, we did not consider this possible . . . But now it is a fact.'

The lunch – and her breakfast with the wife of Iosif Begun, a well-known 'Prisoner of Zion' – were part of the Prime Minister's unorthodox and very personal policy of support for dissidents even at the cost of invoking the fury of communist governments. Her appearance on Soviet television that same week was another example. Three supposedly experienced communist interviewers were lined up against her, but she demolished them in a *tour de force*. 'She charmed the whole of Russia,' said Elena later. She struck a chord too among the British people, which helped her to win the British general election two months later, on 9 June.

The great review of political cases that Sakharov had asked for, according to the estimate he gave me, involved up to 3,000 prisoners, including 'anti-Soviet agitators', conscientious objectors to military service, dissidents convicted of treason or 'religious crime' or on trumped-up criminal charges. About 600 were known by name to Amnesty International. The number, 3,000, was calculated on the basis that there were one or two 'politicals' in each of the country's prisons and camps.

Gorbachev seemed disinclined to listen to Sakharov's plea. As a result, Sakharov spent his first year of freedom in an uncomfortable state of limbo, neither the regime's friend nor its foe. He could do his scientific work. This was encouraged. But he was still not trusted enough to be allowed foreign travel, and the suggestion that he might give secrets to a Western government hurt him deeply. He was still excluded from the government machine, especially from its inner councils, even from those involved in human rights issues.

At the same time he ran the risk of alienating some of his traditional supporters in the West and among the dissidents. 'I am not sure that he is still on our team,' Bukovsky told me. The problem was that reforms were being implemented very slowly and many in the West were still not convinced that serious change was taking place. They certainly doubted whether Sakharov should be making 'compromises' (a dread word in the Soviet dissident vocabulary) with Gorbachev in order to strengthen the Soviet economy by what the latter called perestroyka. Andrey's political influence was thus limited both by his frail state of health and by his uncertain status, neither within the regime nor outside it.

Andrey finally shook hands with Gorbachev on 15 January 1988, at the launch of the International Fund for the Survival of Mankind. It was not the West's favourite fund, backed as it was by Armand Hammer, an American businessman famous for his complicated deals with the Soviet Union, dating back to Lenin's time, and by pro-Soviet individuals from many countries, including Kim Philby's friend Graham Greene. Andrey handed Gorbachev a list of 200 prisoners still detained and made clear his continuing support for those in the same position, but many found it strange to see him, a 'former dissident' as the press now described him,[7] sharing a platform with Western left-wingers who were content publicly to back the Kremlin's foreign policy against that of the US President.

Back to Moscow Again

Returning to the Soviet Union on 9 March 1988, I saw for myself how far the country was from achieving true freedom. Customs officers searched my hand luggage at the airport and became excited when they found copies of *Kontinent*, Kronid Lubarsky's list of political prisoners and other anti-Soviet items. Other passengers gave me a wide berth as a KGB man arrived, neatly dressed in flannel trousers, sports jacket and tartan tie, and turned his attention to this offending material, especially my talk with Andrey fifteen months earlier.

'Who is this man?' he asked, jabbing his finger at the interviewer's name. I told him that it was me. 'You know Academician Sakharov personally?' His mood changed as soon as I confessed that I did. 'What is this book?' I told him that it was my book about the forcible repatriation of Soviet citizens in 1945. It was too deep a problem for so young a man. He had no wish to become involved in the scandal that might ensue, and which he sensed I would be all too happy to encourage. He gave me my books back and sent me through to the bus that had kindly waited, although its passengers were nervous and resented the fact that I had kept them waiting. Later, in the British embassy, officials were visibly horrified when I produced the famous Lubarsky list and told them that I had taken it past a Soviet customs check.

At dinner in the Sakharov kitchen on 13 March 1988, I found that Andrey and Elena (whose father was Armenian) had embraced a new

347

cause, that of Nagorno-Karabakh, an enclave populated mainly by Armenians but situated in the Azerbaijani republic. A few days earlier (20 February) the local Karabakh assembly had passed a resolution calling for the territory to be taken out of Azeri control. Violence erupted immediately in the enclave and at least two Azeris died. Massive retaliation followed against the Armenian population of Azerbaijan, notably in the town of Sumgait, twenty miles north of Baku. On 27 February three days of killing began, leaving thirty-two Armenians dead (according to Soviet figures), maybe many more.

Andrey condemned the Kremlin's policy towards the region as 'unjust, one-sided and provocative'. For the first time since his release he was nursing serious doubts as to the wisdom of his support for Gorbachev's perestroyka. Elena also complained to me that her husband was not being consulted by the leadership, even over matters of special interest to him. They were both becoming impatient about the slow pace of reform and worried about the narrow area where they were forced to manoeuvre, for fear either of alienating Gorbachev's reformers or of being seen to collaborate with them uncritically.

We talked about the dissident movement in its new form. He had no doubt that the remaining prisoners of conscience would soon be released. But what would happen then? Small groups, for instance those of Sergei Grigoryants and Lev Timofeyev, were already conducting open opposition politics and publishing journals without submitting them to censorship. They were straining the limits of allowed freedom under glasnost and the KGB were confused, probably receiving contradictory orders. They harassed these new opponents, arresting them for short periods, confiscating their equipment, which amounted to no more than a photocopier and some items of stationery that would then soon be replenished from 'American sources'. Still, the situation was already a long way from that of 1977, when men were jailed for seven years for uttering the mildest criticism of Soviet policy.

I attended a press conference in Grigoryants's small apartment near Lyotchik Babushkin Street. Also half Armenian, he was offering a news service on the Sumgait massacre and more than fifty Western journalists were hanging on his words. 'It was a pogrom just like those of the end of the nineteenth century,' he said. Members of his team had brought back photographs and video tape from the Baku area.

The journalists, still not allowed to travel freely outside Moscow, were eager to acquire his material. He lacked the basic tools that he needed for his work as a journalist and semi-politician. I gave him a tape recorder and arranged for him to receive boxes of office supplies: telefax paper, ballpoint pens, paperclips, cassettes, string and glue. I also gave him 'magic slates', on which messages not designed for KGB ears could be written and erased by sliding an inside panel.

Andrey told me that he hoped at last to be allowed to visit the United States. In September 1987 he had told Guri Marchuk that he was in 'an embarrassing position' because of all the invitations he received from foreign seats of learning. 'It is a reflection on my integrity.' He also wanted to see his family in Boston and the many American scientists with whom he had corresponded over the years. 'A visit to America would be a pleasure for me and useful to the Soviet Union – a sign of greater openness.'

Marchuk replied that there was still an 'official view' that the very secret nature of Sakharov's work before 1968 precluded his being allowed to travel abroad. Andrey pointed out that another well-known scientist, Yakov Zeldovich, whose work had been equally secret, had recently been allowed a passport. Why then was he being singled out? He resented the idea that his dissident record made him likely to reveal military secrets to the Americans, especially when the secrets were twenty years old. 'It means that I am still in a state of uncertainty and I doubt whether this will change before the end of the year.'[8]

On 21 March Andrey discussed the Armenian claim to Nagorno-Karabakh with Alexander Yakovlev, one of Gorbachev's deputies. Yakovlev did not support any transfer of authority: 'The Caucasus is flooded with arms. They're being brought across the border in great quantities. One match would be enough to light a firestorm.' He then spent that summer working on his writings, much of the time away from Moscow, still unsure of what future lay in store for his country, or what part he might be able to play in it.

In the autumn of 1988 he was at last given permission to go abroad, and on 6 November he flew to New York without Elena, went up to Boston to see her family, and then spent some days in Washington being fêted by President Reagan and others. He received the £30,000 Albert Einstein peace prize. 'I am like a centipede. I cannot make up my mind which foot to put forward next,' he said in his speech. He went on to deliver his usual anti-SDI message and appealed for the release of Vazif Meilanov, a mathematician imprisoned in 1980 for standing in the street with a placard reading 'Free Sakharov' round his neck, an offence for which he had served seven years in jail and was still in exile. 'It is my duty now to support this man and others who remain in prison,' he said. He spoke by telephone to Solzhenitsyn in Vermont and they tried unsuccessfully to resolve some of their differences.

In late November mass expulsions of Armenians from Azerbaijan were taking place, amid considerable bloodshed, followed by the removal of Azeris from Armenia and the creation of a refugee problem several hundred thousand strong on both sides. Then, on 7 December, came a great Armenian earthquake in which 25,000 died and 500,000 were made homeless. Many of the victims were in refugee camps, having fled from Azerbaijan a few days earlier. Andrey and Elena, who were busy in their campaign against Article 6 of the Soviet Constitution, the article which gave the Communist Party a monopoly of power, at once flew to Armenia to visit the stricken area as well as to discuss ways of solving the Karabakh dispute. They sensed, I suppose, an even more powerful earthquake, a political cataclysm that would shake the ground of the entire Soviet Union.

20. The Empire Struck Down

The survival of Soviet power was now finely balanced. The Solidarity movement in Poland had suffered defeat in May 1988, but by the end of that year it was poised, ready to re-emerge as the power it had been in 1980-81, or even greater. In the Baltic states demonstrators were demanding freedom from foreign rule. The Soviet government had agreed to withdraw its troops from Afghanistan by 15 February 1989, while in the country itself elections were due to be held in March 1989. They would still be on a one-party basis, but members of non-communist 'groups' and 'associations' would be allowed to stand. In many districts there would be more than one candidate for each seat. This promised to provide an interesting variation on the previous system. Meanwhile I was involved in a less exotic election myself, for the European Parliament.

I had visions of what might possibly be developing in Europe's eastern lands, but I certainly did not foresee how events were now going to accelerate, making 1989 the year of Eastern Europe's decision to turn its back on the teachings of Marx and Lenin.

On 22 January Andrey Sakharov accepted nomination as a candidate for elections to the Congress of People's Deputies. Speaking to 3,500 people in the Film Makers' Union hall, he called for the abolition of capital punishment, the internal passport system and army conscription. He also demanded the release of Armenian nationalists jailed in Moscow, the so-called 'Karabakh Committee', and parliamentary control over the KGB and Ministry of Defence.

More than half the 120,000-strong Soviet contingent had by now left Afghanistan. The evacuation now intensified and on 15 February, as foreseen in the April 1988 Geneva agreement, the last Soviet soldier drove on to the steel bridge, with red flags flying from his jeep, and crossed the River Oxus into the Soviet border town of Termez. He was Lieutenant-General Boris Gromov. 'We have fully implemented our internationalist duty,' he said in his speech later that day, using the same Marxist jargon as that used by Stalin and

Molotov during the Soviet conquest of eastern Poland in September 1939. This time, though, it was the Soviet army's worst humiliation, comparable to that of the United States in Vietnam. And the conquered super-power, as in Vietnam, had been forced to withdraw leaving several hundred of their prisoners still in enemy hands.

Arriving in Moscow on 1 April 1989, I sensed among the people a deep feeling of relief that the Afghan adventure was now over. The thought was now widespread that Brezhnev and his people had betrayed their country's interest by launching the invasion that had led to the death of 20,000 young Soviet men, not to mention more than one million Afghans. I was not sure if I could myself claim any credit for what had happened, but it was clear that everything that I had hoped to see since 1980 had come to pass. The *mujahedin* had received their anti-helicopter weapons, the famous Stinger missile, and had thus been able to keep up the struggle and maintain control of the countryside. In spite of attempts by many Westerners to dismiss them as ragged and unruly tribesmen, their determination had proved firm and they had survived great hardship. Morale in the Soviet army, on the other hand, had collapsed and was no better than the morale of the American forces had been in South-East Asia. They were no longer the tough men who had torn the guts out of the Nazi German army. Their reputation had been damaged, especially in the Islamic world, and their own people's belief in the wisdom of the Communist Party was shattered beyond repair.

During that April 1989 visit I was amazed to find Soviet officials ready, for the first time, to take my criticisms in reasonable spirit and to begin a dialogue on how their human rights performance could be improved. I found myself invited to the Soviet Foreign Ministry, where their head of human rights told me that a well-known refusenik, Georgi Samoilovich, had just been given permission to leave Russia. I then had the joy of talking to Samoilovich in his flat just as the news was broken to him. I met recently elected People's Deputies from non-communist groups and we discussed previously unthinkable concepts: the merits of the family farm, the right to conscientious objection from army service, democratic control of the KGB, the small business and its compatibility with socialist society, the right to emigrate and to travel abroad, the death penalty, even a possible end to the Communist Party's monopoly of power. I attended mass meetings in Luzhniki Park, where such issues were vociferously debated, and was astonished to note policemen just standing there, allowing the debate to continue. It was still too early to think of abolishing the socialist character of the Soviet Union, but a public argument on all other aspects of the nation's future seemed now to be open.

It was a watershed in my relations with the Soviet Union when, during this same April 1989 visit, I found myself invited to the offices of *New Times*, a weekly magazine published in many foreign languages as well as in Russian. Its traditional aim had been to spread Soviet propaganda in the Third World. It had many KGB people among its staff. However, it had now fallen into the hands of the democratic movement and its editorial line had entirely changed. In March they had attacked me for my article[1] about the KGB's 'black propaganda'. But now in April, with Gorbachev in London promising a new East–West relationship in his Guildhall speech, they were ready to print[2] four pages under the heading 'Lord Bethell's Promise' about human rights and about my hopes to be able to rescue Soviet prisoners still held by the *mujahedin*. *New Times* were well informed about the Afghan war. They knew about Igor Rykov and Oleg Khlan, the two Soviet soldiers who had caused us such worry in 1984, and they knew where they lived. I was excited by the news and we agreed to try to meet them as soon as the June 1989 European elections were over.

These were the days of a 'Moscow Spring' of freedom, but the economy was beginning to crack and many items were unobtainable in the shops: razor blades, soap, toothpaste, butter and salami sausage. Neo-Nazi groups from the 'Pamyat' organization, dressed in black shirts and leather jackboots, were shouting racist propaganda at public meetings. The BBC Russian service was no longer jammed, one man told me, but this was no good to him since he could find no batteries for his radio. The newspapers had indeed improved, he went on, but he and his family could not eat newspapers. In short, Russia was embarked on a voyage into the unknown and the rosy future mapped out by Gorbachev in his Guildhall speech could by no means be guaranteed. I wrote about this, and my article in the *Sun* was predictably headed 'Russian Life Isn't Worth a Sausage'.[3]

A series of manoeuvres removed Sakharov from the list of those who won in the first round on 26 March, but he was eventually elected in a 'run-off' some weeks later and took his place as a People's Deputy. His parliamentary career did not prosper. In one of his first speeches he repeated an unconfirmed Western report that Soviet helicopters had fired on their own troops in Afghanistan, to stop them falling into enemy hands. The reaction was furious. On 2 June the 2,250-man Congress gave a standing ovation to Sergei Chervonopisky, a deputy who had lost both legs in the war, who accused Sakharov of 'irresponsible and provocative statements'. Andrey replied that, though there was no documentary evidence for his claim, he still stood by it, since the nature of his work demanded that he sometimes make statements without evidence.

'I deeply respect the Soviet army and Soviet soldiers,' he protested, his voice almost drowned by the ranks of deputies in military uniform shaking their fists at him and hurling abuse, the old ruling class venting their hatred on the leading figure in the movement that now threatened to take away their lavish privileges and make their lives impossible. They were living in the past, but Sakharov was on unsafe ground over the issue. Even his friends agreed that he had been unwise to touch such a raw nerve among the Russian people at a time of military defeat and austerity. It was the wrong issue at the wrong moment. In those days following the Soviet army's ignominious withdrawal north across the River Oxus, few were able to make the subtle distinction between the soldiers who were good and the war itself which was bad. He was jeered off the podium.

The experience hardened his heart and stiffened his resolve. On 21 June, at Chatham House in London, in a speech often interrupted and amplified by Elena, who was sitting in the audience, he spoke of the 'growing unpopularity' of the Gorbachev regime and described the Soviet Union as 'the last empire on our planet'. He only hoped that it would break up in a relatively peaceful way, as the British Empire had. He warned the West against giving the Soviet Union under Gorbachev too much financial aid on the assumption that the government was already on the right path. Western help might simply prop up a rotten system, he implied. He seemed disillusioned with Gorbachev and to be moving back to the fully dissident position that he had occupied before his release from Gorky.

That same day, 21 June, after another difficult victory in the European elections, I flew to Moscow and took a train to Leningrad

354

the next evening for the meeting with Igor Rykov that *New Times* had arranged for me.[4] It was nearly five years since Igor and Oleg had decamped from London, amid such confusion, and since *Izvestiya* had called me a British secret agent. I therefore expected hostility, or at least controversy, over Igor and his reappearance, none the worse for his redefection. There was no problem. It was now accepted in Russia, apparently without dissent, that the war against Afghanistan had been unjust and that all crimes committed by anyone who participated in it must be pardoned. The harsh words of the Soviet press in 1984 were apparently forgotten.[5]

My next foray was into Afghanistan. The Soviet foreign ministry had shown keen interest, it appeared, in my idea of attempting to release the prisoners they had left behind. I had of course kept the Foreign Office fully informed of these thoughts and John Major, then Britain's Foreign Secretary, wrote to me that the plan had his personal support. On this basis I agreed to visit Kabul under the aegis of, though not at the expense of, the Soviet embassy.

In February 1984 I had entered Afghanistan without the Afghan government's permission, in a jeep from Quetta across an icy pass in Pakistan's northern mountains, to be greeted by bearded men from a rebel group. My second visit, on 29 October 1989, was rather different. With the journalist Chester Stern kindly acting as my 'assistant', we flew to Moscow, then to Tashkent, then on to Kabul in a Soviet Ilyushin military aircraft designed to transport tanks and heavy vehicles, equipped with special defences against the ground-to-air missiles that the *mujahedin* had been given by our own side. To avoid the Stingers we flew above Kabul at high altitude, then corkscrewed down to the airport in descending circles, letting loose every few seconds a flare to confuse missiles seeking the heat of our machine. We had no seat belts, several passengers had no seats, there was a chemical lavatory and our suitcases were roped to the fuselage at the back.

During the next few days I visited the famous Pul-i-Charki prison and listened to many Afghan communists, suddenly humbled by changes in Soviet policy, indicate their wish to cooperate with the *mujahedin* in a government of national unity. Kabul was under constant shelling and windows were taped across, to prevent injuries from shattered glass. I had seen it before, as a small child in London in

1944-5. With great difficulty I shook the bloodstained hand of President Najibullah, the former head of the secret police (KHAD), who released three *mujahedin* prisoners from Pul-i-Charki 'in honour of my visit'. I was even allowed across the threshold of the notorious KHAD building and given documents about prisoners who had disappeared. The entrance, I recall, had a large doormat on it, bearing the word WELCOME in English.

The warmth shown by the Soviet officials who accompanied us was a matter of some confusion, and of grim foreboding, to the Afghans who were our hosts. The Polish communists had already collapsed. People from East Germany were escaping by the thousand, usually through Hungary, their ally, which no longer felt inclined to enforce draconian restrictions on foreign travel. Their own government, the Afghans must have known, would not long survive. And then only God would protect them from the revenge of the *mujahedin*. I left Kabul for New Delhi, then on to the Khyber Pass Hotel in Peshawar to discuss the release of Soviet prisoners with my *mujahedin* friends. On 5 November the *Mail on Sunday* announced that I had been in Kabul 'acting as a special envoy for the Kremlin', albeit 'with the full backing of the British Foreign Secretary'. It seemed like the language of an insane world. Two Soviet soldiers were, however, released through Pakistan a month after my return and I received thanks for this effort from both the British and the Soviet governments.

I flew home from Pakistan on 9 November and the following day my television was showing pictures of happy Germans dancing on the Berlin wall. Then a few days later, on 21 November, I was eating supper in Strasbourg when my German neighbour said, 'Have you heard? It's in Prague too.' The 'velvet revolution' had begun. Alexander Dubček, the ghost from 1968, came back to life addressing the crowds from a balcony in Wenceslas Square, hand in hand with the great Czech dissident and president-to-be, Václav Havel. After all that had gone before, it was not even much of a surprise.

Sakharov's Final Triumph

In early December the European Parliament awarded the Sakharov Prize to Alexander Dubček, father of the 1968 'Prague Spring'. In Strasbourg on 13 December I read Andrey's letter welcoming the award. It was Dubček's belief in socialism with a human face, he wrote, that had inspired his own efforts in those early days of his dissident activity, when 'socialism with a human face' was his highest aspiration. It was his last public utterance. Two days later I was packing my suitcase in readiness for another Moscow visit, my fourth of 1989, thinking to myself both how much Andrey had achieved and how far he had moved politically from Dubček's sad experiment, the 'liberal communist' ideal that had been the intellectual West's dream twenty years earlier. I looked forward to discussing it with Andrey and Elena. The radio was on and suddenly it was announced that Andrey had died of a heart attack in his Chkalov Street flat.

It was in a state of deep sadness that I flew to Moscow. And it was little consolation to find that the Russian people had now at last come to love the noble man who had lived among them, ill-treated and unappreciated, for so long. Their reaction was intense. A table with flowers on it, with a photograph and candles that kept being blown out by the wind, stood in the street by the door to the Sakharov home. A few friends of the family were being allowed through the door and up to the flat, where he lay on the bed in his office. 'A man of conviction and honesty. I valued him,' said Gorbachev. It seemed that now, after he had died, everyone valued him. One after the other, those who had insulted and persecuted him while he was alive made haste to praise him now that he was gone. But even among some of these, I felt, the feeling of grief and loss was genuine. People felt bereft, unprotected, almost fatherless. It was, ironically, the same feeling that they remembered from the moment of Stalin's death in March 1953.

I telephoned the flat from Moscow airport and was able to have a few words with Elena. Andrey would be remembered, I told her, as the man who did more than any other person to rescue Russia from the grip of an evil and destructive political force. 'I think the same as you,' she said. She invited me to come to his *pominki* or 'wake', a memorial supper that would take place the evening after the funeral.

On Sunday, 17 December, I walked past his body as he lay in state on a flower-strewn bier in the central hall of the Palace of Youth. He wore a dark suit and just one medal, the red badge of a People's Deputy of the USSR Supreme Soviet. His other medals were with the family in America. They had anyway not been returned to him after the removal of all his honours in January 1980. Wreaths from the government, from the Supreme Soviet and from Alexander Solzhenitsyn were prominently displayed. At one point the crowd recognized Guri Marchuk, still President of the Academy of Sciences, the man who had spoken threateningly to Andrey even at the moment of his release from Gorky in December 1986, whose duty it was to protect his brother academician, but who had done nothing to help him either before or since. People hissed at him, 'Why are *you* here? Aren't you ashamed?' Men doffed their fur hats, while women lit candles and placed them by the coffin. Elena spent most of those hours sitting in a chair near by, exchanging words with friends. Out in the street placards were displayed, some showing the figure '6' with a cross through it, calling for the repeal of Article 6 of the Soviet Constitution, others with the plaintive appeal, 'Andrey Dmitrievich, forgive us!' Many Russians felt at this point that their whole people had let Sakharov down by their silence during the years of his persecution and that, by recognizing only at the moment of his death how right he had been all along, the whole nation was somehow disgraced.

Pravda, which had reviled him cruelly for so long, printed a poem by Yevgeni Yevtushenko about 'the yawning moral gap in Society' left by his death. The lying-in-state, which began at 1 p.m., was supposed to last until 5 p.m., but it was prolonged deep into the night, by which time about 100,000 had filed past. The coffin was then moved briefly to the Academy of Sciences, where Mikhail Gorbachev came early on the Monday morning to sign a book of condolences. *Moscow News* printed his tribute: 'I feel the loss with great sorrow in my heart . . .'

There had been an unseasonal thaw during the night and a light drizzle was falling as the coffin was taken to the Luzhniki stadium. The nearest metro station was closed. The streets were inches deep in slush and awash with deep puddles of dirty water. There was a vast police and army presence, to the irritation of the mourners, and chaos as people struggled to get into the stadium in time for the non-religious meeting, which at times seemed more like a political rally than a funeral. Several times Elena appealed to the crowd through a microphone: 'This is not 1953. This is Sakharov that you are honouring.' She was referring to the panic in the Moscow streets that had crushed many people to death during Stalin's funeral in March 1953. People in the crowd held up placards with the crossed-out '6'. Others held flags of the republics that were then seeking independence from Moscow. Again Elena had to appeal to the crowd to stop pushing: 'You ask Sakharov to forgive you, but you will not step back three metres!' They obeyed her. After the meeting the coffin was taken to the Vostryakovskoye cemetery and buried. It was already dark.

I came to the Rossiya Hotel that evening to find dinner laid for about 250 people. Gorbachev was not present, but there was an awkward contingent from the communist leadership and the Academy of Sciences, men who had reviled Sakharov while he was alive and were now there to praise him. Boris Yeltsin, then a semi-opposition figure, was there and, for no apparent reason, he detached himself from a group, came over to me, shook my hand and returned to his friends. I was able to exchange a few words with Elena. 'Nicholas, I wanted you to come,' she said. I thought it no more than a politeness, but I was moved, and her daughter Tatyana says, 'I doubt if she was just being polite.' Lech Wałęsa and his then friend Adam Michnik arrived an hour late for dinner. Their flight from Warsaw had been diverted to Leningrad and they had missed the funeral. I was on my own, one of very few foreigners, but eventually I found myself at a table of twelve that included Sergei Kovalyov, Lev Timofeyev, Feliks Svetov, Zoya Krakhmalinova and Dmitri Likhachev, the man who had spoken at the funeral a few hours earlier. All of them had served terms in jail for their political beliefs. By contrast, the twelve at the next table, looking in rather better health and better dressed, were all communists and academics of very high station indeed, all keen to put their Soviet pasts behind them and jump on to the bandwagon of Sakharov's achievement and glory, in the hope that the Russian people would either forgive or forget.

We ate our cold *zakuski* and drank to Sakharov's memory. The Soviet system and empire still existed, but by now almost all the political prisoners had been released, there was little restriction on press freedom and in central Europe the empire had fallen. That very day I had heard BBC reports of anti-Ceauşescu rioting in Bucharest. The Romanian dictator, it was clear, would be the next to go. Every man and woman at that table had personal reason to be grateful to Sakharov for what was happening in all these countries.

Elena went to the microphone and welcomed us. 'I did not expect this to happen so soon,' she said in a voice of strangely quiet complaint. Several of Andrey's friends followed her to the rostrum and spoke for five or ten minutes each. Then Yeltsin spoke. We already knew, I think, that he was the man of tomorrow. Then various members of the Academy of Sciences spoke, one after the other, saying what they had not felt able to say five years earlier. I felt that it was time for me to leave. I went over to Elena. We embraced and I went back to my hotel to pack for a gloomy flight home, listening to BBC World Service prophecies on the imminent demise of Romanian communism.

The dangerous decade was nearly over. It was ten years almost to the day since Brezhnev had upped the stakes in the second cold war, sending troops into Afghanistan and arresting Sakharov in the street. The great scientist was now dead. But, even as I shared Russia's sadness in this bereavement, I felt strangely exhilarated by the thought of the success of this one man who had achieved so much in his battle against the excesses of the Soviet regime. I was happy that I had been there to honour him at his last moment of triumph.

Epilogue

The decade had begun horribly. It ended hopefully, with the beginning of the collapse of the system. It is a convenient place to end this memoir.

My 'war' ended in 1989 too. It was a war against the Soviet system, not against Russia. I like to think that I fought with Russia not in the sense of 'against' Russia, but 'with' its people and against a tyrannical government.

There will now be many problems between Russia and the Western world. We do not know what will emerge from the ruins left by Lenin, Stalin and Brezhnev. There will be poverty and extreme nationalism. There may be fundamentalist Christianity. There could be fascism, or even nostalgia for the Stalinist past. But we can be sure of one thing, I think. There will be no restored Soviet Union. The Soviets lost the cold war.

I could rejoice in how it was won, almost without bloodshed, but this would be wrong. The second cold war may have been 'cold' from the point of view of its main participants. But there *was* a third world war as hot as the first two in the sense that millions perished in regional conflicts directly related to the battle of East against West, most of all in Afghanistan and Vietnam, but also massively in Angola, Estonia, Ethiopia, Hungary, Korea, Latvia and many other lands.

I am happy that the British army wasted its money in teaching me Russian in 1957-8. They never had cause to summon me to interrogate Soviet prisoners or march them from place to place. We won through better ideas and a more successful economy, not by triumph in battle. The balloon never went up. The button was never pressed. Armageddon did not happen. We won by books and radio broadcasts and by thrusting our ideas into the Soviet Union by every available means – and by exposing their violations of human rights, as Sakharov suggested.

I therefore have no regrets at having rushed into the battle, becoming the 'fierce anti-Soviet' spotted by Oleg Gordievsky in KGB papers. If I suffered as a result of my translation of *Cancer Ward* in 1970, it was through an accident that can always happen to anyone who tries to be fair-minded in the context of a bitter conflict. And if, after my attitude to the Soviet system hardened, I was banned from the empire for more than fifteen years, this was a price that had to be paid for refusing to curb my typewriter. It makes no sense to complain.

It was a long exile from a country for which I felt much affection. Until 1989 only Russia's dissidents and émigrés could call me Russia's friend. The rest were at pains to boycott and banish, and their attitude persisted deep into Gorbachev's perestroyka. As late as 1987 the Soviet Foreign Ministry's 'tough guy' in Vienna, Yuri Kolosov, told me that his country would fight against me as his grandparents had fought against mine in the Civil War. In 1988 the KGB were still ready to harass me for taking an article by Sakharov through Moscow airport. After 1989 all this was changed. The dying Soviet Union was not going to be unkind to someone who had been a guest at Sakharov's funeral, who had played a part in saving Soviet army prisoners from the Afghan war. Then when the Soviet Union became the Russian Federation, I had no quarrel with the latter. Vladimir Bukovsky and others returned to Russia as national heroes. And I was their friend.

And so they forgave me, pretending that the quarrel had never taken place, and I was left to walk through Moscow in peace. The Western secret services and their helpers in the journalistic world, even *Private Eye*, had long ago stopped causing me trouble. I had Margaret Thatcher and several dozen Russian dissidents, all of whom gave me their full trust, to thank for that.

Russia then acquired problems of another sort. One of the Soviet Union's merits was that it provided a level, albeit a very low level, of subsistence for the country's citizens. Everyone was entitled to a job, even if it was sweeping snow for 70 roubles a week. Everyone was promised a roof, even if it was a corner of a room in a communal apartment. Bread and other basic foodstuffs were cheap. Heating was organized by the municipality. Bare survival was guaranteed.

These facilities were at risk as soon as the system began to disintegrate. The low price of food now meant simply that most items sold out as soon as the day began. The perennial queueing of Soviet life became more and more arduous. The newspapers were more interesting, but the people of Russia could not eat the newspapers. Hyperinflation was destroying the savings and pensions of the elderly. Even vodka became too expensive for the ordinary working man. And who was to blame for the new poverty? And for the humiliations when country after country voted itself out of the Soviet orbit? There were many who were all too ready to put the blame on the movement towards democratic reform.

Another Soviet achievement was its success in keeping at bay the 'ultra right' and the 'patriots', including the anti-Semites. As Soviet power faded, the fascist movement was free to emerge. I saw this when I interviewed Dmitri Vassiliev, leader of the anti-Semitic 'Pamyat' movement, in April 1989. The forces of extreme nationalism, it was clear, would soon emerge to challenge us.

Elections to the Russian parliament were held in March 1990, but Article 6 of the Soviet Constitution still stood. The Communist Party was the only party allowed to exist and field candidates. Nearly 90 per cent of those elected were Party members. Still, an influential minority of the new assembly believed in a new system based on pluralist democracy and, slowly, the Party membership began to decline as other non-communist groups came into being and established themselves as political forces.

It was still 'a socialist country' and Gorbachev clung to his belief that 'a renewed communist party' could continue as its driving force. However, the likelihood of the Party being brought back to life as the sole source of power diminished quickly as the new decade got under way. There was a haemorrhage of Party members.

In April 1990, the fiftieth anniversary of the Katyń massacres, Gorbachev finally admitted that the mass murders of Poles in 1940 had been ordered by Joseph Stalin, his predecessor in the Kremlin. In June 1990 the Soviet authorities gave me access to these archives and I appeared on Soviet television to discuss the possibility of saving more prisoners held by Afghan groups.

In late 1990 the Soviets complained about my visit to Leila Gordievsky, but they did nothing to prevent it and a year later, after the *coup d'état*, she and her children were released. During the coup itself, on 22 August 1991, I spent several hours with Margaret Thatcher talking about how Gorbachev's life could be saved. Amid the sound of gunfire we spoke to Boris Yeltsin by 'direct dial' from her office to his office in the White House, the Russian parliament building that had by now become a headquarters defending democratic change. I still cannot understand why the plotters left his telephone working.

Then in May 1992 I flew to Moscow with the famous defector Nikolay Khokhlov. He had in 1954 been sent by the KGB to Germany to murder a leading anti-Soviet émigré. He had defected to the Americans and given the world full details of his macabre mission. He had caused the KGB great damage. But now President Yeltsin had pardoned him and articles about how he betrayed the Soviet Union were part of the mainstream of Russian political debate. The old KGB were forced to swallow such humiliations and the new KGB even gave us a tour of the 'Lubyanka', their great headquarters in Moscow on what had until August 1991 been Dzherzhynski Square.[1]

But the people manning the new KGB, and most of the senior positions in the new Russia, were the same ones who had been there in the old Soviet Union. The judge who had sentenced Irina Ratushinskaya for 'distorting Soviet history' was promoted to a senior judicial post in the Ukraine. The doctor who had declared Vladimir Bukovsky insane, on KGB orders, carried on practising as a senior mental health specialist.

Most of these people were quick to adopt the new ideas of the post-Soviet system, showing no repentance for the part that they had played in sustaining the dictatorship. A few former dissidents demanded 'lustration', the exposure and banning from public office of KGB officers and others who had led the oppression. A majority opposed any such idea. Too many people would be hurt by the process. It was safer to forgive and forget.

On 1 January 1992, the Red Flag came down from the Kremlin and the Soviet Union was no more. On 30 January Boris Yeltsin, President of a Russia suddenly and recently freed from the need to govern two dozen neighbouring lands and Soviet republics, asked to see me during a brief visit to London. He thanked me for helping the process of reform in Russian society and presented me with a watch. Things had changed after all, I remember thinking. In December 1984 and again in October 1990 the KGB had denounced me as a British spy.

Now, fifteen months later, the Russian president was thanking me for my years of work.

A month later (February 1992) *The Last Secret* was published by Novosti in Moscow. André Deutsch, who had first published the book in London in 1974, had given me back the Russian-language rights free of charge. The chances of the book ever being published in the Soviet Union, he told me at the time, were too small to be calculated. Novosti paid me a fee of 60,000 roubles, worth about £250 when the contract was signed but about half that amount when they paid it six months later.

Then, in October 1992, I was sent 'the ultimate document', almost the Holy Grail of Sovietology, a paper ordering the Katyń massacres and bearing Stalin's signature. It was the final piece of the gruesome puzzle. We already knew of course in our minds how the picture looked. We just could not prove it. But now it was there on the paper. In 1940 the head of the Russian government had committed the massacre. And in August 1993 the head of the Russian government, Boris Yeltsin, apologized for it, by the Warsaw memorial, like Willi Brandt in 1970.

It was tempting to see this as the dawn of a new life, good rising from the ashes of evil. It indeed had that effect on me personally and often I had to restrain my feelings of euphoria. For years I had been Russia's rejected friend, knocking at the gates of Moscow while government and people turned me away. Only now I was welcome, and my colleagues of the Left, once so keen to disarm British nuclear weapons and jail Russian writers, were no longer invited. These apologists for Brezhnev were made to look foolish for their pro-Soviet behaviour. I enjoyed that turn of fate.

The comedian Spike Milligan called his book of war memoirs *Adolf Hitler: My Part in His Downfall*. He was being absurd, deliberately absurd, but he successfully showed through this absurdity how easy it is for work guided by emotion to drag the worker down into megalomania. Anyone so bold as to crusade can end up looking like Don Quixote at the charge. I hope that I have not fallen into that trap. I know that a single individual cannot fight a great country, or a fierce ideology. I do not claim it. But if I contributed a few blows to the West's effort against the Soviet system, I am happy to have done so.

Notes

NWB: Nicholas Bethell

CHAPTER 1: *The Window Opens*
1. *The Harrovian* (Harrow School Magazine), 5 July 1956.
2. *The Times*, 21 June 1977.
3. *Daily Express*, 8 November 1977.
4. *House Magazine*, Palace of Westminster, London, 11 November 1983.
5. *Spectator*, 19 November 1988.
6. *Sunday Times*, 7 January 1977.
7. *Times Literary Supplement*, 4 January 1963.
8. ibid., 15 March 1963.
9. *Vyecherny Leningrad* (*Evening Leningrad*), 29 November 1963.
10. Introduction by Nicholas Bethell (NWB) to Joseph Brodsky's *Elegy to John Donne . . .*, London, Longmans, 1967, pp. 10–11.

CHAPTER 2: *The Translation of* Cancer Ward
1. Alexander Solzhenitsyn, *The Oak and the Calf*, London, Collins, 1980, p. 204.
2. ibid., pp. 204–5.
3. ibid., p. 209.
4. *Unità* (Italy), 4 June 1968.
5. *Guardian*, 31 March 1969.
6. *New York Times* Magazine, 12 April 1970.
7. Auberon Waugh, *Will This Do?*, London, Century, 1991, p. 229.
8. Article by NWB in *Evening Standard*, 3 February 1993.
9. Solzhenitsyn, *The Oak and the Calf*, p. 497.
10. Patrick Marnham, *The Private Eye Story*, Deutsch, 1982.

CHAPTER 3: *Solzhenitsyn in the West*
1. Alexander Solzhenitsyn, *The Oak and the Calf*, p. 534.
2. ibid., p. 537.
3. ibid.
4. ibid., p. 528.
5. ibid., p. 432.
6. Reinhardt letter to NWB dated 22 November 1974.
7. Solzhenitsyn, *The Oak and the Calf*, pp. 371–4.
8. Article by Peter Reddaway in *New York Review of Books*, 12 December 1974.
9. Solzhenitsyn's letter to NWB dated 25 April 1975.
10. Solzhenitsyn, *The Oak and the Calf*, pp. 310–12.
11. *The Diaries of Auberon Waugh, 1976–85*, London, Private Eye/Deutsch, 1985, p. 167.

CHAPTER 4: *After the Last Secret*
1. Alexander Solzhenitsyn, *Archipelag GULAG* (in Russian), Paris, YMCA Press, p. 261.
2. Public Record Office, London (PRO), PREM 3 364/8.
3. PRO file WO 170 4461, as quoted in NWB's book *The Last Secret*, London, Deutsch, 1974.
4. PRO file WO 170 5025.
5. NWB, *The Last Secret*, p. xii.
6. ibid.
7. BBC Radio 4 interview, 1 April 1976.
8. Davies's letter to NWB, 23 March 1978.
9. Davies's letter to NWB, 4 May 1978.
10. Davies's letter to NWB, 4 July 1978.

CHAPTER 5: *Early Contact with the Sakharovs*
1. Andrey Sakharov, *Trevoga i Nadyezhda* (Alarm and Hope), Moscow, 1990, p. 295.
2. Alexander Solzhenitsyn, *The Oak and the Calf*, p. 534.
3. Sakharov, *Trevoga i Nadyezhda*, pp. 399–405.
4. *The Times*, 10 December 1975.

CHAPTER 6: *Vladimir Bukovsky*
1. *Sunday Times*, 27 June 1976.
2. ibid., 9 January 1977.

CHAPTER 7: *Sakharov and the Helsinki Group*
1. *Sunday Times*, 11 December 1977.
2. *New York Times*, 30 January 1977.
3. ibid., 20 January 1977.
4. *Sunday Times*, 11 December 1977.

CHAPTER 8: *The Helsinki Agreement*
1. *Observer*, 10 August 1975.
2. *Daily Mail*, 23 March 1977.
3. ibid.
4. *New York Times*, 13 February 1977.
5. ibid., 13 January 1977.
6. *Sunday Times*, 3 February 1980.
7. *Sunday Telegraph*, 6 January 1980.

CHAPTER 9: *Human Rights and Political Problems*
1. *Daily Mail*, 17 March 1983.
2. For instance in *The Times*, 17 May 1983.
3. *The Times*, 12 July 1983.
4. *Daily Telegraph*, 2 September 1983.
5. *The Times*, 5 September 1983.
6. *Daily Telegraph*, 3 August 1983.
7. *Le Matin* (Paris), 7 July 1983.
8. Oleg Kalugin's interview with Radio Liberty was on 9 April 1991.

CHAPTER 10: *My First Try at the Pass*
1. Parviz Radji, *In the Service of the Peacock Throne*, London, Hamish Hamilton, 1983, p. 75.
2. *Daily Mail*, 13 February 1979.
3. Radji, *In the Service of the Peacock Throne*, p. 327.
4. Amnesty International's *Report on Afghanistan*, 1986, p. 6.

5. US State Department's *Report on Human Rights*, 1982, p. 1975.
6. *The Times*, 12 August 1980.
7. *The Times*, 22 September 1980.
8. *The Times*, 9 December 1980.
9. *The Times*, 28 December 1980.
10. *The Times*, 30 January 1981.
11. Article by NWB, *Sunday Times*, 1 March 1981.
12. Letter from Margaret Thatcher to NWB, 19 March 1981.
13. *Izvestiya* (Moscow), 20 March 1981.
14. *Izvestiya*, 21 March 1981.

CHAPTER 11: *Two Lonely Soldiers*
1. *The Times*, 12 November 1984.
2. *The Times*, 5 January 1985.
3. TASS report, 1 February 1985.

CHAPTER 12: *My Friend Oleg*
1. Christopher Andrew and Oleg Gordievsky, *KGB: The Inside Story*, London, Hodder & Stoughton, 1988, p. 489.
2. ibid., p. xxxi.
3. *Novoye Vremya* (New Times, Moscow), No. 2, 1992.
4. *Niezavisimaya Gazeta* (Independent Newspaper, Moscow), 14 March 1991.
5. *The Times*, 13 September 1985.
6. Andrew and Gordievsky, *KGB: The Inside Story*, p. xxxii.
7. *Mail on Sunday*, 15 September 1985.
8. Margaret Thatcher, *The Downing Street Years*, London, Collins, 1993, p. 774.
9. *Niezavisimaya*, ibid.
10. *Novoye Vremya*, ibid.
11. *Sunday Express*, 25 November 1990.
12. *Niezavisimaya*, 4 April 1991.
13. *Evening Standard*, 22 July 1991.

CHAPTER 13: *Nelson Mandela*
1. *Mail on Sunday*, 27 January 1985.
2. *The Times*, 29 January 1985.
3. NWB's letter dated 24 October 1984.

4. Letter to NWB dated 6 March 1989.
5. *New York Times* Magazine, 7 July 1985.
6. Radio Addis Ababa, 5 August 1985.
7. Letter from Coetsee to NWB, dated 17 April 1986.
8. *Sunday Telegraph*, 1 April 1990.

CHAPTER 14: *The Katyń Murder Mystery, 1940–92*
1. The O'Malley Report is in the PRO, file FO 371 24467.
2. FO 371 34578.
3. *Evening Standard*, 29 April 1943.
4. FO 371 34572.
5. FO 371 34574.
6. Presidential Archive, Moscow.
7. *Sunday Times Magazine*, 28 May 1972.
8. *Guardian*, 20 September 1976.
9. *The Times*, 17 September 1976.
10. *Daily Mail*, 16 September 1976.
11. *Dziennik Polski*, 18 October 1976.
12. *Mail on Sunday*, 17 June 1990.
13. *Sunday Telegraph*, 2 September 1990.
14. *Observer*, 7 October 1991.
15. *The Times*, 23 October 1992.
16. NWB was made a Commander of the Order of Merit by the President of Poland, Lech Wałęsa, on 19 March 1991. Presenting the award, the Polish ambassador in London, Tadeusz de Virion, said, 'Your crusade for the Katyń massacres to be adequately and truthfully elucidated . . . has won you a permanent and prominent place in British–Polish relations.'

CHAPTER 15: *Poland as a Russian Colony*
1. For instance Tadeusz Walichnowski, *Mechanizm Propagandy Syjonistycznej* (The Mechanism of Zionist Propaganda), Sląsk, Katowice, 1968.
2. *The Times*, 27 January 1971.
3. *Willesden and Brent Chronicle* (London), 19 December 1980.
4. *Daily Mail*, 25 August 1980.
5. *Daily Mail*, 2 September 1980.

6. *Spectator*, 14 February 1981.
7. *Economist*, 11 April 1981.
8. *The Times*, 10 September 1987.
9. *The Times*, 10 September 1987. See also *New Republic* (Washington), 2 November 1987.
10. *Trybuna Ludu* (Tribune of the People), Warsaw, 16 October, 1987.
11. *Sunday Telegraph*, 8 May 1988.
12. *Sunday Telegraph*, 15 May 1988.
13. *Życie Warszawy* (Warsaw Life), 7 June and 14 May 1988.
14. *The Times*, 29 August 1988.
15. *Daily Mail*, 20 September 1988.
16. Margaret Thatcher, *The Downing Street Years*, London, HarperCollins, 1993, p. 778.
17. *Daily Telegraph*, 2 November 1988.
18. See p. 7.
19. Thatcher, *The Downing Street Years*, p. 780.

CHAPTER 16: *The Fall of 'Sir Dracula'*

1. *The Times*, 18 March 1983.
2. *Sunday Express*, 20 March 1983.
3. *Daily Telegraph*, 19/20 March 1983.
4. *Daily Telegraph*, 19 March 1983.
5. Parliamentary Question, 14 March 1989.
6. *The Times*, 20 March 1989.
7. *Spectator*, 6 May 1989.

CHAPTER 17: *Albania – The Last Domino to Fall*

1. Paper by Julian Amery dated 9 October 1991.
2. Kim Philby, *My Silent War*, London, Macgibbon & Kee, 1968, p. 119.
3. Interview with NWB dated 30 June 1983.
4. Interview with NWB dated 19 October 1983.
5. See NWB's book *The Great Betrayal*, London, Hodder & Stoughton, 1984, passim.
6. Letter to NWB from Muhamed Hoxha dated 16 June 1993.
7. *Independent* (London), 11 March 1989. See also *Traveler* (New York), November 1989.

8. *Daily Telegraph*, 4 April 1990.
9. David Smiley, *Regular Irregular*, Norwich, Michael Russell, 1994, p. 198.
10. Amery's paper of October 1991.

CHAPTER 18: *Andrey Sakharov's Arrest*
1. Elena Bonner's interview with NWB, 8 February 1986.
2. *New York Times*, 12 May 1984.
3. *Washington Post*, 13 May 1984.
4. Presidential Archive, Moscow.
5. *The Times*, 30 May 1986.
6. NWB's interview with Sakharov dated 29 December 1986.
7. *The Times*, 15 September 1986.

CHAPTER 19: *Orlov's Release and Marchenko's Death*
1. *Sunday Times*, 12 October 1986. See also *Encounter*, May 1987.
2. *Observer*, 18 January 1987.
3. *Sunday Times*, 21 December 1986.
4. ibid.
5. *The Times*, 28 April 1987.
6. *Sunday Times*, 1 November 1987.
7. *Daily Telegraph*, 16 January 1988.
8. *Sunday Times*, 20 March 1988.

CHAPTER 20: *The Empire Struck Down*
1. *Mail on Sunday*, 12 February 1989.
2. *Novoye Vremya* (Moscow), 21 April 1989.
3. *Sun*, 5 April 1989. See also *Mail on Sunday*, 9 April 1989.
4. *Mail on Sunday*, 16 July 1989.
5. *Izvestiya* (Moscow), 2 December 1984.

Epilogue
1. *Sunday Telegraph*, 24 May 1992.

Chronology

NWB: Nicholas Bethell

1956	October/ November	Soviet troops invade Hungary. British, French and Israeli forces invade Suez. Władyslaw Gomułka is elected leader of Polish Communist Party.
1961	August	Berlin Wall is erected.
1962	November	*A Day in the Life of Ivan Denisovich* by Alexander Solzhenitsyn is published in Moscow monthly *Novy Mir*.
1964	February	Joseph Brodsky stands trial in Leningrad for 'parasitism' and is sentenced to exile.
	October 15	Nikita Khrushchev is deposed as Soviet leader. China explodes its first atomic bomb.
1965	January 12	'The Trial of Joseph Brodsky' is broadcast on BBC Third Programme.
	June 15	Anna Akhmatova reads her poetry in BBC, Broadcasting House, London.
1966	February 14	Andrey Sinyavsky and Yuli Daniel are sent to prison for anti-Soviet agitation.
	March	Anna Akhmatova dies near Moscow.
	June	NWB visits Soviet Union.
1967	March	Pavel Ličko visits Solzhenitsyn in Ryazan.
	November	NWB visits Ličko in Bratislava.
	December	NWB inherits seat in House of Lords.
1968	January	Alexander Dubček succeeds Antonin Novotny as leader of Czechoslovak Communist Party.
	March	Ličko signs *Cancer Ward* contract near Bratislava.

	April 11	Extract from *Cancer Ward* published in *Times Literary Supplement*.
	August 21	Soviet Army invades Czechoslovakia.
	September	*Cancer Ward* published in London.
1969	March	NWB visits Stefan Dubček in hospital.
	June	Solzhenitsyn's play *The Love Girl and the Innocent* published in London.
	July	NWB's biography of Gomułka published in London.
1970	January	NWB visits Moscow.
	June	Edward Heath wins general election. NWB is appointed junior minister.
	September 1	Ličko arrested.
	24	NWB attacked by Auberon Waugh in *Private Eye*.
	October 8	Solzhenitsyn awarded Nobel Prize for Literature.
	11	*The Love Girl and the Innocent* opens at the Tyrone Guthrie theatre, Minneapolis.
1971	January 5	NWB resigns from Edward Heath's government.
	July	NWB visits Moscow.
	September	East–West settlement over Berlin.
	23	NWB's visa to Czechoslovakia is cancelled.
1972	February 7	'Who is Nicholas Bethell?' is shown on Slovak television.
	May	SALT I talks, ABM Treaty.
	June 8	*Private Eye* apologize to NWB in open court.
	November 8	Nixon re-elected US President.
1973	January 1	Britain joins European Community.
	June	Brezhnev–Nixon summit meeting in USA.
	August	Andrey and Maya Sinyavsky emigrate from Soviet Union to Paris.
	September	Russian edition of Andrey Sinyavsky's book *Voice from the Chorus* is published by NWB in London.
	October	Yom Kippur War.

December		Russian edition of *The Gulag Archipelago* is published in Paris.
1974	February	Edward Heath loses general election.
	12	Solzhenitsyn is arrested in Moscow.
	13	Solzhenitsyn arrives in Germany.
	August 8	Nixon resigns as US President.
	11	NWB's book *The Last Secret* is serialized in the *Sunday Express*.
	September	Russian magazine *Kontinent* is launched in London.
	October	*The Last Secret* is published.
	November 17	Election in Greece. Constantine Karamanlis becomes Prime Minister.
1975	February	Heath is voted out of Conservative Party leadership.
	March 17	NWB is appointed to European Parliament by Margaret Thatcher.
	April 25	Solzhenitsyn writes NWB a rude letter.
	August 1	Helsinki Agreement is signed and printed in *Pravda* the following day.
	October 4	NWB visits Elena Sakharov in Florence. Andrey Sakharov is awarded the Nobel Peace Prize on 9 October.
	November	TV film based on *The Last Secret* is shown on BBC2.
	11	Portuguese rule ends in Angola. Cuban and Soviet forces start arriving in Soviet aircraft.
1976	March 1	BBC *Panorama* (Michael Charlton) interviews Solzhenitsyn in London.
	17	House of Lords debates forcible repatriation of Soviet citizens.
	April 1	Solzhenitsyn gives his 'warning to the Western world' on BBC Radio 4.
	May 12	Helsinki Group formed in Moscow.
	July 26	Agostinho Neto, leader of Angolan MPLA, visits Castro in Cuba and asks for more troops.
	October 8	Neto visits Moscow, signs treaty with Brezhnev.
	November	Jimmy Carter is elected US President.

	December		Vladimir Bukovsky is flown to Zurich in exchange for Chilean communist Luis Corvalan.
1977	January	4	KGB search flats of Yuri Orlov and Ludmilla Alekseyeva.
		9	NWB's article 'Bukovsky's Own Story' printed in *Sunday Times*.
	February	3	Alexander Ginsburg is arrested.
		8	President Carter defends dissidents in his first press conference, but says he cannot take up every individual case.
		10	Yuri Orlov is arrested.
		26	Enoch Powell writes in *The Times* about 'the whole monstrous contraption of the European Convention on human rights'.
	March	1	Carter receives Bukovsky in the White House.
		21	'Dignity or Death', series of articles by NWB in *Daily Mail*, tells of KGB suppression of Helsinki Group.
	May	13	Rudolf Nureyev appears before a US human rights commission, highlighting the Kremlin's refusal to allow him to see his mother.
	November		Labour leader Alex Kitson, in Moscow for sixtieth anniversary of October Revolution, praises Soviet society.
		14	US State Department notes airlift of arms to Ethiopia.
		18	European Parliament debate on psychiatric abuse in USSR. Labour MP Tam Dalyell says that the West should not 'lecture Mother Russia on how she should treat her own nationals'.
1978	February		Andrew Young, US Ambassador to the United Nations, says that Cuban troops have brought 'a certain stability' to Angola.
	May	19	Zviad Gamsakhurdia is sentenced to three years in prison, then apologizes on television and denounces his fellow dissidents.
		20	Yuri Orlov is sentenced to seven years in prison, plus five years in labour camps.

June 8 Solzhenitsyn addresses Harvard graduation class. *The Times* prints its text on 16 July.

13 Romanian dictator Nicolae Ceauşescu visits London. Romanian émigré leader Ion Ratiu is arrested outside Claridge's Hotel.

July 11 Trials of Alexander Ginsburg and Anatoli Shcharansky begin in Moscow.

September 7 Bulgarian dissident Georgi Markov is killed on Waterloo Bridge, London.

October 1 Father Gleb Yakunin is arrested in Moscow.

16 Karol Wojtyła elected as Pope John Paul II.

November 8 NWB criticizes Iran's human rights record in House of Lords.

1979 January 16 Shah of Iran leaves the country.

February 12 Revolution in Iran. Prime Minister Shahpour Bakhtiar resigns and escapes from Iran.

April 24 Ginsburg is deported from Soviet Union.

May NWB's book *The Palestine Triangle* is published.

10 British general election. Margaret Thatcher becomes Prime Minister.

28 Alexander Ginsburg, Edward Kuznetsov and three others exchanged for two Soviet UN employees held as spies in USA.

June Places for 982 Vietnam boat people offered in UK.

10 NWB is elected as MEP for London North-West in first European Parliament elections.

22 *The Times* prints editorial on Enoch Powell and boat people.

December 27 Afghan coup overthrows President Amin, installs Babrak Karmal.

27 Airlift of 5,000 Soviet troops into Kabul.

31 Expulsion from Kabul of Western journalists.

1980 January 3 Sakharov calls for Soviet withdrawal from Afghanistan.

4 Carter curtails scientific exchange with Soviet Union.

5 Carter embargoes grain exports to Soviet Union.

11 EC supports grain embargo.

21 US boycott of Olympic Games announced by Carter.

23 Andrey Sakharov is arrested and exiled to Gorky.

February 21 Thatcher writes to NWB approving Yalta Memorial on Crown land.

22 British trade unionist Ray Buckton talks on Czechoslovak TV, attacks the West's proposed boycott of the Moscow Olympic Games.

July 27 NWB appeals in *Daily Telegraph* for funds for Polish workers to be sent to Count Edward Raczyński, former President of Polish government-in-exile.

August 31 Gdańsk Agreement is signed.

November Ronald Reagan elected US President.

17 Leonid Zamyatin on Soviet television accuses the West of pouring millions of dollars into Poland to finance anti-communism.

1981 January Ronald Reagan becomes US President.

29 Reagan in his first press conference says, 'So far, détente has been a one-way street that the Soviet Union has used to pursue its own ends.'

February NWB visits Washington with Afghan *mujahedin* leaders for talks with US Government.

March 11 Reagan addresses Canadian parliament on 'continued Soviet adventurism across the earth'.

April Race riots in Brixton and other London areas.

25 Reagan ends grain embargo on Soviet Union.

May 5 Irish nationalist Bobby Sands dies on hunger strike.

6 *Izvestiya* writes of Sands's death 'in Long Kesh concentration camp' for 'taking part in the struggle against British repression'.

13 Attempt to assassinate Pope John Paul II.

27 Reagan tells West Point students that they are 'holding back an evil force that would extinguish the light we have been tending for 6,000 years'.

December 14 Martial law is declared in Poland.
Lisa Alekseyeva is allowed to leave USSR and marry Elena Bonner's son Aleksey Semyonov.

1982   March 6 Dedication of Yalta Memorial in London.
10 Afghanistan Day in White House.
April 2 Argentina invades Falkland Islands.
11 Mosque of Omar in Jerusalem is attacked.
25 NWB's trip to Pakistan is cancelled on racial grounds.
June 9 Reagan speaks to British parliament in Westminster Hall about the Soviet Union and the Falklands war.
July 4 Bella and Igor Korchnoi, relatives of the famous chess player, are allowed to emigrate.
September 1 Gomułka dies in Warsaw.
October 7 NWB meets Oleg Gordievsky in Brighton.
November 10 Brezhnev dies.

1983   January 10 Gordievsky visits NWB's home.
February 25 KGB Centre orders 'active measures' campaign against American policy. Operation RYAN intensifies, with widespread Soviet belief that West intends to launch a pre-emptive strike.
March 3 Poet Irina Ratushinskaya sentenced in Kiev to seven years in prison and five in exile for 'being critical of Soviet history'.
10 NWB visits Madrid for CSCE Review, meets Sergei Kondryashov, KGB chief.
14 Romanian émigré Stancu Papusoiu is arrested in London, then deported.
29 House of Lords debates the Papusoiu case.
April 18 NWB's visa to USSR is cancelled.
22 NWB's flight to Moscow is booked but not used.
May Valeri Repin forced to 'confess' on Soviet television that money from the Solzhenitsyn Fund is controlled by CIA.
19 European Parliament adopts NWB's report on human rights in USSR by 134 votes to eight. Two British Labour MEPs are among the eight.

June 9	British general election. Thatcher wins in landslide.
July 11/12	Vladimir Promyslov, Mayor of Moscow, visits London. Row at County Hall reception.
August	NWB visits New York and Washington for talks about secret operations in Albania.
September 1	Korean airliner KAL 007 shot down over Sakhalin island.
October 26	US forces invade Grenada.
November 11	Profile of NWB in Palace of Westminster *House Magazine*.
	Book *CIA v. USSR* by Nikolay Yakovlev accuses Sakharovs of being part of CIA plot.

1984	January 29	NWB flies to Islamabad and enters Afghanistan illegally.
	February 8	NWB returns to London from Karachi.
	9	Yuri Andropov dies and is succeeded by Konstantin Chernenko.
	12	NWB's article 'Russia's Lost Legion' appears in *Mail on Sunday*.
	March 13	NWB's report on USSR subversive activities debated in EP and approved by 136 votes to sixty-two. Several Labour MEPs speak against it.
	May 8	USSR announces boycott of Los Angeles Olympic Games.
	June 14	Soviet soldiers Igor Rykov and Oleg Khlan arrive in London. NWB is re-elected in European Parliament elections.
	27	Rykov and Khlan give press conference.
	July	Sir Geoffrey Howe in Moscow. He meets Chernenko and raises questions of Flora Leipman and Oleska Terlezki.
	September	Elena Bonner sentenced to five years' exile for slandering the Soviet state.
	October 3	Oleska Terlezki, father of British MP Stefan Terlezki, comes to England from the Soviet Union to visit the son he has not seen for forty-five years.

		23	Andreas Papandreou visits Warsaw.
		28	Father Jerzy Popiełuszko murdered in Poland.
		30	Prime Minister Indira Gandhi murdered.
	November	6	British minister Malcolm Rifkind visits Poland and lays wreath on grave of Popiełuszko.
		11	Rykov and Khlan return to USSR.
		21	German foreign minister Genscher plans to visit Poland, but cancels visit because he is told he cannot visit Popiełuszko's grave or meet Solidarity activists.
	December	2	NWB attacked as 'staff British intelligence agent' in *Izvestiya* article about Rykov's and Khlan's 'nightmare' visit to England.
		17	Mikhail Gorbachev visits Britain and goes to Chequers for talks with Margaret Thatcher, who says that he is a man with whom she can do business.
1985	January	21	NWB visits Nelson Mandela in Pollsmoor Prison, Cape Town.
	March		Chernenko dies. Gorbachev elected Soviet leader.
	May	8	President Reagan addresses European Parliament. Labour MEPs lead a 'walk-out' during his speech.
	July	20	Gordievsky escapes from Soviet Union.
	September	12	Announcement of 'superspy' Oleg Gordievsky's defection to Britain.
			Elena Bonner's son Aleksey Semyonov on hunger strike in Washington.
	October	23	NWB takes singer Bob Geldof to European Parliament to discuss world famine.
	November	4	KGB agent Vitali Yurchenko announces his redefection in Washington.
		5	Interview with Reagan published in *Izvestiya*.
1986	February	6	NWB meets Elena Bonner in Boston and starts work on material about Sakharov's hunger strike.

	8	Gorbachev is quoted by *L'Humanité* (Paris) to the effect that Sakharov cannot be allowed to travel abroad for reasons of state secrecy.
	9	NWB's article about KGB torture of Andrey Sakharov appears in the *Observer*.
	11	Anatoli Shcharansky and three NATO spies are exchanged in Berlin for five spies held by West.
	16/23	'The Gorky Papers' appear in the *Observer*.
March	17	*The Times* announces death of Oleska Terlezki, father of British MP.
August	2	Second dedication of Yalta Memorial.
	30	Nicholas Daniloff arrested in Moscow, the first such arrest of an American citizen since 1953.
September	12	Daniloff released from Moscow jail.
	29	Daniloff allowed to leave USSR.
October	5	Yuri Orlov flies from Moscow to New York.
	9	Irina Ratushinskaya released from Mordovia labour camp.
	11/12	Reagan and Gorbachev talk in Reykjavik.
December	8	Anatoli Marchenko dies in Chistopol prison.
	23	The Sakharovs return to Moscow from Gorky.
	27	NWB and boys fly to Moscow.
	28/29	NWB meets Sakharov.

1987	January	3	NWB returns from Moscow.
	March		NWB takes Yuri Orlov to meet Margaret Thatcher.
		20	Tony Benn MP writes in Moscow weekly *Novoye Vremya* about British human rights abuses.
		27	Thatcher arrives in Moscow.
		29	Mathias Rust, German amateur pilot, lands his aircraft in Red Square, Moscow.
		30	Margaret Thatcher meets Dr Sakharov.
	April	26	NWB meets Anatoli Koryagin, newly freed dissident psychiatrist, in Lucerne.
	August		NWB flies to Poland, first visit there since 1969, meets Wałęsa near Gdańsk.
	October	22	Joseph Brodsky is awarded Nobel Prize for Literature.

	December	7	Earthquake in Armenia kills 25,000 people.
1988	January	15	Sakharov meets Gorbachev for the first time.
	March	9	NWB flies to Moscow, visits Sakharov.
	May	6	NWB flies to Warsaw for 'round table conference' at Rozalin.
		7	Janusz Onyszkiewicz, Solidarity leader, is jailed. Rozalin conference breaks up. The next day NWB is detained by Polish police in Gdańsk.
	September	25	Anatoli Shustov (Finkelstein), last person on British–Soviet 'bilateral list', flies to London.
	November	1	Polish Prime Minister Rakowski closes Gdańsk shipyard.
		2	Margaret Thatcher flies to Poland.
		18	NWB visits Albania.
1989	April	1	NWB visits Russia, meets Soviet officials, is interviewed by *Novoye Vremya*, meets leaders of racist 'Pamyat' body.
		21	Article about NWB appears in *Novoye Vremya*.
	June	2	Sakharov is attacked in Supreme Soviet for criticizing behaviour of Soviet troops in Afghanistan.
		22	NWB visits Moscow, then meets Igor Rykov in Leningrad, gives him back his guitar.
	August	24	Tadeusz Mazowiecki is elected as first non-communist Prime Minister of Poland since 1939.
	November	3	NWB leaves Kabul for New Delhi.
		10	East German guards no longer man the Berlin Wall.
		21	The 'Velvet Revolution' begins in Prague.
	December	14	Andrey Sakharov dies in Moscow.
		22	Nicolae Ceauşescu is stripped of his GCB and shot three days later.

Index

NWB: Nicholas Bethell